BACK TO WORK

BACK TO WORK

Growing with Jobs in Europe and Central Asia

Omar S. Arias
Carolina Sánchez-Páramo
María E. Dávalos
Indhira Santos
Erwin R. Tiongson
Carola Gruen
Natasha de Andrade Falcão
Gady Saiovici
Cesar A. Cancho

THE WORLD BANK
Washington, D.C.

Contents

Boxes

Figures

Spotlights

Tables

Foreword

Jobs are key to lifting people out of poverty and ensuring that prosperity is shared by all. Jobs are not only the main source of income for individuals and families, but as the 2013 *World Development Report* reminded us, jobs can empower people and enhance their voice and participation in society.

The Europe and Central Asia Region lags behind other middle-income regions and advanced economies in harnessing this transformative power of jobs. Despite impressive reform efforts in many countries and a period of strong economic growth in the past decade, the region has not done well in creating jobs. The international financial crisis and the ensuing Eurozone economic slowdown made matters worse. Today, job creation is weak in most countries and many people find themselves jobless, especially among youth, older workers, women, and some ethnic groups.

Creating more and better jobs has become a top priority for policy makers in the region. This book addresses the timely questions of what steps countries can take to do just that, and how to make work opportunities accessible to all. The book examines these questions through the lens of two factors that make most of Europe and Central Asia unique: the legacy of centrally planned economies (which is related to progress with market economy reforms) and the region's demographic shifts (with some countries' populations aging rapidly, while others experience youth bulges).

With this backdrop, the book underscores five key findings. First, sustained market reforms pay off in terms of greater job creation and increased productivity, although results take time to materialize.

Second, harnessing the potential of entrepreneurship in the region is key to boosting job creation, but, just as in the more advanced economies, not all young firms succeed. Third, many workers, especially younger and older workers, are ill prepared to succeed in today's dynamic labor market because they lack the skills that employers need. Fourth, high labor taxes and the design of pensions and social benefits often discourage employment, and multiple barriers exclude many women, minorities, youth, and older workers from the labor market. Fifth, workers often fail to move to places with stronger job creation potential within their own countries, making it difficult to connect them with jobs in more vibrant regions.

Without downplaying the complexity of the jobs challenge, the report calls for countries in the region to resume the pre-crisis reform momentum in order to (i) lay the fundamentals for the private sector to thrive and create jobs, by enabling existing firms to grow and new firms to emerge and succeed (or fail quickly at low cost); (ii) support workers so they are well equipped to take on the new job opportunities, by having the right skills and incentives, unhindered access to work, and readiness to relocate. The report underscores that there are no one-size-fits-all solutions. Priorities depend on each country's situation, including its demographic outlook and the progress already made with economic and institutional reforms.

The good news is that many countries in the region are already showing the way by making the necessary reforms. Despite the setbacks brought about by the crisis, efforts are underway to continue improving the business climate, reform regulations, reduce labor taxes particularly for low-wage earners, enhance the ability of social protection systems to guard the vulnerable without making work less attractive, make education and training systems more market-driven, remove barriers to work, and to foster social norms more conducive to inclusive labor markets.

The jobs challenge in Europe and Central Asia is pressing, but it is not insurmountable. *Back to Work: Growing with Jobs in Europe and Central Asia* provides a wealth of analysis and references to practical experiences that countries can use to inform their policy making and set their own priorities, and for the World Bank and other development partners to better support their efforts to unleash the potential of jobs to eliminate poverty and promote shared prosperity.

Laura Tuck
Vice President
Europe and Central Asia Region
The World Bank

Acknowledgments

Back to Work: Growing with Jobs in Europe and Central Asia has been prepared by a multisectoral team, co-led by Omar Arias and Carolina Sánchez-Páramo, and comprising Cesar Cancho, María Dávalos, Natasha de Andrade Falcão, Carola Gruen, Gady Saiovici, Indhira Santos, and Erwin Tiongson. The team is grateful for the guidance, support, and technical inputs of Indermit Gill, Ana Revenga, Yvonne Tsikata, Roberta Gatti, and Benu Bidani. The work was carried out under the overall supervision of Philippe Le Houérou as Vice President of the Europe and Central Asia Region.

The authorship of the chapters is as follows: The overview chapter was written by Omar Arias and Carolina Sánchez-Páramo; Chapter 1 was written by Carolina Sánchez-Páramo, with contributions from Cesar Cancho; Chapter 2 was written by Erwin Tiongson, with contributions from Charles Udomsaph (Georgetown University); Chapter 3 was written by Omar Arias, with contributions from Natasha de Andrade Falcão; Chapter 4 was written by María Dávalos and Indhira Santos; and Chapter 5 was written by Carola Gruen, Indhira Santos, Omar Arias, and Gady Saiovici. Robert Zimmerman and Steve Williams edited the overview chapter and the main report, respectively. Substantive inputs to various chapters were provided by Ferhat Bilgin, the BuDDY Team (including Dino Merotto,

Charles Udomsaph, Apirat Kongchanagul, Tao Huang, and Kosuke Konematsu), Tolga Cebeci, Tomas M. Damerau, Giorgia Demarchi, Alexey Dorofeev, Alexandra Fedorets, Julianna Flanagan, Nadeem Karmali, Victor Sulla, and Manami Suga.

Leysan Nigmedzyanova, Irina Rostovtseva, Katerina Timina, and Judy Wiltshire provided invaluable logistical and administrative support.

Background work for four country case studies was conducted for Poland by Piotr Lewandowski (Institute for Structural Research), for Romania by Simon Davis (World Bank) and Nicolaas de Zwager (International Agency for Source Country Information), for Tajikistan by Marina Kartseva (Centre for Economic and Financial Research) and Polina Kuznetsova (Centre for Economic and Financial Research), and Turkey by Cristóbal Ridao-Cano (World Bank).

The team also acknowledges the background papers and/or research undertaken for the report by Hilal Atasoy (Temple University), Pedro Carneiro (University College of London), Tim Heleniak (University of Maryland), Martin Moreno (consultant), Kaspar Ritcher (European Commission), Luz Saavedra (University of St. Thomas), Raimundo Soto (Universidad de Chile), Charles Udomsaph (Georgetown University), and Peter van der Zwan (Erasmus University Rotterdam).

The team is grateful for the insightful advice, comments, and recommendations received from members of the Advisory Board for the report: Georg Fischer (Directorate-General for Employment, Social Affairs & Inclusion, European Commission), John Haltiwanger (University of Maryland), Vladimir Gimpleson (Higher School of Economics), Maciej Bukowski (Institute for Structural Research), and William Maloney (World Bank), as well as from the peer reviewers Gordon Betcherman (University of Ottawa), Isabelle Maquet (DG-Employment, European Commission), Mamta Murthi (World Bank), and Jamele Rigolini (World Bank).

Finally, the team received valuable comments and suggestions throughout the preparation of the report from Cristian Aedo, Gallina Andronova, Paloma Anos-Casero, Nina Arnhold, Roberta Malee Bassett, Sebastian Eckardt, Alvaro González, Jesko Hentschel, Herwig Immervoll, Keiko Inoe, Aylin Isik-Dikmelik, Roumeen Islam, Andrew Mason, Matteo Morgandi, Soren Nellemann, Alberto Rodriguez, Jan Rutkowski, Sophie Sirtaine, Victoria Strokova, Ramya Sundaram, Joanna Tyrowicz, Barbara Viony Kits, participants of the Labor Practice Seminar at the World Bank, members of the Turkey, Poland, and Romania country teams who participated in country consultations, and members of the ECA Regional Leadership Team.

About the Authors

Omar S. Arias has been a Lead Economist in the Human Development Economics Unit for the World Bank's Europe and Central Asia Region since September 2011. Previously he was the Sector Leader of Human Development for Bolivia, Chile, Ecuador, Peru, and República Bolivariana de Venezuela (2008–11); a Senior Economist in the Poverty and Gender Group of the Latin America and the Caribbean Region (2003–07); and a Research Economist in the Inter-American Development Bank in Washington, DC (1999–2003). He was a Fulbright scholar in the University of Illinois at Urbana-Champaign, where he obtained his Master's Degree and PhD in economics.

Carolina Sánchez-Páramo, a Spanish national, is currently a Sector Manager in the Poverty Reduction and Economic Management unit in the Europe and Central Asia Region at the World Bank. Prior to this assignment she was a Lead Economist in the same unit and the Regional Poverty Advisor. She joined the World Bank in 2000 as a Young Professional. Prior to her current assignment, she worked on operations, policy advice, and analytical activities in Eastern Europe, Latin America, and South Asia. She was also part of the core team working on the *World Development Report 2012: Gender Equality and Development*. Carolina has a PhD in economics from Harvard University.

María E. Dávalos is an Economist in the Poverty Reduction and Economic Management Unit (PREM) of the Europe and Central Asia Region at the World Bank since September 2011. Previously she worked in PREM in the Latin America and the Caribbean Region, which she joined in 2010 through the World Bank's Young Professionals Program. She currently leads the economic mobility agenda in Europe and Central Asia and works on the gender and poverty programs for the Western Balkans. She obtained a Master's Degree in economic policy management at the Centre for Studies and Research on International Development (France) and was a Fulbright scholar at Fordham University (New York), where she obtained her PhD in economics.

Indhira Santos is a Senior Economist at the World Bank, where she works on labor markets, skills, and social protection in the Europe and Central Asia Region. She also worked in the South Asia Region after entering the Young Professionals Program in 2009. Prior to joining the World Bank, she was a Research Fellow at Bruegel, a European policy think-tank in Brussels, between 2007 and 2009. She has also worked for the Economic Research Center of the PUCMM University and the Ministry of Finance (the Dominican Republic). She was a Fulbright scholar at Harvard University, where she obtained her PhD in public policy and a Master's Degree in public administration in international development.

Erwin R. Tiongson is a Senior Economist in the Latin America and Caribbean Region of the World Bank. He previously served as Senior Economist in Europe and Central Asia Region, where he worked on issues related to labor markets, enterprise activity, and migration. He was an Associate Professor at the Asian Institute of Management from 2009 to 2011 while on leave from the World Bank.

Carola Gruen works for the Europe and Central Asia Region at the World Bank in Washington, DC. Previously she held positions at the University of Goettingen (Germany), the Institute for Employment Research (Germany), and the University of the Witwatersrand (South Africa). She mainly works on topics in labor economics, poverty, and applied welfare economics and her work has been published in peer-reviewed journals. She holds a PhD in economics from the University of Munich (Germany).

Natasha de Andrade Falcão is a Consultant in the Human Development Unit for the Europe and Central Asia Region of the World Bank. She joined the World Bank in March 2012, after working as a Research Fellow for the Research Department at the

Inter-American Development Bank. Her research interests include returns to education, human capital externalities, poverty, inequality, and income distribution. She holds a PhD and a Master's Degree in economics from the Universidade Federal de Pernambuco (Brazil).

Gady Saiovici has been a Junior Professional Associate in the Human Development Economics Unit for the World Bank's Europe and Central Asia Region since April 2012, working on labor market, social protection, fiscal spending, and aging issues. Prior to joining the World Bank, he was a consultant at the International Labour Organization in Geneva, Switzerland. He obtained his Bachelor's Degree from the University of Sao Paulo, Brazil, and his Master of Research in Economics degree from Pompeu Fabra University, Spain.

Cesar A. Cancho is a Consultant in the Poverty Reduction and Economic Management Unit for the World Bank's Europe and Central Asia Region. His work at the World Bank has focused on measurement and analysis of poverty, the analysis of perceptions of economic mobility, and the estimation of impact on poverty of policies supported by Bank operations. Before joining the World Bank, he worked on different projects in Latin America for the Inter-American Development Bank. He holds a PhD in economics from Texas A&M University and a Bachelor of Science in economics from the Pontifical Catholic University of Peru. He is a former Fulbright scholar and active member of Ankay.

Abbreviations

ADF	Augmented Dickey Fuller
ALMPs	active labor market policies
BEEPS	Business Environment and Enterprise Performance Survey
BES	Business Expectations Survey
BvD	Bureau van Dijk
CEE	Central and Eastern Europe
CIS	Commonwealth of Independent States
DBI	Doing Business Indicator
EAP	East Asia and Pacific
EBRD	European Bank for Reconstruction and Development
ECA	Europe and Central Asia (comprising transition economies and Turkey)
ECD	early childhood development
ECS	European Company Survey
EPL	Employment Protection Legislation
EU	European Union
EURES	European network of public employment services
FCS	Financial Crisis Survey
FE	fixed effects
FYR	Former Yugoslav Republic
GDP	gross domestic product
GEM	Global Entrepreneurship Monitor
HHI	Herfindahl–Hirschman Index
IADB	Inter-American Development Bank
IFC	International Finance Corporation

ILO	International Labour Organization
IZA	Institute for the Study of Labor
LAC	Latin America and the Caribbean
LCU	local currency units
LFP	labor force participation
LFPR	labor force participation rate
LFS	labor force survey
LiTSs	Life in Transition Surveys
LSI	labor shortage indicator
LTU	long-term unemployment
MSME	micro, small, and medium-size enterprises
MTE	Marginal Treatment Effect
NEET	not employed, in education or training
NUTS	Nomenclature of Territorial Statistical Units
OECD	Organisation for Economic Co-operation and Development
OJT	on-the-job training
OLS	ordinary least squares
PATHS	Promoting Alternative Thinking Strategies
PES	public employment services
PIAAC	Program for International Assessment of Adult Competences
PISA	Program for International Student Assessment (OECD)
PP	Phillips Perron
PPP	purchasing power parity
SABER	System Assessment and Benchmarking for Education Results
SAR	special administrative region (China)
SBS	Structural Business Statistics
SEE	Southeastern Europe
SOE	state-owned enterprise
STEM	science, technology, engineering, and mathematics
STEPs	Skills Toward Employment and Productivity
TFP	total factor productivity
TI	transition index
TVET	technical and vocational education and training
WDI	World Development Indicators
WEF	World Economic Forum
WfD	Workforce Development

Note: All dollar amounts are U.S. dollars ($) unless otherwise indicated.

Executive Summary

Creating more and better jobs is arguably the most critical challenge to boosting shared prosperity in Europe and Central Asia (ECA). This report answers two questions: How can the countries create more jobs? Which specific policies can help workers access those jobs? In answering them, the report examines the role of reforms, firms, skills, incentives and barriers to work, and labor mobility through the lens of two contextual factors: the legacy of centralized planned economies and the mounting demographic pressures associated with rapid aging in some countries and soaring numbers of youth entering the workforce in others. The main findings of the report are: (a) market reforms pay off in terms of jobs and productivity, although with a lag; (b) a small fraction of superstar high-growth firms, largely young, account for most of new jobs created in the region—thus, countries, especially late reformers, need to unleash the potential of high levels of latent entrepreneurship to start up new firms; (c) skills gaps hinder employment prospects, especially of youth and older workers, due to the inadequate response of the education and training systems to changes in the demand for skills; (d) employment is hindered by high implicit taxes on work for those transitioning to formal jobs from inactivity or unemployment and barriers that affect especially women, minorities, youth, and older workers; and (e) low internal labor mobility prevents labor relocation to places with greater job creation potential.

The report argues that to get more people *back to work* by *growing with jobs*, countries need to regain the momentum for economic and institutional reforms that existed before the crisis in order to: (a) lay the fundamentals to create jobs for all workers, by pushing reforms to create the enabling environment for existing firms to grow, become more productive, or exit the market, and tap into entrepreneurship potential for new firms to emerge and succeed or fail fast and cheap; and (b) implement policies to support workers so they are prepared to take on the new jobs being created, by having the right skills and incentives, unhindered access to work, and being ready to move to places with the highest job creation potential.

The Employment Problem in Europe and Central Asia

Only 50 out of every 100 working-age individuals is employed in the region. This compares to 59 in Latin America and the Caribbean, 66 in East Asia and Pacific, and 57 in Organisation for Economic Co-operation and Development (OECD) countries. This reflects both high unemployment (14 percent, on average) and low labor force participation rates (58 percent, on average) (figure ES.1). Worryingly, between 40–60 percent of the unemployed have been looking for a job for more than a year. As a result, the region is missing out on its

FIGURE ES.1
Labor Force Participation (Left) and Unemployment Rate (Right)

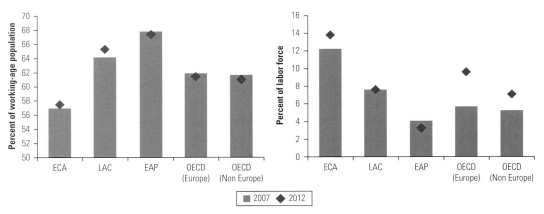

Sources: World Bank 2013b, based on KILM, ILO 2013; World Bank 2013a.
Note: Labor market indicators are for individuals aged 15 and above. The unemployment rate is calculated based on the data available for labor force participation and the employment rates. EAP = East Asia and Pacific; ECA = Europe and Central Asia; LAC = Latin America and the Caribbean; OECD = Organisation for Economic Co-operation and Development.

human capital potential: an average man spends 11 years of his productive life in unemployment or inactivity; a typical woman, 17 years (figure ES.2). Addressing this challenge now is particularly important to sustain the region's economic and social models in the context of a slow economic recovery and uncertain global prospects.

There is significant heterogeneity in employment performance across and within countries. Employment rates range from 68 percent in Kazakhstan to 24 percent in Kosovo. Young and older workers, women, and ethnic minorities are disproportionately likely to be jobless, employed in informal jobs, and/or to earn less. Female activity rates are 16 percentage points below those of men. In Kosovo and Turkey, for example, less than 30 percent of the working-age women are employed or seeking work outside the home. Youth in the region are twice as likely to be unemployed as adults and one in five is neither working, nor searching for work, nor studying. Older workers drop out of the labor force too early, with activity rates falling from

FIGURE ES.2
Average Years of Lost Potential Employment for an Individual, circa 2010

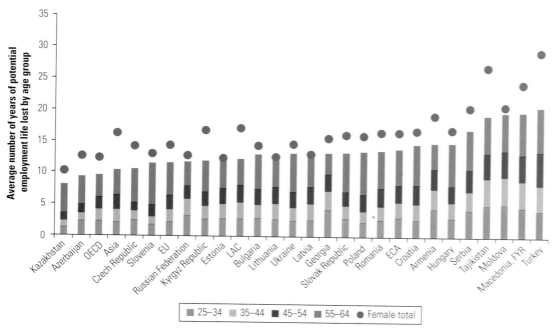

Source: World Bank calculations based on data of the International Labour Organization and household and labor force surveys.
Note: Calculated based on the employment rates by age group (i.e. each age group–specific employment rate indicates average years worked per person in that age group), starting at 15 years old and up to 64 years old, minus the total potential working life. Data for Asia includes Bangladesh, Bhutan, Hong Kong SAR, China, Indonesia, Macao SAR, China, Malaysia, the Philippines, Sri Lanka, and Thailand. Data for LAC includes Argentina, Barbados, Chile, Colombia, Costa Rica, Cuba, the Dominican Republic, Ecuador, El Salvador, Guatemala, Honduras, Mexico, the Netherlands Antilles, Panama, Paraguay, Uruguay, and República Bolivariana de Venezuela. ECA = Europe and Central Asia; EU = European Union; LAC = Latin America and the Caribbean; OECD = Organisation for Economic Co-operation and Development.

an average of 82 percent at ages 45–49 to 61 percent at ages 55–59. Roma earn 56 percent less than the non-Roma population, on average, in countries where they are a significant minority.

How Did the Region Get Here?

The region's poor performance on employment prior to the financial crisis reflects structural factors. While it was the best performing region in terms of economic growth and productivity in the 2000s, it registered one of the lowest employment growth rates. Two factors are important to understand the disconnect between economic growth and employment creation: the legacy of centralized planned economies as countries reform to transit into modern market economies, and the mounting demographic pressures associated with rapid aging in some countries (i.e. over the next 40 years, the working-age population will shrink in the EU-11, the Russian Federation, and other older former Soviet Union countries as much as 20–40 percent) and large numbers of youth in others (i.e. in Turkey and Central Asia, it will increase by 20–40 percent with millions of youth entering the labor market).

In 1990–91, at the start of the transition, open unemployment was rare and labor participation rates, including for women, were high (with the exception of the Western Balkan countries). However, this masked significant unproductive employment in inefficient state-owned enterprises and the public sector. The reform process—in labor markets, business climate, public sector, trade, and finance—required to pave the way for productivity gains advanced at different speed across countries. In the early stages of transition, job shedding from the restructuring of existing enterprises outweighed job creation and thus translated into significant employment losses. In time, however, these reforms paid off in terms of employment creation (figure ES.3). Early reformers— Turkey and most of the new European Union (EU) member states, the latter aided by the EU accession process—moved more quickly toward a virtuous circle of simultaneous productivity growth and net job creation in the late 1990s and the 2000s before the onset of the crisis (figure ES.3a). In contrast, intermediate reformers— Western Balkans, the South Caucasus, Croatia, Romania, and Moldova—were just starting to see fast employment growth when the crisis hit. The late reformers—Belarus, Russia, Ukraine, and most of Central Asia—have for the most part reaped productivity gains with modest or little employment creation (figure ES.3b).

FIGURE ES.3
Job Creation and Job Destruction Rates, 2001–09

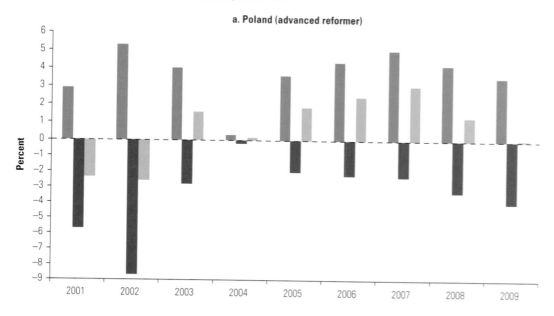

a. Poland (advanced reformer)

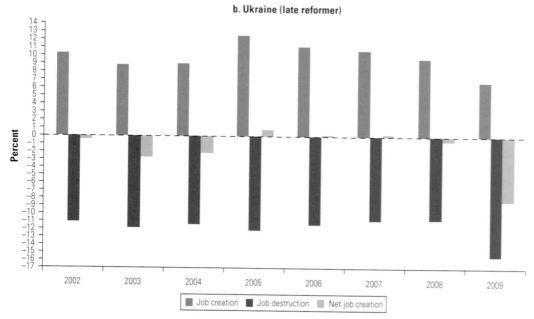

b. Ukraine (late reformer)

■ Job creation ■ Job destruction ■ Net job creation

Source: World Bank 2013b, based on Amadeus database.

What Was the Impact of the Crisis?

The economic crisis led to large employment losses and a significant rise in unemployment (on average, of 2 percentage points, but as much as 20 percentage points among youth in some countries); wages have also fallen albeit less so. The crisis impact on jobs played out mainly through a drop in demand from the negative internal and external shocks to economic activity. Most new EU member states and other countries closest to the Euro Zone were the most affected by the crisis and experienced the largest jobs losses, while Turkey, the South Caucasus, Russia, and other countries from Eurasia bounced back relatively quickly. Job losses were most significant in pro-cyclical sectors, such as construction, and sectors that had expanded rapidly prior to the crisis but they were by no means limited to these sectors. In Turkey, except for the year 2005, exporting firms generally led job creation in the precrisis period. In 2009, however, employment losses among exporting firms far outstripped those among nonexporting firms. Similarly in Romania's manufacturing sector, the subsectors' leading job creation prior to the crisis (apparel and computer-related industries) experienced larger contractions in employment during the crisis.

In addition, the crisis impacted employment by constraining firms' access to finance. Surely younger firms, which had led employment creation in 2000–07, were among the main casualties of the global crisis. Although new firms, innovative firms, and small firms fueled much of the region's job creation during the boom years, they were also less likely to survive during the crisis due to difficulties in accessing credit. In fact, firms that survived the crisis tended to be larger and older firms that had access to finance or could rely on internal sources of finance. New business registrations also fell sharply during the crisis. Between 2004 and 2008, new business registration (measured per 1,000 people) surged by 49 percent, while it fell by over 20 percent, slightly more than all other regions in 2008–09.

What Can Be Done to Create More and Better Jobs in the Region?

Creating more and better jobs calls for a multisectoral policy agenda that goes beyond traditional labor market measures and regulations.

In addition to preserving macroeconomic stability and resuming economic growth, countries—especially intermediate and late reformers—need to regain the precrisis reform momentum to foster competition in product and factor markets, pursue a more effective state, and deepen trade integration. More specifically, they should undertake reforms and policies to improve the environment for existing and new firms to thrive and create jobs, and to support workers to be more adaptable, ready-to-work, and mobile so they can tap into new job opportunities. These reforms have largely paid off for early reformers and are likely to do so for intermediate and late reformers as well.

Enabling Private Sector–Led Job Creation

On average, about 10–15 percent of all firms accounted for over two-thirds of net job creation in the region in the years prior to the crisis (a pattern also observed in other advanced economies). These so-called "gazelles," the engines of new job creation, are mostly younger firms—not necessarily small—that expanded their work-force rapidly. These firms tend to thrive in an enabling business environment and their ability to grow is particularly sensitive to access to finance and the initial quality of management practices. Policies should therefore facilitate the entry of new firms, which have the potential to become the next job-creation superstars, while allowing unprofitable ones to fail quickly and cheaply. Unleashing untapped entrepreneurial potential in the region (e.g. close to a quarter of the labor force would rather be self-employed) represents an opportunity to do so, especially when combined with policies that facilitate the local agglomeration of firms, resources, and talent.

Policy agenda: (a) Continue the process of reforms and enterprise restructuring, including the restructuring of state-owned enterprises in late reformers; (b) Continue reforms to improve the business environment (e.g. competition, property registration, legal system, taxation, infrastructure, economic integration) and the functioning of markets; (c) Promote entrepreneurship by expanding access to prudent finance and business training, improving regulations governing firm entry and exit (e.g. bankruptcy), and promoting more favorable social norms and attitudes toward risk taking; (d) Implement policies to foster agglomeration economies through better infrastructure connectivity and logistics, supply chains, and worker mobility.

Supporting Workers in Acquiring Skills for the Modern Workplace

Across the region, an increasing share of employers cited skills as a major constraint to firms' growth before the crisis. The skills demanded by firms today are rapidly shifting from routine, manual and cognitive skills toward more nonroutine higher-order skills, including socioemotional ("soft") skills. However, most education and training systems in the region have failed to keep up with the fast-changing labor market. In most countries one in five 15-year-olds was functionally illiterate in 2009, reaching up to 40 percent in Bulgaria and Romania and even higher rates in parts of Central Asia (figure ES.4); and students are still tracked too early into vocational education at the expense of weakening generic skills foundations in many countries. On the positive side, higher education still pays in the region, despite a large increase in the number of college-educated workers. Having a university degree is associated with hourly wages that are, on average, 60 percent higher than those earned by a typical person with only secondary education in countries like Albania, the former Yugoslav Republic of Macedonia, Poland, and Turkey. However, there is some evidence that high average returns are not available to everyone. In particular, poor families may accrue returns to their investments in higher education significantly below the average market return that can deem the pursuit of a tertiary degree a bad proposition for a non-negligible group of youth.

Policy agenda: (a) Prepare new labor market entrants with strong generic (both cognitive and socioemotional) skills, by improving early childhood development policies and quality of preschools and basic education, as well as by postponing early tracking into vocational education; (b) Manage the expansion of tertiary education through the strengthening of quality assurance frameworks, the provision of better information on labor market prospects of different fields, and the expansion of access for low-income youth; (c) Address market failures and provide incentives for more on-the-job firm training; (d) Address technical or job specific skills gaps of youth and adults, including more effective age-sensitive training as part of active labor market policies and targeted programs focusing on disadvantaged groups; (e) Create the conditions for the development of a market for adult education and training services.

FIGURE ES.4

Too Many 15-Year-Olds in the Region Remain Functionally Illiterate, 2009

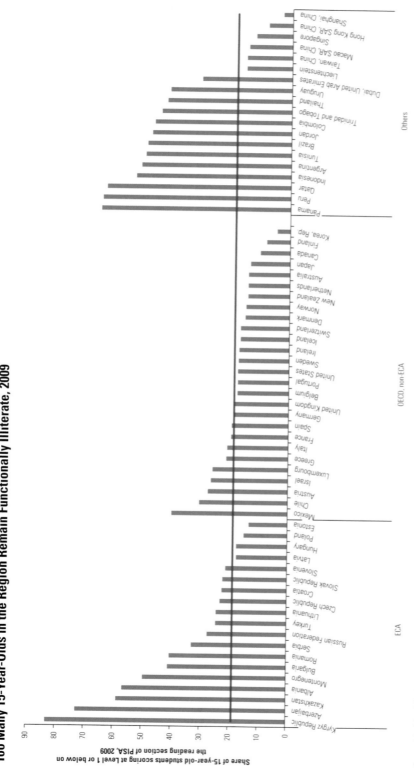

Share of 15-year-old students scoring at Level 1 or below on the reading section of PISA, 2009

Source: Murthi and Sondergaard 2012.

Note: The red line indicates the average share of functionally illiterate 15-year olds in OECD non-Eastern European and Central Asian countries. ECA = Europe and Central Asia, OECD = Organisation for Economic Co-operation and Development. PISA = Program for International Student Assessment (OECD)

Addressing Work Disincentives in Tax and Social Protection Systems and Eliminating Barriers to the Employment of Minorities, Women, Youth, and Older Workers

Taxation and social protection systems do not always make (formal) work pay. A low tax base (for each person contributing to social security, on average, almost three are not) and an often generous social insurance (pensions) system create pressures for high labor taxation rates. On average, income taxes and social contributions in the region amount to 37 percent of labor costs. Importantly, labor taxation is less progressive than in Western Europe, discouraging work among low-wage earners. The design of social protection programs, in turn, also weakens incentives to work formally. Pension systems have encouraged early retirement, undermining work incentives among older workers and cutting working lives short. Meanwhile social assistance and unemployment benefits are not very generous and have limited coverage in most countries, but their design often explicitly or implicitly bans or discourages work. Beyond these disincentives to work, other barriers, mostly outside of the labor market—lack of child and elderly care options; limited flexible work arrangements; imperfect access to productive inputs, networks, and information; and/or adverse attitudes and social norms—can effectively exclude from labor markets some groups, especially women, youth, older workers, and ethnic minorities.

Policy agenda: (a) Reduce labor taxation, especially among low-wage, part-time and second earners; (b) Improve targeting and design of social protection, including pushing forward pension reforms; (c) Improve work regulations to make labor markets more contestable and facilitate flexible work arrangements; (d) Strengthen active labor market programs that address the various obstacles to employment that men and women face during their lifecycle.

Removing Obstacles to Internal Migration

While international migration is an important phenomenon in several countries, internal mobility rates are low in the region. The little internal migration that is observed is often in the "wrong" direction, that is, away from leading regions and/or within lagging regions. Youth are often much more mobile, both internally and internationally, while older workers rarely migrate. Yet, there are significant gains to be made from removing obstacles to internal labor migration, given large disparities within countries in productivity and labor market outcomes. Greater internal mobility would allow workers to go to places with greater job creation potential and in doing so facilitate local agglomeration economies and better labor market matching. Actions should focus on removing existing barriers to migration.

Policy agenda: (a) Support the development of housing/credit markets; (b) Make social benefits portable; (c) Remove barriers that stem from administrative requirements and facilitate access to information about job opportunities across regions through employment services and labor market observatories; (d) Reform regional policies to avoid discouraging mobility; (e) Invest in generic, transferable skills; and (f) Reduce regional disparities in access to basic services.

Establishing Policy Priorities

The successful implementation of a policy agenda that effectively rebalances the work and social protection pillars of the social model in the region requires fitting priorities and tailoring policies to each country's stage of modernization and demographic imperatives (table ES.1).

In all countries, reforms to improve the quality of the business climate, make labor markets more competitive, modernize the public sector, deepen financial development, and increase integration in global markets are a necessary condition for positive and sustained employment creation. These efforts will have to be comprehensive and sustained for the payoff to materialize, as illustrated by the experience of the advanced reformers in the region.

In addition, moving along the modernization path will require further economic restructuring and labor reallocation, irrespective of whether a country is an advanced, intermediate, or late modernizer. These processes can be wasteful and inefficient and lead to significant short-term welfare losses, particularly among specific groups of workers, if they are not accompanied by policies aimed at improving the match between jobs and workers and enhancing the employability of those people who are most affected by the changes. Policies that are sensitive to age and gender can help increase the efficiency and effectiveness of the restructuring process.

TABLE ES.1

Diverse Policy Reform Agendas

Growing quickly, youth bulge	Growing or declining slowly, aging medium term	Declining quickly, aging rapidly
a. Advanced modernizers		
Business climate reform to strengthen and sustain the growth of superstars Ease of entry and exit into entrepreneurship (for example, access to inputs, bankruptcy reform) + social attitudes Strong generic skills + market-driven tertiary education + skills for innovation Remove the barriers to internal mobility Reduce the effects of labor costs and taxation + flexible work arrangements	Business climate reform to strengthen and sustain the growth of superstars Ease of entry and exit into entrepreneurship (for example, access to inputs, bankruptcy reform) + social attitudes Strong generic skills + market-driven tertiary and adult education + skills for innovation Remove the barriers to internal mobility + smart immigration policy Reduce the effects of labor costs and taxation + flexible work arrangements Strong work incentives + pension reforms + improved targeting of safety nets and social protection	Business climate reform to strengthen and sustain the growth of superstars Ease of entry and exit into entrepreneurship (for example, access to inputs, bankruptcy reform) + social attitudes Strong generic skills + market-driven tertiary and adult education + skills for innovation Remove the barriers to internal mobility + smart immigration policy Reduce the effects of labor costs and taxation + flexible work arrangements Strong work incentives + pension reforms + improved targeting of safety nets + social and business attitudes toward older workers
b. Intermediate modernizers		
Deeper integration (with EU, globally) Business climate reform to enable the growth of superstars Ease of entry and exit into entrepreneurship (for example, access to inputs, bankruptcy reform) Strong generic skills + market-driven tertiary education Remove the barriers to internal mobility Reduce the effects of labor costs and taxation + flexible work arrangements	Deeper integration (with EU, globally) Business climate reform to enable the growth of superstars Ease of entry and exit into entrepreneurship (for example, access to inputs, bankruptcy reform) Strong generic skills + market-driven tertiary and adult education and labor training Remove the barriers to internal mobility + smart immigration policy Reduce the effects of labor costs and taxation + flexible work arrangements Strong work incentives + pension reforms + improved targeting of safety nets and social protection	Deeper integration (with EU, globally) Business climate reform to enable the growth of superstars Ease of entry and exit into entrepreneurship (for example, access to inputs, bankruptcy reform) Strong generic skills + market-driven tertiary and adult education and labor training Remove the barriers to internal mobility + smart immigration policy Reduce the effects of labor costs and taxation + flexible work arrangements Strong work incentives + pension reforms + improved targeting of safety nets + social and business attitudes toward older workers
c. Late modernizers		
Public sector restructuring + productive diversification Improved business climate for private sector development Ease of entry and exit into entrepreneurship (for example, access to inputs, bankruptcy reform) Strong generic skills + market-driven tertiary education Remove the barriers to internal mobility Reduce the effects of labor costs and taxation + flexible work arrangements	Public sector restructuring + productive diversification Improved business climate for private sector development Strong generic skills + market-driven tertiary and adult education and labor training Remove the barriers to internal mobility + smart immigration policy Reduce the effects of labor costs and taxation + flexible work arrangements Strong work incentives + pension reforms + improved targeting of safety nets and social protection	Public sector restructuring + productive diversification Improved business climate for private sector development Strong generic skills + market-driven tertiary and adult education and labor training Remove the barriers to internal mobility + smart immigration policy Reduce the effects of labor costs and taxation + flexible work arrangements Strong work incentives + pension reforms + improved targeting of safety nets + social and business attitudes toward older workers

The proposed employment policy agendas follow an incremental approach as countries transition from late to intermediate and advanced modernizers, while differentiating among countries with a youth bulge and countries with a rapidly aging population.

Bibliography

ILO (International Labour Organization). 2013. *Key Indicators of the Labor Market (KILM)*. 7th ed. Geneva, Switzerland: International Labour Office.

Murthi, Mamta, and Lars Sondergaard. 2012. *Skills, Not Just Diplomas: The Path for Education Reforms in Eastern Europe and Central Asia*. Washington, DC: World Bank.

World Bank. 2013a. *World Development Indicators 2013*. Washington, DC: World Bank.

———. 2013b. *World Development Report 2013: Jobs*. Washington, DC: World Bank.

Overview

Introduction

Jobs are at the core of people's aspirations and an imperative for sustained and shared prosperity across all countries in the Europe and Central Asia (ECA) region. In most of the region, during the decades of (socialist) central planning, open unemployment was nonexistent thanks to massive and inefficient labor hoarding in State enterprises. However, during the transition to a market economy, persistent unemployment and labor inactivity emerged as a pervasive labor market feature in most countries. The stellar economic and productivity growth in 2000–07 did not always translate into significant employment creation and, even when it did it failed to make a significant dent on labor force participation and unemployment rates among young and older workers and women. The international financial crisis then erased much of the modest employment creation that had taken place in the 2000s. This report presents new analysis of the jobs challenge in the region and discusses policies that can help countries to *grow with jobs* and get more people *back to work*.

Enhancing Job Opportunities, the last World Bank study on labor markets in the region, analyzed the impact of the transition on labor markets (see Rutkowski and Scarpetta 2005). Then and now, the countries in this region differ substantially in level of income, productive and market structures, and institutional development. Economic restructuring significantly affected labor market outcomes. In some countries, rapid restructuring initially generated more unemployment, but then employment growth followed in some sectors. In other countries, job destruction continued to outpace job creation well into the first decade of the 2000s. Along with restructuring, wage inequality widened; labor force participation declined; and informal employment increased. In the earlier years of the transition, employment was positively correlated with economic growth: it declined as economies contracted in the early 1990s, and then expanded as economic growth picked up in the late 1990s. Thereafter, the association weakened, and some countries experienced a period of nearly jobless growth.

Since the early years of the first decade of the 2000s, significant global and regional forces have been affecting labor markets in the region. The acceleration of growth, the easy access to credit during the financial boom, and improvements in business and labor regulations in some countries boosted labor demand. The steady shift in production and employment toward knowledge-intensive activities and services such as finance, the hospitality industry, and retail trade continued. On the supply side, key factors in some countries included shifts in labor force participation rates, cross-border migration, and changes in social benefits that may affect work incentives.

Three interrelated global forces have been accelerating the changes in labor demand: (a) the spread of information and communication technologies (skill-biased technological change), (b) the adoption of more flexible organizational and workplace structures and practices (skill-biased organizational change), and (c) the reallocation of some or all of the tasks involved in the production of goods and services to countries with lower unit labor costs (outsourcing or offshoring). The ongoing integration with international product and labor markets in 2000–10, particularly the accession of some countries in Central and Eastern Europe to the European Union (EU) and the export boom in countries like Turkey, has accelerated international competition and labor migration. This tends to exacerbate labor reallocations as export-led growth gains importance and firms tap into newly developed higher–value added and technology-intensive activities.

The 2008 crisis and its aftermath have had a dramatic impact on labor market conditions. Employment and wages have fallen substantially in most countries and have been slow to rebound during the modest recovery, with stark differences across countries.

The significance of all these changes for creating jobs and getting people *back to work* across the countries of ECA is the subject of this new regional jobs report. The main findings of the report are: (a) market reforms pay off in terms of jobs and productivity, although with a lag; (b) a small fraction of superstar high-growth firms, largely young, account for most of new jobs created in the region—thus, countries, especially late reformers, need to unleash the potential of high levels of latent entrepreneurship to start up new firms; (c) skills gaps hinder employment prospects, especially of youth and older workers, due to the inadequate response of the education and training systems to changes in the demand for skills; (d) employment is hindered by high implicit taxes on work for those transitioning to work from inactivity or unemployment and barriers that affect especially women, minorities, youth, and older workers; and (e) low internal labor mobility prevents labor relocation to places with greater job creation potential.

The report argues that to get more people *back to work* by *growing with jobs,* countries need to regain the momentum for economic and institutional reforms that existed before the crisis in order to: (a) lay the fundamentals to create jobs for all workers, by pushing reforms to create the enabling environment for existing firms to grow, become more productive, or exit the market and tap into entrepreneurship potential for new firms to emerge and succeed or fail fast and cheap; and (b) implement policies to support workers so they are prepared to take on the new jobs being created, by having the right skills and incentives, access to work, and being ready to move to places with the highest job creation potential.

Confronting the Jobs Challenge: The Transition Legacy, Demographics, and the Crisis Aftermath

There is much to be proud of in the economic performance of countries in the region prior to the financial crisis. ECA has been among the best performers among the regions of the world in economic growth and the expansion of labor productivity during 2000–08. Reforms yielded impressive policy results. Labor market legislation and institutions have gotten into step with the practice in the European countries of the Organisation for Economic Co-operation and Development (OECD), mainly through liberalization of the more rigid labor markets (Fialova and Schneider 2011; Lehmann and Muravyev 2010). The quality of the business climate, measured using the World Bank Doing Business Indicator, improved dramatically in

2006–13 (World Bank and IFC 2013a, 2013b). This has allowed the region to cut this quality gap in half with respect to advanced economies and brought (most of) the region significantly closer to OECD standards.

Strong economic and productivity growth translated into significant wage growth, but the employment gains were modest in 2000–07 and then almost nonexistent in the aftermath of the financial crisis. From 2000 to 2007, real wages more than doubled in the region as real wages recovered and then surpassed pretransition levels, while they grew 16.0 percent globally, 4.5 percent in developed economies, 50.0 percent in East Asia and declined in Latin America (ILO 2013). Although wage growth slowed to an annual average of 5 percent after the 2008 crisis, it still surpassed the growth in labor productivity. In contrast, employment grew by 7 percent between 2000 and 2007 in the region, compared with close to 20 percent in Latin America and the Caribbean and East Asia and the Pacific, 9 percent in the OECD countries in Europe, and 13 percent in the OECD countries outside Europe. This is equivalent to less than 1 percent per year and significantly slower than the growth of the economy, productivity, or even wages. After the onset of the crisis, job losses were significant, and employment returned to precrisis levels only in 2012 in some countries. Limited employment creation across the region meant that countries struggled to provide jobs for all workers even as economies grew. Employment rates remained low, especially among women and young and older workers, and significant unemployment continued to be a problem, particularly among youth.

The apparent disconnect between the strong economic growth and positive record of reform and the weak performance in employment in most of the region in recent years can be better understood through the lens of two important factors. These factors are, first, the common socialist legacy and the related need for modernization during the transition to a market economy and, second, the mounting demographic pressures associated with rapid aging in most countries and the significant increase in the number of youth in a few countries.

The global economic crisis exacerbated labor market challenges in the region and has dampened employment prospects. The financial crisis led to large employment losses, especially in countries more integrated to the Euro Zone and closest to Southern Europe and in pro-cyclical sectors such as construction and sectors that had expanded rapidly in the boom. Younger and smaller firms, which had led employment creation in 2000–07, were among the main casualties. The crisis has heightened fiscal pressures across the region, and may have accentuated skills mismatches in some countries.

The Impact of the Socialist Legacy

No other region of the world has undergone economic and structural change of the magnitude observed in ECA in such a short amount of time. Within the region, countries are at different stages in the transition to a market economy. Some countries embraced reform in a comprehensive manner early on, while others began reforming later or followed a more selective or gradual approach. To capture these differences, we have organized countries into three groups according to information on the reforms in labor market regulation, the business climate, and public sector modernization and on the level of financial development and trade integration. External factors, particularly the promise that membership in the EU holds for many countries in the region, also explain much of the cross-country differences in the speed and scope of reforms. These three country groups may be characterized as follows:

- *The advanced modernizers:* These countries are early reformers that continue to lead in the quality of the business climate and institutional structure, that have made important strides in reducing public sector employment and developing efficient financial markets, and that have effectively integrated into global markets. This group includes Turkey and the new EU member states except Croatia and Romania, that is, Bulgaria, the Czech Republic, Estonia, Hungary, Latvia, Lithuania, Poland, the Slovak Republic, and Slovenia.

- *The intermediate modernizers:* These countries are later reformers that have made significant progress in improving the climate for business and in reforming the public sector, thereby catching up with the early reformers; countries that have established some elements of well-developed financial markets; and that have become more open to international trade and, to a lesser extent, global financial markets. This group includes Albania, Armenia, Bosnia and Herzegovina, Croatia, Georgia, Kosovo, the former Yugoslav Republic (FYR) of Macedonia, Moldova, Montenegro, Romania, and Serbia.

- *The late modernizers:* These countries have initiated reforms relatively slowly or unevenly. Therefore, regulations are still less conducive to an enabling business environment, the public sector still plays a central role in the production sector, and these countries tend to have less well developed financial sectors and are less well integrated globally. In a subset of these countries, natural resources account for a significant share of gross domestic product (GDP). This group includes Azerbaijan, Belarus, Kazakhstan, the Kyrgyz Republic, the Russian Federation, Tajikistan, Turkmenistan, Ukraine, and Uzbekistan.

Armed with this classification, we examine the impact of modernization on employment creation by addressing three questions: Are the early reformers the best performers? Has public sector reform facilitated employment creation in the private sector? Have deeper financial development and integration in global markets translated into more jobs? Although definitive answers to these questions are elusive due to difficulties establishing causal relations, the evidence points to three main conclusions.

First, improvements in the business climate can pay off in better productivity and employment growth, but often with a lag and only among countries that have implemented broad, sustained, and substantive reforms. Among the advanced modernizers, 1 percentage point of GDP growth translated into 0.46 points of employment growth in 2000–07, compared with 0.13 in 1995–99 and with −0.43 among the intermediate modernizers and 0.05 among the late modernizers in 2000–07 (see figure O.1). Among the advanced modernizers, employment growth became more responsive to economic growth only in the first decade of the 2000s as the impact of the reforms implemented in the second half of the 1990s percolated throughout the economy and as many of these countries acceded to the EU. At that point, these countries achieved a more balanced improvement in both employment and productivity. In contrast, the relationship between economic growth and employment growth was weak among the intermediate and late modernizers in the first decade of the 2000s despite significant reforms, particularly among the intermediate modernizers, which also experienced larger employment losses with the crisis (figure O.1). In many of these countries, when productivity gains are achieved they tend to be accompanied by slow rates of net job creation.

Second, differences in employment protection legislation and minimum wage laws are not a first-order factor that explains overall levels of employment, although their role in shaping the composition and dynamics of employment may be more significant.

Third, moving forward the long-term contribution to employment of efforts to restructure the state-owned enterprise sector,

FIGURE 0.1

The Employment Payoff to Reforms during the Boom Years Often Materialized with a Lag and Mostly among Advanced Modernizers

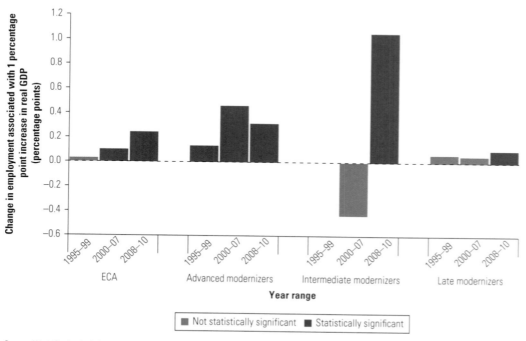

Sources: World Bank calculations based on data of ILO 2011, 2013; World Bank 2013.
Note: Statistical significance at least at the 10 percent level.

develop the financial sector, and open up and diversify trade is likely to be positive and significant, especially among the intermediate and late modernizers.

The Impact of Demographics

The countries in the region can be divided into two groups according to population dynamics projected over the next 20 years: countries that are aging, in some cases rapidly, and countries with large numbers of youth. The combination of aging and low fertility is directly associated with a shrinking working-age population and, without significant changes in participation rates, a shrinking labor force as well. This is the case in Belarus, Moldova, Russia, Ukraine, the new EU member states, and many of the countries in the Western Balkans and the South Caucasus. Increasing youth population shares (the youth bulge), driven by high fertility, are associated with expanding working-age populations and an expanding labor force. This is the case in Albania, Azerbaijan, Turkey, and most of the countries of Central Asia.

The size and demographic composition of the working-age population have a direct impact on labor market outcomes and, ultimately, mediate the relationship between modernization and employment creation. Economic participation is particularly weak among young workers, older workers, women, and minorities, and significant and persistent youth unemployment and long-term unemployment are key challenges in the region. The combination of these factors—low participation especially among women and older workers, high youth unemployment, and long-term unemployment—results in low employment rates and, eventually, substantial losses in the number of hours and years worked over the span of an employment history (figure O.2). Age and gender affect the ability of workers to switch jobs or to find employment after losing a job; young workers and older workers are less likely to find private sector employment relative to workers of prime age, and an older worker is more likely to drop out of the labor force after losing a job relative to a young worker or a worker of prime age. The demographic composition of the working-age population can thus influence the extent to which

FIGURE 0.2

Many Years of Potential Employment Lost, Especially among Older Workers and Women, 2010

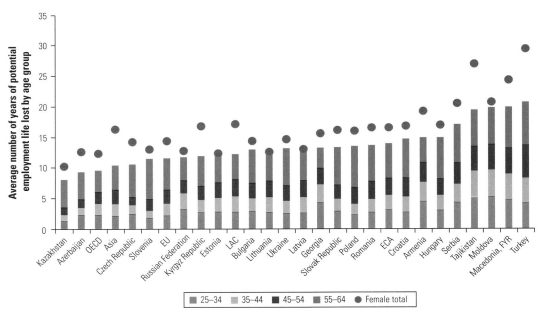

Source: World Bank calculations based on data of the International Labour Organization and household and labor force surveys.

Note: See chapter 1 in the report, figure 1.17. ECA = Europe and Central Asia; EU = European Union; LAC = Latin America and the Caribbean; OECD = Organisation for Economic Co-operation and Development.

labor can be effectively relocated across sectors as the economy restructures or adapts to shocks and firms or workers can be matched with new jobs. Age, gender, and ethnicity influence the ability and readiness of workers to tap into new job opportunities, in terms of their skills, incentives, barriers, and degree of mobility.

The Impact of the Crisis

The economic crisis led to large employment losses and a significant rise in unemployment (on average, of 2 percentage points, but as much as 20 percentage points among youth in some countries); wages have also fallen albeit less so. Most new EU member states and other countries closest to the Euro Zone were the most affected by the crisis and experienced the largest jobs losses, while Turkey, the South Caucasus, Russia, and other countries from Eurasia bounced back relatively quickly. Job losses were most significant in procyclical sectors, such as construction, and sectors that had expanded rapidly prior to the crisis but they were by no means limited to these sectors. In Turkey, except for the year 2005, exporting firms generally led job creation in the precrisis period. In 2009, however, employment losses among exporting firms far outstripped those among nonexistent firms. Similarly, in Romania's manufacturing sector, the subsectors leading job creation prior to the crisis (apparel and computer-related industries) experienced the largest contractions in employment during the crisis.

In addition, younger and smaller firms, which had led employment creation in 2000–07, were among the main casualties of the global crisis. Although new firms, innovative firms, and small firms fueled much of the region's job creation during the boom years, they were also less likely to survive during the crisis due to difficulties in accessing credit. In fact, firms who survived the crisis tended to be larger and older firms that had access to finance or could rely on internal sources of finance. New business registrations also fell sharply during the crisis. Between 2004 and 2008, new business registration (measured per 1,000 people) surged by 49 percent, while it fell by over 20 percent, slightly more than in all other regions in 2008–09.

Several countries in the group of advanced modernizers are grappling simultaneously with high joblessness and vacancy rates. An important question in the offset of the crisis is whether the apparent simultaneous excess demand for some workers and excess supply of others is the result of friction in labor market adjustments, or whether it has a structural component. The so-called Beveridge curve, which is often used to gauge the efficiency of the labor match-ing process, has shifted to the right in several countries indicating that both unemployment and vacancies are increasing (especially in the Baltic states and the Czech Republic), a possible indication of structural mismatches in the labor market.

Against this background, three main messages emerge moving forward. First, *regaining precrisis momentum will require different steps in different countries*. The advanced modernizers should renew their efforts to tackle second-generation investment climate reforms and deal with any pending issues in public sector modernization, while working toward resuming strong economic growth in a fiscally sustainable manner. When necessary, they should also seek to lessen the distortionary effects on the composition of employment that are associated with employment protection legislation and the minimum wage. In contrast, the late modernizers should focus on strengthening macroeconomic and business climate fundamentals, making labor market institutions more flexible, leveling the playing field, and deepening economic restructuring and diversification. The policy agenda among the intermediate reformers should be centered somewhere in between the approaches of these other two groups.

Second, *modernization is a necessary but not always sufficient condition for strong, sustained job creation*. Relative to other middle-income coun-tries and the countries of the OECD, employment rates were low and unemployment remained a stubborn problem even among the advanced modernizers in ECA before the crisis. Demographic shifts promise only to exacerbate the difficulties. The increasing share of older people in the working-age population will continue to exert downward pressure on aggregate labor force participation rates, even if the rates among older workers remain constant or rise slightly, unless there are significant policy and workplace changes to incentiv-ize and enable longer working lives. Similarly, countries with large cohorts of young people entering the labor market will need to implement policies that foster employment creation, while helping the young people to be well prepared and have better access to jobs.

Third, *policies that are sensitive to demographic imperatives such as age and gender can support the job reallocation process, while minimizing the associated negative impacts on specific groups of workers*. Helping workers become more adaptable requires distinct interventions among young workers, older workers, women, and minorities. For instance, addressing skill mismatches among young workers calls for well-designed apprenticeship programs that ease the transition from school to work by developing behavioral skills. Among older workers, it calls for education and training that builds on prior learning and

FIGURE O.3
Continued

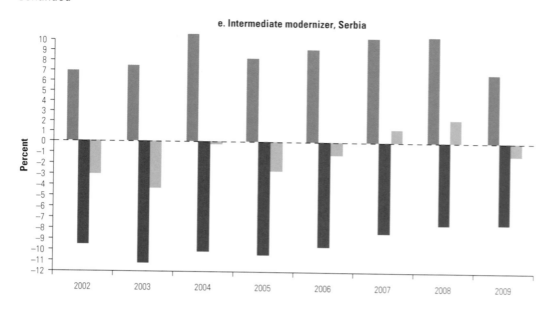

e. Intermediate modernizer, Serbia

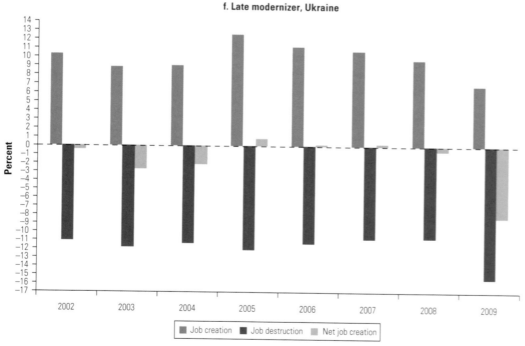

f. Late modernizer, Ukraine

■ Job creation ■ Job destruction ■ Net job creation

Sources: Amadeus (database), Bureau van Dijk, London, https://amadeus.bvdinfo.com/version-2013320/home.serv?product=amadeusneo; for Turkey, Structural Business Statistics (database), Eurostat, Luxembourg, http://epp.eurostat.ec.europa.eu/portal/page/portal/european_business/introduction; for Georgia, Enterprise Surveys (database), World Bank, Washington, DC, http://www.enterprisesurveys.org/Data/ExploreEconomies/2008/georgia; World Bank calculations.

Even among this handful of firms, performance has been affected by the quality of the business environment. Firms that have been faced with a less burdensome regulatory environment and less corruption have experienced more rapid growth. In particular, a one-standard-deviation improvement in each dimension of the business environment is associated with a significant improvement in firms' employment and profitability (Udomsaph 2012). Greater competition, access to higher-quality infrastructure, and judicial efficiency are also associated with better performance. These results are consistent with the aggregate evidence discussed above on the impact of reform on productivity growth and job creation.

In addition, many of the young productive firms that drove employment creation up to 2008 were put out of business by the credit crunch during the financial crisis. In good times, the financial sector is able to allocate resources toward young innovative firms that have growth potential. However, the crisis distorted this allocation process, and, as a consequence, the region lost many of these enterprises, including enterprises with great promise of growth that could have become drivers of employment expansion. The firms that survived the crisis tended to be larger and older firms that had access to finance or could rely on internal sources of financing.

Finally, job creation prospects in the near term generally remain dampened. Although these are difficult to assess, there is evidence that hiring expectations data from Business Expectation Surveys can be useful leading indicators. On average, for countries for which the relevant data are available which are mostly the Advanced Modernizers, they indicate that hiring prospects are not yet back to their precrisis levels. For example, net balances (or the net share of firms that expect to hire more people) in the construction sector, a key driver of job creation in the boom years, are hovering around zero through the first quarter of 2013, far below their precrisis peak of about 16 percent. There are similar patterns in the manufacturing sector. In the retail and services sector, the net hiring balances are more diverse and, in some cases, are back or near their precrisis peak (such as in the Slovak Republic's service sector). More generally, however, aggregate hiring prospects remain subdued almost everywhere, especially in Southern Europe.

Latent Entrepreneurship and Business Startups

Because of the central role of younger firms in new job creation and the loss of young firms during the crisis, fostering higher rates of entrepreneurship plays an essential role. Business startups can help expand and sustain a modern enterprise sector that absorbs those out of work, including workers displaced from restructured enterprises. New entrepreneurs can help replace some of the youngest, most dynamic, and most innovative firms that the region lost to the global financial crisis. In the current period of uncertain economic prospects, entrepreneurial initiatives can once again fuel economic growth and job creation.

Rates of entrepreneurship in the region are thought to be generally lower than those in other emerging and high-income economies. However, the region's record is more ambiguous than generally thought, as cross-country comparisons are often hampered by variations in data sources and definitions. Led by the advanced modernizers, entrepreneurial activity in the region has, along certain measures, compared favorably with that in many other countries, particularly in recent years.

There is evidence of substantial latent entrepreneurship in the region (figure O.4). Close to a quarter of the labor force in the region would rather be self-employed than wage employees. The desire to be self-employed does not appear to be driven by necessity or at least not by necessity alone (survival entrepreneurship). As many as a fifth of the wage-employed declare they prefer self-employment, and a large fraction of this group is highly educated or highly skilled professionals employed as directors or managers. This compares well with countries in Western Europe on which comparable data are available. In addition, over a quarter of these latent entrepreneurs have previously attempted to start a business, and nearly two-thirds of those who tried succeeded.

Both latent entrepreneurship and the likelihood of succeeding in starting a business among latent entrepreneurs are associated with particular attitudes and demographic characteristics and with the quality of the local business climate. Older married men and individuals willing to take risks are more likely to self-report latent entrepreneurship. While there is no consistent relationship between educational attainment and latent entrepreneurship, educational attainment is positively correlated to the probability of starting a business and succeeding. Working in the private sector is associated with higher latent entrepreneurship rates relative to working in state enterprises. Latent entrepreneurship is also greater in areas with a higher concentration of economic activity. The gap between starting a business and succeeding is largest among late modernizers and narrowest among advanced modernizers.

FIGURE O.4

High Latent Entrepreneurship but Low Rates of Startups in the Region in 2010

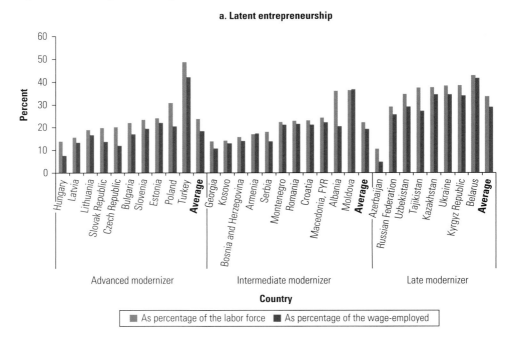

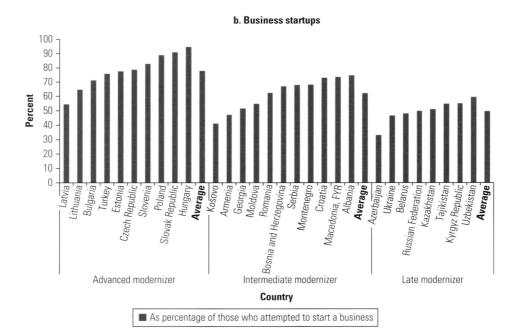

Sources: Life in Transition Survey (database), European Bank for Reconstruction and Development, London, http://www.ebrd.com/pages/research /economics/data/lits.shtml; Atasoy et al. 2013.
Note: Latent entrepreneurship refers to people's dormant entrepreneurial spirit, measured by an individual's preference for self-employment. Business startups refer to the number of succesful business startups as a percentage of those who took steps toward this goal.

In this environment, there is a role for policy in strengthening job creation and entrepreneurship. *Business climate reforms that lower the cost of starting and closing a business,* including reforms in regulations on business registration, insolvency, and bankruptcy procedures, can allow businesses with high potential to thrive and create jobs, while allowing others to fail rapidly and fail cheaply. Similarly, policies that *facilitate and promote economic agglomeration and increase business density* also hold promise in the effort to close the gap between latent and actual entrepreneurship as new firms are more likely to thrive in areas with higher levels of concentration in economic activity. *Investing in business skills* (for example, through the creation of business schools) and *shifting social norms and attitudes about risk taking and failure* can be effective in increasing the number of entrepreneurs and fostering the creation of new businesses.

Provided the conditions exist for businesses to create jobs, workers need to be prepared, adaptable, willing, and mobile to tap into newly created job opportunities. Foremost, they must possess the skills that the jobs require.

Developing the Skills for the Job

The global and regional forces that affect labor markets require adaptable workers. Trade and technological and organizational change have led to a decline in the demand for more routine manual skills and a growing demand for new economy skills, that is, higher-order analytical and organizational skills that cannot be easily automated (Autor, Levy, and Murnane 2003). In the region, significant structural transformations and changes in production, job creation and destruction, and integration with international markets—for example, the accession of countries in the region to the EU—have also affected the demand for skills. The response of education and training systems to these trends is determining the extent to which there are mismatches in the supply and demand for skills. Two main questions arise: Are skill gaps a constraint on employment in the region? Who is more affected, youth or older workers?

The evidence indicates that skill gaps are hindering labor performance among youth and older workers in the region, though the importance of the gaps varies across countries. There are three main reasons for this outcome. First, employers say that the skills of workers are at the top of their concerns regarding the growth of their businesses. Second, in many countries, but especially in the advanced reformers, businesses are increasingly requiring modern workplace skills. Third, education and training systems have not kept up with the pace of the changes in the demand for skills.

On the eve of the financial crisis, enterprises in the region reported that finding workers with the skills they needed was one of the top constraints on the growth of their businesses. There was a substantial increase in the share of firms reporting that finding workers with adequate skills was a top constraint on their businesses in all countries in the region, except Hungary, between 2005 and 2008. In fact, lack of skilled workers became the second most common constraint on growth cited by firms (Mitra, Selowsky, and Zalduendo 2010; Murthi and Sondergaard 2012). Close to 3 in 10 firms reported that skills were a major or severe constraint, slightly less than infrastructure and corruption. The increase was greater in several CIS countries and new EU members, where the share of firms citing skills as a major or severe constraint rose by 20–30 percentage points. In particular, skills were the most binding constraint on firms in countries that were better integrated with external markets (such as Lithuania and Poland), that had underperforming education and training systems, and that were experiencing rapid out-migration (such as Kazakhstan and Romania), or in which a large share of the adult labor force had low educational attainment or secondary vocational schooling (such as Moldova and Russia).

Much like their peers in advanced economies, when employers in the region complain that workers do not have the appropriate skills, they are not reflecting only on educational attainment. More than ever, workers are matched to jobs based on a multiplicity of skills, not merely educational attainment. Employers value generic skills, including cognitive skills, such as literacy, numeracy, and problem-solving abilities, and socioemotional skills, such as self-discipline, perseverance, dependability, and teamwork (also known as noncognitive or soft skills), besides technical skills, including vocational and career qualifications and job-specific skills. There is mounting evidence that employers in OECD countries and countries in the region view the lack of socioemotional skills as at least as much of a binding constraint as the lack of cognitive and technical skills.[1]

The demand for new economy skills has increased in the advanced modernizers, particularly among young workers. For instance, Lithuania has experienced a substantial expansion in the higher-order skill content of employment since the country's EU accession (figure O.5). This likely reflects its gradual, but consistent shift toward a knowledge-based economy with special emphasis on biotechnology. Other countries that experience similar trends, though with varying

FIGURE 0.5

Skills of Older Cohorts Are at Risk of Obsolescence in Several Countries in the Region

a. Lithuania, cohort born after 1974

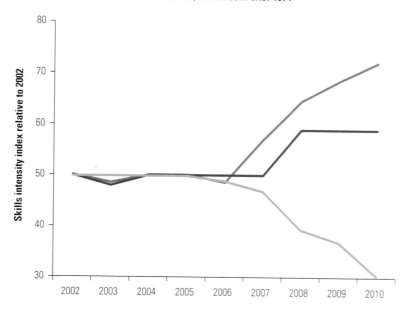

b. Lithuania, cohort born before 1955

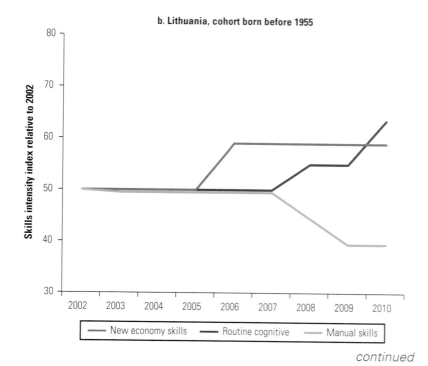

continued

FIGURE 0.5
Continued

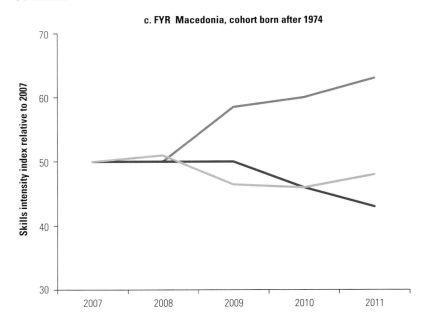

c. FYR Macedonia, cohort born after 1974

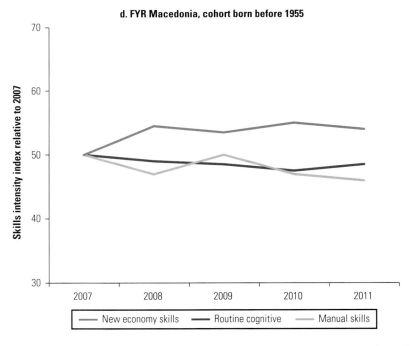

d. FYR Macedonia, cohort born before 1955

New economy skills — Routine cognitive — Manual skills

continued

FIGURE 0.5
Continued

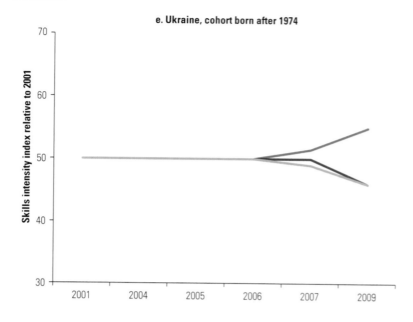

e. Ukraine, cohort born after 1974

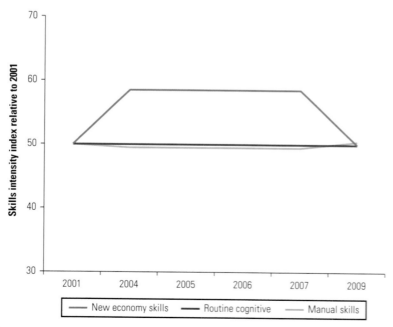

f. Ukraine, cohort born before 1955

—— New economy skills   —— Routine cognitive   —— Manual skills

Source: World Bank estimates based on labor surveys.
Note: The y-axis plots the percentile of the distribution of the skills intensity of jobs held by any given cohort for each year.
The index uses as a base the respective median of the skills intensity distribution in the initial year. Chapter 3 of the full
report provides details on the methodology.

intensity, are the Czech Republic, Estonia, Georgia (in urban areas), Latvia, Poland, and Slovenia. In addition, the shift toward the higher intensity of jobs in new economy skills and in routine cognitive skills is stronger (or only occurs) among younger cohorts, while work intensity in manual skills is mostly falling or is flat among younger and older cohorts.[2] Thus, older workers have not benefited as much from the increasing availability of jobs that require higher-order skills, and they are losing out as jobs requiring traditional skills disappear.

In contrast, the intermediate and late modernizers, such as FYR Macedonia and Ukraine, have not yet experienced significant changes in the skill intensity of jobs (see figure O.5). As they embark on the agenda of pending reforms, these countries are likely to experience age-differentiated shifts in the demand for skills similar to the shifts experienced by the advanced modernizers. This may leave some older workers at a disadvantage because they are at higher risk of skills obsolescence.

This longer-term trend in skills demand has been aggravated by the recent financial crisis: some countries are grappling with high joblessness rates and significant job vacancy rates simultaneously. A labor shortage indicator derived from the European Commission's Business and Consumer Surveys shows that about 8 percent of EU manufacturing firms considered labor shortages a factor limiting their production in the years preceding the crisis (European Commission 2012a). The indicator showed a drop to 2 percent in 2009 and then climbed up to around 5–6 percent in 2012 despite the persistent economic sluggishness and rising unemployment. Whether the apparent simultaneous excess demand for some types of workers and the excess supply of others is the result of structural mismatches or of friction in labor market adjustments is unclear.

The inability of the supply of skills to keep up with shifts in demand has led to skill gaps. At first look, such skill gaps in the region seem puzzling. Except for a few countries, the region fares well in international comparisons of basic education attainment and average student learning outcomes, and the region has also registered a substantial expansion in tertiary education enrollments. However, digging deeper, several studies have argued that the response of the education and training systems in the region to the shifts in the demand for skills has been uneven (Cedefop 2012; European Commission 2012a; Murthi and Sondergaard 2012; Quintini 2011). For instance, a recent World Bank report indicates that many education and training systems are failing to achieve quality and relevance because they are not developing the appropriate skills among new entrants in the labor market and adults already in the workforce (Murthi and Sondergaard 2012).

Age profiles of the population are important in identifying skill gaps in most of the region. Nearly 60 percent of the potential workforce is of prime adult age (35–54) or older (55+), except in the young CIS countries and Turkey, where the share is only one-third. This group has an average mid-level education in most countries (over two-thirds had completed secondary education). The older population (55+) comprises 15–20 percent of the potential work-force, except in the young CIS countries and Turkey, and 20–40 percent had not completed secondary education. New, younger entrants in the labor market (ages 15–24)—the cohort edu-cated largely post-transition—attain higher education in greater pro-portions, but are a shrinking share of the workforce in the EU-11 and the older Balkan and CIS countries.[3] These young people already comprise fewer than 20 percent of the potential workforce in the Central European countries, between 20–30 percent in the other EU-11 countries and the CIS, and nearly 40 percent in the younger CIS and Turkey. These shares are projected to shrink quickly below 15 percent in the EU-11 and the older Balkan and CIS countries over the next three decades. The emigration of more well educated youth aggravates the skill constraints in some rapidly aging countries in the region.

Many youth often acquire inadequate generic and technical skills. Too many children are not acquiring basic generic skills. According to the 2009 reading assessment of the OECD's Program for International Student Assessment (PISA), over 20 percent of 15-year-olds in sev-eral countries in the region fail to acquire basic functional literacy skills and thus do poorly relative to corresponding youth in OECD countries (figure O.6). The share of youth who are functionally illit-erate reaches 40 percent in Bulgaria and Romania, 30 percent in Russia, and dramatically higher levels in other countries participating in PISA in the CIS and the Balkans. This failure in the provision of basic skills disproportionately affects disadvantaged groups such as the Roma and other ethnic minorities. Yet, the basic education system in several countries continues to overemphasize the teaching of facts and imparting knowledge, rather than the development of the kinds of analytical and problem-solving skills that will help young people acquire knowledge and other skills later on in postsecondary educa-tion or on the job (Murthi and Sondergaard 2012). And in several countries, poorly performing students continue to be directed into vocational schools rather than being encouraged to finish general upper secondary education.

FIGURE 0.6

Too Many 15-Year-Olds in the Region Remain Functionally Illiterate, 2009

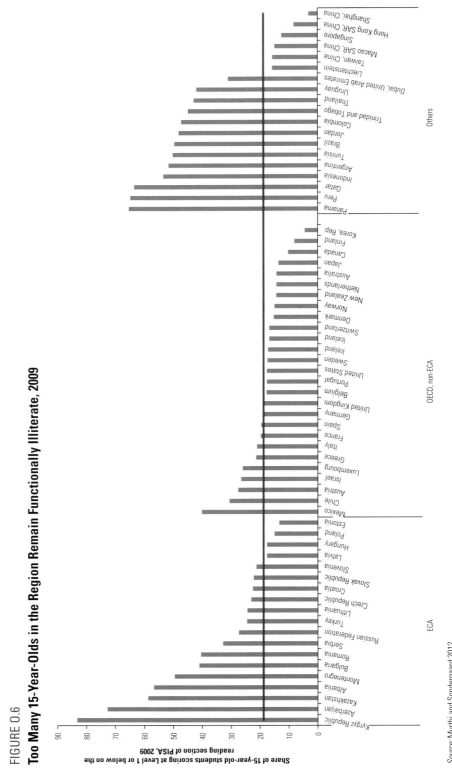

Source: Murthi and Sondergaard 2012.

Note: The red line indicates the average share of functionally illiterate 15-year-olds in OECD non–ECA countries. ECA = Europe and Central Asia; OECD = Organisation for Economic Co-operation and Development.

Tertiary education among youth has expanded rapidly, but with varying quality and relevance. The coverage of tertiary education has expanded more rapidly in the region than in other parts of the world over the last two decades. However, this occurred while there were weak or nonexistent mechanisms to maintain quality. Much of the expansion has occurred among private, for-profit providers of tertiary education, especially among part-time (including weekend) students or through distance learning programs. For instance, in 2009, half the undergraduate students in Poland were enrolled in weekend programs, while, in Romania, around two-thirds of students enrolled in private universities (42 percent of total enrollment) were part-time students or were participating in distance learning (Murthi and Sondergaard 2012).

The quality of these programs is undocumented, but likely heterogeneous. For example, a recent survey of university students in several countries in the region found that more than 60 percent of respondents knew other students who had purchased their entry to university or paid to obtain specific grades (Murthi and Sondergaard 2012). This raises doubts about the capacity of some of the new providers to ensure that students graduate with the requisite skills.

Concerns about the existence of an oversupply or the overqualification of university graduates for available jobs in the region are misplaced, but there is evidence that not all individuals would benefit in the same way from a college education. There is little evidence that the rapid expansion of tertiary education is driving down the average returns to university education overall. In most countries in ECA, the average wage premiums associated with tertiary education remained unchanged or increased in 2000–10 with only a few exceptions (figure O.7). The wage premiums are generally higher among the more advanced modernizers, such as most of the EU-11 countries and Turkey, and are low, though still significant, in a smaller group of late modernizers. However, novel findings using unique data for Bulgaria and Poland show that the high average returns to college education are not available to everyone. In Bulgaria, tertiary education is quite a lucrative investment for graduates who are able to land jobs at the upper end of the salary scale in their fields, but it may turn out to be an unattractive investment for those graduates who take on jobs at the lower end, particularly when tuition and the other direct costs of tertiary education are factored in. The pursuit of a tertiary degree may thus be a poor proposition for a nonnegligible share of youth even if it constitutes a valuable investment for most.[4]

There is a major gap in the data on skills, especially the skills of the older working-age population and the socioemotional skills of youth

FIGURE O.7
Tertiary Education Delivers High Average Returns in Most Countries

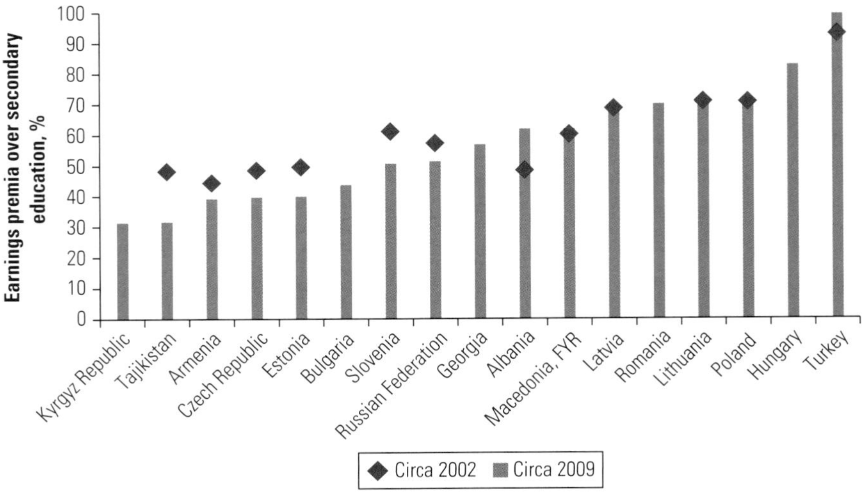

Source: World Bank based on labor force and households surveys, latest available years.

and adults. Since the onset of the transition, skills upgrading among adults and older workers on or off the job has been inadequate or underdeveloped. Adult education and training programs are not being adequately promoted although they are critical in economies with an aging labor force, and on-the-job skills formation through firm training has filled the gap only partially. Information on the impact of either public or private training is limited. Similarly, soft skills should be systematically assessed, and education and training interventions at schools, at home, and through training programs should be evaluated to find ways to foster the development of these skills effectively.[5]

In light of these challenges, there is a need to rethink the fundamentals of education, training, and lifelong learning systems. There are three key directions: (a) stronger policy coordination between government, training providers, and the enterprise sector, with a sound regulatory regime for the development of private provision; (b) appropriate incentives for firms to engage more in training adults and older workers; and (c) a concerted effort by employers, governments, and workers to invest more effectively in training at older ages. A policy framework is sound only if it is not restricted to narrow, fragmented educational, training, and labor policies and integrates policies into a long-term strategy for skills development. Lifelong skills development should be at the center of the policy agenda in the region. Policies must help build skills for the workplace by focusing on the development of a strong foundation of generic skills, an expansion of tertiary education systems that ensures quality and relevance, and the promotion of training systems that are responsive to markets and sensitive to demographics so as to enable the lifelong upgrading of skills.

The priorities depend on the age profile of a country's workforce. In all countries, it is critical to develop the shrinking youth workforce to its full potential by ensuring that the basic education system lays a strong base in the new economy skills that are fundamental to the modern workplace. The access of youth to tertiary education should respond to employer needs and take advantage of the niches a country can exploit in global external markets to create jobs. An important effort should be dedicated to providing individuals and families with timely, relevant information on the market returns to various career paths and on appropriate education and training programs that have been monitored to ensure quality. In rapidly aging economies, where the population shares of workers of prime age and older workers are becoming larger, adult education and training should be a priority. Training for adults needs to be delivered in ways that acknowledge that older adults learn differently from younger adults. Advanced modernizers that are facing a demographic decline should use regulation and financing to facilitate the emergence of an adult education and training market that is oriented to the private sector. Late modernizers experiencing a demographic decline (that is, many countries in Southeastern Europe and the middle-income CIS countries) can focus on the introduction of a strategic policy framework for adult learning and the creation of tools needed to implement this framework (for example, coordination mechanisms, plus the initial regulatory steps). In all countries, participation in the OECD Program for International Assessment of Adult Competencies or the World Bank Skills Toward Employment and Productivity (STEP) surveys would help in understanding the current skills and competencies of the workforce and in adapting education to the needs of a modern economy.[6]

Making Work Pay and Jobs Accessible

In addition to being prepared with the skills needed to tap into new job opportunities, workers must see that work actually pays and be able to access jobs that fit their skills. Market institutions, tax and social protection systems, and the rules and norms that govern employment in most countries in the region have been mainly designed for men of prime age. This raises two questions: Do tax and social protection systems in the region undermine work incentives? Do some groups face additional barriers to employment?

There is evidence that taxes and social protection systems, as well as other market, social, and institutional factors, do not always make work pay or make jobs accessible. Across the region, labor taxes and the design of social protection systems can create disincentives to (formal) employment. Labor taxes remain high in some countries; this is often particularly so among low-wage, part-time, and second earners. Additionally, in some cases, if a person starts to work even one hour per week, social assistance or unemployment benefits are fully withdrawn. In other cases, social assistance benefits are withdrawn abruptly as formal labor income increases. Pension systems that encourage early retirement also undermine work incentives among older workers. Other barriers render labor markets unattractive or inaccessible among women, youth, older workers, and ethnic minorities, thereby inadvertently excluding or discouraging many from work.

The design of labor taxes and social protection systems, often more than the benefit levels themselves, can create work disincentives. In many cases, labor taxes remain high, and are less progressive relative to labor taxes in the EU-15 and OECD countries.[7] High taxes among low-wage earners, combined with the high cost involved in relinquishing social protection benefits in favor of (formal) employment, mean that work disincentives are greater among low-wage and part-time workers (usually younger workers, older workers, women, and ethnic minorities) and second earners in families (usually women). In some cases, the eligibility criteria for social benefits effectively prohibit or discourage work. For instance, a common benefit eligibility requirement is proof of unemployment status or registration with public employment services. Additionally, benefits are often open-ended or of long duration. In Russia, Serbia, and Slovenia, a person may receive unemployment benefits for up to two consecutive years. In the case of pensions, low retirement ages shorten the working lives of older workers by a substantial amount. The average statutory retirement age in the region is 59 years for women and 62.5 years for men compared with the OECD average of 64 for women and 65 for men, with significant variation in the effective retirement age across countries partly because of early retirement schemes. This is a missed opportunity in the quest to promote employment because the labor market decisions of these groups are also the most responsive to tax and benefit rules and to changes in these rules.

Social assistance beneficiaries are discouraged from abandoning labor inactivity because of the significant forgone benefits, especially among low-wage and part-time earners. This inactivity trap is illustrated in figure O.8a for the average and low-wage earners. In Latvia, Lithuania, and Slovenia, an individual who takes up work at an average wage loses the equivalent of 70–85 percent of his labor income through a combination of income taxes and lost benefits. While less severe among average earners in the region than in OECD countries, the formal work disincentives are disproportionately greater (70 percent, on average) for low-wage earners, part-time workers, and second earners on social assistance. The implicit tax rates are significantly higher for workers earning only half the average wage compared with workers earning higher wages. In Latvia, for example, low-wage earners on social assistance gain practically nothing by taking on a formal job because the combined implicit tax—the taxes paid on their new earnings, plus the forgone social benefits—is 100 percent.

In FYR Macedonia, Montenegro, and Serbia, the implicit tax rates are greater than 70 percent among low-wage earners so that a household's total income increases by only 30 percent of the worker's new earnings in a formal job. Second earners in the household—usually women—also face weak incentives if they have the possibility of taking a formal job and relinquishing social assistance and unemployment benefits. For example, in Turkey, the inactivity trap is five percentage points higher among the second earners in a household relative to the first earners.

Especially among low-wage and part-time earners, leaving unemployment to take on a formal sector job is also strongly discouraged by poorly designed tax and benefit systems. Even if unemployment benefits are not generous, an individual who takes up a formal sector job may abruptly lose them entirely. On average in the countries in the region on which data are available, the equivalent of almost two-thirds of labor income for an average wage earner is taken away if one makes the leap from unemployment benefits to formal employment (figure O.8b). This unemployment trap is more significant in the region than in non-European OECD countries. As in the case of the inactivity trap, the work disincentives linked to the unemployment trap are more substantial among low-wage and part-time earners, particularly among prime-age and older workers whose labor market histories make them eligible for unemployment benefits. Disincentives are especially serious in Bulgaria, Latvia, FYR Macedonia, Serbia, and Slovenia, where the implicit tax rate is above

FIGURE O.8

The Costs of Moving Out of Social Assistance or Unemployment Benefits Could Be High, Especially for Low-Wage Earners and Part-Time Workers, 2010

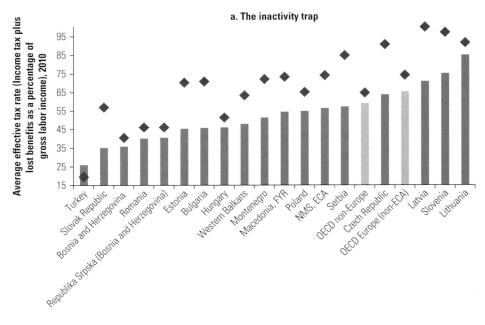

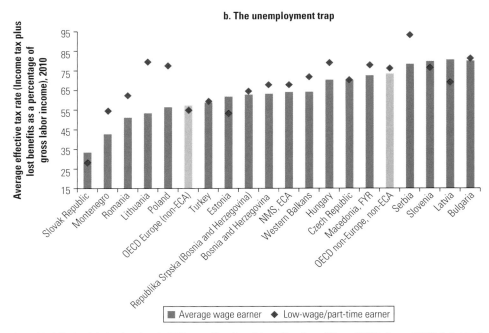

■ Average wage earner   ◆ Low-wage/part-time earner

Source: World Bank calculations based on the OECD tax and benefit model; see "Benefits and Wages: OECD Indicators," OECD, Paris, http://www.oecd.org/els/benefitsandwagesoecdindicators.htm.
Note: See chapter 4 of the report for details on the methodology of the calculations. The Western Balkans refers to Albania, Bosnia and Herzegovina, Kosovo, the former Yugoslav Republic of Macedonia, Montenegro, and Serbia. Republika Srpska is a political entity of Bosnia and Herzegovina. NMS = new EU member states in Central and Eastern Europe.

business, but also workers. For example, BMW has piloted adjustments to production lines to address the health, skills, workplace
environment, and other challenges associated with their aging
workforce. The adjustments, which have included the addition of
special chairs to reduce physical strain, the use of magnifying lenses
along assembly lines, and the introduction of stackable transport
containers, led to a 7 percent increase in productivity among older
workers within one year to match the productivity levels of production lines with younger workers. Modern technology and new
management practices have opened up a wide array of alternative
and more flexible work arrangements, including new types of contracts, such as on-call contracts, freelance contracts, and telework.
Among white-collar workers, computers, mobile devices, Internet
access, videoconferencing, and other technologies have made it
possible for people to work productively outside of the traditional
office space. Similarly, among blue-collar workers, technological
advances have allowed the automation of many processes so that
work shifts can become more flexible.

The region can also learn from the experience of countries that
have adopted a more comprehensive approach to incorporating
women into the labor market. For instance, in Canada between 1995
and 2004, the already high female labor force participation rate rose
by almost 6 percentage points to a large extent because of more
family-friendly policy initiatives and tax reforms. Tax wedges for
second earners (usually women) were cut, and the prioritization of
early childhood development paved the way for the expansion of
child care and family benefits. In Southern Europe, substantial
increases in employment among women in recent decades have
been attributed partly to gradual but steady changes in cultural and
social norms in favor of greater women's participation in the labor
force.

Specific policy priorities, across and within the pillars described
above, will depend on a country's reform path and the demographic
composition of its workforce. Figure O.10 shows aggregate indexes
for work disincentives and barriers for countries in the region and
benchmark EU countries. While only indicative, it shows that the
challenges vary significantly across countries. In addition to removing
barriers to employment that affect specific groups, the key challenge
is balancing employment and protection: for countries with high
work disincentives, the main task is to reduce these disincentives, but
not at the expense of social protection; in contrast, for countries with
low protection, the task lies in expanding protection without creating
more disincentives to work.

FIGURE O.10

A Diverse Agenda on Disincentives and Barriers to Employment in the Region

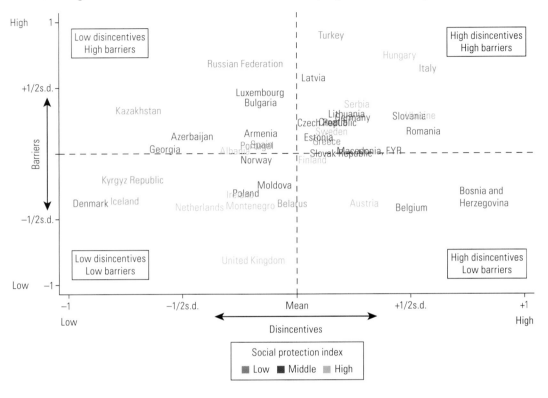

Social protection index

Low	Middle	High
Belarus, Spain, Greece,	Armenia; Azerbaijan; Belgium;	Albania, Austria, Finland,
Iceland, Italy, Kazakhstan,	Bulgaria; Bosnia and Herzegovina;	United Kingdom, Hungary, Ireland,
Kyrgyz Republic, Portugal, Russian Federation,	Czech Republic;	Montenegro, Netherlands, Serbia,
Turkey	Germany; Denmark; Estonia;	Sweden, Ukraine
	Georgia; Croatia; Lithuania;	
	Luxembourg; Latvia; Moldova;	
	Macedonia, FYR; Norway; Poland;	
	Romania; Slovak Republic; Slovenia	

Source: See chapter 4 in the report for data sources and details on the methodology.
Note: The indices for disincentives, barriers, and protection have been obtained as the average of subindicators. For each index, a higher value means a higher level of disincentives, barriers, or protection. Each indicator has been standardized by subtracting the mean and dividing by the standard deviation, so that all indicators have a mean of 0 and a standard deviation (s.d.) of 1. OECD = Organisation for Economic Co-operation and Development.

Leading Workers to Better Jobs

In addition to helping workers acquire the right skills and making employment more attractive and accessible, policy makers need to develop an environment that facilitates internal labor mobility and leads workers to jobs. Many workers in the region cross international borders in search of better economic opportunities: many Belarussians, Moldovans, Tajiks, and Ukrainians, for example, migrate permanently or temporarily to Russia; many Poles and Turks go to Germany; many people from FYR Macedonia and many Romanians work in Italy. However, in labor markets, internal migration can be as important as international migration: economic development occurs through the agglomeration of economic activities (World Bank 2009b). When workers move to cities and leading regions within a country, they help bring knowledge and human capital closer together, which generates productivity gains through agglomeration and better labor market matching, as well as higher wages and living standards for themselves and their families. Internal mobility is especially relevant for those countries in the region in which demographic pressures are placing a social premium on a larger domestic labor force.

This raises two main questions: Can enhanced internal labor mobility improve employment outcomes in the region? What can policy makers do to ensure that markets, institutions, and policies foster rather than hinder internal mobility?

Labor mobility in the region is generally low. A Eurobarometer survey conducted in 2009 revealed that people in the region view geographical mobility positively (European Commission 2010). However, when asked during the 2010 round of the Life in Transition Survey about their willingness to move for employment reasons, a large majority (74 percent) had no intention of going elsewhere in the country for a job, which is below the reported intentions in Western European countries.[8] As shown in figure O.11, even after adjustments are made for differences in the size of geographical units or population across countries, countries in the region show internal migration rates below the rates in Western European and other peer countries. People move much less frequently within their own countries in the region relative to people in other parts of the world, such as Australia, Canada, Chile, China, the United States, and some countries in northwestern Europe. In the 2010 round of the Life in Transition Survey, between 10 and 20 percent of the population in the region said they had moved away from the place of their birth over the last 20 years. The corresponding share is nearly 30 percent

FIGURE O.11

The Population in Europe and Central Asia Is Less Internally Mobile Than in the Rest of the World, 2009

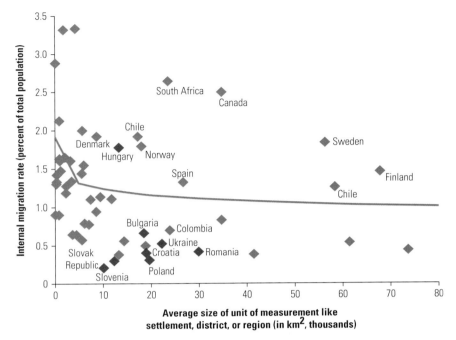

Source: World Bank 2012b, based on United Nations, Eurostat, and national-level data.
Note: See chapter 5 in the report for details on the methodology. Red dots are for ECA countries; blue ones are for the rest of the world.

in Germany and Sweden, 40 percent in the United Kingdom, and 60 percent in France. In the United States, 32 percent of the population is living outside the state in which they were born.

The internal migration observed in the region does not always lead to the types of agglomeration economies that are crucial to economic development. This is especially the case in intermediate and late modernizers, where, respectively, 47 and 37 percent of all migration takes place from urban to rural areas and within rural areas (compared with 28 and 31 percent among the early modernizers and the Western European countries, respectively). Because productivity growth is often concentrated in cities, this type of migration is likely to have only limited effects on growth and living standards. Indeed, in some countries, most of the migration is not to urban areas: in Estonia and Poland, over half of all migration (55 percent) is to or within rural areas; in Tajikistan, almost three-quarters (72 percent) is this sort of migration. The latter may be associated with some groups, particularly older individuals, who are moving to places with a lower cost of living.

International migration and commuting are important alternatives to internal labor mobility, but are far from perfect substitutes. On average, about 10 percent of the population in the region is living in countries other than their birth countries. By this metric, several countries appear quite mobile, especially countries in Central Asia and some EU-11 countries. Similarly, available data from household surveys show that commuting is important in the Czech Republic, Hungary, the Kyrgyz Republic, and the Slovak Republic. While commuting and emigration can help relieve labor market pressures and improve resource utilization, they cannot substitute for healthy rates of internal mobility. Emigration can deprive the local economy of increasingly scarce local talent and exacerbate demographic shifts in rapidly aging countries with shrinking working-age populations. Commuting generally occurs across localities that are not so distant, but rarely across distant provinces or regions. It cannot therefore be expected to reduce all gaps in economic opportunities between leading and lagging areas within a country; it is necessary to remove barriers and constraints to full internal mobility. Neither commuting nor international migration are conducive to the agglomeration economies and resource reallocations that internal labor mobility can foster.

Internal labor mobility and labor market performance reinforce each other. Greater internal labor mobility correlates with lower unemployment and higher employment rates. People move to places with better job opportunities, higher wages, and less unemployment. At the same time, internal mobility can improve labor market outcomes through a more accurate matching of workers and firms and through increases in productivity. Internal labor mobility may also facilitate the adjustment to economic shocks because, for example, workers can move away from the hardest hit areas into less affected ones.

Significant employment and productivity gains may be realized in the region through greater internal labor mobility. There are important gaps within countries in the region in terms of unemployment rates and labor productivity, and these gaps—especially in labor productivity—are larger in the region than in the EU-15 countries (figure O.12). In Ukraine, for example, the most productive areas are more than twice as productive as the rest of the country (World Bank 2012b). In ECA, only 6 percent of productivity gains between 1999 and 2008 were associated with intersectoral productivity growth and labor mobility. In contrast, in East Asia, 42 percent of the overall growth in labor productivity has been associated with job reallocations across sectors, a key ingredient of the success of East Asia in the

FIGURE O.12

Relatively Large Regional Disparities in Labor Productivity, 2002 and 2009

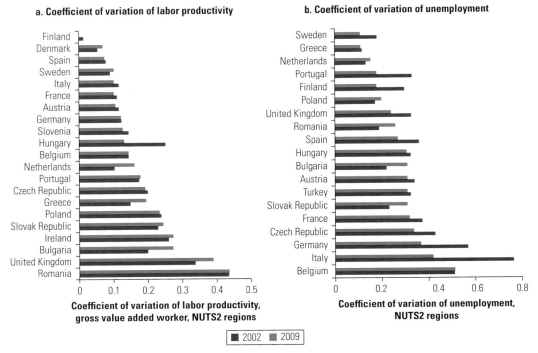

Source: World Bank calculations using Eurostat data.

Note: The coefficient of variation is the ratio of the standard deviation to the mean and is a measure of inequality. The larger the coefficient, the larger the regional disparities. Data on unemployment for Turkey refers to 2006 and 2009; data on productivity for Sweden refers to 2002 and 2007. The NUTS classification (Nomenclature of territorial units for statistics) is a hierarchical system for dividing up the economic territory of the EU. NUTS2 is the base for the application of regional policy.

past decade. Much of this involved shifts in the labor share in agriculture and low-productivity services in rural and lagging areas to more productive uses in manufacturing and services in urban and leading zones. An untapped potential exists in the region: enterprise surveys show that firms located in large cities where capital and labor are agglomerated grow more quickly (IFC 2013). Realizing the gains from greater internal labor mobility is particularly relevant for late modernizers that must still undertake significant economic reforms and promote productive restructuring.

While the reasons behind the low internal labor mobility in the region warrant more research, there is evidence that demographics, incentives, and institutional factors play a role. Age is a prominent factor in internal mobility: youth and younger adults are much more mobile, and even older individuals who have ever migrated largely did so when they were younger. Individuals with a tertiary-level degree are 1.7 times more likely to have migrated to urban areas than people with less than lower secondary education. Individuals who tend to take more risks and who are healthier are also more likely to migrate. Homeowners are less likely to migrate. People in the region are generally more driven to migrate internally because of schooling or family reasons than because of job opportunities.

Incentives matter and people do move from lagging to leading regions, although the flows are smaller than one might expect given the regional gaps in opportunities. If we consider net regional migration flows, the wealthier regions appear to function as poles of migration, attracting younger cohorts in particular. The high unemployment rates in the region seem to influence the migration decisions of individuals of prime age, but not those of youth. This is consistent with migration among younger cohorts that is driven by mobility among students. In contrast, older migrants (closer to retirement age) tend to leave wealthier regions to go to less well-off regions, which is consistent with the high shares of rural-to-rural and urban-to-rural migration.

On the institutional side, strict administrative requirements and shallow housing and real estate credit markets stemming from the legacy of central planning, as well as insufficient labor market information and lack of portability in social benefits, have all deterred greater internal mobility in at least some countries in the region. In Ukraine, for example, administrative procedures require people to register at their place of residence, but many people prefer not to register (for various reasons related to trust, taxes, and so on), and underdeveloped housing and credit markets make it difficult to rent or buy housing in leading regions.

To facilitate internal labor mobility, countries in the region should focus on removing the barriers arising from market, institutional, and policy failures that inadvertently keep people in place. Workers must face positive work incentives and be equipped with the skills they need to succeed in labor markets in leading regions and economic centers, but policies are also necessary to tackle other market, institutional, and policy failures that deter internal labor migration in the region. These would include urban policies to help sustain functional cities that provide the benefits of agglomeration economies, but limit the downside of urbanization; policies to strengthen housing and credit markets, which, if underdeveloped, increase the cost of migration, especially among people with liquidity constraints; social benefits and regional policies, which, if poorly designed, can discourage mobility, but, if properly designed, can foster mobility; policies to promote information sharing and networks, which are critical for successful labor market transitions, while the lack of reliable and timely information about job vacancies, job requirements, and living conditions at potential destinations can be a barrier to mobility; policies that strengthen labor market institutions, which, if too rigid, can make labor markets less dynamic by making it difficult for people without employment to find a job or which dampen wage signals by compressing wages, thereby reducing the potential payoff from migration.

The demographic imperative also calls for a smarter cross-border migration policy that complements efforts to increase internal labor mobility. As the working-age population begins shrinking in Western Europe, the higher wages and better benefits that are available there will likely become increasingly attractive to younger workers in the New Member States. This, in turn, will accelerate the shrinking of the workforce in the latter. A similar situation exists in Belarus, Moldova, and Ukraine, for example, where populations are also aging rapidly and from which a great number of younger workers are migrating, mostly to Russia. Rapidly aging countries in the region, even more than Western Europe, need to attract global talent to stem the steep decline of the local workforce. The region attracts fewer immigrants than many OECD countries. Since the competition for talent is global, there are lessons to be drawn from successful immigration countries: Australia, Canada, New Zealand, and the United States, for example, where immigration rates are higher, but where the typical migrant is also more well educated. Almost half the adult EU immigrant population originating from outside the EU has only primary education, while only 25 percent have secondary education, and 21 percent have tertiary education. In contrast, about 40 percent of the immigrants to Australia, New Zealand, and the United States have a tertiary education.[9] To compete successfully, policy makers need to be proactive in searching out talent or filling skill gaps and flexible in adapting to changing labor market conditions.

Critical to an integrated migration policy is the strengthening of links between the diaspora and the local economy and the creation of incentives for migrants to return and invest productively at home. Remittances are already having a significant impact in some countries in the region; the challenge for policy makers is to create incentives for gearing remittances toward more productive investments and to strengthen links with the diaspora. Many workers may also want to return to their home countries, and public policies can concentrate on making these transitions easier, focusing, for example, on making it easier to maintain social benefits, buy property, and start a business.

A Diverse Jobs Policy Agenda

The successful implementation of an *employment agenda that effectively rebalances the work and social protection pillars of the social model in the region in order to grow with more jobs and get more people back to work* requires solid macroeconomic fundamentals and an adequate rule of law. It also requires, a combination of short-term measures in support of macrostabilization and fiscal consolidation to resume growth and long-term measures aimed at accelerating job creation, making workers more adaptable and mobile, and strengthening the incentives and eliminating the barriers to work. At the country level, *specific policies linked to each one of these goals will have to respond and be tailored to the country's stage of modernization and to the demographic imperatives,* as detailed in table O.2.

However, *some basic principles apply to all countries.* In all cases, reforms to improve the quality of the business climate, make labor markets more competitive, modernize the public sector, deepen financial development, and increase integration in global markets are a necessary condition for positive and sustained employment creation. These efforts will have to be comprehensive and sustained for the payoff to materialize, as illustrated by the experience of the advanced reformers in the region. In addition, moving along the modernization path will require further economic restructuring and labor reallocation, irrespective of whether a country is an advanced, intermediate, or late modernizer. These processes can be wasteful and inefficient and lead to significant short-term welfare losses, particularly among specific groups of workers, if they are not accompanied by policies aimed at improving the match between jobs and workers and enhancing the employability of those people who are most affected by the changes. Policies that are sensitive to age and gender can help increase the efficiency and effectiveness of the restructuring process.

In addition, *the proposed employment policy agendas follow an incremental approach as countries transition from late to intermediate and advanced modernizers, while differentiating among countries with a youth bulge and countries with a rapidly aging population.* The basic elements of this approach are summarized as follows:

- *Business climate, labor market, and public sector reforms; financial development; and global integration:* The late modernizers are expected to focus on public sector restructuring and productive diversification (particularly among resource-rich countries), as well as on

TABLE 0.2
Diverse Policy Reform Agendas

Population growing quickly, youth bulge	Population growing or declining slowly, aging medium term	Population declining quickly, aging rapidly
a. Advanced modernizers		
Business climate reform to strengthen and sustain the growth of superstars Ease of entry and exit into entrepreneurship (for example, access to inputs, bankruptcy reform) + social attitudes Strong generic skills + market-driven tertiary education + skills for innovation Remove the barriers to internal mobility Reduce the effects of labor costs and taxation + flexible work arrangements	Business climate reform to strengthen and sustain the growth of superstars Ease of entry and exit into entrepreneurship (for example, access to inputs, bankruptcy reform) + social attitudes Strong generic skills + market-driven tertiary and adult education + skills for innovation Remove the barriers to internal mobility + smart immigration policy Reduce the effects of labor costs and taxation + flexible work arrangements Strong work incentives + pension reforms + improved targeting of safety nets and social protection	Business climate reform to strengthen and sustain the growth of superstars Ease of entry and exit into entrepreneurship (for example, access to inputs, bankruptcy reform) + social attitudes Strong generic skills + market-driven tertiary and adult education + skills for innovation Remove the barriers to internal mobility + smart immigration policy Reduce the effects of labor costs and taxation + flexible work arrangements Strong work incentives + pension reforms + improved targeting of safety nets + social and business attitudes toward older workers
b. Intermediate modernizers		
Deeper integration (with EU, globally) Business climate reform to enable the growth of superstars Ease of entry and exit into entrepreneurship (for example, access to inputs, bankruptcy reform) Strong generic skills + market-driven tertiary education Remove the barriers to internal mobility Reduce the effects of labor costs and taxation + flexible work arrangements	Deeper integration (with EU, globally) Business climate reform to enable the growth of superstars Ease of entry and exit into entrepreneurship (for example, access to inputs, bankruptcy reform) Strong generic skills + market-driven tertiary and adult education and labor training Remove the barriers to internal mobility + smart immigration policy Reduce the effects of labor costs and taxation + flexible work arrangements Strong work incentives + pension reforms + improved targeting of safety nets and social protection	Deeper integration (with EU, globally) Business climate reform to enable the growth of superstars Ease of entry and exit into entrepreneurship (for example, access to inputs, bankruptcy reform) Strong generic skills + market-driven tertiary and adult education and labor training Remove the barriers to internal mobility + smart immigration policy Reduce the effects of labor costs and taxation + flexible work arrangements Strong work incentives + pension reforms + improved targeting of safety nets + social and business attitudes toward older workers
c. Late modernizers		
Public sector restructuring + productive diversification Improved business climate for private sector development Ease of entry and exit into entrepreneurship (for example, access to inputs, bankruptcy reform) Strong generic skills + market-driven tertiary education Remove the barriers to internal mobility Reduce the effects of labor costs and taxation + flexible work arrangements	Public sector restructuring + productive diversification Improved business climate for private sector development Strong generic skills + market-driven tertiary and adult education and labor training Remove the barriers to internal mobility + smart immigration policy Reduce the effects of labor costs and taxation + flexible work arrangements Strong work incentives + pension reforms + improved targeting of safety nets and social protection	Public sector restructuring + productive diversification Improved business climate for private sector development Strong generic skills + market-driven tertiary and adult education and labor training Remove the barriers to internal mobility + smart immigration policy Reduce the effects of labor costs and taxation + flexible work arrangements Strong work incentives + pension reforms + improved targeting of safety nets + social and business attitudes toward older workers

first-generation business climate and labor market reforms aimed at promoting private sector development. The intermediate modernizers are expected to implement more well targeted policies geared toward enabling the growth of superstar firms and to deepen integration with the EU and with other potential markets (such as Asia and the Middle East and North Africa). The advanced modernizers are expected to focus on strengthening and sustaining the growth of superstar firms, which, in the current context, involves policies to promote the stabilization of financial and credit markets. All three types of countries should also pursue reforms that ease the entry into and the exit out of entrepreneurship, including increased access to credit and bankruptcy reform, to allow businesses with high potential to thrive and create jobs and others to fail quickly and fail cheaply.

- *Skills:* The late, intermediate, and advanced reformers are expected to focus on promoting the acquisition of strong generic skills and on enhancing the alignment of academic curricula with market demands, particularly at the tertiary level. All countries, but especially countries with aging populations, need to revamp training systems, including the role of firm training, to enable the lifelong, market-driven upgrading of skills. In addition, the advanced reformers should pay attention to the production of skills for innovation, and all countries with an aging workforce should invest in improving adult education and existing training systems and ensuring that they are not age blind.

- *Incentives and barriers to work:* All countries need to pay attention to the potentially negative impact on labor market participation and employment outcomes among specific groups generated by the interaction between existing disincentives and barriers to work. This requires the implementation of reforms that level the playing field regarding the effects of labor taxation. In addition, countries with an aging workforce should reform their pension systems and improve the targeting and other design features of existing safety nets and social protection programs to encourage longer working lives. There is a role for evidenced-based policies in removing the barriers to work, including adapting the workplace to the needs of an aging workforce, addressing social norms regarding the access to economic opportunities among women and older workers, promoting flexible work arrangements and the access to productive inputs, information and networks.

- *Mobility:* All countries are expected to implement reforms that remove the barriers to internal mobility, such as the simplification or elimination of registration requirements and the development of a well-functioning housing market, including rental housing. Those countries with a fast-aging workforce should also implement immigration policies to tap into young international talent, fill local skill gaps, and leverage national diasporas.

In the short term, macro policies will be mediated by the need to resume growth and improve the fiscal stance. This is especially the case for countries more integrated to the Euro Zone and closest to Southern Europe. A balanced approach combining policies to reignite internal and external demand while maintaining fiscal discipline and to regain the momentum for structural reforms is essential to resume economic growth with more and better jobs and to get more people back to work in the region.

Notes

1. This is reflected in recent employer surveys in Bulgaria, FYR Macedonia, Georgia, Kazakhstan, Poland, Russia, and Ukraine that delve more deeply into the skills that are scarce or most valued (World Bank 2009a, 2011a).
2. Skill intensity refers to the skill requirements that are associated with the tasks carried out in jobs. For instance, a job with high intensity in new economy skills requires more higher-order skills.
3. The EU-11 are Bulgaria, Croatia, the Czech Republic, Estonia, Hungary, Latvia, Lithuania, Poland, Romania, the Slovak Republic, and Slovenia.
4. These results come from an econometric analysis that exploits the geographic and cohort variation in access to college from the expansion in the number of public and private universities in Poland over the last 50 years.
5. There is evidence that the performance captured on tests such as PISA is also partly the result of differences in persistence and motivation among the students taking the tests (for example, see Borghans et al. 2008). So, PISA scores reflect a combination of cognitive and socioemotional skills that cannot be sorted out directly.
6. For the OECD program, see the website at http://www.oecd.org /education/skills-beyond-school/piaacprogrammefortheinternational assessmentofadultcompetencies.htm. For the World Bank STEP framework, see http://go.worldbank.org/0D2PFCULF0.
7. The EU-15 are Austria, Belgium, Denmark, Finland, France, Germany, Greece, Ireland, Italy, Luxembourg, the Netherlands, Portugal, Spain, Sweden, and the United Kingdom.
8. Life in Transition Survey (database), European Bank for Reconstruction and Development, London, http://www.ebrd.com/pages/research /economics/data/lits.shtml.

9. Database on Immigrants in OECD and non-OECD Countries: DIOC, Organisation for Economic Co-operation and Development, Paris, http://www.oecd.org/els/mig/dioc.htm.

Bibliography

Abras, Ana, Alejandro Hoyos, Ambar Narayan, and Sailesh Tiwari. 2012. "Inequality of Opportunities in the Labor Market: Evidence from Life in Transition Surveys in Europe and Central Asia." Background paper for *World Development Report 2013*, World Bank, Washington, DC.

Aedo, Cristian, and Ian Walker. 2012. *Skills for the 21st Century in Latin America and the Caribbean*. Washington, DC: World Bank. https://openknowledge .worldbank.org/handle/10986/2236.

Atasoy, Hilal, Erwin Tiongson, Peter van der Zwan, and Carolina Sanchez-Paramo. 2013. "Latent Entrepreneurship in the East Central Asia Region." Unpublished working paper, World Bank, Washington, DC.

Autor, H. David, Frank Levy, and Richard T. Murnane. 2003. "The Skill Content of Recent Technological Change: An Empirical Exploration." *Quarterly Journal of Economics* 118 (4): 1279–333.

Blom, Andreas, and Hiroshi Saeki. 2011. "Employability and Skill Set of Newly Graduated Engineers in India." Policy Research Working Paper 5640, World Bank, Washington, DC.

Borghans, Lex, Angela L. Duckworth, James J. Heckman, and Bas ter Weel. 2008. "The Economics and Psychology of Personality Traits." *Journal of Human Resources* 43 (4): 972–1059.

Bowles, Samuel, Herbert Gintis, and Melissa Osborne. 2001. "The Determinants of Earnings: A Behavioral Approach." *Journal of Economic Literature* 39 (4): 1137–76.

Brunnelo, Giorgio, and Martin Schlotter. 2011. "Non Cognitive Skills and Personality Traits: Labour Market Relevance and Their Development in Education and Training Systems." IZA Discussion Paper 5743, Institute for the Study of Labor, Bonn, Germany.

Cedefop (European Center for the Development of Vocational Training). 2012. "Skill Mismatch: The Role of the Enterprise." Cedefop Research Paper 21, Publications Office of the European Union, Luxembourg.

European Commission. 2010. *Geographical and Labour Market Mobility*. Special Eurobarometer 337, June. Brussels: European Commission.

————. 2012a. *Employment and Social Developments in Europe 2012*. Brussels: Directorate-General for Employment, Social Affairs and Inclusion, European Commission.

————. 2012b. *Discrimination in the EU in 2012*. Special Eurobarometer 393, November. Brussels: European Commission.

Fialova, Kamila, and Ondrej Schneider. 2011. "Labor Institutions and Their Impact on Shadow Economies in Europe." Policy Research Working Paper 5913, World Bank, Washington, DC.

Gallup Organization. 2010. *Employers' Perception of Graduate Employability: Analytical Report*. Flash Eurobarometer 304. Brussels: European Commission.

Goos, Maarten, Alan Manning, and Anna Salomons. 2009. "Job Polarization in Europe." *American Economic Review* 99 (2): 58–63.

Handel, Michael. 2012. "Trends in Job Skill Demands in OECD Countries." OECD Social, Employment and Migration Working Papers 143, Organisation for Economic Co-operation and Development.

Heckman, J. James, Jora Stixrud, and Sergio Urzua. 2006. "The Effects of Cognitive and Noncognitive Abilities on Labor Market Outcomes and Social Behavior." *Journal of Labor Economics* 24 (3): 411–82.

IFC (International Finance Corporation). 2013. *IFC Jobs Study: Assessing Private Sector Contributions to Job Creation and Poverty Reduction*. January. Washington, DC: IFC.

ILO (International Labour Organization). 2011. *Key Indicators of the Labour Market*. 7th ed. Geneva, Switzerland: ILO.

———. 2013. *Global Wage Report 2012/13: Wages and Equitable Growth*. Geneva, Switzerland: ILO.

Lehmann, Hartmut, and Alexander Muravyev. 2010. "Labor Market Institutions and Labor Market Performance: What Can We Learn from Transition Countries?" Working Paper 714, Dipartimento Scienze Economiche, University of Bologna, Bologna, Italy.

Mitra, Pradeep, Marcelo Selowsky, and Juan Zalduendo. 2010. *Turmoil at Twenty: Recession, Recovery, and Reform in Central and Eastern Europe and the Former Soviet Union*. Europe and Central Asia Studies. Washington, DC: World Bank. https://openknowledge.worldbank.org/handle/10986/2682.

Murthi, Mamta, and Lars Sondergaard. 2012. *Skills, Not Just Diplomas: The Path for Education Reforms in ECA*. Washington, DC: World Bank.

Quintini, Glenda. 2011. "Right for the Job: Over-Qualified or Under-Skilled?" OECD Social, Employment, and Migration Working Papers 120, Organisation for Economic Co-operation and Development, Paris.

Rutkowski, J. Jan, and Stefano Scarpetta, with Arup Banerji, Philip O'Keefe, Gaëlle Pierre, and Milan Vodopivec. 2005. *Enhancing Job Opportunities: Eastern Europe and the Former Soviet Union*. Report, November. Washington, DC: Europe and Central Asia Region, World Bank.

Udomsaph, Charles. 2012. "Local Governments and Firm Performance: Evidence from Eastern Europe." Working paper, Georgetown University, Washington, DC.

World Bank. 2009a. Ukraine: Labor Demand Study. Washington, DC: World Bank.

———. 2009b. *World Development Report 2009: Reshaping Economic Geography*. Washington, DC: World Bank.

———. 2011a. *Strengthening Skills and Employability in Peru*. Report 61699-PE, Washington, DC: World Bank. https://openknowledge.worldbank.org /handle/10986/12533.

————. 2011b. *World Development Report 2012: Gender Equality and Development*. Washington, DC: World Bank.

————. 2012a. *World Development Report 2013: Jobs*. Washington, DC: World Bank.

————. 2012b. *Summary Report*. Vol. 1 of *In Search of Opportunities: How a More Mobile Workforce Can Propel Ukraine's Prosperity*. Washington, DC: World Bank.

————. 2013. *World Development Indicators 2013*. Washington, DC: World Bank.

————. Forthcoming. *The Inverted Pyramid: Pension Systems in Europe and Central Asia Facing Demographic Challenges*. Washington, DC: World Bank.

World Bank and IFC (International Finance Corporation). 2013a. *Doing Business 2013: Smarter Regulations for Small and Medium-Size Enterprises*. Washington, DC: World Bank.

————. 2013b. *Doing Business 2013, Smarter Regulations for Small and Medium-Size Enterprises: Regional Profile, Eastern Europe and Central Asia (ECA)*. Washington, DC: World Bank.

FIGURE 1.2

Significant Across-the-Board Reform Efforts

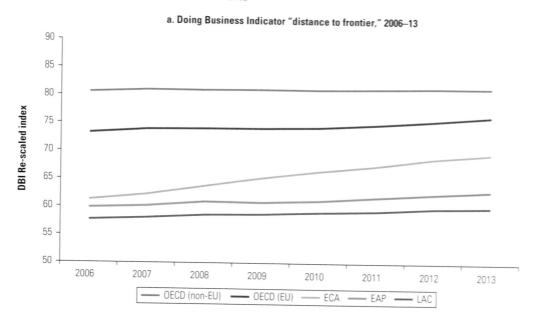

a. Doing Business Indicator "distance to frontier," 2006–13

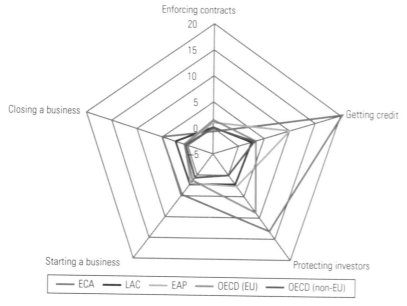

b. Changes in Doing Business Indicator components in 2006–13

Sources: World Bank 2013a, 2013b.

Note: The "Distance to Frontier" measure shows how far on average an economy is from the best performance achieved by any economy on each Doing Business Indicator (DBI) since 2005. The measure is normalized to range between 0 and 100, with 100 representing the best performance (the frontier) (World Bank 2013a). EAP = East Asia and Pacific; ECA = Europe and Central Asia; LAC = Latin America and the Caribbean; OECD = Organisation for Economic Co-operation and Development; EU = European Union.

FIGURE 1.3

Rapid Real Wage Growth Characterized the Early 2000s in ECA

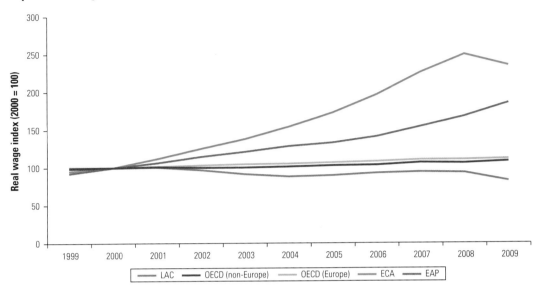

Source: ILO 2013b. Real Monthly Average Wages in local currency units. Base year 2000.
Note: Data for ECA includes Albania, Armenia, Azerbaijan, Belarus, Bulgaria, Croatia, Estonia, Georgia, Hungary, Kazakhstan, the Kyrgyz Republic, Lithuania, Moldova, Poland, Romania, the Russian Federation, Serbia, Tajikistan, and Ukraine. For LAC, Costa Rica, the Dominican Republic, Jamaica, Panama, Paraguay, Peru, and República Bolivariana de Venezuela. For EAP, China, Indonesia, Malaysia, Mongolia, and Thailand. For OECD (Europe), Austria, Belgium, Denmark, Finland, France, Germany, Iceland, Italy, Luxembourg, the Netherlands, Norway, Portugal, Spain, Sweden, Switzerland, and the United Kingdom. For OECD (non-Europe), Australia, Canada, Israel, Japan, and New Zealand. EAP = East Asia and Pacific; ECA = Europe and Central Asia; LAC = Latin America and the Caribbean; OECD = Organisation for Economic Co-operation and Development.

(ILO 2013a). As a result, hourly direct pay remains relatively low in the region: among ECA countries, a worker employed in manufacturing gets paid between $4.74 per hour in Hungary and $6.10 per hour in the Czech Republic, compared to $5.41 per hour in Brazil, $8.68 per hour in Argentina, or $14.53 per hour in Spain (all amounts in real 2010 U.S. dollars; ILO 2013a).[3]

In contrast, employment gains were only modest in 2000–07 and almost null in the aftermath of the crisis. Employment grew by 7 percent between 2000 and 2007 in ECA, compared to close to 20 percent in LAC and EAP, 9 percent in OECD countries in Europe, and 13 percent in OECD countries outside Europe (figure 1.4a). This is equivalent to less than 1 percent per year and significantly lower than GDP, productivity, or even wage growth. During and following the crisis, job destruction was significant and employment numbers reached precrisis levels only in 2012.

Given that ECA experienced strong economic growth during 2000–07, these numbers suggest that the relationship between GDP growth and employment creation is relatively weak in the region.

In fact, during this period 1 percentage point of GDP growth translated into 0.10 percentage points of employment growth in ECA, compared to 0.19 in LAC, 0.47 in OECD countries in Europe, and 0.29 among OECD countries outside of Europe (figure 1.4b). Caution is needed, however, in interpreting these numbers since low net employment creation can mask significant gross employment creation and destruction as labor is relocated across sectors and firms in the transition to a market economy.

Indeed evidence presented below and in chapter 2 supports the notion that both gross employment destruction and creation continue to be important elements of economic restructuring in the region, with job creation outpacing destruction in some countries, albeit only modestly.

Limited employment creation across the region meant that countries struggled to provide jobs for all workers even as economies grew. With few (additional) jobs to go around, employment rates remained low and high unemployment continued to be a problem across the region during the first decade of the 2000s. Only 50 out of every 100 working-age adults are employed in ECA, compared to 59 in LAC, 66 in EAP, and 57 in OECD countries (figure 1.5a). Among those in the labor force, 14 out of every 100 are unemployed, 50 percent more than in LAC and twice the number in EAP or OECD (figure 1.5b). And the crisis only aggravated the situation, sending unemployment rates even higher and adding significantly to the number of long-term unemployed, which climbed from close to 5 in every 100 to 7 in every 100 between 2007 and 2011 (figure 1.5c). These trends are the more worrisome against the backdrop of low and stagnant labor force participation rates (LFPRs). Labor force participation in ECA, at 58 percent, is several points below that of other middle-income regions and the OECD and has increased only minimally over the decade (figure 1.5d).

Most countries in the region enjoyed both positive economic and employment growth in 2000–07, but employment creation rates varied significantly across countries—even for countries with similar growth experiences. For instance, employment growth was significantly higher in Albania than in Bosnia and Herzegovina, even though they both grew at similar rates during the period (figure 1.6a). Similarly, the impact of the crisis was felt very differently across the region. Some countries (e.g., Poland, Turkey, and Turkmenistan) recovered rapidly and enjoyed overall positive economic and employment growth in 2008–11, while others (e.g., Latvia and Croatia) struggled to overcome the negative effects of the crisis (figure 1.6b). There were also important cross-country differences in

FIGURE 1.4

Limited Employment Creation Due to a Weak Relationship between Economic and Employment Growth and to the Crisis

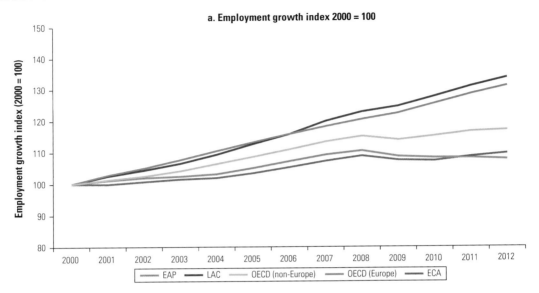

a. Employment growth index 2000 = 100

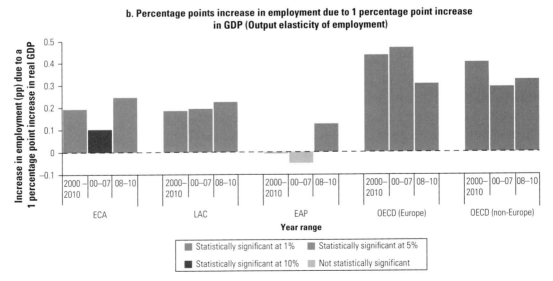

b. Percentage points increase in employment due to 1 percentage point increase in GDP (Output elasticity of employment)

Sources: Calculations based on data from ILO 2013b; World Bank 2013c.
Note: Data for ECA include Albania, Armenia, Azerbaijan, Belarus, Bosnia and Herzegovina, Bulgaria, Croatia, the Czech Republic, Estonia, Georgia, Hungary, Kazakhstan, the Kyrgyz Republic, Latvia, Lithuania, the former Yugoslav Republic of Macedonia, Moldova, Poland, Romania, the Russian Federation, the Slovak Republic, Slovenia, Tajikistan, Turkey, Turkmenistan, Ukraine, and Uzbekistan. For LAC, Argentina, Belize, Bolivia, Brazil, Chile, Colombia, Costa Rica, Cuba, the Dominican Republic, Ecuador, El Salvador, Guatemala, Guyana, Haiti, Honduras, Jamaica, Mexico, Nicaragua, Panama, Paraguay, Peru, Suriname, Uruguay, and República Bolivariana de Venezuela. For EAP, Cambodia, China, Fiji, Indonesia, the Republic of Korea, the Lao People's Democratic Republic, Malaysia, Mongolia, Papua New Guinea, the Philippines, the Solomon Islands, Thailand, Timor-Leste, and Vietnam. For OECD (Europe), Austria, Belgium, Denmark, Finland, France, Germany, Greece, Iceland, Ireland, Italy, Luxembourg, the Netherlands, Norway, Portugal, Spain, Sweden, Switzerland, and the United Kingdom. For OECD (non-Europe), Australia, Canada, Israel, Japan, New Zealand, and the United States. EAP = East Asia and Pacific; ECA = Europe and Central Asia; GDP = gross domestic product; LAC = Latin America and the Caribbean; OECD = Organisation for Economic Co-operation and Development.

FIGURE 1.5

Labor Force Participation and Employment Rates Are Low and Unemployment Is High

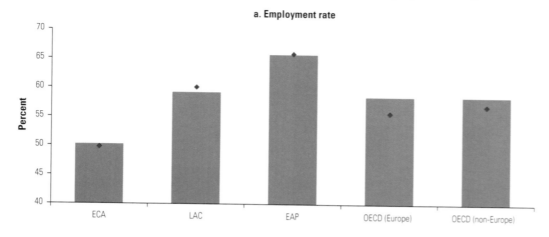

a. Employment rate

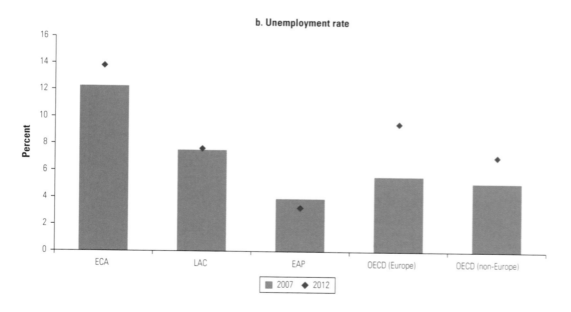

b. Unemployment rate

continued

FIGURE 1.5
Continued

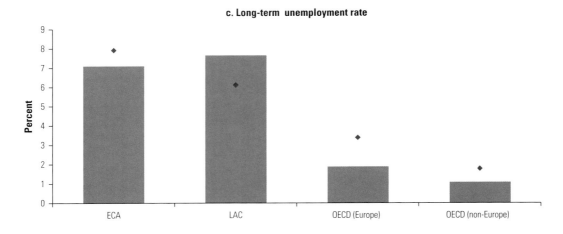

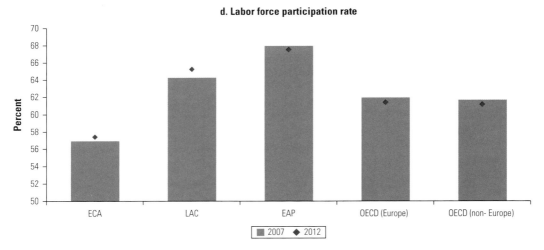

Sources: Calculations using data from ILO 2013b; World Bank 2013c.
Note: See annex 1A for details on the data used. EAP = East Asia and Pacific; ECA = Europe and Central Asia; LAC = Latin America and the Caribbean; OECD = Organisation for Economic Co-operation and Development.

the relationship between labor productivity growth and wage growth. In some countries wage growth was significantly higher than productivity growth both before and after the crisis (e.g., Russia, Belarus, and Georgia), while in others both have been more aligned (e.g., Hungary, Estonia, and Lithuania) (figure 1.6c and d).

Taken together, these numbers reveal fundamentally different realities about the functioning of labor markets in the region. Labor markets can respond to changes in GDP (and labor productivity) in multiple ways: via changes in prices (wages), via changes in quantities (either jobs or hours work), or via changes in both. Wage changes,

FIGURE 1.6

Cross-Country Differences in Growth and Labor Market Performance

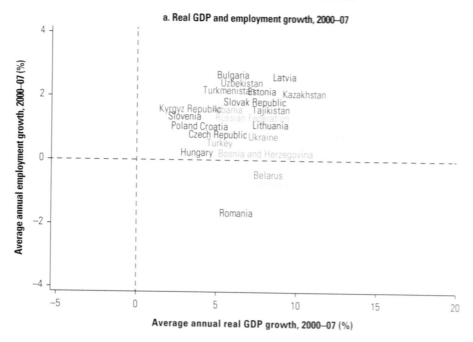

a. Real GDP and employment growth, 2000–07

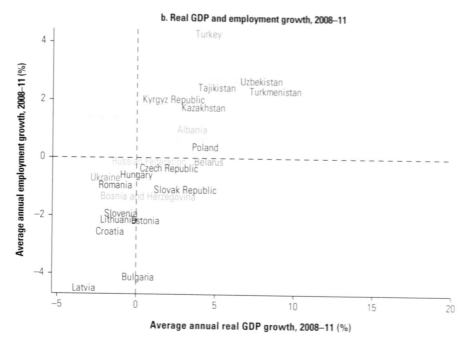

b. Real GDP and employment growth, 2008–11

continued

FIGURE 1.6
Continued

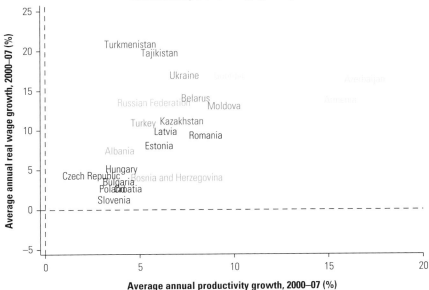

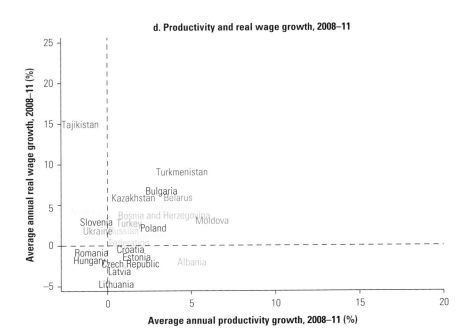

Sources: Calculations using data from ILO 2013b; World Bank 2013c.
Note: Gross domestic product (GDP) growth calculated using real GDP at constant 2000 US$ from World Bank 2013c. Employment growth calculated using data from ILO 2013b. Productivity growth estimated using GDP (constant 1990 purchasing power parity (PPP) US$) per person employed from World Bank 2013c. Real wage growth calculated using nominal wages from ILO 2013b, deflated using average consumer prices inflation from IMF 2013.

combined with and to some extent facilitated by changes in hours worked, seem to characterize the adjustment process in Russia and other Commonwealth of Independent States (CIS) countries and, to a lesser extent, in the Western Balkans. As a result, boom times are associated with rapid wage growth and limited employment creation, while down times are associated with wage stagnation (or even declines) and rising underemployment (Gimpelson and Kapeliushnikov 2011; Lehmann and Pignatti 2007). In contrast, among new European Union (EU) member states, changes in GDP are usually accompanied by changes in both wages and employment. As a result, boom and down times are associated with more marked changes in employment and unemployment and (limited) changes in wages (Rutkowski 2006; World Bank 2005).

Equally significant cross-country differences exist regarding labor force, employment, and unemployment rates—both in levels and in changes. Labor force participation and employment rates are highest among the Central Asia countries and lowest in the Western Balkans, while the opposite is true for unemployment rates (figure 1.7). In contrast, changes in employment and (long-term) unemployment rates were largest among the new EU member states following the crisis. As discussed later in the chapter and in chapter 4, country averages hide significant heterogeneity in outcomes across age and ethnic groups and between men and women.

Against this background, how should one then think about jobs in ECA? The rest of this chapter aims at providing a framework and a country typology to do just that. This framework is built on the premise that there are two contextual factors that characterize ECA and make it stand apart from other regions, while allowing for significant cross-country differences within the region: (a) a socialist legacy common to all countries and (b) mounting demographic pressures associated with either rapid aging (in most countries) or significant youth bulges (in a few countries).

Thinking about Jobs in ECA

With the exception of Turkey, all ECA countries shared a socialist past and a legacy of state planning at the time of transition and faced similar challenges in a number of areas. Existing institutions were inadequate to facilitate the creation and support the functioning of markets, economic activity was dominated by the state with the private sector playing a limited role at best, and the level of integration with the rest of the world was extremely low.

FIGURE 1.7

Significant Cross-Country Differences in Labor Force Participation, Employment, and Unemployment Rates

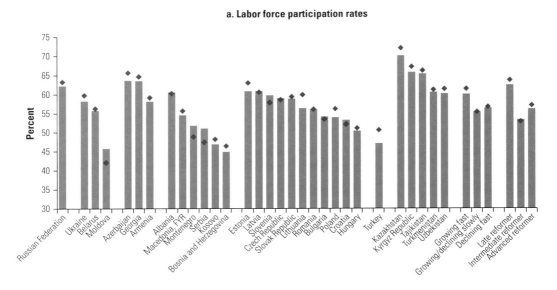

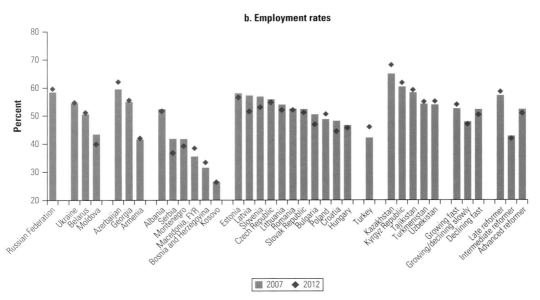

2007 ◆ 2012

continued

FIGURE 1.7
Continued

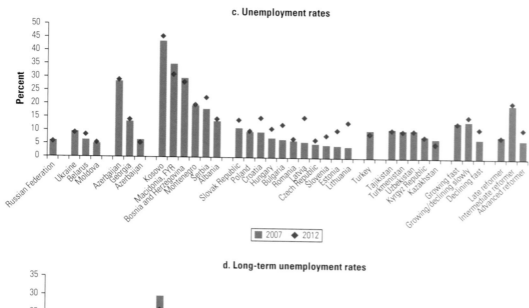

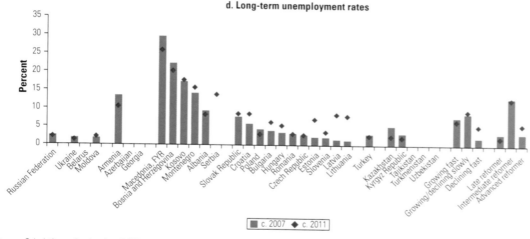

Sources: Calculations using data from ILO 2013b; World Bank 2013c.
Note: See annex 1A for details on the data used.

The Impact of Legacy and Modernization

Overcoming these challenges required the implementation of a comprehensive reform agenda capable of supporting the development of
a new economic system. To some extent, most countries in the region
have made progress over the past two decades in implementing
different components of this agenda. At the same time there are
significant differences across countries in terms of the pace of reform
and economic restructuring. Data on the European Bank for

Reconstruction and Development (EBRD) Transition Index (TI) for 2000–12 suggest that some countries started walking down the path of modernization as early as the mid-1990s and have since come a long way in the transition to a market economy. This is the case for most new EU member states. Other countries, such as Serbia, Montenegro, Bosnia and Herzegovina, or Armenia, lagged behind initially but have caught up during the early 2000s. Yet others continue to face important reform challenges. This group includes, among others, Turkmenistan, Belarus, and Uzbekistan (figure 1.8a).

The scope of reforms varied significantly across countries as some embraced wholesale reform while others implemented changes more sequentially and/or selectively. New EU member states had already implemented significant elements of the transition reform agenda across a wide range of issues and sectors by the late 1990s or early part of the 2000s and continued to do so. Similarly, countries in the Western Balkans made significant progress along all reform areas captured by the TI but did so only after 2000. In contrast, Russia made great progress on policies related to trade and foreign exchange but limited progress in other reform areas (figure 1.8a and b).

External factors, and particularly the presence of the European Union and the promise it holds for many countries in the region, have played an important role in explaining cross-country differences in the speed and scope of reforms efforts. The process of EU accession undoubtedly provided a strong momentum for fast and comprehensive reform among new member states in the late 1990s and early 2000s, as these countries aimed at complying with the EU *acquis communautaire*. Something similar has happened in Turkey and, to a lesser extent, the Western Balkans over the past decade as part of the accession negotiation process (Gill and Raiser 2012).

Changes in labor market institutions were also significant during the 2000s, increasing overall levels of labor market flexibility. Contrary to what has been sometimes argued, the rigidities in the national labor laws that characterized the region in the 1990s were not the product of a socialist legacy but rather were introduced in the late 1980s and early 1990s, at the early stage of transition, when governments attempted to combat looming unemployment. The evolution of labor regulations then followed an inverted U-shaped pattern since transition, with the peak of rigidity occurring in the 1990s, followed by liberalization of labor laws and increased flexibility in the 2000s—sometimes in dramatic proportions, as has been the case in Georgia and Kazakhstan (Lehmman and Muravyev 2011; Muravyev 2010). As a result, most transition countries are in the middle of the labor market flexibility scale, with levels similar to

FIGURE 1.8

Important Reforms Efforts Were Made in the 2000s but with Differences in Speed and Scope

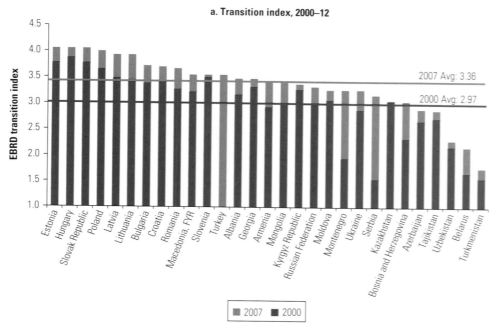

a. Transition index, 2000–12

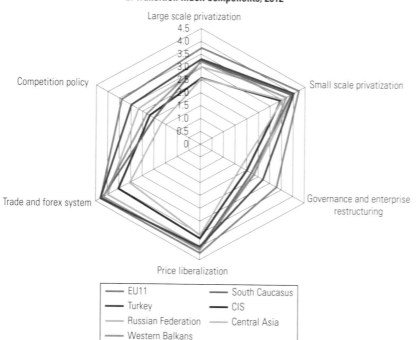

b. Transition Index components, 2012

continued

FIGURE 1.8
Continued

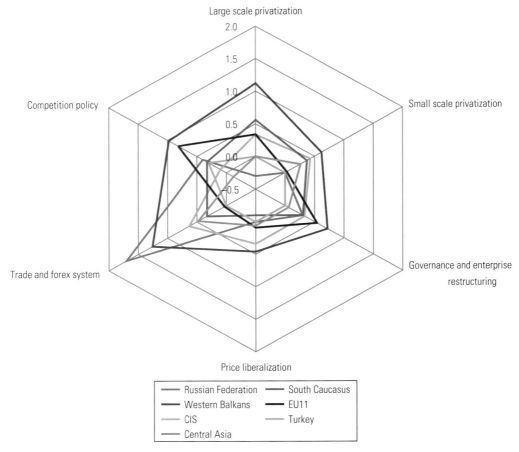

c. Changes in transition index components, 2000–12

Large scale privatization

Competition policy

Small scale privatization

Trade and forex system

Governance and enterprise
restructuring

Price liberalization

	Russian Federation		South Caucasus
	Western Balkans		EU11
	CIS		Turkey
	Central Asia		

Source: Calculations using data from EBRD 2013.
Note: CIS = Commonwealth of Independent States; EBRD = European Bank for Reconstruction and Development.

those of EU-15, at least as judged by the existing estimates based on the OECD Employment Protection Legislation (EPL) methodology. There are significant differences across countries. Similarly, minimum wages increased during 2000–10 but remain low (below 40 percent of average wage), with the exception of a few countries (figure 1.9).

Regulatory and institutional reforms in turn facilitated deeper structural change through the relocation of productive factors. Public employment, which was extremely high in the wake of the transition, declined significantly in most countries throughout the 1990s and first decade of the 2000s. In 1989 the public sector accounted for

FIGURE 1.9

Intermediate Levels of Labor Market Flexibility and Low Minimum Wages

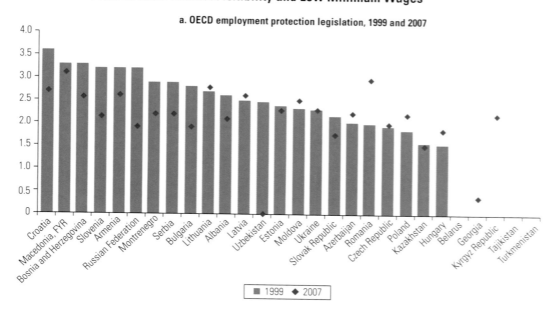

a. OECD employment protection legislation, 1999 and 2007

■ 1999 ◆ 2007

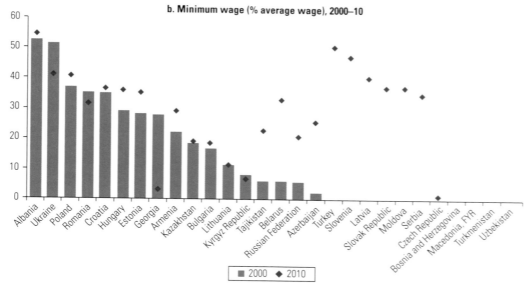

b. Minimum wage (% average wage), 2000–10

■ 2000 ◆ 2010

Sources: Calculations using data from OECD 2007; ILO 2013b.
Note: Data not available for Bosnia and Herzegovina, Macedonia FYR, Turkmenistan, Tajikistan, and Uzbekistan.

60–90 percent of total employment—the one exception being Turkey at 40 percent. Over the next two decades, public employment dropped dramatically, with declines ranging from 20 percent in Belarus and 30 percent in Azerbaijan to over 70 percent in Albania, Georgia, and Poland (figure 1.10). And, consistent with the process

FIGURE 1.10

Public Sector Employment Declined Significantly over the Past Two Decades

Share of public employment in total employment, %

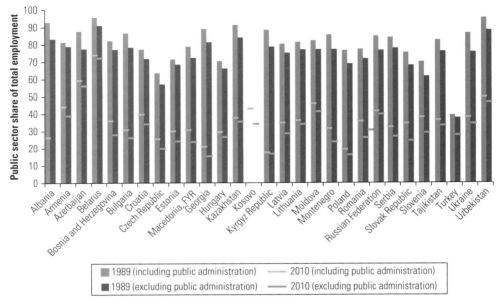

Sources: Calculations using data from Life in Transition Surveys (EBRD 2006, 2010).

of economic restructuring and privatization of public enterprises, most of this decline was driven by a reduction in public employment outside the public administration sector.

Finally, the transformation of domestic productive structures was accompanied by higher levels of international trade and financial development. Foreign trade rose markedly over the past decade across the region, but it did so more rapidly in the EU new member states (20 percent growth between 2000 and 2011), Turkey (30 percent growth), and the Western Balkans (25 percent growth) than in CIS countries (2 percent growth). In addition, EU countries traded significantly more than Turkey, CIS countries, or the Western Balkans. Exports by new EU economies in the period 2000–11 (measured as a share of GDP) were on average 10 percentage points of GDP higher than those of the CIS (including energy exports) and 20 percentage points of GDP higher than those in the Balkan countries. These differences can partly be attributed to higher access to the EU trading area but are also indicative of higher levels of competitiveness among producers in these countries (World Bank 2013c). Similarly, financial development in ECA (as measured by the Financial Development Index prepared by the World Economic Forum) was below OECD levels (4.20 versus 5.30) but higher than in

LAC (4.05) or EAP (4.08) in 2008; it suffered a significant drop as a consequence of the crisis, however. Within ECA, the EU countries exhibit the highest levels of development (4.63), followed by the Western Balkans (4.13), Turkey (4.11), and the CIS countries (3.73).

Taken together, these data suggest that ECA has undergone very significant economic and structural change in a compressed period of time, and yet, within the region, countries are still at very different stages in the transition to a market economy. To capture this idea, this chapter organizes countries into three groups: advanced modernizers, intermediate modernizers, and late modernizers. Country groupings are constructed using the information on EPL, business climate, public sector reform, international integration, and financial development discussed above. A detailed description of the approach followed for the exercise is provided in spotlight 1.1. A very succinct description of the main characteristics of each group follows:

- *Advanced modernizers*: These are early reformers that continue to be in the lead regarding the quality of their business climate and institutional structure. They are countries that have made important strides in reducing public sector employment and developing efficient financial markets and that have effectively integrated into global markets. This group includes the new European Union member states except Romania and Croatia, and Turkey.

- *Intermediate modernizers*: These are countries that got off to a late start but have made significant progress when it comes to business climate and public sector reform, hence catching up with the early reformers. They are countries that have some (but not all) of the elements of well developed financial markets and that have become increasingly open to international trade and, to a lesser extent, to global financial markets. This group includes Albania, Armenia, Bosnia and Herzegovina, Croatia, the former Yugoslav Republic of Macedonia, Georgia, Kosovo, Moldova, Montenegro, Romania, and Serbia.

- *Late modernizers*: These are countries whose reform efforts have moved relatively slowly and/or unevenly and where the public sector still plays an important role in the productive sphere. They also have less developed financial sectors and are less integrated globally. In addition, in some countries natural resources account for a significant share of GDP. This group includes Azerbaijan, Belarus, Kazakhstan, the Kyrgyz Republic, Russia, Tajikistan, Turkmenistan, Ukraine, and Uzbekistan.

The question then arises as to whether employment performance differs across these three groups—or, more specifically, as to whether the advanced modernizers are the best performers. To answer this question, the chapter analyzes the impact on employment growth of the three key elements underpinning the modernization agenda: (a) business climate and labor reform legislation and regulatory reform, (b) public sector modernization, and (c) financial development and integration into global markets. The evidence discussed below suggests that, indeed, the advanced modernizers have managed to more effectively translate economic and productivity growth into jobs—although there are limits to the impact of modernization on employment creation.

Can Business Climate Legislative and Regulatory Reform Strengthen Employment Creation?

The short answer to this question is "yes": countries with better-functioning market-oriented institutions and a stronger business climate have enjoyed longer periods of positive and sustained employment growth over the first decade of the 2000s. Specifically, while some intermediate and late modernizers experienced relatively high employment growth during a specific year or years, the advanced modernizers were the only group that systematically enjoyed positive and significant annual employment growth rates (between 1.5 percent and 2.5 percent per year) over a period of six to eight years in the early 2000s (figure 1.11).

To explore the relationship between a country's reform record and its employment performance, this report first measures the direct impact of reforms on employment creation by regressing employment growth on both GDP growth and the level of different reform indicators, such as the Doing Business (DBI) and the Transition (TI) Indicators and their different components. Parameter estimates suggest that a number of reforms can boost employment. Specifically, reforms that make it easier to close a business, measures related to large-scale privatization and governance, and measures concerning enterprise restructuring are positively and significantly correlated with employment growth. In other words, countries that have implemented deeper reforms in any of these three areas have enjoyed higher employment creation, other things being equal. Employment growth is also positively correlated with several governance indicators, including more corruption control, better quality of regulation, more government effectiveness, and higher levels of voice and accountability (Richter and Witkowski 2013).

FIGURE 1.11

Advanced Modernizers Experienced Longer Episodes of Positive and Sustained Employment Creation in the 2000s

Total duration in years and average annual employment growth rate (%) of longest positive employment-creation episode, 2000–11

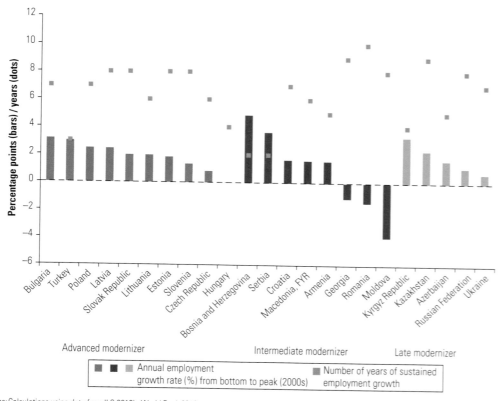

Sources: Calculations using data from ILO 2013b; World Bank 2013c.

In addition, certain reforms have a positive impact on employment growth for some groups of countries but not others. For instance more flexible hiring regulations and banking reform are associated with higher employment creation among advanced modernizers, while better competition policy and improved governance lead to higher employment creation among intermediate and, especially, late modernizers (Richter and Witkowski 2013).

Second this report examines the *indirect* impact of reforms on employment creation by allowing the relationship between GDP growth and employment growth to vary across countries at different stages in the reform process, measured using the Doing Business and Transition Indicators and their different components. In all cases, the deeper and more advanced the reform, the stronger the relation between growth and employment. And consistent with the results pertaining to the direct impact of reform, this effect is significant for reforms related to large- and small-scale privatization, governance and enterprise restructuring, and competition policy. Parameter values and significance levels are quite sensitive to the model specification, however. Similar results are obtained if indicators related to EPL (as measured by the Institute for the Study of Labor [IZA]) are used instead. In that case, both hiring and firing restrictions diminish the impact of growth on employment, although only the first one is significant (EBRD 2012).

Taken together, these results suggest that reforms that (a) lowered the cost of restructuring (e.g., privatization and enterprise restructuring), (b) leveled the playing field in product markets (increased competition), and (c) improved the overall governance structure had the most impact on employment creation. In addition, reforms that directly tackled rigidities and imperfections in the labor and capital markets also had positive impacts, but mostly among countries that had already implemented the so-called first generation reforms mentioned earlier—i.e., the advanced modernizers.

In reality, however, the relationship between reform efforts and employment creation is not as straightforward as the discussion above may have suggested, since the payoff to reform often materializes with a lag and only among countries that have managed to implement and sustain broad reform agendas. One way to see this is to compare the impact of 1 percentage point of GDP growth on employment growth across countries and over time. Among advanced modernizers, 1 percentage point of GDP growth translated into 0.46 points of employment growth in 2000–07, compared to 0.13 in 1995–99, or to −0.43 among intermediate modernizers and 0.05 among late modernizers in 2000–07 (figure 1.12). In other words, among advanced modernizers, employment growth became more responsive to economic growth only in the early 2000s as the impact of reforms implemented in the second half of the 1990s percolated throughout the economy and as many of these countries gained access to the EU (Havlik 2004). In contrast, the relationship between economic and employment growth remained weak among intermediate and late modernizers in the early 2000s despite significant reforms efforts, particularly among the former.

The fact that reform does not automatically lead to higher employment creation should not be surprising. In most ECA countries, the most immediate effect of reform efforts was to facilitate economic restructuring, which initially meant large job destruction and little employment creation. As unproductive firms died and

FIGURE 1.12

The Employment Payoff to Reforms Often Materializes with a Lag and Only among Advanced Modernizers

Output elasticity of employment by country groups and over time

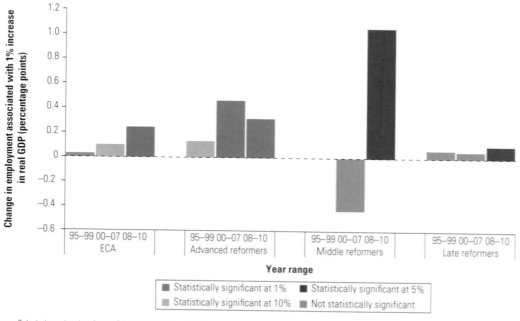

Sources: Calculation using data from ILO 2013b; World Bank 2013c.
Note: ECA = Europe and Central Asia; GDP = gross domestic product.

others became more efficient in their use of labor (primarily by shedding some of it), total employment actually fell while labor productivity increased. Later on, as productivity gains consolidated and economic growth resumed, existing firms started hiring again and new businesses were created.

Data on productivity growth and employment growth confirm this view. At the aggregate level, advanced modernizers—countries where job destruction has subsided and job creation is gaining pace—enjoyed contemporaneous positive productivity and employment growth more often than intermediate or late modernizers. And this difference was more marked in 2000–10 than in the 1990s, as the positive impact of reforms on employment creation was felt more intensely.

For instance, the Czech Republic experienced both positive productivity and positive employment growth during 30 percent of the years in the 1990s and 60 percent of the years in the 2000s, while these same figures are 12 percent and 50 percent for FYR Macedonia and 12 percent and 17 percent for Belarus (figure 1.13a and b). Interestingly, some of the natural-resource-rich CIS countries, such

FIGURE 1.13

Modernization Increases the Correlation between Productivity Growth and Employment Creation

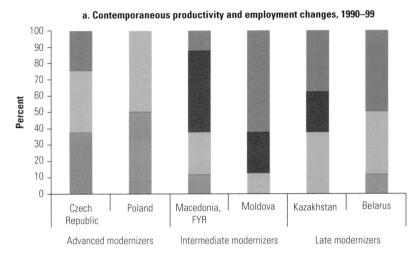

a. Contemporaneous productivity and employment changes, 1990–99

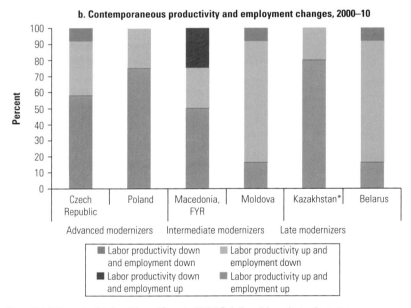

b. Contemporaneous productivity and employment changes, 2000–10

■ Labor productivity down and employment down
■ Labor productivity up and employment down
■ Labor productivity down and employment up
■ Labor productivity up and employment up

Source: Calculations using data from Arias and Saavedra 2013. * Excluding mining and extractive sector.

as Kazakhstan, defy this pattern in the early 2000s, as they experienced high productivity growth but (relatively) modest employment growth during the decade. When the mining and extractive sector is excluded from the analysis, the number of years for which employment and productivity exhibit positive growth is smaller, although still significant. Periods of positive productivity growth and negative employment growth are also more likely to be followed by periods of both positive productivity and employment growth among advanced modernizers than among other countries.

Sectoral and firm-level data on productivity and employment growth show similar patterns. Sectoral employment responds positively to both contemporaneous sectoral and total productivity growth among advance modernizers but not among other countries (Arias and Saavedra 2013). And firm-level evidence discussed in chapter 2 shows that firms that are leading job creation (such as exporting firms in Turkey or foreign firms in Ukraine) also tend to be more productive.

In addition, data on sectoral productivity and employment suggest that the process of relocation of labor across sectors and firms has been more intense among advanced modernizers than among the other two groups of countries. Specifically, the share of total employment in agriculture is smaller and the share of total employment in manufacturing and, especially services, is larger among advanced modernizers than among other countries. The same can be said about labor productivity in manufacturing and services (figure 1.14). This suggests that these countries have been more successful in both relocating labor from low productivity to high productivity sectors and fostering labor productivity growth in manufacturing and services. Having said this, the construction sector also played an important role in the years leading to the crisis in terms of employment creation, particularly among advanced reformers, so that not all new jobs created during this period were high productivity and/or stable jobs.

The same argument applies if changes in sectoral employment shares and productivity levels are considered instead (not shown). The decline in agricultural employment and the increase in the employment share and the productivity of manufacturing and services are most marked among advanced modernizers. In contrast, among intermediate modernizers agricultural employment fell throughout the decade, but productivity in manufacturing and services remained fairly constant, while labor relocation and productivity gains in non-agriculture were relatively modest among late modernizers. Despite these differences, wherever relocation happened, it led to important productivity and ultimately GDP gains. For example in Romania,

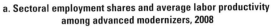

FIGURE 1.14

Relocation of Labor from Low to High Productivity Sectors Has Been More Intense among Advanced Modernizers

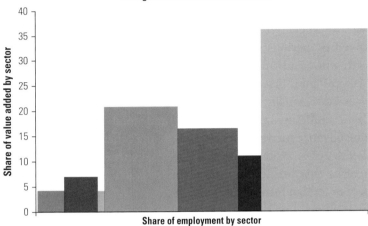

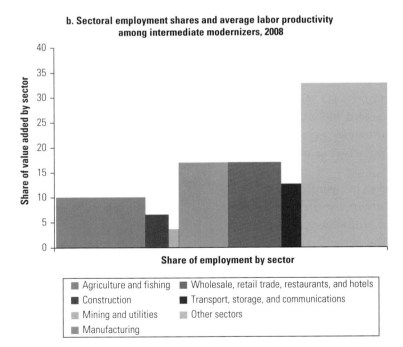

continued

FIGURE 1.14
Continued

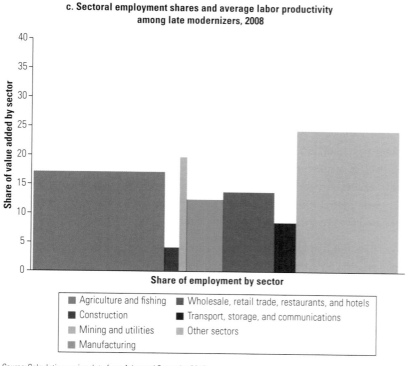

c. Sectoral employment shares and average labor productivity among late modernizers, 2008

Legend:
- Agriculture and fishing
- Construction
- Mining and utilities
- Manufacturing
- Wholesale, retail trade, restaurants, and hotels
- Transport, storage, and communications
- Other sectors

Source: Calculations using data from Arias and Saavedra 2013.
Note: Advanced modernizers include Turkey, the Czech Republic, Estonia, Hungary, Poland, the Slovak Republic, Slovenia, Bulgaria, Latvia, and Lithuania. Intermediate modernizers include Croatia, the former Yugoslav Republic of Macedonia, Romania, Georgia, and Moldova. Late modernizers include Azerbaijan, Kazakhstan, the Kyrgyz Republic, the Russian Federation, and Ukraine. Value added and employment in 2008 are calculated using growth rates estimated in Arias and Saavedra (2013) applied over observed values in 2000.

an intermediate modernizer, there is evidence of significant structural change associated with the relocation of labor from low productivity to high productivity sectors between 2002 and 2010, and this relocation may have boosted growth by up to 2 percentage points per year.

What is the Impact of Employment Protection Legislation and Other Labor Market Institutions on Employment?

The laws, practices, policies, and conventions that fall under the umbrella of labor market institutions determine what kinds of employment contracts are permissible; set boundaries for wages and benefits, hours, and working conditions; define the rules for collective representation and bargaining; proscribe certain employment practices; and provide for social protection for workers. The discussion here focuses on the role of EPL and minimum wages, while a discussion on the role of labor relations is provided in box 1.1.[4]

BOX 1.1

Labor-Employer Relations: New Approaches to Collective Representation

The debate on the impact of unions and collective bargaining on firms' productivity is not new, and it has received some attention in *Jobs, World Development Report 2013* (WDR). On the one hand, it is argued that giving "voice" to labor can address information failures at the workplace, thus generating efficiency gains, stimulating innovation, and resolving potential conflicts. On the other hand, higher union coverage and bargaining tends to result in increased regulation and higher wage premiums, which are deemed to influence employment levels. The "union wage effect," indeed, can be rather high (e.g., around 15 percent in Germany, where collective bargaining covers almost 60 percent of workers). The OECD concludes that a 10 percentage point decline in union coverage is associated with a 0.8 percentage point increase in employment. In South Africa, for example, the unemployment rate would decrease by 1.5 percentage points if the employment effect of bargaining councils was to be eliminated.

While the discussion on this trade-off is not new, changes are emerging across the world in the structures for collective bargaining institutions. Traditional forms of collective bargaining are firm-level bargaining or industry-based bargaining with national coverage. However, new arrangements are emerging and were captured in the *WDR 2013* discussion.

In China, local, sector-based collective bargaining agreements have appeared since 2003, when the first of such agreements was negotiated in the wool-sweater manufacturing industry in the Xinhe district. The successful development of "local-sectoral" forms of collective bargaining allowed firms to overcome key challenges they faced and resulted in more stable labor-employer relations, a more reliable labor supply, and more transparent changes in labor costs.

Another development in the institutional structure of collective representation is the emergence of associations of self-employed workers. Traditional trade unions, in fact, fail to provide voice to the self-employed and to workers in the informal sector. These categories represent a large proportion of workers in developing countries, including within Europe and Central Asia (ECA). Several associations have therefore emerged, including India's Self-Employed Women's Association, Peru's groups of street vendors, and Bogotá's waste pickers association. The latter managed to aggregate claims to negotiate with government authorities and resorted to litigation in the courts to uphold waste pickers' rights.

Innovative forms of collective bargaining such as these could offer ECA countries and their changing labor markets new ways of striking the balance among workers' rights, firms' productivity, and employment creation.

Source: World Bank 2012a.

The past two decades have been witness to significant controversies over the role and impacts of labor market institutions. Research in the 1990s typically found that strong protective legislation slowed job growth and increased unemployment in OECD countries, thus leading to policy recommendations in support of flexible rules for protecting employment and setting wages and hours and unemployment and welfare systems that minimized work disincentives. A parallel body of evidence did not yet exist for developing countries, but the dominant policy message was similar: while institutions were introduced with good intentions and had a role in addressing market failures, they often had unintended negative consequences in terms of both efficiency and equity.

However, new evidence produced over the past decade suggests that the overall impact of EPL and minimum wages is smaller than the intensity of the debate would suggest (see Betcherman 2012 for a comprehensive review of existing literature). Most estimates of the impacts of EPL and minimum wages on employment levels tend to be insignificant or modest, while both are associated with a decline in wage inequality. Impacts on the composition of employment and on employment dynamics are somewhat more sizeable. EPL and minimum wages can shift employment away from young people, women, and the less-skilled and toward prime-age men and the better educated, although the effects vary across countries. And stringent EPL can potentially reduce labor market flows, increase durations in both employment and unemployment, and ultimately slow down labor reallocation and limit the efficiency gains from creative destruction, although the evidence on the impact of EPL on productivity is at best mixed (Betcherman 2012).

Where does ECA fit into this picture? The evidence on how labor market institutions and policies have affected labor market outcomes in ECA is scarce but points toward the presence of distortions. There are only a handful of cross-country studies that analyze this question (Cazes and Nesporova 2003; Fialová and Schneider 2009), and of those only one has data for CIS countries, and only for some (Lehmann and Muravyev 2010, 2011). Evidence for new EU member states suggests that distortions introduced by minimum wages, although present, are limited (Packard, Koettl, and Montenegro 2012). In contrast, the strictness of EPL has a negative impact on the overall employment rate (Lehmann and Muravyev 2011) and can affect the effectiveness of other labor market policies, such as active labor market interventions—i.e., if EPL is less flexible, firms could be less willing to hire from the unemployed pool (Lehmann and Muravyev 2010).

EPL and minimum wages also affect the composition and dynamics of employment in ECA. The strictness of EPL is positively correlated with youth unemployment (Lehmann and Muravyev 2011) and with the size of the informal sector; the latter in the new EU member states (Packard, Koettl, and Montenegro 2012). There is also evidence that differences in the strictness and nature of EPL across countries in the region can explain some of the observed differences in the way that labor markets respond to business cycles—particularly whether the adjustment falls primarily on prices (wages), quantities (jobs), or both (Gimpelson and Kapeliushnikov 2011; Lehmann and Pignatti 2007). Finally, it is likely that employment legislation and regulation will become a more binding constraint as other barriers to employment related to the overall business environment disappear. In fact, the discussion in chapter 2 suggests that firms in advanced modernizers are more likely to identify labor regulation as a binding constraint to employment creation than firms in intermediate and late modernizers, while the latter are more likely to complain about the negative impact of, say, corruption.

Having said this, the best performers in terms of employment creation in the region are also countries with relatively high EPL and minimum wages, which suggests that labor market institutions are not the only or even the most important determinants of labor market performance. This is consistent with the international evidence that suggests that most countries set EPL and minimum wages in a range where impacts on employment or productivity are modest but distributional impacts could be more significant.

Moving forward, countries in the region should introduce reforms that minimize the negative distributional impacts associated with current EPL levels and nature while increasing flexibility where needed (i.e., Western Balkan and some CIS countries). In doing so, these countries should think carefully about introducing flexibility at the margin through, for instance, the use of temporary contracts versus following a more comprehensive approach that takes into account the interaction between EPL and minimum wages and other labor market institutions and programs. A review of the European experience regarding temporary contracts is provided in box 1.2, and box 1.3 provides a description of Denmark's "flexicurity" model, which shifts protection away from jobs to the incomes of people who lose employment and combines it with efforts to get them back to work.

BOX 1.2

Do Temporary Contracts Increase Overall Flexibility in the Labor Market?

Employment protection legislation (EPL) reform in Europe during the past few decades has proceeded along a two-tier system, as defined by the World Bank's *Golden Growth* report. While maintaining strict protection for permanent work contracts, many European countries deregulated the use of temporary contracts to increase labor market flexibility. The outcome of these reforms is mixed.

Golden Growth presents the example of Spain as illustrative of the dualism in EPL reforms. Spain liberalized the use of temporary contracts in 1984, leading to an increase in temporary jobs from 11 percent to 35 percent of total employment in 1995. Much of the increase in the number of temporary contracts affected young workers, in Spain and elsewhere: in most EU member states, 40 percent of young people (ages 15–39) are on temporary contracts. Similar reforms took place in other European countries, but their effects varied. It appears that countries with less strict regulations for permanent contracts (e.g., Denmark and the United Kingdom) did not witness a sharp increase in temporary employment.

The impact of temporary contracts is mixed. On the positive side, they can give firms an opportunity to evaluate workers' suitability for jobs or cushion firms from demand fluctuations that would otherwise require costly adjustments to their core labor force (i.e., severance payments and legal costs). They can also help increase new recruitments and reduce long-term unemployment, as was the case in Spain during the period of high growth between 1987 and 1994. However, temporary contracts can have adverse effects, especially when firms use them to reduce labor costs. This practice can be especially harmful for productivity, decreasing marginal returns for labor, as was found to be the case in Italy, and for human capital development.

Source: Gill and Raiser 2012.

Does Public Sector Modernization Facilitate Private Sector Employment Creation?

In the wake of the transition, countries in ECA faced important challenges regarding existing state-owned enterprises (SOEs). These firms employed large numbers of workers, in many cases well above what would be considered efficient, with significant negative impacts on labor productivity and competitiveness. Labor hoarding in SOEs threatened to slow down the relocation of labor from less to more productive sectors and firms in the absence of reform. More broadly, in many cases governance problems and biased regulation that favored SOEs undermined competition, reducing incentives to reduce costs, innovate, and become more efficient. These problems were

BOX 1.3

Denmark's Flexicurity

Over the past few decades, new approaches emerged in several European countries to balance flexibility for employers and income security for workers. Denmark is often portrayed as a successful pioneer in such practice, called *flexicurity*. Its successful example is presented in the World Bank's *Golden Growth* report.

The Danish arrangement, which emerged in the 1990s and is often called the "Golden Triangle," combines three elements: flexible hiring and firing laws, generous unemployment benefits, and active labor market programs. The employment protection legislation index for Denmark, compiled by the OECD, fell from 2.4 in 1983 to 1.5 in 2009, which indicates relatively flexible hiring and firing regulations. At the same time, unemployment insurance, financed from contributions, and taxes cover around 80 percent of the labor force. It provides up to four years of unemployment benefits, which average close to two-thirds of earnings and are capped at €2,173 a month. The last element of this triangle is a solid set of active labor market programs, including job search assistance and training, which absorb about 75 percent of the €13 billion spent on labor market programs in 2010.

Flexicurity seems to work well in Denmark. The unemployment rate declined from 10 percent in 1993 to just over 3 percent in 2008, and long-term unemployment dropped from a third to a tenth of total unemployment in the 1994–2009 period.

Despite this success, however, the sustainability of the Danish model and its applicability to other countries are debatable. The *Golden Growth* authors raise three main concerns. First, there is a gap between actual unemployment and official unemployment statistics that is likely to overestimate the decline in unemployment. Second, it is hard to establish whether the sizeable decrease in unemployment was due to flexicurity on its own or a combination of flexicurity and strong economic performance. Last, the Danish model represents a significant fiscal burden: it costs 4.5 percent of GDP in terms of active and passive labor market measures. These should be key considerations for other countries when designing their labor market policies along the lines of the Danish model.

Source: Gill and Raiser 2012.

particularly acute in network sectors, such as energy and transport, which have a large impact on the performance of the private sector. Over the 1990s and first decade of the 2000s, nonadministrative public employment declined significantly in most countries but on average it did relatively more so among advanced modernizers. Nonadministrative public employment fell between 53 percent (Slovenia) and 76 percent (Poland) among advanced modernizers, between 46 percent (Moldova) and 80 percent (Georgia) among intermediate modernizers, and between 20 percent (Belarus) and 58 percent (Kazakhstan) among late modernizers. In addition, because countries differed substantially in terms of the initial share of public employment in total employment, important differences still remain. In 2010, public sector employment accounted for 16 percent (Poland) to 34 percent (Lithuania) of total employment among advanced modernizers, for 15 percent (Georgia) to 41 percent (Moldova) among intermediate modernizers, and for 33 percent (Tajikistan) to 72 percent (Belarus) among late modernizers.

Efforts to reform SOEs and reduce public sector employment paid off significantly in the form of employment growth in the private sector. Results from an accounting decomposition exercise suggest that GDP growth and changes in public sector employment are the two largest contributors to changes in private sector employment over 2000–10 (Soto 2013). On average, 1.00 percentage point reduction in public employment is associated with a 0.53 percentage point increase in private employment. As a result, actual changes in public

FIGURE 1.15

Public Sector Retrenchment Is Positively Correlated with Private Employment Growth

Share of predicted changes in private employment explained by changes in public sector employment

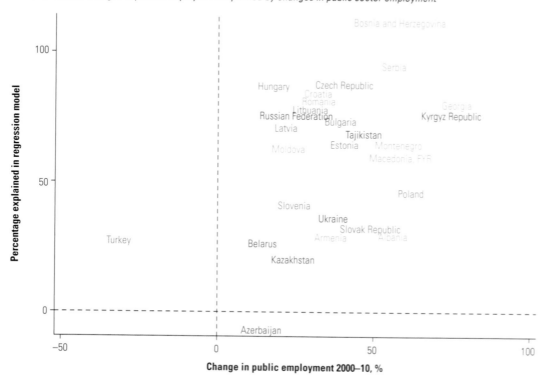

Sources: Calculations using data from LiTS (EBRD 2010); Soto 2013.

employment can account for approximately 60 percent of the predicted change in private employment among advanced modernizers and intermediate modernizers and for 40 percent of the predicted change among late modernizers (figure 1.15). Having said this, it is possible that in some cases the dismantling of SOEs in capital intensive sectors may have (temporarily) led to a decline in labor productivity.

In contrast, countries that have so far failed to successfully reform the SOE sector are paying a high price in terms of productivity and employment growth. In Belarus, overemployment in SOEs is estimated to stand at more than 25 percent in the industry and construction sector alone. Labor hoarding in SOEs continues to undermine sectoral and aggregate productivity growth—labor productivity among private among private firms is between 1.5 and 4.5 times higher than among SOEs operating in the same sector—and to hinder productive labor relocation—approximately 15 percent of those employed in SOEs are in loss-making enterprises (World Bank 2012b).

Have Deeper Financial Development and Integration in Global Markets Translated into More Jobs?

Higher levels of financial development and integration in global financial markets contributed to positive employment creation in the years preceding the crisis but exacerbated the negative impact of the crisis on jobs and could undermine employment creation moving forward. Availability of finance can facilitate new business creation and growth and can therefore intensify competition and boost labor demand (Gatti and Love 2008; Levine 2005; Love 2003). Indeed, increased domestic credit to the private sector (a common measure for financial depth) had a positive impact on employment creation in 2000–07; a 1 percentage point increase in the ratio of domestic credit to the private sector to GDP was associated with a 0.7 percentage increase in the employment rate (Love 2013). Other financial indicators, such as foreign direct investment and private capital flows (both in percentage of GDP) did not have a significant effect on employment (Love 2013). In contrast, countries with higher precrisis levels of financial development (for the most part advanced modernizers) experienced larger employment contractions during the crisis (Love 2013). These results are consistent with the firm-level evidence discussed in chapter 2. During 2000–07, businesses with access to credit were more likely to create employment than otherwise comparable businesses. However, because these were often new and/or small firms with little or no self-financing capacity, they were also the most affected by the credit crunch that followed the crisis.

The impact on employment creation of increased integration among ECA countries and with the rest of the world, especially with Western Europe, was positive but modest and concentrated among advanced reformers. In the 2000s export growth was associated with higher employment levels in all countries in the region except the Western Balkans, while the opposite is true about import growth, particularly among CIS countries (Soto 2013). Consequently the net impact of trade on employment was positive in those countries where export growth surpassed import growth, namely, the advanced modernizers and some late modernizers, and it was negative in those countries where the opposite happened. The overall impact of trade on employment was relatively modest, however. Results from an employment growth accounting-decomposition exercise suggest that increased openness can explain at most 16 percent of the predicted change in private employment in 2000–11 (Soto 2013)—a relatively small percentage compared to the effect of economic growth and public employment reductions measured in the same exercise and discussed above.

Moving forward, the impact of financial markets and trade on employment creation is likely to remain limited. Persistent weakness in the financial sector, such as a large fraction of nonperforming loans, and the reluctance of many institutions to allow credit to grow back to precrisis levels could undermine prospects for stronger employment creation in the near future, particularly among small and medium enterprises in advanced modernizers. Similarly, the estimated impact of converging to world trade patterns (as predicted using a gravity model on the basis of economic size, level of development, and transportation costs) on employment growth is also relatively small and would affect only a few countries, mostly intermediate and late reformers, conditional on further reform that allows for sustainable expansion in trade volumes and a (significant) shift in trade patterns (Soto 2013).

When considered together, the evidence on the impact of modernization on employment creation points toward three main conclusions. First, business climate reforms do pay off in the form of stronger (productivity and) employment growth, but they do so only with a lag and for countries that have implemented broad and substantive reforms. Second, the impact of EPL and minimum wages on overall employment is modest, although their impact on employment composition and dynamics could be more significant. Third, the employment impact of additional efforts to restructure the SOE sector, to develop the financial sector, and to open up to and further diversify trade is likely to be positive and significant among intermediate and late modernizers but limited among advanced modernizers.

Consequently regaining the precrisis momentum will require different things from different countries. Advanced modernizers should minimize distortionary distributional effects associated with EPL and minimum wages and renew their efforts to tackle second-generation investment climate reforms and to deal with any pending issues concerning public sector restructuring. In contrast, late modernizers should focus on strengthening macro fundamentals and governance, making labor market institutions more flexible where they are not, leveling the playing field, and deepening economic restructuring and diversification. Not surprisingly, the agenda for intermediate modernizers would fall somewhere in between those of the other two groups.

Having said this, the impact of modernization on labor market performance and ultimately employment creation will be mediated by the second contextual factor that characterizes ECA countries; namely, demographic pressures associated with aging (in most countries) and youth bulges (in some countries). For instance, even among advanced modernizers, employment rates continued to be low and unemployment remained a stubborn problem relative to other middle-income countries and the OECD in the years leading to the crisis. This implies that modernization should be understood as a necessary but not always sufficient condition for stronger and sustained employment creation and that complementary policies will be needed to effectively align the modernization process with demographic imperatives.

The Impact of Demographics

The second contextual factor that has shaped labor markets' performance and dynamics in ECA and will continue to do so in the decades to come is demographics. Workers of different ages, men and women are affected by and respond to labor market developments (and shocks) differently. The transition to a market economy has required and will continue to require intense labor relocation across sectors and firms. Labor relocation can be a wasteful and painful process for workers if not managed adequately. Policies that take into account and adapt to changes in the size and composition of the working-age population and the labor force (i.e. policies that are age and gender sensitive) can support the relocation process while minimizing the negative impact that it can have on (specific groups of) workers.

Fewer and Older: What Is the Impact of Demographics on the Size and Composition of the Working-Age Population?

Countries in ECA can be divided in two groups according to their projected population dynamics over the next 20 years: countries that are aging, in some cases very rapidly, and countries with large numbers of youth. Increasing life expectancy means that larger numbers of individuals are living longer and, when combined with low and declining fertility rates, that the elderly account for a growing share of the total population. In contrast, where fertility rates remain high the size of younger cohorts is expected to continue to grow over the next two decades, despite higher life expectancy. Of course, population dynamics are to some extent endogenous as both fertility and migration respond to social and economic changes. For the purpose of this chapter, projections are taken as given, while a more extensive discussion on migration is provided in chapter 5.

Population dynamics have a direct impact on the size of the working-age population and the labor force. Aging is directly associated with a shrinking working-age population and, without significant changes in participation rates, a shrinking labor force as well. This is the case in Russia, Ukraine, Belarus, Moldova, the new EU member states, and most of the Western Balkans and South Caucasus. Youth bulges driven by high fertility are associated with growing working-age populations and labor forces. This is the case in Albania, Azerbaijan, and Central Asia (figure 1.16a).

Demographic pressures also affect the composition of the working-age population and the labor force. Although the share of older workers will increase and the share of young workers will decline in all countries, they will do so at very different speeds. Twenty years from now, the share of older workers (ages 55–64) in the working-age population of aging countries will be as large (around 14–16 percent) as the share of young workers (ages 15–24)—and it will be more than double the size of the share of young workers if all individuals above the age of 55 are taken into account. In contrast, young workers will account for 20–25 percent of the working-age population in countries with youth bulges, compared to 10–12 percent for older workers (figure 1.16b and c).

FIGURE 1.16

Demographic Pressures Impact the Size and Composition of the Working-Age Population

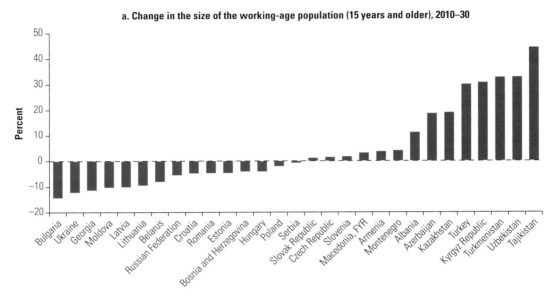

a. Change in the size of the working-age population (15 years and older), 2010–30

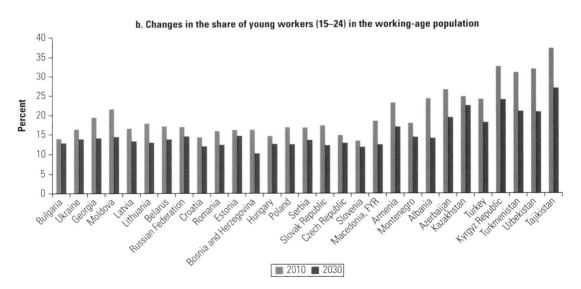

b. Changes in the share of young workers (15–24) in the working-age population

■ 2010   ■ 2030

continued

FIGURE 1.16
Continued

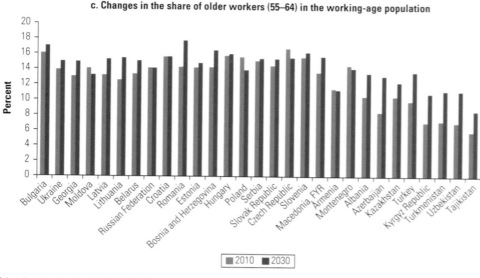

c. Changes in the share of older workers (55–64) in the working-age population

Legend: 2010 | 2030

Sources: Calculation using data from UN 2013; ILO 2013b.

The question then arises as to the impact of demographics on labor market outcomes and dynamics. To answer this question we examine the impact of demographics on labor force participation, employment and unemployment rates, labor relocation, and ultimately economic restructuring. The evidence suggests that demographics have indeed played an important role in shaping labor market performance over the past decade, as different groups have adapted and fared differently to the effects of reform and modernization.

Can Demographics Explain Low Employment Rates in the Region?

Low employment rates result from the combination of low participation and high unemployment and translate into significant losses in hours and years worked in ECA. A typical person in ECA spends one-third of his or her productive years out of work, either in inactivity or in unemployment. These low employment rates translate into significantly fewer working hours and work years in a lifetime. In ECA, people work 14 years less than a fully employed working life, approximately two full years less than the average for the non-ECA EU countries, and four years less than in OECD countries outside of Europe. For example, in FYR Macedonia, Moldova, and

FIGURE 1.17

Many Years of Potential Employment Are Lost, Especially among Older Workers and Women

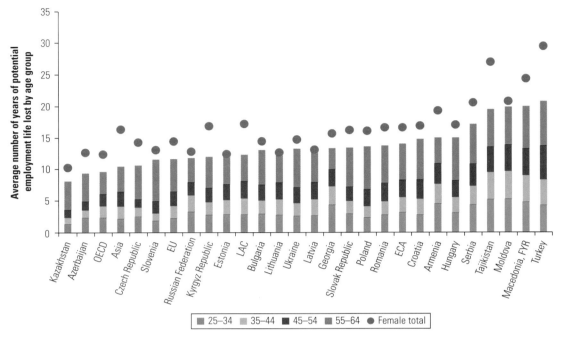

Source: World Bank calculations based on data of the International Labour Organization and household and labor force surveys.
Note: Calculated based on the employment rates by age group (i.e., each age group–specific employment rate indicates average years worked per person in that age group), starting at age 15 and ending at 64 years, minus the total potential working life. Data for Asia include Bangladesh; Bhutan; Hong Kong SAR, China; Indonesia; Macao SAR, China; Malaysia, the Philippines; Sri Lanka; and Thailand. Data for LAC include Argentina, Barbados, Chile, Colombia, Costa Rica, Cuba, the Dominican Republic, Ecuador, El Salvador, Guatemala, Honduras, Mexico, Netherlands Antilles, Panama, Paraguay, Uruguay, and República Bolivariana de Venezuela. ECA = Europe and Central Asia; EU = European Union; LAC = Latin America and the Caribbean; OECD = Organisation for Economic Co-operation and Development.

Turkey, 20 years of potential employment are lost on average over a lifetime—as much as 29 years for Turkish women. Much of this loss of productive years happens among older workers and women. In fact, the number of years lost after an individual turns 55 is twice as high in ECA as in OECD countries, and the number of years lost among women is 50 percent higher (figure 1.17).

Participation is particularly weak among young and older workers and among women. These groups are more than twice as likely to be out of work than prime-age workers (25–54 years), and activity gaps are particularly large for men: younger men are five times more likely to be inactive than those in prime age. Participation rates among youth and older workers are also low by international standards—only 37 percent of young workers (ages 15–24) in ECA seek work or are employed, 12 percentage points below rates in LAC and EAP and 13 percentage points below OECD countries. Similarly, participation rates among older workers (55–64), at 50 percent, are far below the average for other regions (60 percent in OECD, 62 percent in LAC, and 65 percent in EAP). In contrast, participation rates for prime-age individuals are close to 80 percent and in line with international norms (figure 1.18).

Across all age groups, women continue to have only limited access to economic opportunities. Half of women in the region remain inactive. As a consequence, female labor force participation is 20 percentage points below that of men and significantly

FIGURE 1.18

Low Labor Force Participation Rates among Young and Older Workers and Women

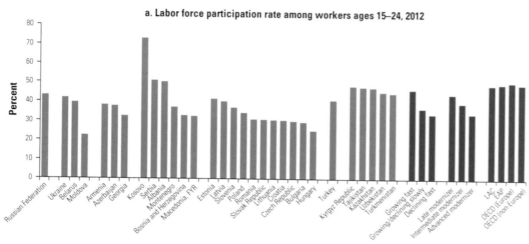

a. Labor force participation rate among workers ages 15–24, 2012

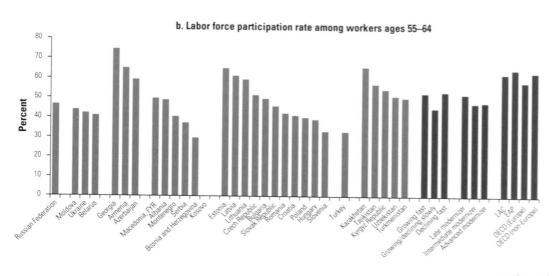

b. Labor force participation rate among workers ages 55–64

continued

FIGURE 1.18
Continued

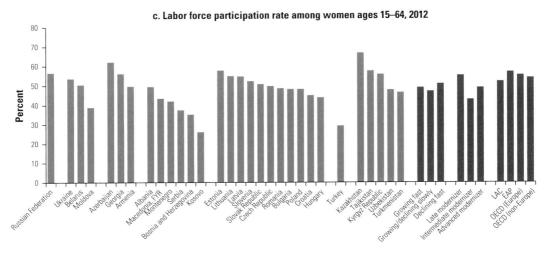

c. Labor force participation rate among women ages 15–64, 2012

Sources: Calculations using ILO 2013b; World Bank 2013c.
Note: Missing bars indicate data is not available for that country. EAP = East Asia and Pacific; LAC = Latin America and the Caribbean; OECD = Organisation for Economic Co-operation and Development. Blue bars show country data; red bars show region/group data.

lower than that of women in OECD countries and most regions in the world. Participation rates for women are particularly low in Kosovo (26 percent), Turkey (30 percent), Bosnia and Herzegovina (42 percent), and Moldova (44 percent). Moreover, contrary to the rest of the world, the gap in labor force participation between men and women remained unchanged between 1999 and 2009.

High and persistent youth unemployment and long-term unemployment (LTU) remain important challenges in the region. Changes in youth unemployment mimic those of total unemployment, but youth unemployment rates are several percentage points higher than the average unemployment rate in most countries. They are not however disproportionately higher than total unemployment by international standards, which suggests that to some extent high youth unemployment rates reflect broad structural problems in the labor market (figure 1.19). The incidence of LTU is also high by international standards, especially among young and older workers and among women. And although the years prior to the crisis were witness to an overall improvement, the young and the long-term unemployed were the hardest hit by the crisis, which sent rates back to historically high levels.

Many countries suffer from either low participation rates (especially among older workers) or high youth unemployment, but ECA

workers to remain employed, while those who continued working through the transition often dropped out of the labor force relatively early on in their lives. And once an older worker left the labor market, it became increasingly difficult to bring them back.

But the impact of age on the ability of workers to transition from job to job and to move from the public to the private sector continued to be felt in the 2000s, even as job destruction subsided and job creation gained strength. An examination of the labor histories of individuals ages 18–24, 25–54, and 55–64 during 2000–06 (EBRD 2006) reveals that young (18–24) and older (55–64) workers were less likely to find a job in the private sector in year t than prime-age workers, irrespective of the activity or employment status in year $t - 1$. In addition, being employed in the public sector or being unemployed in year $t - 1$ significantly diminished the probability of finding a private sector job in year t, particularly among older workers (figure 1.21a).

Age also had an impact on the ability to find employment after being separated from a job. In the case of involuntary job loss at year t (firing), young workers were 15 percent less likely to find private employment in year $t + 1$ than prime-age workers, and older workers were 33 percent less likely. And when they did find a job, they were respectively 1.5 and 1.3 times more likely than prime-age workers to be working informally, often with low protection and/or limited (re)training options. This is particularly detrimental for young workers for whom it is often difficult to transition into formal employment with higher wages. In contrast, when the separation was voluntary, young workers were as likely to find a private job as prime-age ones, suggesting that the separation was motivated by the move to a better job. In fact, evidence for Russia suggests that voluntary separations (quitting) motivated by job-to-job transitions are quite common, particularly among younger workers (Gimpelson and Kapeliushnikov 2011). In contrast, older workers were 46 percent less likely to leave for other jobs than prime-age workers, most likely due to the fact that many of these separations were motivated by early retirement.

Data on labor market transitions in 13 European Union countries during 2010–11 (including Bulgaria, the Czech Republic, Estonia, Hungary, Romania, and the Slovak Republic) reveal similar patterns. Permanence in employment is higher among prime-age workers, who also have very low transition rates to inactivity. In contrast, among young workers, transitions from employment to unemployment and to inactivity, including education, are relatively more frequent (8 percent and 10 percent, respectively). Older workers exiting employment go mainly to inactivity, with most of

FIGURE 1.21

Finding Private Employment Is Harder for Young and, Particularly, Older Workers

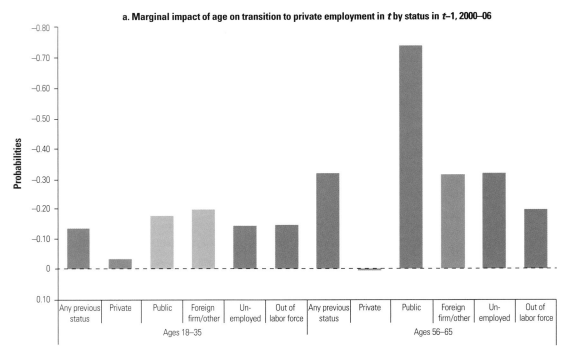

a. Marginal impact of age on transition to private employment in *t* by status in *t*–1, 2000–06

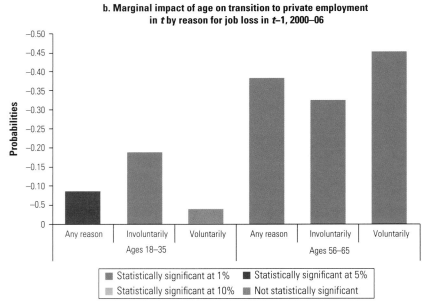

b. Marginal impact of age on transition to private employment in *t* by reason for job loss in *t*–1, 2000–06

Statistically significant at 1% Statistically significant at 5%
Statistically significant at 10% Not statistically significant

Source: Calculations using data from EBRD 2006.

them entering normal retirement schemes. For the unemployed, the probability of remaining unemployed increases only slightly with age. However, unemployed young people have much higher rates of return to employment than older workers, while both groups have lower rates than prime-age workers (EC 2013).

Going forward, demographic pressures will only exacerbate these problems. Other things being equal, the increase in the share of older workers in the working-age population will continue to put downward pressure on aggregate participation rates, even if rates among older workers remain constant or even increase slightly. The share of older workers in the labor force will also increase. Only a combination of policies aimed at increasing participation rates among both older workers and other workers with relatively low participations rates (such as women) will have the potential to reverse the impact of the aging tide (Cancho and Sánchez-Páramo 2013). Similarly, countries with large cohorts of young workers entering the labor market will be hard pressed to implement policies that not only foster employment creation and but also help these workers find jobs.

Conclusion: Building a Country Typology to Think about Jobs in ECA

The discussion in this chapter has been built on the premise that to understand labor market performance in ECA countries one must take into account the two contextual factors that characterize the region: the socialist legacy and growing demographic pressures. The legacy and the extent to which countries have moved away from it and toward a market economy have fundamentally affected the relationship between growth and employment creation across different countries. Changes in the size and composition of the working-age population and the labor force have shaped labor markets and outcomes, particularly the extent to which the restructuring process has been associated with large dislocations of labor.

When combined, these two contextual factors generate a country typology in which each country is characterized by its level of modernization and its demographic status (table 1.2). Although significant differences exist between the countries in each cell (see spotlight 1.1), these countries share some common institutional and economic features and, more importantly, face common challenges.

The discussion in the rest of the report will make use of this typology to interpret the existing evidence and to develop country-type specific policy agendas aimed at strengthening employment creation in the region.

TABLE 1.2

The Importance of Legacy and Demographics: Proposed Country Typology

		Working-age population		
		Growing fast (youth bulge)	Growing/declining slowly (aging medium term)	Declining fast (aging rapidly)
Stages in modernization	Late	Azerbaijan, Kazakhstan, Kyrgyz Republic, Tajikistan, Turkmenistan, Uzbekistan	Russian Federation	Belarus, Ukraine
	Intermediate	Albania, Kosovo	Armenia; Bosnia and Herzegovina; Croatia; Macedonia, FYR; Montenegro; Romania; Serbia	Georgia, Moldova
	Advanced	Turkey	Czech Republic, Estonia, Hungary, Poland, Slovak Republic, Slovenia	Bulgaria, Latvia, Lithuania

SPOTLIGHT 1.1

Advanced, Intermediate, and Late Modernizers: Who Are They?

Over the past two decades, political, economic, and social events have propelled countries in the Europe and Central Asia (ECA) region at different speeds down the path of transition to a market economy and modernization. Change has been driven by both domestic policy and international developments. In some cases, reform efforts have encompassed a wide range of sectors and policies, while in others they have followed a piecemeal approach.

Both the extent to which countries have been able to modernize and the way in which they have done so matters for labor market performance. To examine this issue, information on labor market institutions, business climate, public sector reform, natural resource dependency, trade openness, and financial development is used to organize countries into three country groupings: advanced modernizers, intermediate modernizers, and late modernizers.

The purpose of this exercise is to identify countries that share a common reform experience and that are relatively similar in terms of their current institutional structure and modernization level. Having said this, it is important to remember two things regarding these country groupings. First, even if countries in the same group share some common features, there is still significant within-group heterogeneity. The proposed groupings are constructed around the variables considered most relevant to the functioning of labor markets but do not capture many other defining features of a country's economy. Second, to some extent differences across groups reflect differences in the initial conditions immediately after transition (i.e., 1989–90) rather than

continued

reform efforts since then. Focusing on the first decade of the 2000s, instead of the full two decades since transition, helps "mute" the direct impact of initial conditions on performance (especially among those countries that have moved further along with reforms) but does not make them disappear entirely.

Constructing these country groupings is as much an art as it is a science, as inevitably some judgment calls need to be made when the existing quantitative information is incomplete and/or inconclusive. Cutoffs separating countries into different groups have been chosen in one of two ways—to coincide with a significant break in the value of the indicator between two contiguous countries when countries are ranked according to the value of the indicator, or, in the absence of such breaks, to produce relatively evenly distributed groups of countries.

Five modernization areas and their six indicators (the first area has two indicators) are considered for the purpose of building the country groupings. Details on each of the indicators used and the cutoffs applied to group countries into different categories are provided in the list of modernization areas that follows and in table S1.1.1.

1. **Labor market institutions and efficiency:** Two indicators are used to measure the degree of flexibility of existing labor market institutions and the extent to which labor markets function efficiently. The first is the Employment Protection Legislation Indicator developed by the Organisation for Economic Co-operation and Development (OECD) and applied to countries in the ECA region by Institute for the Study of Labor (IZA). This indicator focuses on regulation pertaining to the hiring and, particularly, the firing of workers; the use of temporary contracts; the functioning of temporary work agencies; and collective dismissals. Most recent data is available for 2007–09, depending on the country. The second indicator is the Labor Market Efficiency Indicator developed by the World Economic Forum. This indicator captures information on labor market flexibility (cooperation in labor-employer relations, flexibility of wage determination, hiring and firing practices, redundancy costs, and extent and effect of taxation) and on efficient use of talent (pay and productivity, reliance on professional management, brain drain, and female participation in labor force). Most recent data are available for 2012–13.

2. **Quality of business climate:** This is assessed using the Transition Index (TI), developed by the European Bank for Reconstruction and Development (EBRD). The index contains information on reforms pertaining to large and small-scale privatization efforts, enterprise restructuring, price liberalization, and trade and foreign exchange policy. Most recent data are available for 2012. Information on the change in the TI in 2000–12 is also used selectively to assess the intensity and nature of business climate reforms efforts over the last decade. The TI are preferred to other indices that also focus on the quality of business climate, such as the Doing Business Indicator, because it is designed to capture institutional elements and processes specific to transition economies. Having said this, country groupings are generally robust to the use of other indices.

continued

SPOTLIGHT 1.1 *continued*

TABLE S1.1.1
The Numbers behind the Country Groupings

Dimensions of modernization			Stage of modernization		
			Advanced	Intermediate	Late
Area	Indicator	Total range and ECA minimum (m) and maximum (M)	Cutoff values		
Labor market institutions and efficiency	Employment Protection Legislation Index (IZA)	0 (not stringent) to 6 (most stringent) m(0.4) M(3.1)	Less than 2	2–2.5	More than 2.5
	Labor Market Efficiency Index (WEF)	1 (lowest) to 7 (highest) m(3.8) M(5.1)	More than 4.5	4.5–4.2	Less than 4.2
Business climate	Transition Index (EBRD)		More than 3.5	3.5–3	Less than 3
Public sector reform	Share of public employment in total employment (%)	0–100 m(18) M(73)	Less than 30	30–40	More than 40
Trade openness and competitiveness	Export as a share of GDP (%)	0–100 m(15) M(92)	More than 50	50–30	Less than 30
Financial development	Financial Markets Development Index (WEF)	1 (lowest) to 7 (highest) m(3.2) M(4.6)	More than 4	4.0–3.5	Less than 3.5

3. **Public sector reform:** The presence of the public sector in the productive sphere is measured using information on the share of nonadministrative public sector employment in total employment from the EBRD's 2010 Life in Transition Survey. Data on the change in this share in 2000–10 are also used selectively to identify countries where public sector reforms efforts were particularly significant.

4. **Trade openness and competitiveness:** This is proxied by the share of total exports to GDP in 2011 (latest year available in the World Development Indicators database). The share of total exports was preferred to the share of total exports plus total imports as it is more closely related to a country's ability to compete in international markets.

5. **Financial development:** This is measured using the Financial Market Development indicator developed by the World Economic Forum. This indicator captures and summarizes information on market efficiency (availability and affordability of financial services, financing through local equity markets, and ease of access to loans and venture capital availability) and trustworthiness and confidence (soundness of banks, regulation of securities exchange, and legal rights). Most recent data are available for 2012–13. Groupings are consistent with those

continued

SPOTLIGHT 1.1 *continued*

produced by combining information on various financial market indicators, such as foreign direct investment, private capital flows, and the share of formal firms that have access to credit.

6. **Natural resources:** Information on the share of natural resources rent in GDP is also taken into account selectively to assess the degree to which natural resources account for a large fraction of economic activity. In 2010 (the last year for which data are available) this share was higher than 10 percent of GDP in only five countries in the region: Azerbaijan, Kazakhstan, the Russian Federation, Turkmenistan, and Uzbekistan. Although a high share is not per se an indicator of good or bad performance, it is a useful proxy for the level of diversification in the economy.

For each indicator, countries are classified as advanced, intermediate, or late modernizers with respect to that specific area and this information is consolidated across areas and indicators to produce final, aggregate groupings. An overview of the indicator-specific and the aggregate groupings is provided in table S1.1.2. For example, Bulgaria is in the top performing group for labor markets (both indicators), business climate, and trade openness and in the intermediate group for public employment reform and financial development. Based on this information, it is considered to be an advanced modernizer. Similarly, the former Yugoslav Republic of Macedonia is in the top performing group for business climate; in the intermediate group for public sector reforms, trade openness and competitiveness, and financial development; and in the bottom group for labor markets. Based on this information, it is considered to be an intermediate modernizer. Finally, Uzbekistan is in the bottom group for labor markets, business climate, public sector reform, and trade openness and competitiveness. No data are available for financial development. In addition, it is one of the five countries with a large natural resource sector. Based on this information, Uzbekistan is considered to be a late modernizer. In the cases of Belarus, Kosovo, and Turkmenistan, where only limited information or no information was available for three out of the six indicators, countries were assigned to different groups after consulting with the World Bank economic and country team.

More generally, a characterization of the three groups and a complete list of the countries in each group is as follows:

- **Advanced modernizers:** Early reformers that continue to be in the lead regarding the quality of their business climate and institutional structure; countries that have made important strides in reducing public sector employment and that have effectively integrated into global (and financial) markets; countries with a well-developed financial market. This group includes the new European Union member states (except Romania and Croatia) and Turkey. This should not be surprising as the accession process provided significant impetus to reform as these countries sought to comply with the EU *acquis communautaire.*

continued

SPOTLIGHT 1.1 *continued*

TABLE S1.1.2

Advanced, Intermediate, and Late Modernizers

	Indicators						Classification		
	TI (EBRD) 2012	EPL (IZA) 2007	Labor market efficiency (WEF) 2012–13	Public employment, % total (LiTS) 2010	Exports, % GDP 2011	Fin dev (WEF) 2012–13	Advanced	Intermediate	Late
Albania								X	
Armenia								X	
Azerbaijan		NA							X
Belarus			NA			NA			X
Bosnia and Herzegovina								X	
Bulgaria							X		
Croatia								X	
Czech Republic	NA						X		
Estonia							X		
Georgia			NA					X	
Hungary							X		
Kazakhstan									X
Kosovo	NA	NA						X	
Kyrgyz Republic									X
Latvia							X		

CHAPTER 2

Enterprises and Job Creation

Introduction

Dynamics in the enterprise sector play a central role in the economies of the Europe and Central Asia (ECA) region. The pace of restructuring in this sector has been a key driver of the region's broader transformation, facilitating the reform of the older industries and the entry of new private enterprises.

More than two decades since the beginning of the economic transition, however, countries in the region still find themselves at different points of the transformation process. As explained in chapter 1, the pace of reforms across countries in the region has varied widely. Some countries have implemented comprehensive reforms and achieved extensive improvements in their business environment, institutional structures, and the efficiency of their public sector while others have implemented reform programs more selectively or have entered late into the modernization process. As the region recovers from the global financial crisis and responds to looming structural challenges, the unfinished transition has both immediate and longer term implications for the region's capacity to find productive employment for its labor force.

This chapter addresses the following questions:

- *What are the patterns of job creation in recent years?* The chapter documents the patterns of net job creation in the enterprise sector over the past few years, including the underlying patterns of gross job creation and gross job destruction. It brings together information drawn from several enterprise data sources—reflecting different relative strengths and weaknesses—and identifies a few striking patterns of employment growth among enterprises despite a number of data constraints. It characterizes the profile of those that have experienced expansions in employment, particularly those that have led job creation. It links such patterns of job flows with the pace of modernization and finds striking patterns that likely reflect the gains from early reforms.

  The chapter also devotes special attention to the role of new private firms that have emerged over the past decade. New enterprises appear to have played a leading role in job creation ahead of the crisis, but there is evidence that many of them may have been lost during the crisis years. This chapter underscores the importance of the entry of new firms into markets and the emergence of new enterprises to help sustain employment growth in the postcrisis period.

- *Why is there limited firm entry and why are there so few entrepreneurs in ECA?* Although new enterprises have played a key role in the transformation process, providing productive employment as old industrial enterprises have diminished in importance, it is generally thought that rates of entrepreneurship in the region lag behind those of more advanced economies or those of other countries at similar stages of development. This is seen as an "attitudinal legacy" of central planning, holding country and institutional characteristics constant. The chapter explores this phenomenon more fully along two dimensions.

  First, it consolidates several cross-country measures of entrepreneurship to reexamine the claim that there are few entrepreneurs in the region. There are a few commonly used indexes of entrepreneurship, and they differ widely in definition, data source, and country coverage, thus hampering cross-country comparison.

  Second, the chapter explores a new data source that suggests the existence of a sizeable pool of "latent entrepreneurs" in the region who could be the drivers of new job creation and new enterprises. Although the measure of latent entrepreneurship is arguably imperfect, the chapter provides evidence that it can be a reasonable measure of *potential* entrepreneurial activities. The correlates of such latent entrepreneurship and the correlates of successful efforts to start a business together provide compelling evidence of the individual and demographic drivers of entrepreneurship as well as the policy drivers of and constraints to greater entrepreneurial activity.

- *How can public policy help strengthen job creation and entrepreneurship?* The chapter discusses the role for public policy in strengthening employment generation in the enterprise sector. It brings together the relevant findings from the preceding sections to identify opportunities for the public sector to help boost the potential of enterprises in the region. The policy opportunities reflect a diverse policy agenda, reflecting varying stages of the modernization process.

The findings presented in this chapter show that the region experienced net job creation in the years prior to global financial crisis, but with significant variations across countries. The varying magnitudes of net job creation during this period reflect, in part, the pace of enterprise restructuring and structural transformation. *Advanced modernizers* generally experienced sustained net job creation while *intermediate modernizers* reached the state of balanced job flows on the eve of the crisis. Where restructuring had lagged behind, the enterprise sector experienced much less or no net job creation, underpinned by sizeable gross job destruction. Invariably, however, the global financial crisis weakened job creation everywhere. As the region continues to recover from the crisis, its capacity to create net employment will be driven in part by its stage of the restructuring process, along with its competitiveness, its capacity to innovate, and so forth.

Net job creation in the region appears to be typically led by a handful of firms, many of which are young firms. On average, about 10–15 percent of all firms account for over two-thirds of net job creation. This pattern holds regardless of whether the entire enterprise sector is experiencing net job creation or net job destruction. Although an earlier strand of the literature observed that these few firms were typically young and small—the so-called gazelles—and firms at the technological frontier were thought to be potentially significant drivers of job creation, in fact the data suggest diverse profiles across countries. In some countries, market services have led job creation, while in other countries construction has led the way. It is clear, however, that recently established or relatively younger firms have played an important role. Due to data constraints, their role is indicated here by the number of jobs created alone and not to the quality of jobs created. There is some evidence, though weak, that suggests that more productive firms may have created more jobs.

As a consequence of the crisis, however, the region lost many of its youngest and newest firms. During good times, the financial sector is able to allocate resources toward young, innovative firms that have the potential to be high-impact companies. However, a crisis can distort this allocation process, and as a consequence there is evidence that the region lost many of its young, innovative enterprises, including those with high-growth potential and those that could have been future drivers of employment growth. Nonetheless, many inefficient firms could also have closed as a result of the crisis, and some of the firm exits could eventually prove to be productivity enhancing for the sector as a whole. The lack of postcrisis enterprise data prevents one from exploring this more fully.

Business startups and new firm entry can help expand and sustain a modern enterprise sector, but rates of entrepreneurship in the region are thought to be generally lower than those of emerging and high-income economies. However, the region's record is more ambiguous than generally thought, as cross-country comparisons are often hampered by different data sources and definitions. Along certain dimensions, the ECA region's entrepreneurial activity compares favorably with many other countries, particularly in recent years, led by the advanced modernizers.

In addition, there is evidence of substantial latent entrepreneurship in the region, that is, a fairly large pool of entrepreneurs waiting to enter the market. Numerous workers who profess to want to be self-employed are among those currently gainfully wage-employed. Of these, the fraction of those who actually took steps to start a business and successfully managed to do so vary substantially across countries, reflecting individual-level and demographic characteristics, on one hand, as well as features of the respective country's business environment and its stage in the modernization process, on the other.

In this environment, there is a role for policy in strengthening private sector–led job creation and promoting entrepreneurship. This includes reducing costs for business startups, simplifying the business registry requirements, and streamlining insolvency procedures. Ensuring that firms with high-growth potential have access to finance will also be important. Where a burdensome business environment constrains enterprise operations, there is much room for policy reform.

The chapter is organized as follows. The second section analyzes patterns of net job creation in recent years, ahead of the crisis and in the current period for which the relevant data are available. The third explores the entrepreneurial process and quantifies the magnitude and drives of actual and potential (or latent) entrepreneurship. Finally, the fourth section provides concluding observations on the role for public policy in helping facilitate job creation and entrepreneurship.

Patterns of Net Job Creation

This section presents the patterns of net job creation in the enterprise sector observed in recent years, including the underlying trends in gross job creation and gross job destruction. It brings together information drawn from multiple enterprise data sources which, despite data constraints, reveal striking patterns of job creation.

The Region Has Experienced Substantial Variations in Overall Net Job Creation Reflecting, in Part, the Pace of Enterprise Restructuring

In the years immediately following the 1998 Russian crisis, the region was still struggling with insufficient job creation. Gross job creation was generally outpaced by gross job destruction, which in turn was driven largely by the job destruction that accompanied enterprise restructuring (see, for example, Alam et al. 2008 and Rutkowski et al. 2005). Whatever little job creation took place during that period also was observed to be clustered around selected geographic areas, tending to reinforce regional labor market disparities.

In the precrisis boom years, there were substantial variations in overall net job creation across countries. Figure 2.1 depicts rates of gross job creation and job destruction underpinning net job creation for the enterprises for which employment data are available. The countries were selected to represent the relevant reform subgroups in the region; annex 2A provides summary figures for all countries for which data are available. In the absence of census data on enterprises, the patterns reported here refer to job creation and destruction among surviving firms and exclude those flows due to firm entry or firm exit. They are therefore different from those patterns in the literature that have been calculated using enterprise census data. (See also box 2.1 for the data sources, their strengths, and their weaknesses.) Enterprise data can be reported in a number of ways, using either surviving firms from year to year or using a longitudinal sample of firms over selected time periods. This study finds that the patterns are generally consistent, whether using all available data each year or using data from a smaller longitudinal sample.

FIGURE 2.1

Precrisis Net Job Creation in Selected ECA Countries

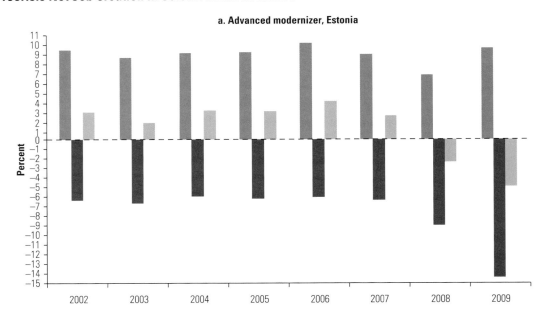

a. Advanced modernizer, Estonia

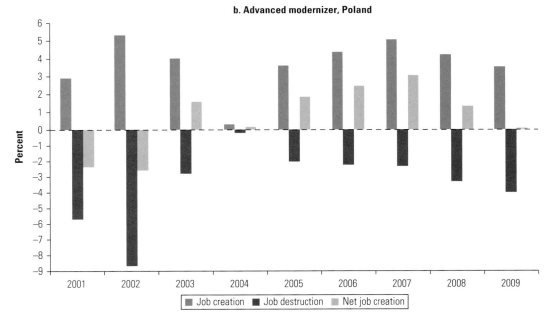

b. Advanced modernizer, Poland

■ Job creation ■ Job destruction ▨ Net job creation

continued

FIGURE 2.1
Continued

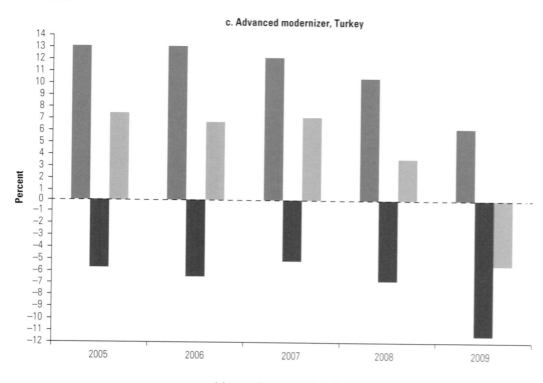

c. Advanced modernizer, Turkey

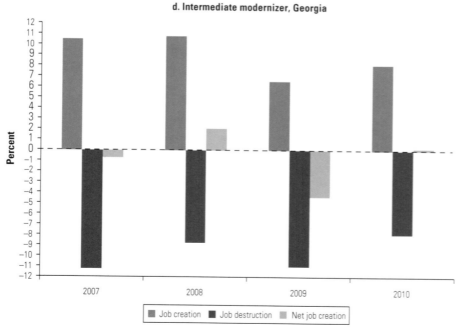

d. Intermediate modernizer, Georgia

Job creation   Job destruction   Net job creation

continued

FIGURE 2.1
Continued

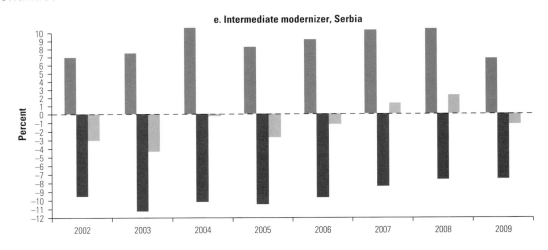

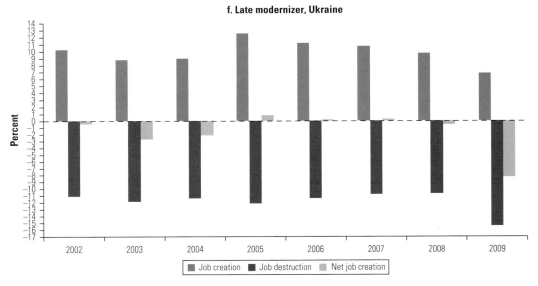

Sources: Amadeus database; Turkey Structural Business Statistics (SBS) data; Georgia enterprise survey data; and World Bank calculations. See box 2.1 and annex 2A for a description of the data sources.

As the panels in figure 2.1 show, there are notable disparities in net job creation across countries, along with striking differences in the underlying gross job destruction and gross job destruction rates. Poland and Turkey had experienced years of net job creation ahead of the crisis, while little or no net job creation took place in Georgia and Ukraine. In turn, the underlying dynamics have been quite different. Gross job creation rates have been highest in Turkey.[1] The enterprises in Ukraine have gross job creation rates that are comparable to those

BOX 2.1

Main Data Sources

The chapter relies on four principal sources of microeconomic data. First, the chapter draws on firm-level data from the Business Environment and Enterprise Performance Survey (BEEPS). The BEEPS database now spans four rounds, the most recent of which is the 2008–09 round, covering some 11,800 enterprises in 29 countries. In six countries (Bulgaria, Hungary, Latvia, Lithuania, Romania, and Turkey), BEEPS data are supplemented with three rounds of a Financial Crisis Survey (FCS) through mid-2010, which provides information on enterprise adjustment during the crisis and performance in the initial stage of the recovery period. Second, it uses information from the Amadeus database. The Amadeus database is a cross-country database managed by Bureau van Dijk (BvD), a private company in the business information industry. Amadeus provides detailed information on enterprise performance and operation, including financial performance. To date, it covers mostly the EU-10 countries, some countries in the Western Balkans, Moldova, the Russian Federation, and Ukraine. Third, BEEPS and Amadeus data are supplemented with enterprise census and enterprise survey data in a handful of countries. For most countries in the Amadeus database, the estimation of job flows will be based on continuing firms alone. In countries for which census data are available, a detailed analysis of firm entry and exit is possible. Finally, the analysis of entrepreneurship draws on new individual-level data from the Life in Transition Surveys (LiTSs). The LiTS is a nationally representative survey first conducted in 29 countries in 2006, a joint undertaking by the European Bank for Reconstruction and Development and the World Bank, to measure household well-being and public attitudes during a period of significant political and economic transformation. A second wave was conducted in 2010, again to capture measures of household welfare during the global financial crisis. Some 1,000–1,500 households were surveyed in each country in the Europe and Central Asia (ECA) region and in selected Western European countries, producing a sample of about 39,000 households from 34 countries.

Each data source has its own strengths and weaknesses. For example, BEEPS provides comparable data across countries in the ECA region. However, the period covered by BEEPS generally ends just before the financial crisis (except for six countries for which data from the crisis period are available). In addition, although BEEPS provides useful information about firms' perception of the characteristics of the business environment, information on the economic activities of the firms are limited, some of them based on recall of activities that took place a few years prior to the survey.

In contrast, Amadeus provides more detailed information about firm activities, and the same firms can be tracked over time. However, it includes only firms that have reported financial statements within a particular four-year period. The main four-year window coverage for the latest version of the database purchased by ECA-PREM (Poverty Reduction and Economic Management) is 2005–08. Specifically, as companies exit or stop reporting their financial statements, the

continued

BOX 2.1 *continued*

agency that collects Amadeus data puts a "not available/missing" for four years following the last included filing. Firms that have not been reporting for at least five years (since 2004 or earlier) are then removed from Amadeus. Therefore, the current database does not include firms that closed down before 2005, and all data from 2004 and earlier come from firms that must have been in business over the period 2005–08. In other words, the sample before 2005 exhibits survivorship bias. Consequently, this survivorship bias restricts the scope of analysis that can be conducted with any particular version of Amadeus. For example, the estimation of job flows from job creation and destruction between and within industries can be estimated but is limited to the particular four-year period. Strong assumptions also need to be made regarding the nonreporting by firms, namely that exit is the cause rather than incomplete or not up-to-date firm registries. Similarly, the determination of entry and exit at the firm level is limited to the four-year window as well. Meanwhile, LiTS data provide a snapshot of entrepreneurship in 2010. In the absence of suitable data for other periods, it is not immediately clear whether the magnitude of entrepreneurship (whether latent or actual) and its drivers in 2010 are the same as in other periods. Where entrepreneurial bent may be a function of the business cycle, the statistical portrait may not be wholly accurate.

Where multiple sources of data exist, the rate of change may not always be at the same level. In general, BEEPS data suggest faster employment growth rates than those of Amadeus, suggesting that BEEPS may be more representative of the more successful firms.

of Turkey, but they have been offset or outstripped by equally large gross job destruction rates. It is clear, however, that net job creation fell in all countries during the global financial crisis (that is, around 2009).

Differences in net job creation across countries may be driven in part by differences in the pace of restructuring. As is well known in the literature on the enterprise sector in the ECA region, job destruction rates rise as enterprises downsize or close down while job creation rates surge as businesses expand or as new enterprises enter the market. The relative size of job creation and job destruction—whether or not job creation exceeds job destruction—and the timing are seen to vary across countries, depending on their stage of the transition process. At the beginning of the restructuring process, job destruction exceeds job creation, as workers employed by obsolete industrial enterprises are retrenched. As the pace of restructuring gains momentum, new enterprises enter the market and efficient enterprises expand job creation that offsets job destruction, and the economy reaches a state of balanced job flows. Over time, as enterprise sector reform is completed, job creation exceeds job destruction.

Following the typology developed in chapter 1, this study classifies the countries in figure 2.1 according to the stage they have reached in the modernization process. Although the typology in chapter 1 is based on a consolidated assessment of reforms along several dimensions (i.e., reforms with respect to the enterprise sector, the public sector, the degree of economic integration, and the level of financial development), in fact, it is broadly consistent with specific transition indicators most closely linked to enterprise activity and enterprise sector reform. In particular, during this period, the values of the European Bank for Reconstruction and Development (EBRD) transition index for the indicator "Governance and enterprise restructuring" suggest that Estonia, Poland, and Turkey were leading this sample of countries (with ratings of 3.7 out of 4.0), Georgia and Serbia were trailing (2.3 out of 4.0), and very little restructuring had taken place in Ukraine (2.0 out of 4.0). Perhaps not surprisingly, the advanced modernizers tend to be disproportionately represented—in those countries, enterprise data tend to be more readily available for stable sample sizes over longer periods of time.

The evidence shows that job flows indeed reflect in part the stage of the enterprise sector reform process. At the beginning of the transition period, Poland was one of the first to go through a period of enterprise restructuring. As a result, the economy's rate of gross job creation also outstripped gross job destruction earlier, resulting in positive net job creation several years ahead of the crisis. In contrast, Georgia had just reached the state of balanced job flows on the eve of the financial crisis—when job destruction and labor shedding in older sectors were proportionally offset by job creation in the new sector—as it carried out intensive enterprise restricting relatively later than other countries in the region (see Rutkowski 2008, 2012b; Rutkowski et al. 2005). Meanwhile, Ukraine has generally lagged behind other transition economies in the restructuring of its enterprise sector. A recent study of firm dynamics in Ukraine provides complementary evidence drawn from census data that entry and exit rates have been lower than those of neighboring countries (World Bank 2010; see also Bartelsman and Kilinc 2009). As a consequence, large, inefficient firms continue to operate, many of which are state-owned enterprises. In this economic environment, financial and human resources are not reallocated to newer firms or more productive firms with higher growth potential. Although the job flows do reflect the enterprise sector reform process, the relationship is not perfectly linear, as evidenced by intermediate modernizers performing as well as or better than some advanced modernizers.

A Few Characteristics of Growing Firms Stand Out

Despite the heterogeneity of experiences with net job creation, a few characteristics of growing firms stand out. Common features among growing firms with respect to age, ownership, and size, among other characteristics, are documented below, drawing from Amadeus, the Business Environment and Enterprise Performance Survey (BEEPS), or other enterprise data sources as appropriate. As explained in box 2.1 each source has its own respective strengths and weaknesses. A relatively large longitudinal sample of firms can be drawn from the Amadeus data, but only for a handful of countries and mostly from among the advanced modernizers. (These countries include those in figure 2.2—four countries each from among the advanced and intermediate modernizers and two from among the late modernizers—or subsets of these 10 countries, depending on the availability of the relevant data.) The enterprise-level information, as presented in the Amadeus database, prevents the classification of enterprises by

FIGURE 2.2

The Upper Tail by Pace of Reform, 2006–08

Percent of enterprises and percent of net jobs created by those enterprises

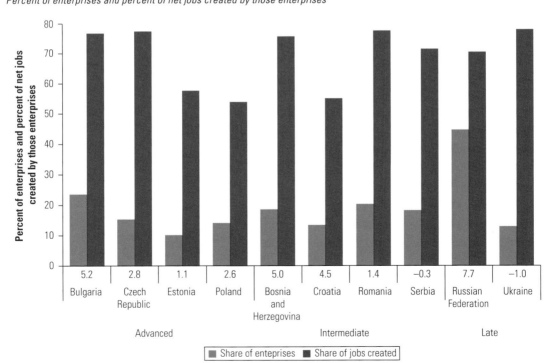

Source: Amadeus and World Bank calculations.
Note: The number above each country names indicates the average annual growth rate for the period.

ownership or by export orientation.[2] In contrast, BEEPS data cover the entire region, and enterprises can be readily classified by ownership and so forth. On the other hand, the sample sizes by country are typically small and for the purposes of this chapter, they are analyzed as cross-sectional data, using retrospective information on employment growth to understand job creation. Notwithstanding these weaknesses, one does find some notable patterns that are often complementary across the data sources.

Net Job Creation Appears to Be Typically Led by a Handful of Firms

First, a handful of firms accounts for the majority of net job creation. On average, about 15 percent of firms account for over two-thirds of net job creation, according to information drawn from the Amadeus database. In figure 2.2, the "upper tail" refers to enterprises that have been growing at 20 percent or more over the precrisis period. While this may seem somewhat arbitrary, the general conclusions—that a few firms account for most of employment growth—hold whether the upper tail is defined as the upper 5 percent or upper 10 percent along the distribution of firms by employment growth or the upper tail is identified based on a particular threshold.[3] In addition, these patterns hold across various periods, though only the 2006–08 period is reported in figure 2.2 (see table 2A.1 in annex 2A for the full summary statistics). There is some heterogeneity across countries and the Russian Federation is an outlier as the Amadeus sample is not nationally representative.[4]

The role played by high-growth firms is true in both expanding and shrinking enterprise sectors, irrespective of the stage of the enterprise transformation process. In figure 2.2, the number above the country names report the average annual growth rate for the 2006–08 period for the entire sample of enterprises. As the numbers indicate, enterprises in the EU-10 countries experienced net job creation during this period while Serbia and Ukraine experienced little or no job creation. Across all countries, however, a small number of firms created all or most of the net employment growth.

These patterns are consistent with a small but growing literature on a few high-growth firms, usually thought to be young and small, that are leading job creation. The literature refers to such high-growth or high-impact firms as *gazelles*. They are observed to create all or most of employment growth in economies where they have been identified (see, for example, Henrekson and Johansson 2010). There is ongoing debate as to whether there are dominant characteristics of the gazelles, in particular, whether they are necessarily small or young. There is rising evidence, however, drawn from patterns of enterprise growth in the United States and from a meta-review of empirical evidence to date in a handful of advanced economies, that it is the young age of the firms more than their size that is associated with rapid growth (see, for example, Haltiwanger, Jarmin, and Miranda 2012; see also Henrekson and Johansson 2010). This suggests a more careful interpretation of the role of small business as drivers of jobs growth. In contrast, the importance of young age suggests the contribution of business startups to employment growth, consistent with what we know of the evolution of industries, including the role of firm entry, learning and selection (see Haltiwanger, Jarmin, and Miranda 2012).

High-growth firms in the region are also generally young. In Poland, for example, the average age of enterprises in the upper tail or upper end of the distribution of firms by employment growth during the precrisis period is 8.4 years, according to Amadeus data. In contrast, all the other enterprises are 16.4 years old, on average. In Bulgaria, the average age of the upper tail is about five years, compared to 12 years for all other enterprises. There is also some evidence that enterprises in the upper tail are relatively small (defined in this case as employing fewer than 50 workers). In Poland, such small firms account for 75 percent of the upper tail, in contrast to the rest of the firms, of whom only about half of the sample consists of small firms. The differences are statistically significant.

High-growth firms tend to operate in construction and market services, as well as a few other industries. This is not surprising as these sectors also tend to be labor-intensive, meaning sizeable employment growth can take place. This pattern holds across all countries, in expanding and contracting countries alike, independent of the stage of transformation process, though a few marginal variations can be observed across countries (figure 2.3). In Estonia, Romania, and Ukraine, for example, the construction sector represents a larger share of high-growth firms. In contrast, these firms play a smaller role in Poland and Serbia. On average, the distribution of high-growth firms across industries is similar to the distribution of all other growing firms, though there are marginal differences in shares.

Complimentary Evidence from BEEPS Confirms the Role of Young Startups in Employment Creation

Complementary evidence from BEEPS suggests that young firms have indeed been leading job creation. Over the precrisis period for which self-reported employment growth data are available, firms that

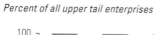

FIGURE 2.3

The Upper Tail by Sector, 2006–08

Percent of all upper tail enterprises

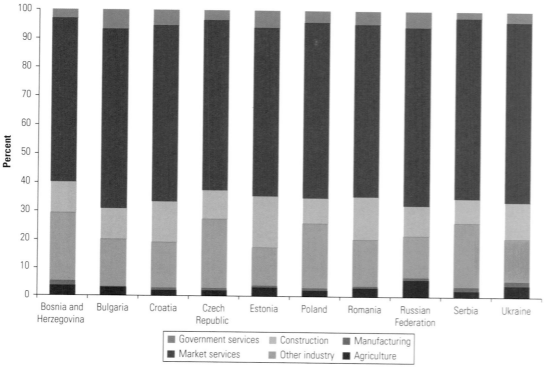

Source: Amadeus and World Bank calculations.

were recently established experienced more rapid employment growth than their older counterparts. Newer firms grew at an annual growth rate of 12 percent while older firms grew at an average annual rate of 5 percent. More generally, newer firms have led job creation across all countries independent of the enterprise restructuring reform, following the typology of countries developed in the previous chapter (figure 2.4). The results of an econometric analysis confirm these patterns (figure 2.5).

State-Owned Enterprises Grew More Slowly While Foreign-Owned Firms Played an Important Role in Leading Job Creation Where Enterprise Reforms Have Lagged Behind

State-owned enterprises have grown more slowly than all other enterprises. For the region as a whole, state-owned enterprises grew by about 5 percentage points more slowly than other enterprises, controlling for a number of firm characteristics. This likely reflects

FIGURE 2.4

Patterns of Job Creation by Firm Age: Evidence from the Business Environment and Enterprise Performance Survey

Annual average geometric growth rate, 2004–07

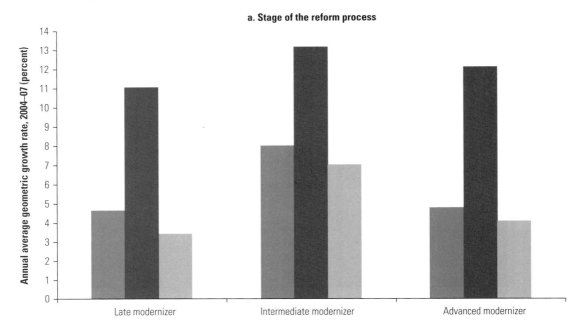

a. Stage of the reform process

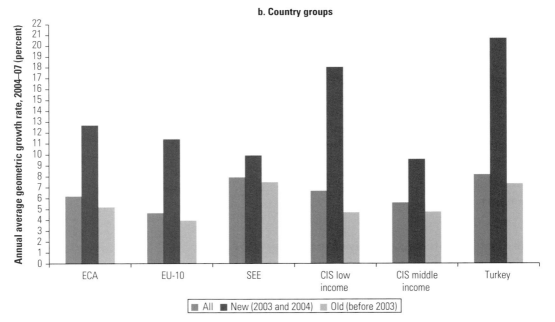

b. Country groups

Source: BEEPS and World Bank calculations.

Note: CIS = Commonwealth of Independent States; ECA = Europe and Central Asia; EU = Europe Union; SEE = Southeastern Europe.

Younger and smaller firms were among the casualties of the global crisis. The results, which are presented in figure 2.7, are based on the Financial Crisis Survey (FCS), a longitudinal survey that tracked manufacturing and service sector firms through 2010 in Bulgaria, Hungary, Latvia, Lithuania, Romania, and Turkey. Although new

FIGURE 2.7

Exit Patterns during the Crisis per the Financial Crisis Survey

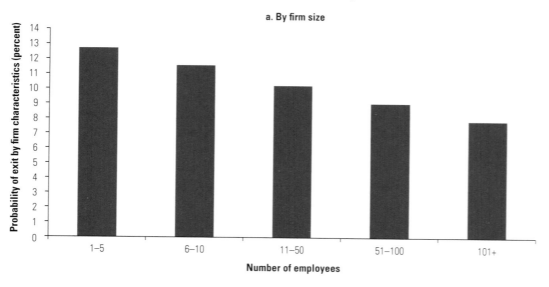

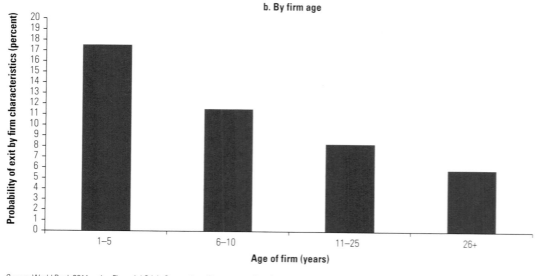

Source: World Bank 2011, using Financial Crisis Survey data. These are predicted probabilities of exit from the regression analysis of actual firm exits in 2009.

firms, innovative firms (defined using the relevant FCS variables as those that introduced new products or engaged in R&D), and small firms fueled much of the region's job creation during the boom years, they were also less likely to survive during the crisis. The results of the econometric analysis of FCS data suggest that the smallest firms were 63 percent more likely to fail, compared to their larger counterparts. Younger firms were also more likely to fail, as they had weaker access to finance.

In addition to young firms closing down, the results of the analysis of FCS data suggest that nonexporting firms and domestic firms were more likely to reduce their workforces. Nonetheless, once again substantial heterogeneity exists across countries. In some countries, the firms that up until the crisis were leading the job creation also suffered larger job losses as a consequence of the crisis. In Turkey, except for the year 2005, exporting firms generally led job creation in the precrisis period. In 2009, however, employment decline among exporting firms far outstripped that of nonexporting firms. In Romania's manufacturing sector, the subsectors leading job creation prior to the crisis (apparel and computer-related industries) also experienced larger contractions in employment during the crisis, according to data from the Amadeus database.

In fact, firms that survived the crisis tended to be the larger— and older—firms that had access to finance or could rely on internal sources of finance. Because of rapid financial sector deepening experienced by the ECA region in the previous decade, enterprises reported easy access to finance in 2005. Conditions gradually changed over time, closer to the beginning of the crisis in 2008, reflecting major changes in the global financial environment (World Bank 2011). In the current period, as banks in the region (and foreign banks in Western Europe) recover from or address the consequences of the Euro Zone crisis, and central banks tighten prudential requirements, it is not likely that the period of easy access to credit will reemerge soon, and younger, smaller firms will be vulnerable. More generally, the ECA region appears to be lagging behind all other regions with respect to financial depth (figure 2.8).

In addition to firm exits, new business registrations fell sharply during the crisis. Between 2004 and 2008, new business registration (measured per 1,000 people) surged by 49 percent. Between 2008 and 2009, however, new business registration in ECA fell by over 20 percent, slightly more than all other regions and most income groups.[8]

FIGURE 2.8

Financial Depth across Regions

Percentage of regional GDP

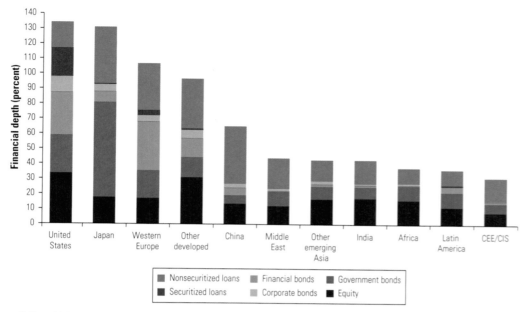

Source: McKinsey 2013.

Note: CEE = Central and Eastern Europe; CIS = Commonwealth of Independent States.

Moving Forward, Prospects for Job Creation Appear Subdued

Economic prospects in the postcrisis period remain fragile, which does not bode well for the employment prospects of the enterprise sector. The summary data on job flows reported in figure 2.9 suggest that all countries experienced contractions in employment during the crisis. Where data exist through 2010 or 2011, the evidence indicates that employment has not fully recovered.

Beyond 2009 or 2010, however, and in the near term, one generally knows little else about patterns of job creation in the enterprise sector. Real-time data on employment growth in the enterprise sector are typically not available because a census of enterprises is conducted only every few years, if at all. Where surveys of enterprises exist, the data are typically made public belatedly. The latest enterprise survey data, for example, cover only the period through 2010, at best, and provide little information on the new drivers of job creation in the recovery period. Some centralized information on vacancies may exist, but they are rare and often not readily available. They are also constrained by the willingness of private enterprises to share information with public employment agencies.

To assess employment growth prospects in the enterprise sector, one option is to use employment expectations information from high-frequency business expectations data. The results from the time-series analysis of employment expectations in ECA provide encouraging evidence that they are leading indicators of employment growth (spotlight 2.1). This empirical exercise included a preliminary assessment of the predictive value of employment expectations using monthly or quarterly sector-level manufacturing and construction data from the

SPOTLIGHT 2.1

Where Are the Jobs Going to Come From?

Labor demand is, of course, difficult to predict; in general we know labor demand, ex post, by examining the hiring decisions of enterprises to date. The World Bank and national authorities typically do not have real-time information on job creation and labor demand because the enterprise surveys are conducted only every few years, if at all, and data are made publicly available belatedly. The latest enterprise survey data, for example, cover only the period through 2010, at best, and provide little information on the drivers of job creation in the aftermath of the global financial crisis. For welfare monitoring, national development planning, and social policy making, the lack of high-frequency data is a substantial handicap.

One option is to use readily available high-frequency data on firms to monitor labor demand and job creation. Rather than allocate large amounts of resources to collect new information, the idea is to make better use of firm-level data already being collected regularly by the authorities. Data from Business Expectations Surveys (BESs)—sometimes referred to as Business Confidence or Business Tendency Surveys—include detailed information about employment expectations of respondent enterprises and represent an underutilized source of information on employment growth prospects. Central banks (or chambers of commerce) routinely conduct such surveys (on a quarterly basis or on a monthly basis in some cases) using a broad cross-sectional sample of enterprises, about 1,000 or more, representing different sectors. The results of the survey are usually aggregated into an index of business confidence, the movements of which are reported alongside real-time information on financial and economic variables. This confidence index is underpinned by a wealth of information provided by enterprises about their economic and financial outlook, including their expected

continued

FIGURE 2.9
Continued

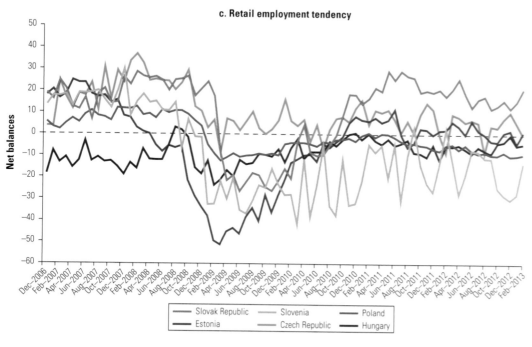

c. Retail employment tendency

Legend: Slovak Republic — Slovenia — Poland — Estonia — Czech Republic — Hungary

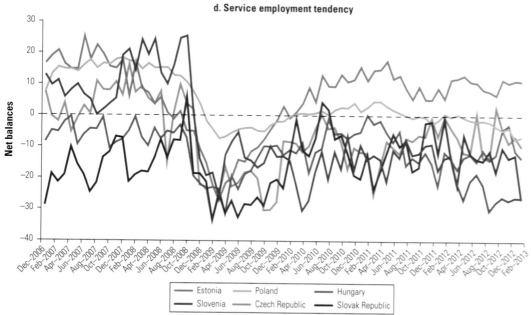

d. Service employment tendency

Legend: Estonia — Poland — Hungary — Slovenia — Czech Republic — Slovak Republic

Sources: OECD Business Tendency Survey data and World Bank calculations.

FIGURE 2.10

Aggregate Net Employment Outlook, 2008–13

Net balances by country or country groups

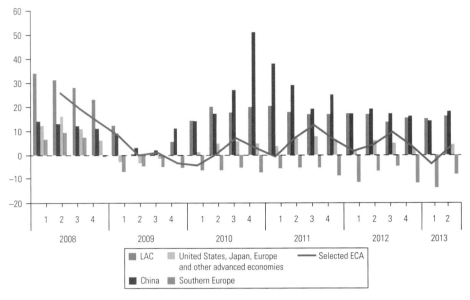

Sources: Manpower Group and World Bank calculations.
Note: ECA = Europe and Central Asia; LAC = Latin America and the Caribbean.

precrisis levels. Net balances in the construction sector, for example, a key driver of job creation in the boom years, are hovering around zero through the first quarter of 2013, far below their precrisis peak of about 16 percent. There are similar patterns in the manufacturing sector. In the retail and services sector, the net employment balances are more diverse and in some cases are back or near their precrisis peak (for example, services in the Slovak Republic), but in many cases they are also hovering around zero.

More generally, employment prospects remain subdued almost everywhere. Summary data from a private firm that conducts employment outlook surveys across a broad sample of countries worldwide are presented in figure 2.10. The net employment outlooks for ECA countries in the sample are consistent with information in figure 2.9: net employment prospects are down, well below their precrisis peak. However, this seems to be generally true everywhere, except China. Net employment outlook in Latin America and the Caribbean (LAC) region and in advanced economies are below their recent peaks. In Southern Europe, the net employment outlook has been negative since the beginning of the crisis.

For late modernizers in ECA, however, the employment outlook is made more difficult by the unfinished restructuring process. Where the enterprise sector is yet to be restructured or where large, inefficient, state-owned enterprises continue to exist, there will be little room for the entry of more productive firms with high growth potential. This is true in economies like Ukraine, for example, where large and inefficient state-owned enterprises are yet to be restructured. In addition, workers employed by these inefficient firms will be retrenched, thus exacerbating gross job destruction for at least some time. All these need to be taken into account, as economies take stock of what is reasonable to expect in the coming years.

Firm Entry, Business Startups, and Latent Entrepreneurship

With the recent loss of young firms as a consequence of the crisis, higher rates of firm entry and entrepreneurship can play an important role in sustaining private sector development and creating new jobs. New entrepreneurs can help replace some of the youngest, most dynamic, and most innovative firms that the region lost to the global financial crisis. In the current period of uncertain economic prospects, entrepreneurial initiatives activities can once again help fuel economic growth and create jobs.

Some Claim That There Are Too Few Entrepreneurs in the Region

More generally, new private firms and entrepreneurs have played a key role in the transition process. During the central planning period, enterprise sectors in the region were dominated by large, state-owned industrial enterprises, with no room for small or medium-size enterprises. As the central planning period ended, new private enterprises, more than privatized firms, have led industries in investment activity and employment creation. New business creation and entrepreneurial activities have been important building blocks for structural change and innovation to replace collapsing manufacturing industries. Entrepreneurs have provided new consumer goods, introduced new production and management processes, challenged the market dominance of state-owned enterprises, and, more generally, helped sustain the reform momentum (see, in particular, McMillan and Woodruff 2002).

Despite the importance of new private firms and entrepreneurs, many have claimed economies in the ECA region have low rates of entrepreneurship compared to high-income economies or other emerging markets. Whether due to the legacy of central planning, the demographic and socioeconomic characteristics of the population, or the business environment, lower rates of entrepreneurship and entrepreneurial entry rates have been documented in the ECA region compared to more advanced economies or other emerging market economies, even more than two decades after the beginning of the transition period and holding constant a number of country and institutional characteristics.[10] A recent EBRD paper on successful business startups in the ECA region also provides evidence that the share of successful business starters (in percentage of the total population) is much lower in relation to comparators in Western Europe, based on Life in Transition Survey (LiTS) data. While the Western European average is close to 16 percent, the ECA averages range from 3.5 percent (Armenia) to a little over 14 percent (Albania).[11] To explain this observed phenomenon, some turn to institutional and attitudinal explanations, in particular, the general lack of trust, which then hinders the development of networks and constrains the provision of entrepreneurial finance (see, for example, Aidis, Estrin, and Mickiewicz 2008; Estrin and Mickiewicz 2010; Estrin, Meyer, and Bytchkova 2006). They have also quantified a general lack of confidence and autonomy in contrast to more developed market economies, traits that are perceived to be essential ingredients in risk taking and entrepreneurship.

The Region's Entrepreneurial Record Actually Compares Well with Other Countries, Led by the Advanced Modernizers

In fact, the region's entrepreneurial record is clouded by a number of measurement issues. Part of the confusion may be due to the proliferation of various data sources and measures of entrepreneurship. There are debates, for example, on whether it is appropriate to use self-employment as an approximation of entrepreneurship. Depending on the source, the unit of analysis is either the individual or the enterprise, the country coverage varies substantially, and the reference periods differ widely. For example, the Global Entrepreneurship Monitor (GEM) conducts its own survey worldwide using a representative sample of about 2,000 working adults in each country. It then examines the entrepreneurial process, quantifying the number of months business have been in operation, the number of months they have paid salaries or wages, and so on, and calculating rates of nascent entrepreneurship, new business ownership, and early-stage entrepreneurship. Some studies use the

International Finance Corporation's (IFC's) index of micro, small, and medium-size enterprises (MSMEs) per 1,000 people, while other studies use indicators of business registry density (per 1,000 people). As a result, summary figures are often inconsistent and contradictory.

Along some dimensions, the ECA region's entrepreneurial record is comparable to those of high-income economies and other market economies. Using data on recent entrepreneurial activity from the GEM database, the ECA region, on average, compares favorably with Western and Southern Europe (figure 2.11). However, the region, as a group, does lag behind the East Asia and the Pacific Region and the LAC Region—with respect to early-stage entrepreneurship and established business ownership in the case of East Asia and across all measures in the case of LAC. Meanwhile, using MSME density (per 1,000 people) as a measure of entrepreneurship, the ECA region compares well with other regions, though it lags behind Western and Southern Europe. In terms of new business registry, it leads all other regions, except the high-income economies. Finally, its rates of self-employment are comparable to those of Western Europe and other advanced economies, but they lag behind those of other regions. Among the self-employed, the employers more or less account for a similar fraction of all employed.

Despite ECA's mixed record of entrepreneurship in comparison with those of other country groups, within the region, advanced modernizers appear to perform consistently well across indexes of entrepreneurship (figure 2.12). For two of the measures of entre-preneurial activity presented above, advanced modernizers in the region are the highest end of the distribution. On the other hand, the stage of the demographic transition is not correlated with any perceptible pattern relative to entrepreneurship. Among the advanced modernizers in the sample, Estonia and Latvia perform exceptionally well in the GEM-based measures of entrepreneur-ship. With respect to the density of MSMEs, the Czech Republic surpasses all other countries at 84 (per 1,000 people). At the low-est end of the distribution are late modernizers the Kyrgyz Republic and Belarus at 1 and 4, respectively. These are striking patterns as they are robust irrespective of the measure of entre-preneurship and may reflect in large part the payoffs to an earlier round of enterprise sector transformation. This is a point we take up more fully in the next section.

In addition, advanced modernizers promote more business startups compared to other countries in the ECA region. Advanced moderniz-ers do not necessarily see more of their workforce attempting to start a business (figure 2.13). However, among those who do attempt to start

FIGURE 2.11

The ECA Region's Comparative Entrepreneurial Record

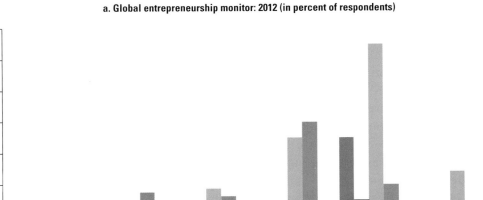

a. Global entrepreneurship monitor: 2012 (in percent of respondents)

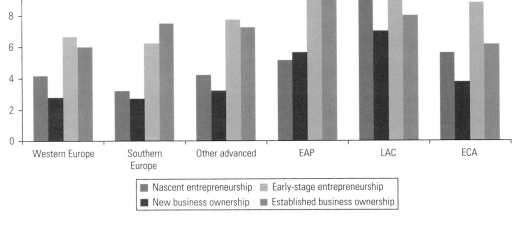

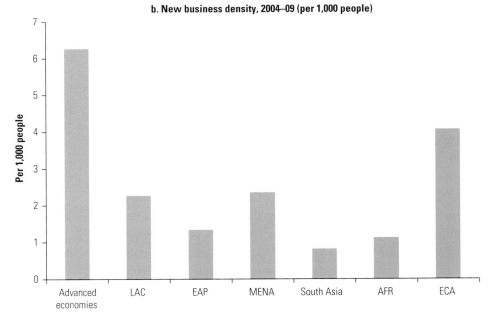

b. New business density, 2004–09 (per 1,000 people)

continued

FIGURE 2.11
Continued

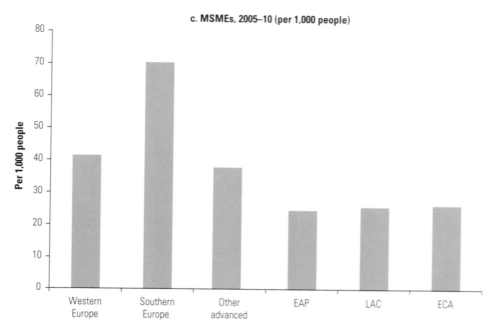

c. MSMEs, 2005–10 (per 1,000 people)

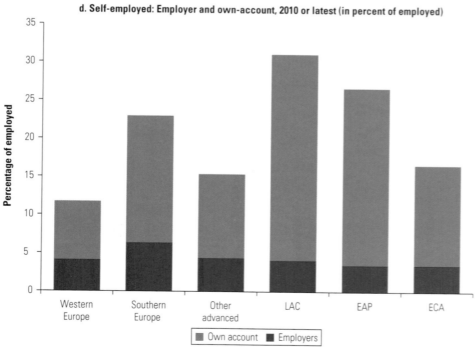

d. Self-employed: Employer and own-account, 2010 or latest (in percent of employed)

Sources: International Finance Corporation micro, small, and medium-size enterprises (MSME) database, GEM database, and World Bank calculations.
Note: EAP = East Asia and Pacific; ECA = Europe and Central Asia; LAC = Latin America and the Caribbean; MENA = Middle East and North Africa.

FIGURE 2.12

Entrepreneurship in ECA by Stage of Transformation

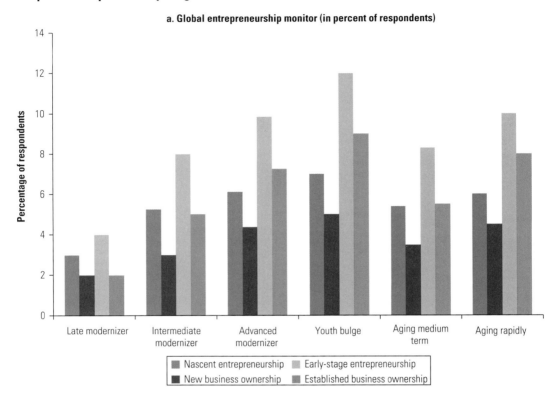

a. Global entrepreneurship monitor (in percent of respondents)

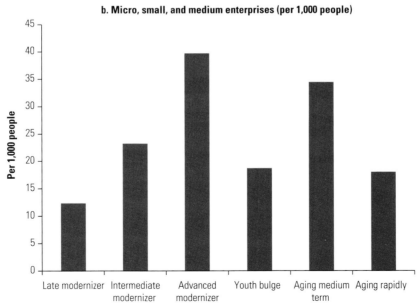

b. Micro, small, and medium enterprises (per 1,000 people)

Source: Life in Transition Survey data and World Bank calculations.

FIGURE 2.13

Business Startups by Stage of Transformation

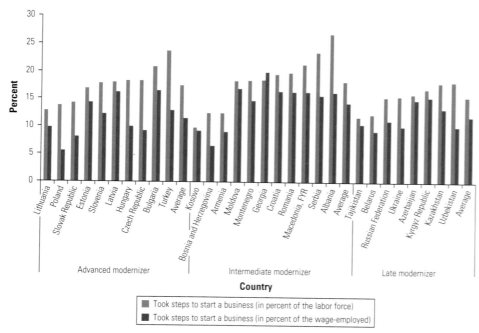

Source: Life in Transition Survey data and World Bank calculations.

a business, over three-quarters succeeded, just slightly below their Western European comparators. This outstanding success rate surpasses that of late modernizers by more than 25 percentage points. In Hungary, nearly everyone who attempts to start a business succeeds. In contrast, in Azerbaijan, about two-thirds of those who make an effort to start a business fail.

A Large Pool of "Latent" Entrepreneurs May Be Waiting to Enter the Market

An examination of business entry and new enterprise activity alone may overlook the entrepreneurial potential of the region. Despite the wealth of new insights from a very large literature on enterprise activity, the literature recognizes that analyses to date focus largely on existing firms and entrepreneurs alone. These firms are therefore self-selected into the sample while those firms facing enormous constraints never enter the market at all and are excluded from the analysis. This issue has come to be known as the "hippopotamus versus camel" problem, which suggests that analyses based on those present in the sample ("camels in the desert") may miss an important fraction of the population, the potential or "latent" entrepreneurs. More than a decade ago, a promising new literature on latent entrepreneurship emerged, making use of unusual survey data that collected information across countries on whether members of the labor force preferred to be self-employed as a measure of potential or latent entrepreneurship. This research program covered about 20 countries, including a handful of ECA countries: four of the new EU member countries and Russia.[12] The study concluded that there are large numbers of people who would like to be entrepreneurs—up to 80 percent of the wage-employed workers in one country—but the entrepreneurial spirit remained dormant. In the absence of suitable data, the literature has largely remained stagnant, and few ECA countries have ever been analyzed from this perspective. The inclusion of a number of related questions in LiTS provides a window of opportunity to revisit this literature.

Evidence from recent LiTS data suggests that the pool of latent entrepreneurs in the region—those who prefer to be self-employed—may be quite large. Close to a quarter of the labor force in the ECA region would rather be self-employed, as evident in figure 2.14 (see also box 2.2 for the operational definition of latent entrepreneurship). This is comparable to the size of the latent entrepreneurs among the Western European comparators in LiTS.

Though some may object to this measurement of latent entrepreneurship, it arguably captures the pool of all *possible* entrepreneurs. Some may rightfully argue that not all forms of self-employment may be considered entrepreneurship. In difficult labor markets, self-employment may be an alternative to joblessness or unemployment and may represent little more than a survival strategy rather than an opportunity-driven, job-creating business activity. As such, many self-employed activities will never be the kind of high-impact and high-growth activity that entrepreneurship can help spur. Nonetheless, the pool of those who would rather be self-employed may also be thought of as representing the entire pool of all possible entrepreneurs. Every successful venture has arguably grown from the initial efforts of self-employed individuals, as the first studies of latent entrepreneurship also argued. Those who prefer to be self-employed represent all latent entrepreneurs, in other words, "survival" or subsistence entrepreneurs and "opportunity" entrepreneurs are alike, and their success appear to be driven by similar individual-level and policy correlates (EBRD 2011).

FIGURE 2.14

Latent Entrepreneurship in ECA

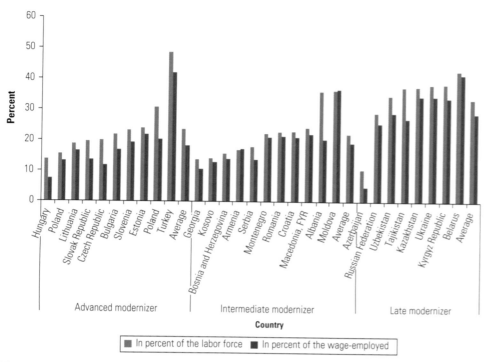

Sources: Life in Transition Survey data and Atasoy et al. forthcoming.

Furthermore, the desire to be self-employed does not appear to be driven by necessity alone, based on their individual characteristics. A large fraction of latent entrepreneurs among the wage-employed are highly skilled professionals—employed as directors or managers of their companies—and highly educated. In addition, many of those already in the labor force or already gainfully wage-employed prefer to run their own business. As much as a fifth of the wage-employed workers would prefer to be self-employed.

More generally, latent entrepreneurs and the employers share many similar characteristics. The results of this econometric analysis do not yield any discernible differences between the characteristics of the latent entrepreneurs in the region and the characteristics of the employers among the self-employed (in other words, those who are already entrepreneurs, by virtue of being self-employed and creating jobs for other people). The latent entrepreneurs share many similar individual characteristics with the employer self-employed, including educational attainment, network membership, and other

BOX 2.2

Who Wants to Be an Entrepreneur?

Data from the 2010 wave of the Life in Transition Survey (LiTS) provide information on latent entrepreneurship that is fully consistent with the earlier literature. The survey's specific question that can be used is the following (question 5.26): "Suppose you were working and could choose between different kinds of jobs. Which of the following would you personally choose?" The choices include self-employed, employee in a small private enterprise, employee in a large private enterprise, employee in a state-owned enterprise, and government employee. Those who prefer to be self-employed are therefore thought of as potential or latent entrepreneurs.

   Though there are clear shortcomings to this measure of entrepreneurship—and the literature since Baumol (1968) has referred to broader views of entrepreneurship to include innovation and leadership—the merit of this measure, as has been argued by Blanchflower, Oswald, and Stutzer (2001) and many others, is its simplicity. Every successful venture has arguably grown from the initial efforts of self-employed individuals. Furthermore, this measure of entrepreneurship is comparable across countries. It has the added advantage of allowing this study to be comparable with the literature that has emerged over the past decade using this measure. Finally, though biases may exist in the interpretation of this question, Blanchflower, Oswald, and Stutzer (2001) and others have argued that those biases are likely similar across countries and the relative magnitudes and rankings of countries are then still informative.

Source: Atasoy et al. forthcoming.

characteristics. Their trust in institutions such as courts and the financial system—a defining characteristic, if one is to believe a strand of the literature that has explained low rates of entrepreneurship as a function of social values—is also statistically the same as those of the employers.

However, employers and latent entrepreneurs do differ in their attitudes toward risk, with the employers more willing to take on risks. The employers are also more likely married, the head of the household, richer, and less likely to be female, compared to the latent entrepreneur, though this last characteristic is only marginally significant. This, and how the business environment can enable more of the latent entrepreneurs to transition successfully into employer self-employment, is a point explored more fully below.

Within the ECA region, there are large variations in the rates of latent entrepreneurship. At the highest end of the distribution, close to half of all wage-employed people in Turkey would rather be

FIGURE 2.16
Marginal Impact of the Business Environment on Employment Growth

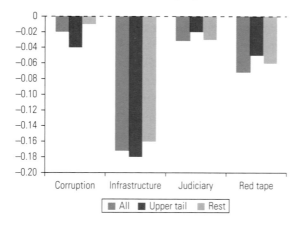

Source: Staff estimates.

country, sector, city type, city size, and firm size. It then applies principal component analysis to produce four indicators representing geographic outcomes: indexes of (a) corruption, (b) infrastructure, (c) judicial efficiency, and (d) red tape. Using firm-level data from Amadeus, this exercise also constructs indexes of tax administration and competition. It then controls for a vector of firm-level and industry-level characteristics that are seen to be important drivers of employment growth, following the existing literature, including the log of firm wage, log of tangible fixed assets, log of output, labor market power, four- and two-digit level peer wages, and four- and two-digit level industry output.[14] It utilizes dynamic panel estimation methods as a way to control for unobserved fixed effects (these fixed effects drop, as the exercise focuses on differences rather than levels) and minimize the endogeneity bias by including fixed effects to control for province, industry, and country trends. Finally, the exercise accounts for persistence over time in firm performance by specifying a first order autoregressive distributed lag model, that is, by factoring in lagged values of firm performance.

The results indicate that firms that were confronted with a less burdensome regulatory environment and less corruption experienced faster growth.[15] Decreased incidence of corruption, increased access to higher quality of infrastructure and judicial efficiency, and greater bureaucratic efficiency were also associated with better performance. In particular, a one-standard improvement of each dimension of the business environment is associated with substantial growth in employment as well as profitability.

Moreover, the drivers of employment growth are important for both the high-growth firms (the upper tail) as well as all other firms. The results to date suggest that broad-based improvements in the business environment matter to both the upper tail and the average growing firms. The results are robust to the use of different samples. Some evidence implies that competition may matter more to the average firms and tax rates matter less to the high-impact firms, but these results are more fragile. This suggests that there is not necessarily a separate policy agenda to foster the growth of the upper tail. The reforms that sustain employment growth among firms in general are the same reforms that boost the performance of the upper tail. This is similar to what the literature documented previously with respect to entrepreneurship activities—the individual and community drivers of entrepreneurship hold for both subsistence and opportunity-driven entrepreneurship. There is no risk of encouraging the emergence of lower-impact entrepreneurship any more than sustaining the growth of only the lower-impact enterprises.

In addition, increased competition helps foster employment growth. As documented widely in the literature, greater competition can help promote the incentive to adopt new technology, greater efficiency and productivity, and more rapid expansion (see, for example, Gill and Raiser 2012; Klapper, Laeven, and Rajan 2006; and Poschke 2010). The results of the econometric analysis of employment growth using the data described above and using the Herfindahl–Hirschman Index (HHI) as a measure of market concentration indicate that the greater concentration of market power is significantly associated with lower growth.

Lower tax rates are also associated with employment growth. The results of the same econometric analysis of employment growth also suggest that lower tax rates (using information on tax liability reported by the firms themselves) are associated with employment growth, controlling for firm characteristics. Not surprisingly, tax rates are high on the list of obstacles to doing business reported by firms in the BEEPS survey.

The Evolving Relative Importance of Various Obstacles to Doing Business Suggests a Differentiated Policy Agenda

During the boom years, it became evident that the legacy of skilled workers and infrastructure did not keep pace with the needs of the enterprise sector in the region (Mitra, Selowski, and Zalduendo 2010; World Bank 2011). During the precrisis period, as has been previously documented using BEEPS data, complaints about the education of the workforce and the quality and quantity of infrastructure, notably electricity, soared and are now among the top obstacles to doing business, along with tax rates and corruption. This was true across the reform typologies, in advanced and late modernizers alike.

First, there was a marked increase in firms reporting skills shortages, particularly among enterprises at the technological frontier. Those who introduced new products, engaged in research and development, and upgraded their existing products were more likely to report that the inadequate skills of the workforce were a severe obstacle to their business activities (figure 2.17). More generally, across all enterprises and across countries, the dissatisfaction with the quality of labor surged during the boom years. This is thought to reflect a structural transformation in the enterprise sector, as jobs with higher skill content rose in the years prior to the crisis. Some firms have managed to respond by providing training to their workforce, though not all firms have adequate resources to do so. On average, firms in high-income economies are more likely to provide training, suggesting that, left unchecked, the gaps in enterprise productivity and performance may be exacerbated.[16] These issues are explored more fully in the next chapter.

FIGURE 2.17

Workforce Education as an Obstacle to Business Activity

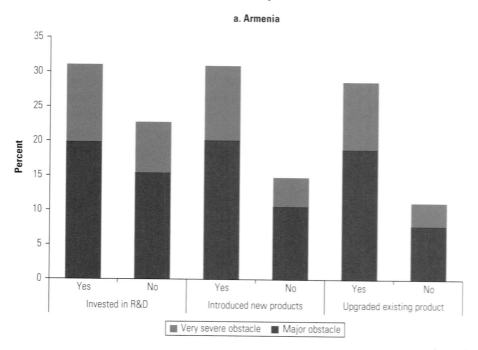

a. Armenia

■ Very severe obstacle ■ Major obstacle

continued

FIGURE 2.17
Continued

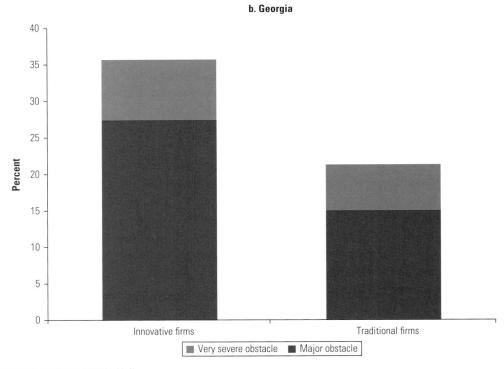

Sources: BEEPS data; Rutkowski 2012a, 2012b.
Note: R&D = research and development.

Second, complaints about electricity rose particularly sharply among expanding firms (Mitra, Selowsky, and Zalduendo 2010). This signifies the increasing complaints and reflected the rapid enterprise growth reaching infrastructure capacity constraints and not just the global fuel hikes during that period. Meanwhile, expanding and contracting firms alike across countries complained about the quality of the workforce, suggesting that there were essential structural deficiencies in the education system. Escalating complaints about infrastructure and skills have been interpreted as reflecting the exhaustion of the benefits of infrastructure and human capital inherited from the planning era.

Meanwhile, complaints about tax administration and trade regulation—previously high among the list of perceived obstacles to doing business—have fallen in importance. Once again, this is generally true across all the reform groups, as both dimensions of the business environment ranked low in relative importance. This has been taken to mean that, at least along these dimensions, there has been progress in building a market economy.

Although such a reading of the evidence—noting an escalation or diminishing of complaints where there are common trends—is valid, it may, however, conceal significant disparities among the reform groups. In other words, in reforming and unchanging economies alike, enterprises will certainly complain about selected dimensions of the business environment. Assessing the changes in ranking over time can be instructive, but it can also mask real improvements where they have taken place or hide unfinished reform programs where they have lagged behind.

Late Modernizers Have Lagged Behind along Several Dimensions of the Business Environment That Hinder Firm Growth

A comparison of the known obstacles to doing business among the three reform groups is instructive: Late modernizers have lagged behind advanced modernizers in numerous dimension of the business environment (figures 2.18 and 2.19). For example, comparing the intensity of complaints between firms among advanced modernizers and late modernizers, many more firms in the latter complain about the business environment along almost every dimension. A large percentage of firms complain about electricity everywhere, but complaints are about 10 percentage points more among enterprises in late modernizers. Few firms complain about customs and trade regulation, but complaints are about 10 percentage points higher among firms in late reforming countries. Firms in late reforming countries also complain about corruption and crime by over 15 percentage points more than firms in advanced modernizers, on average. Only with respect to a single dimension of the business environment do firms in advanced modernizers complain more: labor regulation. This is not surprising, as it is in these countries where labor regulations are much more strictly enforced.

In contrast, intermediate modernizers and advanced modernizers have much more in common in their perception of obstacles to doing business. Although along several dimensions enterprises in intermediate modernizers complain more about the business environment than their counterparts in the advanced modernizers, the gap is much narrower than that between late and advanced modernizers. On average, complaints outstrip those of advance reformers by only about 5 percentage points. In fact, along several dimensions, enterprises in the advanced modernizers complain more, such as with respect to tax rates, practice of formal competitors, and the education of the workforce.

FIGURE 2.18

Major or Severe Obstacles to Enterprise Operations, by Level of Modernization

a. Advanced modernizers

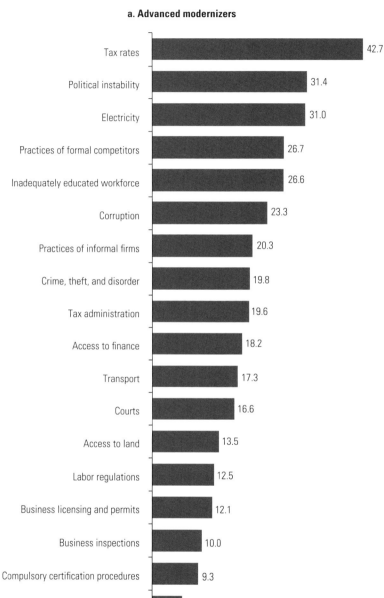

Percent of all firms

continued

FIGURE 2.18
Continued

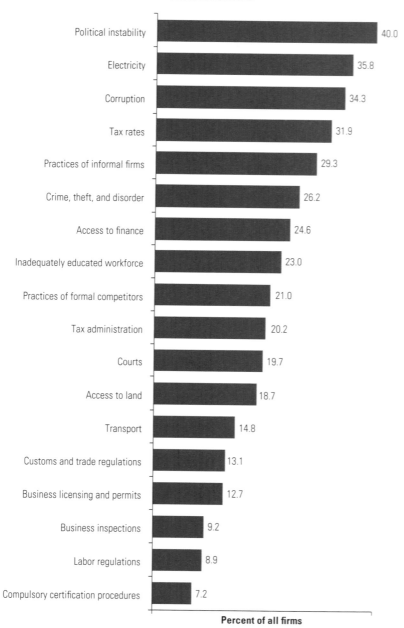

b. Intermediate modernizers

	Percent of all firms
Political instability	40.0
Electricity	35.8
Corruption	34.3
Tax rates	31.9
Practices of informal firms	29.3
Crime, theft, and disorder	26.2
Access to finance	24.6
Inadequately educated workforce	23.0
Practices of formal competitors	21.0
Tax administration	20.2
Courts	19.7
Access to land	18.7
Transport	14.8
Customs and trade regulations	13.1
Business licensing and permits	12.7
Business inspections	9.2
Labor regulations	8.9
Compulsory certification procedures	7.2

continued

FIGURE 2.18
Continued

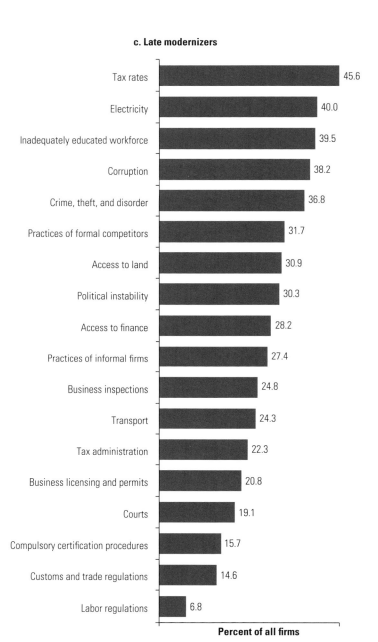

c. Late modernizers

Tax rates	45.6
Electricity	40.0
Inadequately educated workforce	39.5
Corruption	38.2
Crime, theft, and disorder	36.8
Practices of formal competitors	31.7
Access to land	30.9
Political instability	30.3
Access to finance	28.2
Practices of informal firms	27.4
Business inspections	24.8
Transport	24.3
Tax administration	22.3
Business licensing and permits	20.8
Courts	19.1
Compulsory certification procedures	15.7
Customs and trade regulations	14.6
Labor regulations	6.8

Percent of all firms

Sources: European Bank for Reconstruction Development (EBRD) and World Bank calculations.

Comparisons within the same countries over time confirm that real progress has been achieved among advanced modernizers (figure 2.20). Not every dimension can be compared over time, because of changes in the survey instruments. However some comparison can be made with respect to a number of obstacles to

FIGURE 2.19

Major or Severe Obstacles to Enterprise Operations

Percent of all firms

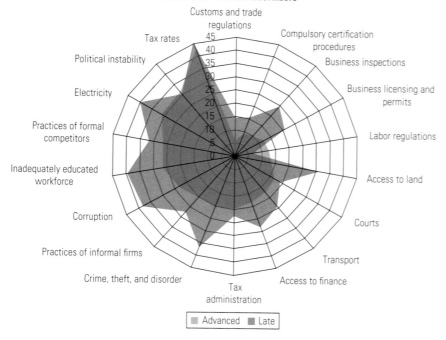

a. Advanced vs. late modernizers

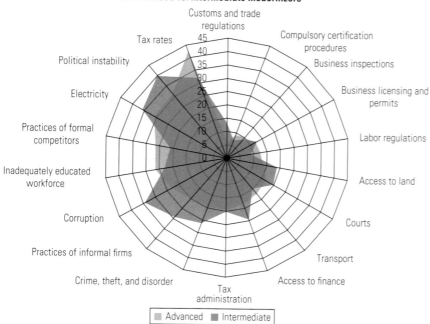

b. Advanced vs. intermediate modernizers

Sources: European Bank for Reconstruction and Development (EBRD) and World Bank calculations.

enterprise operation. Figure 2.20 shows that although tax rates, the education of the workforce, and corruption are high among the advanced modernizers' list of complaints, in fact, on average, about 12 percentage points fewer firms complained about them in 2008 compared to 2002. More generally, the intensity of complaints has fallen everywhere, by about 15 percentage points on average. In turn, they reflect real reforms that have taken place in recent years. In Poland, for example, in the period coinciding with BEEPS, the authorities consolidated registrations information, combining company registry and statistics with tax and social security information. In Estonia, startup time dropped from 35 days to 7. Only in the areas of transport and electricity have complaints risen among advanced modernizers, which confirms previous findings that the infrastructure inherited

FIGURE 2.20

Major or Severe Obstacles to Enterprise Operations: Change over Time

Percent of all firms

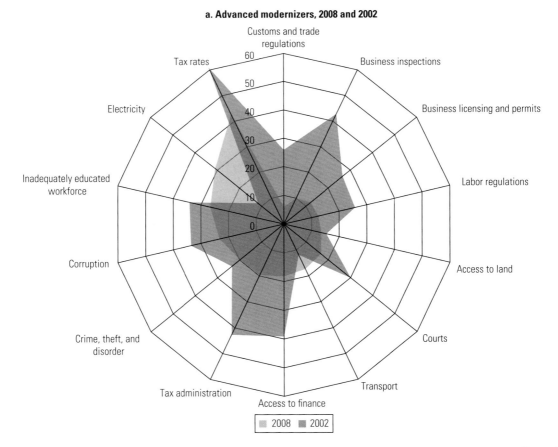

a. Advanced modernizers, 2008 and 2002

continued

FIGURE 2.20
Continued

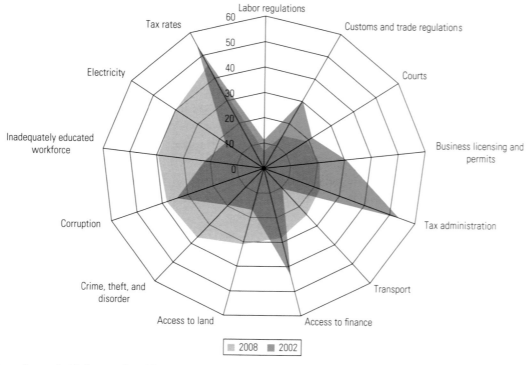

b. Late modernizers, 2008 and 2002

■ 2008   ■ 2002

Sources: European Bank for Reconstruction and Development (EBRD) and World Bank calculations.

from the planning era is nearing its capacity constraints and will have important growth consequences, particularly for growing firms.

On the other hand, progress has lagged behind among the late modernizers. Along certain dimensions, there is progress, as measured by decreasing intensity of enterprise complaints. Customs regulation, judicial efficiency, business licensing, and tax administration are the areas where there is diminishing complaint among enterprises. However, along many other dimensions, there is growing complaint among firms. In 2002, only about a fifth of all firms thought that crime was an important obstacle to doing business. In 2008, close to 40 percent thought that crime was a major obstacle to their operations. While some of this rising intensity of complaints may reflect the growth of enterprises, the gap between late modernizers and advanced modernizers as well as the rising complaints along selected dimensions are a cause for concern.

Together, this suggests a need for a differentiated policy agenda to sustain growth in the enterprise sector. Although the relative ranking of obstacles to doing business are important, assessing the intensity of such complaints—the fraction of enterprises that they constrain, how the complaints may have expanded or contracted over time, and how they differ across countries—will be equally important. The comparisons and contrasts in this section suggest that along many fronts, particularly those related to the creation of a market economy and the provision of a level playing field, advanced modernizers have made significant progress. However, rising capacity constraints in infrastructure should be an important item in their policy agenda. In addition, labor regulations, despite ranking low among the reported obstacles to doing business, constrain a greater share of enterprises in advanced modernizers. Meanwhile, late modernizers confront the reality that as complaints about business obstacles have risen, so have their intensity along many fronts. Addressing these challenges will be both urgent and important.

Across Countries in the Region, There Is a Role for Policy in Facilitating New Firm Entry and Promoting Entrepreneurship

As previously reported, there are substantial variations in the prevalence of successful startups in the region.[17] As a group, the advanced modernizers lead other countries in the success rate of attempts to start a business (figure 2.21). In turn, the success rate of intermediate modernizers outstrips later reformers by more than 10 percentage points. Within each group, however, there are substantial variations as well. Among advanced modernizers, Hungary and the Slovak Republic lead other countries. Among intermediate modernizers, Croatia and the former Yugoslav Republic of Macedonia compare well with advanced modernizers, although Kosovo is well below the late reformer average. Azerbaijan compares very poorly with all other countries in the region. In this economy, few there seem inclined to start a business, few actually attempt to start a business, and those who do are more likely to fail.

Understanding the drivers of entrepreneurship is critical for supporting the conditions for enterprise growth and job creation. Finding the conditions that encourage and enable entrepreneurship—from latent entrepreneurship to successfully starting a business—is critical. Because of the role that entrepreneurial activity has played in facilitating structural change through the first two decades of the transition process in the ECA region and the role it could play to sustain economic recovery in the current period characterized by weak labor markets, the implications of this information could be significant.

FIGURE 2.21
Successful Business Startups

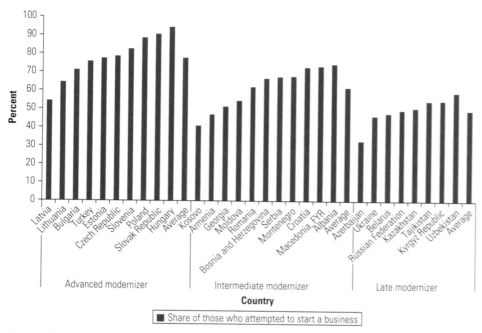

Sources: Life in Transition Survey; Atasoy et al. forthcoming.

The gap between attempts to start a business and successful startups reflect in large part differences in the business environment.

Improving the business environment could yield potentially large payoffs in private sector development, both in easing the entry of new firms and in facilitating the exit of inefficient firms. The results of the econometric analysis of LiTS data, controlling for individual and demographic characteristics, show that the ease of doing business is positively related to latent entrepreneurship. In particular, the reduced number of procedures required starting a business, higher investor protection, and higher rates of resolved insolvency in a country are all associated with latent entrepreneurship rates. This is true for the entire sample as well as for the samples of men and women alike (figure 2.22).

Although the importance of the business environment as a correlate of successful business startups is consistent with the existing literature on actual entrepreneurship, the statistical relationship with latent entrepreneurship is striking. This seems to suggest that the inclination to start a business—when individuals elect to consider the possibility of becoming an entrepreneur—already takes into consideration the entire cycle of enterprise birth and death: the costs of both

FIGURE 2.22

Entrepreneurship, the Business Environment, and Access to Finance

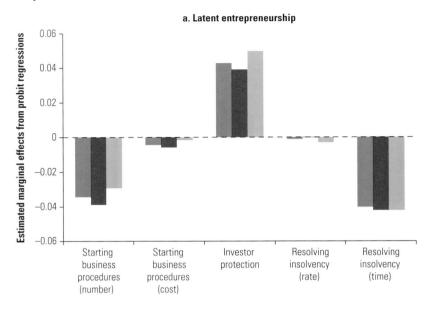

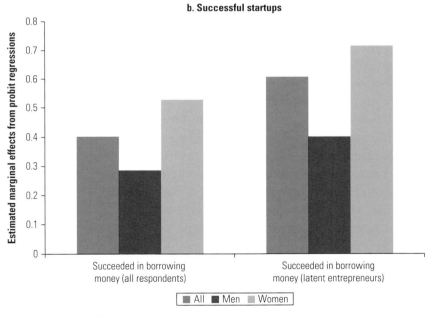

Sources: Life in Transition Survey; Atasoy et al. forthcoming.

creating a new business and eventually closing the business down, when necessary. As discussed earlier, much of the literature on binding constraints to entrepreneurship and new business entry often miss those who opt out of the entire process from the beginning, thus underestimating the binding constraints to enterprise growth. Meanwhile, the importance of business density—where there are more entrepreneurs, one sees more latent entrepreneurship—suggests that some communities may be locked in a bad equilibrium, which public policy can help redress.

Addressing Specific Challenges in the Labor Market May Help Promote Entrepreneurship, Particularly among Women

Promoting access to finance supports more entrepreneurial activities. Access to finance—as approximated in the LiTS database as the self-reported successful attempt to borrow money—is one of the strongest determinants of successful startups. People who succeeded in borrowing money are 60 percent more likely to be actual entrepreneurs (figure 2.22). As we saw in the second section of the chapter, firms with access to credit to finance their investment activities also tended to grow faster.

Improvements in access to finance may have large dividends, particularly among women. Women in the ECA region are less likely to be latent entrepreneurs and less likely to attempt to start a business, but they are more likely to succeed once they try. Understanding the conditions that allow women to succeed is then an important policy question. The evidence suggests that access to finance matters more to women: On average, women who manage to gain access to credit are 70 percent more likely to successfully set up a business, controlling for other individual and community characteristics. Access to finance matters to men as well, but less so: Those who are able to borrow are 40 percent more likely to succeed in starting a business.

One possibility is that certain policy interventions matter more to women, as they help to redress existing gender-based labor market disparities. As explained more fully in chapter 4, women in the region are much less likely to have access to finance, along with young workers and ethnic minorities. When they do gain access to credit, they are also subject to tighter requirements. At the same time, male heads of household are more likely to own lands compared to their female counterparts, thus constraining access to women's collateral that, in turn, may curb access to credit. This argues for greater assistance in the form of access to credit to promote greater female entrepreneurship (see also EBRD 2011). This has the potential to yield multiple payoffs, promoting the well-being and labor market participation among women, which can then be a source of further employment creation and enterprise sector growth.

Other forms of labor market disadvantages translate into lower entrepreneurial activities, suggesting a multipronged strategy for addressing the jobs challenge. For example, as the results in the preceding section suggest, those in the private sector are more likely to be latent entrepreneurs, suggesting that private sector experience likely facilitates the acquisition of requisite skills. This advantage carries over through various stages of the entrepreneurship process. Conditional on being a latent entrepreneur, whether one attempts to start a business is also significantly associated with private sector employment. Finally, successful transitions from attempting to start a business to actually starting a business are also associated significantly with private sector experience.

Finally, Innovations in Other Countries Offer Some Evidence That Promoting Entrepreneurship Directly Can Yield Large Payoffs

There is growing evidence that entrepreneurship—or at least better management practice—can be taught. Some recent field experiments from other regions, for example, suggest that consulting advice on management practice provided to randomly selected manufacturing firms can help boost productivity by up to 17 percent (Bloom et al. 2013). They also found important spillover benefits among firms that were not part of the field experiment but adopted the new technologies anyway and experienced rapid productivity growth. The researchers also found that lack of information and strong preferences for existing practice often constrained the adoption of more efficient management practice, suggesting that there may be a role for policy to make relevant management information more widely available.

Some countries promote startup ideas directly and are welcoming of foreign entrepreneurs and their ideas. A program in Chile, for example, has since 2010 hosted 500 firms and 900 entrepreneurs from about 37 countries (*The Economist* 2012). It selects young firms with promising new ideas and provides them with a year's worth of stipend to explore their ideas in Chile. The program has spurred new ideas among local companies as well. About two-fifths of recent applications were from local firms. Similarly, the United Kingdom, New Zealand, and Singapore offer special visas to entrepreneurs and investors.

Annex 2A: Figures and Tables

FIGURE 2A.1
Net Job Creation in Selected ECA Countries: Evidence from Amadeus Data—All Available Data

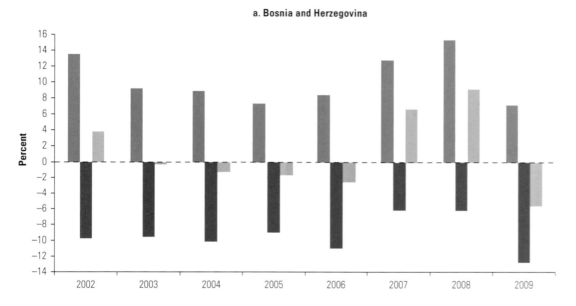

a. Bosnia and Herzegovina

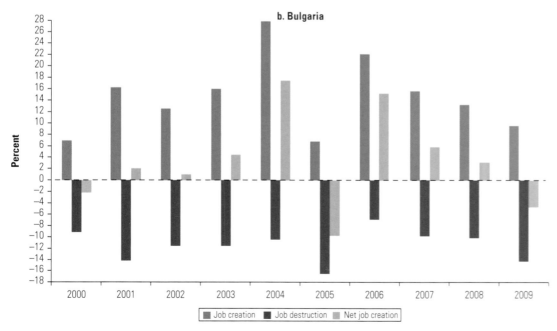

b. Bulgaria

Job creation Job destruction Net job creation

continued

FIGURE 2A.1
Continued

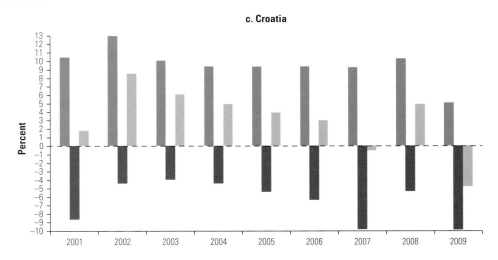

c. Croatia

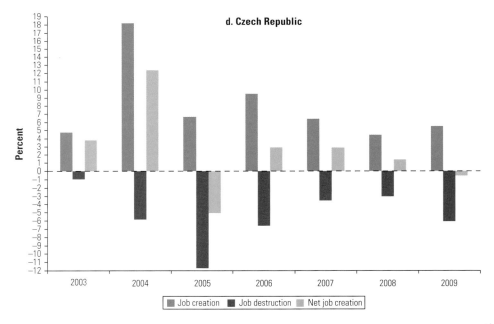

d. Czech Republic

■ Job creation   ■ Job destruction   ■ Net job creation

continued

FIGURE 2A.1
Continued

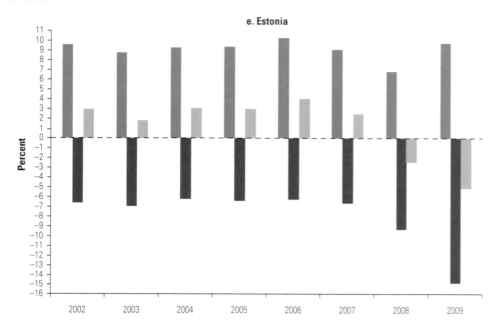

e. Estonia

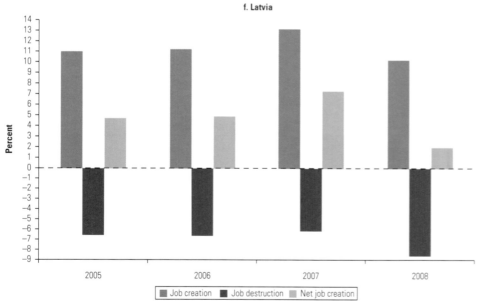

f. Latvia

■ Job creation ■ Job destruction ■ Net job creation

continued

FIGURE 2A.1
Continued

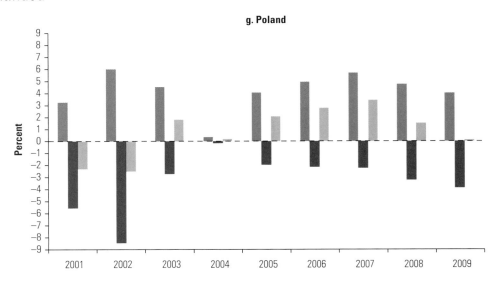

g. Poland

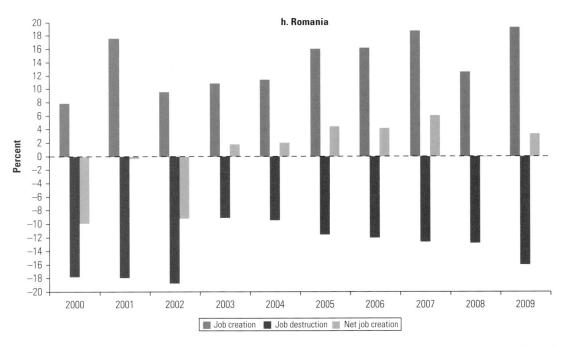

h. Romania

Job creation   Job destruction   Net job creation

continued

FIGURE 2A.2
Continued

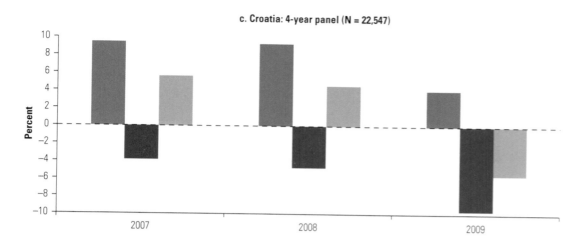

c. Croatia: 4-year panel (N = 22,547)

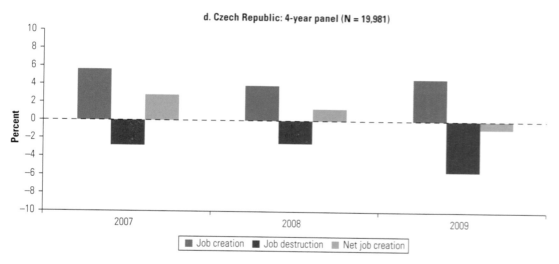

d. Czech Republic: 4-year panel (N = 19,981)

■ Job creation   ■ Job destruction   ■ Net job creation

continued

FIGURE 2A.2
Continued

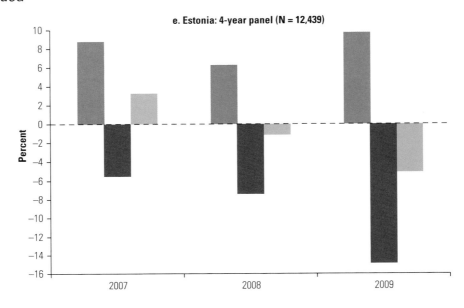

e. Estonia: 4-year panel (N = 12,439)

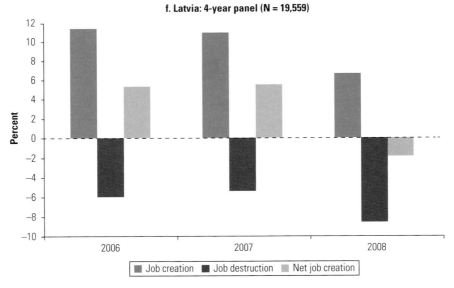

f. Latvia: 4-year panel (N = 19,559)

■ Job creation ■ Job destruction ■ Net job creation

continued

FIGURE 2A.2
Continued

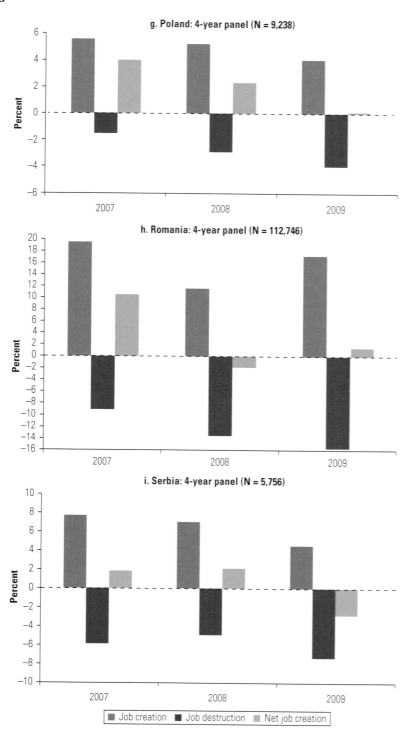

g. Poland: 4-year panel (N = 9,238)

h. Romania: 4-year panel (N = 112,746)

i. Serbia: 4-year panel (N = 5,756)

■ Job creation ■ Job destruction ■ Net job creation

continued

FIGURE 2A.2
Continued

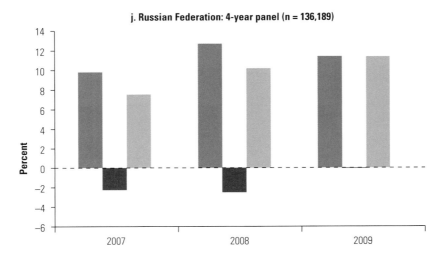

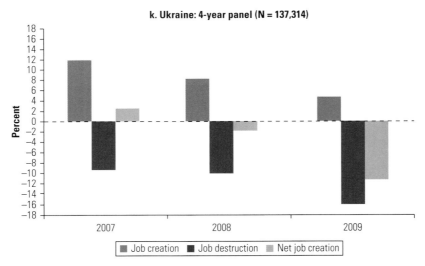

Source: Amadeus and World Bank calculations.

Annex 2B: Technical Notes[18]

Amadeus

The version of the Amadeus database purchased from Bureau van Dijk (BvD) for this analysis (with the first round received in the summer of 2010 and four rounds of updates from June 2010 to June 2011) contains financial information on 5,414,319 firms across 21 countries in the ECA region. The database includes up to 10–12 years of information per company, although coverage varies significantly by country. Amadeus is useful because it covers a large fraction of new and small and medium-size enterprises across all industries. The Amadeus database is created by collecting standardized data received from 30 specialist regional information providers. The local source for these data is generally the office of the Registrar of Companies.

The Amadeus database includes firm-level accounting data in standardized financial format for 25 balance sheet items, 27 income statement items, and 24 financial ratios. The accounts are transformed into a universal format to enhance comparison across countries, though coverage of these items varies significantly across countries. Monetary values are expressed in thousands of local currency units (LCUs). Period average official exchange rates of a U.S. dollar per LCU and a euro per LCU are provided for all countries and years covered. In addition to financial information, Amadeus provides other firm-level information, such as company name, address, zip code, city, region (e.g., province, county, oblast), legal status and form, date of incorporation, and NACE Rev.1 code—the European standard of industry classification since 2008—at the four-digit level. All NACE sections are covered. Data on ownership and export activity are largely unavailable and effectively insufficient for the purposes of empirical analysis.

Particular Four-Year Window Coverage and Survivorship Bias

Amadeus includes only firms that have reported financial statements within a particular four-year period. The main four-year window coverage for this version of the database is 2005 through 2008. Specifically, as companies exit or stop reporting their financial statements, BvD puts a "not available/missing" for four years following the last included filing. Firms that have not reported for at least five years (i.e., since 2004 or earlier) are removed from Amadeus. Therefore, the current database does not include firms that exited before 2005, and all data from 2004 and earlier comes from firms that must have been in business over the period 2005–08. In other words, the sample before 2005 exhibits survivorship bias.

Consequently, this survivorship bias restricts the scope of analysis that can be conducted with any particular version of Amadeus. For example, the estimation of job flows from job creation and destruction between and within industries can be estimated but is limited to the particular four-year period. Strong assumptions also need to be made regarding the nonreporting by firms, namely that exit is the cause rather than incomplete or not up-to-date firm registries. Similarly, the determination of entry and exit at the firm level is limited to the four-year window as well.

Sample Bias

Amadeus is generally not the ideal data set to conduct international comparisons of aggregate performance across countries. Samples may not be representative of the economy in a given year (during the 2005–08 four-year window), because BvD may have access to a specific data source only in certain years. Depending on the country, data availability and types of sources may have varying coverage from year to year. For example, new sources can be created or obtained that increase coverage, resulting in large increases in sample size that are not due to high rates of entry but rather new registries becoming available. Therefore, an investigation of entry and exit, nationwide reallocation, and macro-type studies where firm-level data is aggregated at the industry, sector, or national level, such as the decomposition of aggregate TFP seen in Foster, Haltiwanger, and Krizan (2001) and Olley and Pakes (1996), are difficult and likely to suffer from sample bias.

Nevertheless, a handful of countries have relatively consistent sample sizes with low variance over the 2005–08 window: Bosnia and Herzegovina, Croatia, Estonia, Latvia, Romania, and Ukraine. Samples size for Poland, Russia, and the Slovak Republic show some stability over 2006–08. For these select countries, job flows, including job creation and destruction from firm entry and exit, were calculated and are reported in the main text. In the case of Russia, however, Amadeus covers only western Russia, specifically the Central Federal District, the North Caucasian Federal District, the Northwestern Federal District, the Southern Federal District, and the Volga Federal District. Amadeus does not cover the Far Eastern

Federal District, the Siberian Federal District, and the Ural Federal District. The corresponding summary data should therefore be interpreted with caution.

TFP Estimation and Employment Determination

TFP estimation: Variables necessary for the estimation of a three-factor Cobb-Douglas production function of firms in manufacturing industries (NACE Rev.1 15–37) were available for several countries in Amadeus. Output, labor, materials, and capital are proxied, respectively, by operating revenues (opre), the number of employees (empl), material cost (mate), and tangible fixed assets (tfas). Because up to 10–12 years of data were available for firms operating in the 2005–08 window, both structural (e.g., Levinsohn and Petrin 2003) and dynamic panel (e.g., Arellano and Bond 1991; Blundell and Bond 2000) estimators were possible to obtain. In particular, TFP figures cited in the text are computed as the Solow residual of a log-linear Cobb-Douglas production function (Solow 1956). It is well known that analytical results are sensitive to assumptions underlying the exact timing and dynamic implications of input choices and unobserved productivity shocks. Six methods are utilized to estimate the coefficients on capital and labor: ordinary least squares (OLS), fixed effects (FE), difference General Method of Moments (GMM) (Arellano and Bond 1991), system GMM (Blundell and Bond 1998), Levinsohn and Petrin (2003, henceforth LP), and last, the Wooldridge (2009) variant of the LP estimation algorithm (Wooldridge-LP). Based on the Amadeus database, a log-linear Cobb-Douglas production function for each two-digit manufacturing industry (NACE Rev.1 15–37) in each country for which data is available is estimated separately to allow for differences in manufacturing technologies and input elasticities across industries and countries. Value added is selected as the measure of firm output in the computation of TFP and is computed as operating revenue minus material costs, each deflated using country-specific two-digit industry-level producer price indices. Labor input is measured as the total number of employees, and capital input is measured as the value of tangible fixed assets (deflated using country-specific price indices for gross fixed capital formation).

Employment determination: Variables necessary for the estimation of employment demand functions—such as those specified in Arellano and Bond (1991) and Nickell and Wadhwani (1991)—for firms in industry, construction, and market services are available for several countries in Amadeus. The main firm-level variables are the number of employees (empl), average wage (ace), capital (tfas), output (opre), liquidity ratio (liqr), solvency ratio (solr), noncurrent liabilities (ncli), and total shareholders' funds (shfd). Industry- and sector-level variables can either be based on aggregated firm-level data from Amadeus or collected from external sources, such as Eurostat or statistical yearbooks. Because up to 10–12 years of data were available for firms operating in the 2005–08 window, dynamic autoregressive distributed lag models were estimated using difference and system GMM (e.g., Arellano and Bond 1991; Blundell and Bond, 2000).

Amadeus versus BEEPS

For international, regionwide comparisons, the sample bias of Amadeus and coverage of countries in the ECA region are problematic, and therefore BEEPS is a more appropriate data set for these comparisons. In contrast to earlier rounds, the implementation of BEEPS 2009 has gone to great length to ensure representativeness of the universe of firms in each country and provides survey weights in the data set. Sample selection is stratified on three criteria: sector of activity, firm size, and geographical location. Although the sample sizes are much smaller when compared to Amadeus, they are sufficient to ensure estimates of proportions with 5 percent and 7.5 percent precision in 90 percent confidence intervals, assuming maximum variance. For example, with 5 percent precision, the minimum sample size tends to a sample size of 270, as population size increases; with 7.5 percent precision the sample size tends to 120. In all 29 ECA countries, this sampling methodology was implemented, and an identical survey instrument was used. Therefore, unlike Amadeus, empirical findings can be generalized and extended for the country as a whole and used for cross-country comparisons.

In addition, data on foreign/government ownership, export activity, technology/innovation, training, and many other variables unavailable in Amadeus are collected in the BEEPS. Industry coverage includes only the nonagricultural private sector, specifically the following ISIC rev.3.1 Sections: all manufacturing sectors (D); construction (F); services (G and H); transport, storage, and communications (I); and subsector 72 (from section K). The sampling frame for each country excludes establishments with fewer than five employees—in order to limit the surveys to the formal economy—and also excludes fully government-owned enterprises. More information regarding the sampling methodology and coverage of the BEEPS can be found at http://www.enterprisesurveys.org/Methodology/.

The main weakness of BEEPS 2009 compared to Amadeus is the lack of information on firm inputs and performance, specifically, balance sheet items, income statement items, and financial ratios. Moreover, many firm inputs and performance variables that are available in the BEEPS are collected only for manufacturing. In contrast, the BEEPS is strong on the measurement of the business environment, such as indicators of governance, regulatory burden, and the quality of public services. For example, qualitative and quantitative variables on bribe payments, time spent on dealing with regulations, and the frequency of power outages are available in the BEEPS.

Amadeus and BEEPS

Data from Amadeus and BEEPS can be combined in order to exploit the relative strengths of both. Following Anós-Casero and Udomsaph (2009) and Udomsaph (2012b), indicators of the business environment from the BEEPS can be merged with Amadeus on a set of criteria, for example, country, municipality/region, firm size, and year, in order to measure the effect of changes in the business environment on productivity growth. In this way, among other things the impact of policy reforms in areas covered by the BEEPS—corruption, infrastructure quality, judicial effectiveness, and regulatory burden—on firm-level employment can be estimated, as is done in the main text.

Notes

1. This is calculated using a panel of 16,713 continuing firms between 2004 and 2009. In Turkey's enterprise survey, firms with fewer than 20 employees are resampled every year and are therefore excluded from the summary figures.
2. Owners are listed individually, for example, rather than providing aggregate-level information about the ownership of a particular enterprise.
3. The threshold is comparable to those in the literature. See, for example, OECD (2006), "A Proposed Framework for Business Demography Statistics."
4. The job creation patterns in the Amadeus data for Russia are different from what aggregate employment data suggest. This is because the Amadeus sample is not nationally representative. See annex 2B.

5. The figures were calculated using value-added as a measure of output. However the patterns hold, irrespective of whether the output is measured using revenue and whether labor productivity is measured in logs or levels.

6. This is based on the BuDDy template for Ukraine. See Merotto and Boccardo (2012).

7. These are employment determination models following Nickell and Wadhwani (1991) and Arellano and Bond (1991). Roodman (2006) uses a similar model to demonstrate the use of the Stata routine for difference and system General Method of Moments (GMM). The specification includes controls for firm-level characteristics (such as financial variables) and industry characteristics (industry output, concentration indexes, etc.).

8. Data on new business density are from the World Development Indicators (WDI) database, http://data.worldbank.org/data-catalog/world-development-indicators.

9. Employment expectations data from the other sectors in the OECD database (retail and services) are yet to be tested, pending the availability of more complete information.

10. See for example Aidis, Estrin, and Mickiewicz (2008); Estrin and Mickiewicz (2010); Estrin, Meyer, and Bytchkova (2006); and Ireland, Tihanyi, and Webb (2008). The literature on new firm creation in the ECA region is fairly recent. See, for example, Meyer and Peng (2005).

11. There are similar patterns in relative performance, in percentage of the labor force, as shown in the narrative.

12. A series of papers by Isabel Grilo, Roy Thurik, Peter van der Zwan, and their associates build and improve on the earlier work by Blanchflower, Oswald, and Stutzer (2001) using EU data and including the new EU member countries. Szarucki (2009) studies entrepreneurial motives in Poland while Baltrušaitytė-Axelson, Sauka, and Welter (2008) examine "nascent entrepreneurs" in Latvia. However, the majority of countries in the ECA region—including those in the Western Balkans and the CIS countries, both low-income and middle-income economies—have not yet been studied.

13. This builds on and expands the EBRD analysis of business startups.

14. This follows the specification in Nickell and Wadhwani (1991); Arellano and Bond (1991); and Roodman (2006).

15. This is based on the recent work of Udomsaph (2012b) and background work for this chapter.

16. As noted in chapter 3, current vacancies and unemployment profiles indicate lingering structural and skills mismatches, at least in some countries. Not all vacancies require cutting-edge skills. As reported in this chapter's second section, many of the high-growth firms operate in industries that do not particularly require higher education, such as in construction and market services. In Georgia, almost half of all unemployed workers have tertiary education. There is, however, weak labor demand for skilled workers. The sectors and many firms creating new employment require no more than secondary or vocational education.

17. This section builds on the analysis of the EBRD, by exploring other dimensions of the business environment which may help explain successful startups.
18. This draws heavily and reproduces verbatim sections from the background technical notes prepared by Udomsaph (2012a).

Bibliography

Ahmad, Nadim. 2006. "A Proposed Framework for Business Demography Statistics." OECD Statistics Working Paper, OECD, Paris.

Aidis, Ruta, Saul Estrin, and Tomas Mickiewicz. 2008. "Institutions and Entrepreneurship Development in Russia: A Comparative Perspective." *Journal of Business Venturing* 23: 656–72.

Alam, Asad, Paloma Anós Casero, Faruk Khan, and Charles Udomsaph. 2008. *Unleashing Prosperity: Productivity Growth in Eastern Europe and the Former Soviet Union.* A World Bank Study. Washington, DC: World Bank.

Anós-Casero, Paloma, and Charles Udomsaph. 2009. "What Drives Firm Productivity Growth?" Policy Research Working Paper 4841, World Bank, Washington, DC.

Arellano, Manuel, and Stephen Bond. 1991. "Some Tests of Specification for Panel Data: Monte Carlo Evidence and an Application to Employment Equations." *Review of Economic Studies* 58 (2): 277–97.

Atasoy, Hilal, Carolina Sanchez-Paramo, Erwin R. Tiongson, and Peter van der Zwan. Forthcoming. "*Latent Entrepreneurship in the Europe and Central Asia (ECA) Region.*" Washington, DC: World Bank.

Baltrušaitytė-Axelson, J., A. Sauka, and F. Welter. 2008. "Nascent Entrepreneurship in Latvia. Evidence from the Panel Study of Entrepreneurial Dynamics 1st Wave." Working Paper, Stockholm School of Economics in Riga, Riga.

Bartelsman, Eric, and Umut Kilinc. 2009. "Firm Dynamics, Reallocation and Productivity." Ukraine CEM Background Paper, World Bank, Washington, DC.

Baumol, J. William. 1968. "Entrepreneurship in Economic Theory." *American Economic Review* 58 (2): 81–106.

Bilgin, Ferhat, Alexey Dorofeev, and Erwin Tiongson. Forthcoming. "Where are the Jobs Going to Come From? Employment Expectations as Leading Indicators of Labor Demand." World Bank, Washington, DC.

Blanchflower, J. David, and Andrew J. Oswald. 1998. "What Makes an Entrepreneur?" *Journal of Labor Economics* 16 (1): 26–60.

Blanchflower, J. David, Andrew J. Oswald, and Alois Stutzer. 2001. "Latent Entrepreneurship across Nations." *European Economic Review* 45 (4–6): 680–91.

Bloom, Nicholas, Benn Eifert, Aprajit Mahajan, David McKenzie, and John Roberts. 2013. "Does Management Matter? Evidence from India." *The Quarterly Journal of Economics*, Oxford University Press, 128(1): 1–51.

Blundell, Richard, and Stephen Bond. 1998. "Initial Conditions and Moment Restrictions in Dynamic Panel Data Models." *Journal of Econometrics* 87 (1): 115–43.

———. 2000. "GMM Estimation with Persistent Panel Data: An Application to Production Functions." *Econometric Reviews* 19 (3): 321–40.

Cizmesija, M., N. Erjavec, and V. Bahovec. 2010. "EU Business and Consumer Survey Indicators and Croatian Economy." *Zagreb International Review of Economics and Business* 13 (2): 15–25.

Claveria, Oscar, Ernest Pons, and Raul Ramos. 2007. "Business and Consumer Expectations and Macroeconomic Forecasts." *International Journal of Forecasting* 23: 47–69.

Correa, Paulo, Mariana Iootty, Rita Ramalho, Jorge Rodríguez-Meza, and Judy Yang. 2010. "How Firms in Eastern and Central Europe Fared through the Global Financial Crisis: Evidence from 2008–2010." Enterprise Note 20, World Bank, Washington, DC.

EBRD (European Bank for Reconstruction and Development). 2011. "Entrepreneurship in the Transition Region: An Analysis Based on the Life in Transition Survey." In *Transition Report 2011: Crisis and Transition: The People's Perspective*, Chapter 4. London: EBRD.

Economist, The. 2012. "Entrepreneurs in Latin America: The Lure of Chilecon Valley." October 13, 2012. http://www.economist.com/node/21564589 /print.

Estrin, Saul, Klaus E. Meyer, and Maria Bytchkova. 2006. "Entrepreneurship in Transition Economies." In *The Oxford Handbook of Entrepreneurship*, edited by M. Casson, 693–723. Oxford, U.K.: Oxford University Press.

Estrin, Saul, and Tomasz Mickiewicz. 2010. "Entrepreneurship in Transition Economies: The Role of Institutions and Generational Change." IZA Discussion Paper 4805, Institute for the Study of Labor, Bonn, Germany.

Foster, Lucia, John C. Haltiwanger, and C. J. Krizan. 2001. "Aggregate Productivity Growth. Lessons from Microeconomic Evidence." In *New Developments in Productivity Analysis*, edited by Charles R. Hulten, Edwin R. Dean, and Michael J. Harper. Chicago, IL: University of Chicago Press.

Gelb, Alan, Vijaya Ramachandran, Manju Kedia Shah, and Ginger Turner. 2007. "What Matters to African Firms? The Relevance of Perceptions Data." Policy Research Paper 4446, World Bank, Washington, DC.

Gill, Indermit, and Martin Raiser. 2012. *Golden Growth: Restoring the Luster of the European Economic Model.* Washington, DC: World Bank.

Grilo, Isabel, and Jesus-Maria Irigoyen. 2006. "Entrepreneurship in the EU: To Wish and Not to Be." *Small Business Economics* 26 (4): 305–18.

Grilo, Isabel, and A. Roy Thurik. 2005a. "Latent and Actual Entrepreneurship in Europe and the US: Some Recent Developments." *International Entrepreneurship and Management Journal* 1 (4): 441–59.

———. 2005b. "Entrepreneurial Engagement Levels in the European Union." *International Journal of Entrepreneurship Education* 3 (2): 143–68.

———. 2008. "Determinants of Entrepreneurial Engagement Levels in Europe and the US." *Industrial and Corporate Change* 17 (6): 1113–45.

Looking forward, the chapter derives implications for skills policies. Technological change will continue to change the bundle of skills demanded in the labor market. These trends will impact the labor market prospects of older workers as well as those currently in their 30s and 40s over the next couple of decades, raising concerns about skills obsolescence. In the late reformers, a pending reforms agenda is likely to drive age-differentiated changes in skills demand as seen in early reformers. There is an imperious need to rethink education and training systems in the region to attune them to these global trends as well as to the life-cycle nature of skills formation and the region's demographic outlook, particularly how learning—and its neurological and social foundations—varies as people age. The focus should be on developing strong generic skills foundations of the increasingly scarce cohorts of youth, ensuring quality and relevance in expanding tertiary education systems, and revamping training and adult education systems to make them market responsive and age sensitive, including on-the-job training (OJT). The chapter is based on the premise that education lays the core foundation to acquire valuable skills for the workplace over a person's working life but it is not the only channel of skills acquisition. The work experience and skills acquired on the job, through OJT or learning by doing, are too often neglected because they are not well measured. However, these can and should play a fundamental role for life-long skills acquisition in aging economies.

Skills Wanted: Changes in the Demand for Skills

The technological and organizational change, trade, and innovation that have taken place over the past two decades call for new types of skills. There is evidence from the Organisation for Economic Co-operation and Development (OECD) and emerging economies that, in a constantly changing economic environment, many jobs involve less routine tasks and have become more interactive, with implications on skills requirements (box 3.1).

In ECA the significant structural productive transformations during and after the economic and political transition have led to substantial resource reallocation. Coupled with the global change in labor demand, job creation and destruction have impacted the demand for skills as firms restructure and turnover and declining sectors (e.g., agriculture) lead way to those in expansion (e.g., services). In many countries, the further integration into international product and labor markets during the 2000s—particularly via the

BOX 3.1

Jobs, Tasks, and Changes in Skills Demand in the Global Economy

The rapid pace of technological change and changes in business organization and trade over the past two decades has spurred an active debate about the key labor competencies needed in a dynamic labor market. The skill content of jobs is heavily determined by the technologies used in production processes. As technology evolves, new occupations appear, and the required skill mix is constantly changing. The production and occupational structures of most developed economies have undergone significant change: a steady shift in value added and employment toward knowledge-intensive activities and services (e.g., finance, hospitality, retail). The ensuing changes in the demand for skills have been primarily attributed to three forces: (i) the spread of information and communication technologies, known as skill-biased technological change (Katz and Murphy 1992), (ii) changes to more flexible forms of organizational and workplace practices, or skill-biased organizational change (Caroli and Van Reenen 2001), and (iii) relocation of all or some of the tasks involved in the production of goods and services to countries with lower unit labor costs: outsourcing or off-shoring (Grossman and Rossi-Hansberg 2008).

This has led labor economists to go beyond the common use of educational attainment and experience as crude proxies of skills to a so-called task approach to skills and jobs. This focuses on the tasks workers actually do in a job and on the set of skills required to complete these tasks. The earliest example of this task-based approach is the seminal 2003 study of Autor, Levy, and Murnane, building on Levy and Murnane (1996). They measure the average task content of jobs and the associated skill requirements in order to uncover how changes in the U.S. occupational structure induce shifts in skills demand: new technologies reduce demand for routine cognitive and manual tasks that can be easily automated and increase demand for nonroutine tasks. New occupations with high content of analytical and interpersonal skills are becoming more prevalent, while occupations that are intensive in repetitive tasks are increasingly being performed by computers. Acemoglu and Autor (2011) connect this to the literature on "trade in tasks" and technological change and derive implications for employment, skills demand, and earnings. One implication is "jobs polarization" in the form of faster rising employment in high- and low-skill occupations and stagnation or decline in middle-skilled occupations, which is well-documented in numerous advanced countries, including most of Western Europe (Goos and Manning 2007; Goos, Manning, and Salomons 2009; Handel 2012).

In a more recent study, Autor and Handel (forthcoming) extend the approach to measure task demands within an occupation as well as across occupations. They collect data for a representative sample of U.S. workers on three broad task domains: cognitive, routine, and manual. Their findings illustrate the power of the tasks approach to understand the labor market dynamics affecting skills demand. For instance, 24 percent of salary workers in their sample use higher level math in their job, 37 percent regularly read documents longer than six pages, and 29 percent predominantly manage or supervise others. While education is a strong determinant of the

continued

BOX 3.1 *continued*

task content of jobs, broad occupation categories are more strongly correlated with how frequently tasks are performed in the job than worker's education level, and tasks remain significant predictors of wages after controlling for education and other worker characteristics.

This emerging literature is changing the way economists, educators, and policy makers think
about skills policy and the consequences of technological change and economic development
for labor demand. This new understanding should enrich the design of education and training
programs.

accession to the European Union (EU) of the new member states and
export booms in countries like Turkey—has further accelerated internal economic forces through international competition and emigration. This may have led to mismatches in the supply and demand of
skills, which could exacerbate as export-led growth gains importance
and firms tap into newly developed higher value-added and technology intensive activities. ECA countries are not alone. Throughout
Western Europe and other advanced economies, education and
training systems are pressed to equip workers with the skills needed
to adapt in fast changing labor markets.[2]

Have these global and regional forces changed the demand for
skills in ECA? This chapter answers the question in two steps.
First, it examines the data on what employers say about how easy
it is to find workers with the skills they need. Then it analyzes
changes in skills demand during the early 2000s on the basis of
changes in the occupational structure of jobs in several ECA
countries.

On the eve of the financial crisis, enterprises in ECA reported
that skills had become one of the top constraints to their business
growth. As shown in Mitra, Selowsky, and Zalduendo (2010),
there was a substantial increase in the share of firms reporting that
finding workers with adequate skills was a major or very severe
constraint to business growth in virtually all ECA countries (except
Hungary) over the latter half of the first decade in the 2000s. This
trend was stronger in Eurasian countries and several new EU
members, where the percentage of firms citing skills as a major or
severe constraint increased between 20 and 30 percentage points.
Figure 3.1 presents data from the EBRD–World Bank Enterprise
surveys covering a representative sample of ECA firms in the

FIGURE 3.1

Skills Are an Important Constraint for Many Firms in ECA Countries

Distribution of firms that consider skills as a major or very severe constraint to their business, 2008

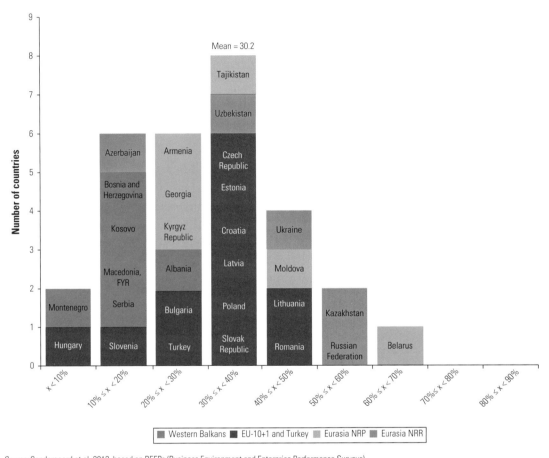

Source: Sondergaard et al. 2012, based on BEEPs (Business Environment and Enterprise Performance Surveys).
Notes: The percentages on the x-axis are the shares of enterprises in the relevant bars that say skills are a major or very severe constraint to their business. EU-10+1 comprise the new member states of Eastern Europe. Eurasia NRR = Eurasian natural-resource-rich countries; Eurasia NRP = Eurasian natural-resource-poor countries.

manufacturing, services, and construction sector in 2008. About 3 out of 10 firms in the region reported skills as a major or very severe constraint, just behind infrastructure and corruption. Skills were most binding for firms in countries more integrated to external markets (such as Lithuania and Poland), with underperforming education and training systems and experiencing rapid emigration (such as Romania and Kazakhstan), or with a high share of the adult labor force having low education or a vocational secondary schooling (such as the Russian Federation and Moldova).

Manufacturing firms in the new EU member states report skills constraints to be as binding as in the older EU member states. Data from the European Company Survey (ECS) reveal that in 2009, in the manufacturing sector, about 37 percent of firms in the EU-15 had difficulties in hiring workers for skilled jobs and 10 percent had trouble hiring workers for low-skilled or unskilled jobs.[3] The corresponding figures were 40 percent and 13 percent, respectively, among the EU-10 countries, ranging from nearly 60 percent and 15 percent in Bulgaria to below 30 percent and 10 percent in Lithuania. In a special Eurobarometer survey in late 2010, recruiters of recent higher education graduates in the EU-27 were asked to name the two most important challenges they faced in filling their vacancies.[4] About 4 out of 10 respondents said the main reason was a shortage of applicants in their country with the right skills and capabilities to do the job, followed by 31 percent who saw a difficulty in being able to offer a competitive starting salary.[5] A shortage of applicants with the right skills was most important in Turkey, Germany, Austria, and Norway while the difficulty in offering a competitive starting salary was most prevalent in Hungary, Romania, Poland, and the Slovak Republic. The latter reason might be an indication of competition for a reduced pool of suitable candidates.

When employers complain that workers do not have the right skills, they are reflecting not only on education credentials or technical qualifications. Employers value a multiplicity of skills, both generic and technical. The former comprise both cognitive (e.g., literacy, numeracy, problem-solving) and socioemotional (e.g., self-discipline, perseverance, dependability, teamwork) skills—also called "soft" or "noncognitive." The latter consists of vocational and job-specific skills and career qualifications. These skills are a core requirement in most jobs in modern economies. Recent employer surveys in Bulgaria, Georgia, Kazakhstan, Poland, the former Yugoslav Republic of Macedonia, Russia, and Ukraine delve more deeply into which skills are scarce or most valued. The findings clearly indicate that employers in these countries see the lack of socioemotional (soft) skills at least as binding as cognitive and technical skills (World Bank 2009, 2011; Arnhold et al. 2011). Similar evidence from employer surveys in OECD countries and non-OECD middle-income economies point to the importance of generic cognitive and socioemotional skills aside from technical skills in firms' hiring decisions.[6] For instance, in a recent study based on a survey of employers of engineers in India, socio-emotional skills were ranked at or above technical qualifications and credentials in terms of their significance for the employability of recent graduates (Blom and Saeki 2011). Several studies using new labor force data that include measures of these skills have found that they carry earnings returns as significant as the returns to cognitive skills in the U.S. and European labor markets and other emerging economies.[7]

The importance employers attach to generic skills should factor into strategies to make education and training more market relevant. It would be unrealistic to expect the education and training system to deliver workers who know everything there is to thrive on a job, particularly young recruits. Much of skills acquisition (behavioral and technical) happens on the job. At the same time, firm training is less likely to cover general training on cognitive or socio-emotional skills since there is a higher risk the investment is captured by other employers. These skills are a prerequisite for learning-readiness or trainability of prospective workers. As documented later in the chapter, it is possible for schools and labor training programs to develop the types of generic skills that would enable further skills acquisition through training or learning on the job.

Next the chapter examines whether the concerns of ECA employers are reflected in the overall labor market trends in skills demand. In light of lack of data on firm demand for specific skills, the chapter applies the tasks-based approach pioneered by Autor, Levy, and Murnane (2003), as refined by Acemoglu and Autor (2011), to a group of ECA countries with the required labor force microdata (see box 3.2). Rather than using educational attainment as a crude proxy of skills, the analysis derives the evolution of the skills intensity of jobs from changes in the employment structure by occupation using the catalogue of specific skills requirements of occupations in the United States. Autor, Levy, and Murnane (2003) find that from 1960 to the early 2000s the U.S. saw a dramatic rise of jobs in occupations that are more intensive in higher order analytical and organizational skills (nonroutine cognitive analytical and interpersonal skills)—new economy skills—and a sharp decline of those intensive in skills associated with repetitive and manual tasks (routine cognitive, routine manual, and nonroutine manual). Similar trends have been documented in several Western European economies and some emerging economies (see box 3.1).

BOX 3.2

Measuring Changes in Skills Demand

Lacking direct measures of skills, the skills demand analysis of the chapter relies on a methodology first developed in a well-known study by Autor, Levy, and Murnane (2003), and expanded by Acemoglu and Autor (2011). This analysis employs the skills requirements of different occupations in the United States as a benchmark, defined by the O*NET dictionary of occupations. The latter is based on a systematic peer assessment of the importance, in a scale 1–5, of different skills for the performance of tasks in each occupation. These tasks are then assigned to five categories of skills: Nonroutine Analytical (tied to tasks requiring abstract thought processes, processing, and decision-making), Nonroutine Interpersonal (personality traits and behaviors underlying teamwork and personnel and client relationships), Routine Cognitive (repetitive non-physical tasks, structured and unstructured), Routine Manual (require speed, repetitive movements, and physical abilities), and Nonroutine Manual (adapt and react to changing circumstances using tools, manual dexterity, and spatial orientation). Table B3.2.1 presents skills definitions, the tasks associated with these skills, and examples of occupations for each category.

TABLE B3.2.1

Taxonomy of Skills, Tasks, and Occupations

| Skills | New economy skills | | Routine cognitive | Manual skills | |
	(Nonroutine cognitive) analytical	(Nonroutine cognitive) interpersonal		Routine manual	Nonroutine manual
Tasks	Analyzing data/ information	Establishing and maintaining personal relationships	Importance of repeating the same tasks	Pace determined by speed of equipment	Operating vehicles, mechanized devices, or equipment
	Thinking creatively	Guiding, directing, and motivating subordinates	Importance of being exact or accurate	Controlling machines and processes	Spend time using hands to handle, control, or feel objects, tools, or controls
	Interpreting information for others	Coaching/ developing others	Structured versus unstructured work (reverse)	Spend time making repetitive motions	Manual dexterity Spatial orientation
Examples of occupations demanding high levels of these skills		Lawyers Teachers Medical doctors Managers	Telephone operators Bookkeepers Meter readers (utilities) Cashiers	Industrial truck operator Cutting and slicing machine settlers, operators, and tenders Shoe machine operators Food cooking machine operators and tenders Construction workers, carpenters	

Source: Based on Aedo et al. 2013, adapted from Acemoglu and Autor 2011.

continued

BOX 3.2 *continued*

These specific skill requirements are then imputed to the occupational structure using labor force surveys in countries with at least three surveys and detailed data on workers' occupations to match international occupational classifications over time (two-digit international ISCO codes defined by the ILO). Averages for each skills category are then computed using the survey weights (and thus the share of each occupation in total employment). The exercise is conducted for different cohorts of workers according to their birth year. Changes in skills requirements are measured through the change in the relative position of the median skills intensity of jobs held by a cohort between the baseline year (first survey) and each other year in each country, which can be interpreted roughly as an index of percentile changes in skills requirements.

No country-specific applications of the O*NET equivalence table exist for ECA countries, so the analysis assumes that the skill content of a given occupation in each country is comparable to that in the United States. This means a medical doctor or a bank cashier are assumed to carry out tasks that contain similar skill intensities in the U.S. and ECA countries. A recent analysis by Handel (2012), using dictionaries of occupations for European countries and other data sources on skills requirements, strongly supports this assumption. Although the skills content of occupations in ECA may differ from the United States, the use of the same classification of the skill content of occupations allows systematic tracking over time within a country and cross-country trend comparisons. Naturally, there is no implication as to the actual skills workers have. For the latter, new household surveys such as the Program for International Assessment of Adult Competences (PIACC) by the Organisation for Economic Co-operation and Development (OECD) (measuring cognitive and technical skills) and Skills Toward Employment and Productivity (STEPs) (which also measures socioemotional skills) by the World Bank attempt to measure the skills workers have.

Given that economic developments post-transition, particularly international integration, may render obsolete the skills of many adult workers in the region,[8] the chapter applies the approach to different age cohorts separately. Figure 3.2 illustrates the typical findings for three archetypical ECA countries and table 3A.1 presents the main results for all countries with available data. It depicts the change during the 2000s in an index of the task-skills intensity of jobs held by a given cohort relative to the skills intensity of jobs held by the cohort at the beginning of the period, measured in "centiles" (or less precisely, the percentile change in skills requirements in jobs held by a given cohort). Only the youngest cohort (born after 1974) and oldest cohort (born before 1955) are discussed.[9] These cohorts correspond to workers who were (i) in their late 40s and older or (ii) between 25 and their mid-30s at the time of the labor survey. Given the cross-sectional nature of the data it is not possible to disentangle age from cohort effects. Although the available data only spans part of the 2000s decade, the fast economic transformation in a number of countries results in meaningful changes in the skills intensity of jobs. The findings are informative about how changes in skills demand differ across countries (e.g., early versus late reformers) and across cohorts within countries (e.g., the match to new skills demand). Two broad groups of countries can be distinguished.

One group of countries shows a pattern of changes in skills demand similar to that found in developed economies, although largely among the youngest cohort. That is, the demand for new economy and/or routine cognitive skills (often those in modern manufacturing and services) increases and routine manual skills (often in low productivity agriculture and retail services) decline. These countries tend to be among the advanced reformers that are more integrated to external markets, particularly to the EU. This is illustrated by Lithuania (see figure 3.2), which shows an impressive expansion in the higher-order skills content of employment after EU accession. This likely reflects the country's gradual but consistent shift toward a knowledge-based economy with special emphasis on biotechnology. Other countries in this group are the Czech Republic, Estonia, Georgia (urban areas), Hungary, Latvia, Poland, and Slovenia. The trend toward a higher demand for skills adds up to the shift that had occurred during the early transition of these countries to market economies. As discussed further below, studies have found that the returns to education increased significantly after the transition. For instance, a study for Hungary found that returns to skill increased 75 percent from 1986 to 2004, primarily among those with a college or university education (younger workers who acquired a higher education after the main market reforms) while workers with only a primary or vocational education experienced falling returns to their education (Campos and Jolliffe 2007).

These trends show a distinctive age-cohort pattern. The shift toward higher intensity in "new economy" and routine cognitive skills is stronger (or even only occurring) among younger cohorts, while jobs intensity in manual skills falls or is flat for young and/or older cohorts. In these countries, older workers have not benefitted as much from the expansion of jobs that require higher-order skills and are losing out as jobs requiring traditional skills disappear. There are qualified exceptions where the older cohort experiences a modest increase in employment with a high intensity in new economy skills (Lithuania) or routine cognitive skills (Poland). These countries are said to have had better performing education systems before the transition.

A second group of countries show no changes in the demand for skills, or the visible changes are too recent to discern a trend or are not clear cut across cohorts. This group comprises some late reformers or less externally integrated countries like Ukraine and FYR Macedonia (shown in figure 3.2), Bulgaria, and Romania. In these countries, overall net employment creation has been sluggish across all ages, and a pending reforms agenda is likely to drive age-differentiated changes in skills demand as seen in early reformers, which could possibly leave some older workers short-changed as their skills are at higher risk of becoming obsolete. Turkey also falls in this group, as the change toward jobs with a higher intensity in new economy skills is apparent only in the last three years of the period with available data. Its less skilled workforce may impinge some inertia in the skills-intensity of overall employment.

Among "new economy skills" the cognitive/analytical have increased the most in the first group of countries and among the younger cohort (see table 3A.1). Jobs intensity in interpersonal skills has increased in most countries among the younger cohort—consistent with the expansion of the service sector—and has remained relatively more stable in the older cohort. The weight of manual skills in the employment structure has decreased across most countries for both the young and older cohorts (except in Croatia).[10]

Analyzing by groups with different education levels, the increase in the job intensity of higher order skills in the first group of countries occurs largely among those with tertiary education. Meanwhile, all workers but especially the less educated (with secondary education or less) experienced a falling or constant trend in manual skills. This again is consistent with the documented trend toward jobs polarization in developed economies.

In sum, the analysis shows that the shifts in skills demand during the early 2000s in ECA are consistent with those observed in OECD countries, in those countries with the most modern economies (early reformers) and a relatively more skilled labor force. Technological change, through the more prevalent use of computers, has dramatically changed the bundle of skills potentially demanded in the labor market.

in ECA countries due to both technological progress and the adoption of new production processes. Some degree of skills mismatch is natural and unavoidable in every growing and restructuring economy due to adjustment costs and the delayed response of national educational systems. Especially in the context of fast-changing technology, changes in the skill structure of the labor supply tend to lag behind those of labor demand, even in a well-performing labor market. The chapter now turns to analyzing the extent to which the supply of skills has been able to adapt to these shifts in demand.

The Gaps in Skills Development in ECA

Has the skills supply, nurtured by education and training systems, adapted well to changes in skills demand in ECA? Several studies, including the recent World Bank report *Skills Not Just Diplomas* (Sondergaard et al. 2012), have argued that it has not and that this has led to emerging skills gaps.[11] If so, in a first look, the existence of skills gaps in the ECA region poses a puzzle. It is well documented that, except for several countries, the region fares well in international comparisons of basic education coverage and attainment, student learning outcomes, and the expanding enrollment in tertiary education.[12] Sondergaard et al. (2012) discuss in great detail numerous reasons for this apparent disconnect. Chiefly, it points to gaps in how education and training systems achieve quality and relevance and translate these into market-valued skills. In what follows, the chapter recasts the main pieces of evidence underscoring a life-cycle lens in the development of skills for the workplace, starting with three observations.

A first observation is the importance of being mindful of the distinction between the flow of future workers—those of school age and youth still in school—and the current stock—youth and middle age and older adults already outside the formal education system. The labor force comprises workers who went through the education system and have continued to acquire or have eroded their skills in different times (spanning decades) and contexts. This can result in rather heterogeneous stocks and pathways of skills acquisition. Moreover, when employers complain about gaps in workers' skills, they are reflecting on their perceived skills shortage among both new entrants and the adult work force.[13] As discussed in chapter 1, the demographic outlook of most ECA countries makes this an even more important consideration when diagnosing skills gaps and policies to address them.

A second observation is that skills beget skills (Cunha, Heckman and Schennach 2010). Skills formation is a cumulative life-cycle process; as individuals age they build on the skills developed in each step to move up to the next step. Skills gaps can therefore start very early in life due to inadequate nurturing and learning environments often faced by disadvantaged families and a deficient quality of basic education (especially in excluded communities and lagging areas).[14] The development of the brain's cognitive capacities is highly influenced by maternal and child health and nutrition from the womb through the first years of life. The quality of nurturing environments at home during infancy and childhood further shapes cognitive and socioemotional skills. While basic cognitive ability is well set by the teen years, basic education provides a person with subject knowledge, tools, and experiences that enhance both cognitive and socioemotional skills. Socioemotional skills continue to develop and remain malleable through the adolescence and adult years (see World Bank 2011). As discussed further below, the latter can be influenced cost-effectively through public intervention over this period of life. A solid foundation of generic skills determine a person's "readiness to learn" and thus enables the acquisition of technical and job-specific skills through tertiary schooling, training, and on-the-job experience.

A third related observation is that skills gaps can take many forms, and educational attainment is a readily available but imperfect proxy to assess them. There can be gaps in generic (cognitive and socioemotional) skills and in technical skills. While these skills are complementary, they can affect different groups of workers and manifest in isolation. Gaps in generic skills are particularly troublesome since they lay the foundation for a "well-educated" labor force that is well prepared to adapt in the rapidly changing labor markets of the 21st century global economy. These skills correlate with higher educational attainment and enable individuals to "learn how to learn" and to adapt to different tasks and problem-solving environments. This is crucial in a constantly changing economic environment where specific skills can be rendered obsolete. The international evidence suggests that without a minimum base of generic skills, technical skills training alone often fail to address the skills gaps and to increase the employability of workers (see World Bank 2013a; OECD 2012a).

Keeping these ideas in mind, where are the skills gaps of the workforce in ECA? As noted by World Bank (2011), the data gaps are enormous. To begin, it is useful to examine the distribution of the potential labor force (working-age population, 15–64) by age groups and levels of educational attainment. Figure 3.3 depicts these breakdowns for the EU-10 and several accession and CIS countries, from which one can draw a few useful patterns.

FIGURE 3.3

Potential Workforce in ECA by Education and Age, circa 2010

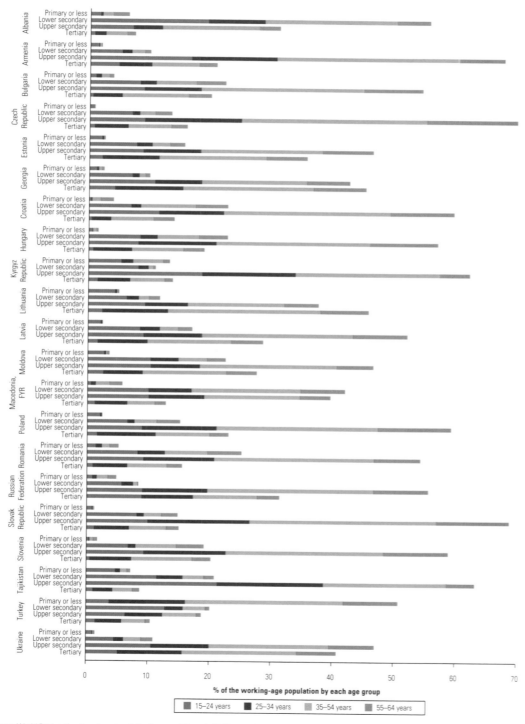

% of the working-age population by each age group

■ 15–24 years ■ 25–34 years ▨ 35–54 years ▨ 55–64 years

Source: World Bank estimations based on Labor Force and Households Surveys, latest years available.

Nearly 60 percent of the potential workforce members are into their prime-age adult years (35–54) or older (55 and over), except in the young CIS countries and Turkey, where they make up only one-third. This group has a mid-level of education in most countries (over two-thirds obtained a secondary education) and one-third to one-half in the Baltics, Georgia, and Ukraine have tertiary schooling. Roughly half of them have less than a secondary education in FYR Macedonia. The older population (55 and over) already comprises 15–20 percent of the potential work force in most countries (except in the young CIS countries and Turkey) and has an education profile similar to the prime-age adult group. Still, between 20 and 30 percent of older individuals did not complete a secondary education, reaching up to 40 percent in Romania.

Younger, new entrants to the labor force in the EU-10 and accession countries, the only group educated largely in the post-transition, are a shrinking but better educated group. Youth (ages 15–24) comprise somewhat less than 20 percent of the potential workforce in the Central European countries, between 20 and 30 percent in the other EU-10 and the CIS countries, and nearly 40 percent in the younger CIS countries and Turkey. The fractions are projected to shrink fast in the EU-10 and older CIS countries over the next three decades. Although the majority of youth remain in the education system, they are set to outdo the prime-age and older adults in educational attainment. This is not always the case for young adults (age 25–34)—comprising around 20 percent of the working-age population, most already in the labor force—which in half of these countries have educational profiles relatively similar to the prime-age adults (including college attainment). Notable exceptions are FYR Macedonia, Poland, Romania, Russia, the Slovak Republic, and Slovenia, where young adults are 1.5–2 times more likely than prime-age adults to have a tertiary education, reflecting the massive expansion of tertiary education over the last two decades.

Skills Gaps among Prospective Workers (the Flow)

Although the former characterization is based on the quantity of education, it helps to think about the nature of skills gaps in the workforce and policies to address them. One can begin with prospective and recent new entrants to the workforce. This is the group for which there is more, albeit still incomplete, data. In fact, existing student assessments are mostly informative about the generic (cognitive) skills that recent new entrants are bringing to the workforce. In this respect, the evidence points to disparate performance in the development of generic skills of this shrinking segment of the future workforce. As discussed in Chapter 5, emigration of better educated youth compounds skills constraints in some fast-aging countries.

While many ECA countries fare relatively well in international student assessments, too many children are not acquiring minimum generic skills. This is illustrated in figure 3.4, taken from Sondergaard et al. (2012), which compares the proportion of 15-year-olds who scored at or below the threshold for functional literacy (Level 1) on the 2009 reading test of the Program for International Student Assessment (PISA). This captures the ability to read and draw useful information from a simple text. With a handful of exceptions, in ECA countries over 20 percent of 15-year-olds fail to acquire even this generic skill, and fare worse than OECD countries. The proportion of functionally illiterate reaches 40 percent even in Bulgaria and Romania, 30 percent in Russia, and dramatic levels in the participating CIS and Balkan countries. This poor performance tends to be concentrated among disadvantaged groups like the Roma population and other ethnic minorities.[15] These are serious deficiencies that will hinder the ability of these young people to acquire knowledge and other skills, whether through further schooling or on the job. Sondergaard et al. (2012) note that this underperformance may reflect a persistent emphasis of education systems in the region on teaching facts and knowledge rather than on developing the kinds of higher-order skills that new jobs require in order to solve new problems in new environments.

In addition, ECA countries have lost ground to other middle-income economies that have achieved significant gains in cognitive skills measured by international assessments. A few countries have improved their international test results consistently, but a majority is losing ground to those improving fastest. Only Latvia, Lithuania, Poland, and Slovenia made it near the top of a recent McKinsey ranking of best improving education systems in the world on the basis of achieving results in skills development (McKinsey 2011). This list was topped by East Asian economies. A majority of ECA countries have either inconsistent or deteriorating results in PISA over the early 2000s. However, in the last round of PISA 2009 (OECD 2010), several countries (including Bulgaria, Romania, Serbia, the Kyrgyz Republic, and Turkey) achieved large improvements over their 2006 test results. Further sustained improvement is critical for the region to tap the potential of its scarce young workforce to find niches in global external markets on the basis of the new economy skills that modern jobs require.

A major gap is the lack of data on the socioemotional—"soft"— component of the generic skills of new entrants to the workforce.

FIGURE 3.4

Too Many 15-Year-Olds in the Region Remain Functionally Illiterate, 2009

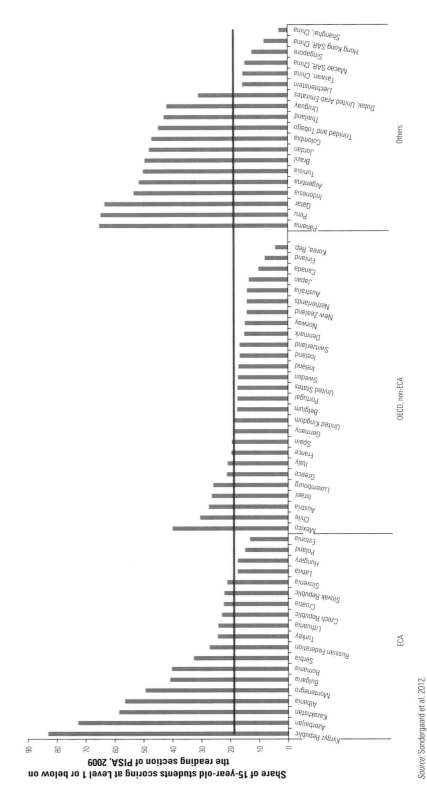

Source: Sondergaard et al. 2012.

Notes: The red line indicates the average share of functionally illiterate 15-year-olds in OECD non–ECA countries. ECA = Europe and Central Asia; OECD = Organisation for Economic Co-operation and Development.

PISA and other student tests are designed to measure directly cognitive skills. Actually, there is evidence that the performance in tests such as PISA captured, in part, differences in attention, persistence, and motivation of students taking the tests (Borghans et al. 2008). Thus, in reality PISA scores reflect a mix of cognitive and socioemotional skills, which is not easily disentangled. Only recently are socioemotional skills—such as self-discipline, persistence, and interpersonal traits—starting to be measured in some national labor force surveys (LFSs) using standardized instruments long developed by psychologists. New household surveys under the Skills Toward Employment and Productivity (STEPs) initiative by the World Bank are designed to measure these socioemotional skills among the working-age youth and adults and how they relate to their labor market performance. As discussed below, not only can these skills be systematically assessed, but there are also effective interventions to foster them at schools, at home, and through training programs.

The development of technical skills among new entrants has also been affected by the shift from vocational toward general secondary education. Enrollment in terminal vocational schools (that do not link up to further tertiary education) has fallen significantly in many ECA countries during the transition. During the first decade of transition (1989–99), enrollment in vocational schools declined sharply across all countries, from 60 to 40 percent of total enrollment at the upper secondary level. In some important ways, this has been a welcomed development, since the quality of vocational schooling was very heterogeneous and because general secondary education can have a big impact on foundational generic skills. This has been shown by the experience of countries like Poland, where the postponement of the early tracking of students has been shown to improve the country's cognitive skills development as measured by PISA (Jakubowski et al. 2010.). However, it has recently been argued that the pendulum might have shifted too far. Advocates for revising the role of technical and vocational secondary education point to the experience of Germany and Austria's dual education vocational systems, which are said to have helped maintain lower levels of unemployment even during the recent crisis. Yet in several countries vocational education is still a default option for weak-performing students—who are redirected into vocational schools rather than finishing upper secondary education. These students have often attended poor quality elementary schools and come from families with lower socioeconomic status. To reduce this explicit income-based selection into vocational schools, it is critical to even out the quality of primary and lower secondary schools.

There is a trade-off and a balance to strike between vocational and general education. On the one hand, vocational education can develop specific job-related skills that can facilitate the school-to-work transition, but these can become obsolete at a faster rate than generic skills. On the other hand, general education stresses generic skills as the foundation for further learning, OJT, and more adaptable work lives, but these may come at a cost of slower transitions to first employment. Figure 3.5 illustrates this trade-off for EU-10 countries; the initial labor-market advantage of vocational relative to general secondary and postsecondary education tends to evaporate at older ages, except in Bulgaria and Latvia. The higher rates of employment among youth going into vocational rather than the general track do not seem to suffice to impart job-specific skills in schools: such skills deteriorate rapidly without use. However, these results are just suggestive correlations due to the known nonrandom

FIGURE 3.5

Technical-Vocational and General Education May Offer Different Lifetime Employment Paths

Employment rates by age group, 2010

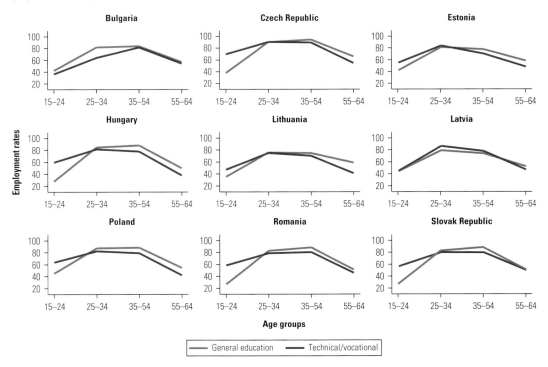

Source: World Bank estimates based on labor force data, from Eurostat 2010.

selection of individuals into technical and general secondary tracks. The weaker later labor performance of these workers may be the result of having attended poor quality elementary schools and of their families' socioeconomic background.

This issue has been carefully studied recently by Hanushek, Woessmann, and Zhang (2011). Using microdata for 18 countries from the International Adult Literacy Survey, they show that for the well-known European "dual-systems" of vocational education and apprenticeships there is indeed a trade-off between short-term and long-term benefits: the initial labor-market advantage of vocational relative to general education decreases with age. Adult workers with narrower vocational skills tend to have more difficulties transiting back to employment when they lose their job later in their working life. With rapid technological change, employment gains from vocational education in the youth years may be offset by less adaptability and difficult job transitions at older ages. These latter costs can easily offset by a big margin the short-term benefits in an increasingly dynamic labor market where job transitions are and will continue to be the norm. There is a qualified consensus in the literature that too early vocational tracking ends up harming lifetime employment prospects.[16] Fortunately, it is possible to avoid an either-or choice, as discussed later in the policy section of this chapter.[17]

Although we lack direct measures of the technical skills of new entrants to the workforce, there are reasons to suspect that skills gaps have built up at the tertiary level. There are no internationally comparable data on skills acquired through tertiary education or training and their fit for modern jobs. However, as argued by Sondergaard et al. (2012), the characteristics of the very fast expansion of the coverage of tertiary education in the region—the largest in the world in the past two decades—probably led to skills gaps among some recent tertiary graduates. The study argues that significant deficiencies in the functioning of education and labor markets lead to disconnects between individual investments in tertiary education and labor market demands. These market failures involve the lack of strong quality assurance and of information on the returns to different careers and postsecondary vocational training offered by institutions to guide students' choices. These have two main consequences: high variation in the quality of provision and misguided career choices that result in imbalances in the skills supply of graduates.

The rapid expansion of the supply of tertiary education in ECA took place with nonexistent or weak mechanisms of quality assurance (Sondergaard et al. 2012). Much of the expansion of tertiary education has occurred in private, profit-based tertiary education providers, especially in part-time (including weekend) and long-distance programs of study. For instance, in 2009 half of Poland's undergraduate students were enrolled in weekend programs, while in Romania about two-thirds of students enrolled in private universities (42 percent of total enrollment) were part-time or long-distance students. The quality of these programs is undocumented, but there is likely a lot of variation. When quality assurance mechanisms for tertiary education were put in place, they revealed widespread noncompliance with minimum quality standards by numerous higher education institutions. There were reports of fraud, corruption, and plainly unethical behavior (Sondergaard et al. 2012). For example, a recent survey of university students in several ECA countries found that more than 60 percent of respondents knew other students who had purchased either entrance to the university or a specific grade.[18] This raises serious doubts about the capacity of some of the new providers to ensure that students graduate with the requisite skills and not just diplomas. Also, it feeds a perception that the tertiary education system in many countries is fragmented and offers a widely divergent array of access and levels of quality in the development of technical skills of the young population.

Too many youth in tertiary education are said to be pursuing the "wrong" careers with limited labor market prospects. For a start, the fast expansion of tertiary enrollment probably drew from the pool of less-college-ready students. The deficits in generic skills of high school graduates impact their capacity to further develop these generic skills and acquire new technical skills in their pursue of a tertiary education. Moreover, the popular claim is that too often many of these youth go into presumably saturated or dead-end professions (such as law, pedagogy, or communication) and end up in jobs unrelated to their acquired qualifications (the so-called "horizontal qualification mismatch"). Meanwhile, the returns to some technical skills and careers (such as engineering, technicians) remain very high.

There is particular concern for skill shortages related to professionals and technicians in science, technology, engineering, and mathematics (STEM) fields (OECD 2011b). These are deemed critical to the region's capacity to develop knowledge-intensive industries through national science and innovation systems in the context of the global patterns of trade and technology diffusion. Figure 3.6 shows the change in the percentage of tertiary graduates in ECA countries during the early 2000s, compared with some Western European countries and the United States. Indeed, in most ECA countries the share of graduates in science and engineering fields declined while the share in business, law, social sciences, and service-related fields increased

FIGURE 3.6

Recent Tertiary Graduates in ECA Are Choosing Fields of Study Like Their Western European and U.S. Peers

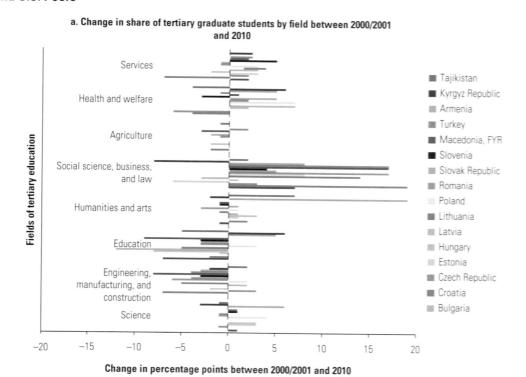

a. Change in share of tertiary graduate students by field between 2000/2001 and 2010

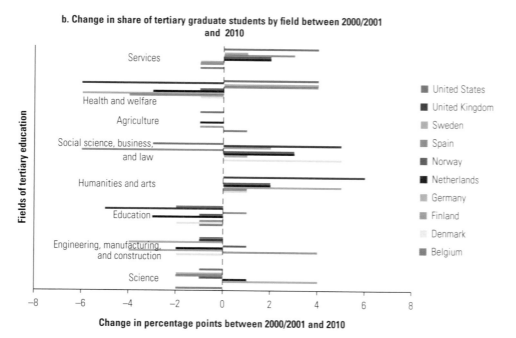

b. Change in share of tertiary graduate students by field between 2000/2001 and 2010

Source: World Bank estimates based on UNESCO Education Digest, 2003, 2012.

significantly. Much of the expansion in private schools was a response to a sharp increase in demand in specific areas not requiring expensive investments (such as law, business, accounting, languages, economics, and management). However, a similar pattern is observed in Western Europe and the United States. As important as these technical skills are for productivity-driven competitiveness, one cannot discern from these data root cause of these trends. They may be a result of a supply-driven shortage in STEM-related skills or a response to changes in skills demand from the shift of economic activity to services and a low capacity to generate innovation-based economic clusters (due to an unfavorable business environment).

Skill mismatches are a more relevant problem than "overqualification" or disconnects in the choice of fields of study in tertiary education. Commonly claimed mismatches in technical skills are not always real. An individual holding a job that does not directly match his professional qualifications need not be a mismatch. As discussed before, broad shifts in skills demand are driven by the need to match workers' skills to the tasks they need to perform in a job. More than ever, workers are matched to jobs based on a multiplicity of skills, not just their educational qualifications. For several years now, the finance industry has been hiring math graduates and physicists into relatively high-paying "quant" jobs. Economists and statisticians are known to permeate the world of sports. These apparently mismatched workers typically earn more because they increase the productivity (and profitability) of business. The move spearheaded by the European Qualifications Framework toward defining and accrediting qualifications tied to workers' skills should maintain the focus on the skills employers required from workers to perform tasks in their jobs.

Skill mismatches are best addressed by following the market signals captured by the returns to the various types of tertiary education. A key indicator to judge if a skill is in short supply is the premium the labor market places on it, or better yet, whether skills investments pay off in terms of their private and social benefits. This is clearly relevant from a policy perspective, especially in the context of ECA countries where education is heavily subsidized. The chapter returns to this topic in the next section.

Skills Gaps among the Adult Population (the Stock of Workers)

Data gaps are particularly severe with regard to the skills of adults and the older population. PISA and, for that matter, all other international assessments are hardly informative about the skills gaps of the prime-age and older adults in the workforce. Tests like PISA, designed to measure generic functional skills, go back only to the year 2000, so they may capture the cognitive skills that current young adults brought into the labor market (early test takers would be in their late 20s today). If anything, those earlier results for most ECA countries (with exceptions like Poland) were either similar or actually lower than in the most recent tests. However, this cohort of young adults continued to develop skills through tertiary education, training, or on-the-job experience, so that earlier test results cannot really be taken as accurate measures of their skills today. There is a blind spot in the knowledge about the skills of the older adult population, which was educated decades ago and has since acquired skills on-the-job. The data gap is equally acute with regard to socioemotional skills of the adult workforce. Again, only recently are these vast gaps in measuring skills of the labor force starting to be addressed through new household surveys under the Program for International Assessment of Adult Competences (PIAAC) of the OECD (measuring cognitive and technical skills) and the World Bank STEPs initiative (which in addition measures socioemotional skills).

The pace of economic change and how the education and training systems operated in a centrally planned economy raise concerns about the skills of older workers. Rapid economic change renders skills obsolete. The capacity to maintain a workforce with adequate skills depends on how the education and training system adapts to economic change and to aging. There is concern that after the transition in several ECA countries the obsolescence of technical skills has not been addressed and vocational education systems have not performed well. The European Commission (EC) reports results of a 2011 pilot survey carried out by Cedefop in Hungary and other Western European economies which found that, based on a self-assessment of skills, a significant share of workers experiences skills obsolescence (EC 2012a). About 12 percent of respondents believe that the current match of their skills to the requirements of their job is worse than what it was when they first started their current line of work. Lower-skilled workers and older individuals are at greater risk of skills obsolescence, but it also affects prime-age workers and about 9 percent of tertiary education graduates. Those who report lacking opportunities to develop their skills throughout their careers and who had lengthy career interruptions (due to unemployment, child rearing, and so forth) are most affected.

Many adult and older workers may have been unable to offset the obsolescence of their skills through training and on-the-job learning, especially in the late reformers countries. A large international literature documented by empirical evidence—largely for OECD countries—shows that firm-led training is often most effective in developing skills (see, for example, Almeida, Behrman, and Robalino 2012; Dearden, Reed, and Van Reenen 2000; OECD 2009). Postschool learning is an important source of skill formation that accounts for as much as one-third to one-half of all skill formation in an economy (see the discussion in Heckman, Lochner, and Taber 1998). However, the ability of adult workers to upgrade their skills has been limited by the characteristics of workplace training before and after the transition. Under centrally planned economies, this focused exclusively on continuing vocational training of the employed workforce. With the exception of socialist Yugoslavia, unemployment was nonexistent by definition, hence training of the unemployed was not a feature of education and training systems. Even in modern market economies market failures tend to lead to underinvestment in training by both individuals and firms. The countries of ECA are no exception. Sondergaard et al. (2012) report evidence from available comparable national surveys of training in firms that puts ECA behind Western European countries in the training of their workers. There is wide variation between the Czech Republic and Estonia, on the one hand, where about 70 percent of firms report that they provide such training, and Azerbaijan, on the other, where only about 10 percent do so. Large firms integrated into external markets are considerably more likely to train. For example, Almeida and Aterido (2010) estimate that the probability of investing in OJT is approximately 40 percentage points higher in Eastern Europe for large firms (more than 250 employees) than for microfirms (fewer than 10 employees). The incidence of job training is around 10 percentage points higher among firms present in foreign markets or with foreign participation. Finally, both the share of workers who participate in training and the actual hours of training are limited. Altogether, this raises questions about the actual coverage and quality of the firm-led training that adult workers have received since the transition.

Even today access to training for the unemployed in the ECA region is limited. While countries have long funded industrial training institutes that train or retrain unemployed workers, these institutes were rarely designed to meet the needs of the modern workplace. The introduction of passive and active employment policies in ECA at the start of the transition gave priority to interventions that retrained workers who had lost their jobs as part of privatization and enterprise restructuring. There is evidence that these often had positive impacts on employment when well designed (Betcherman, Olivas, and Dar 2004; Card, Kluve, and Weber 2010). Today, in most countries training programs for the unemployed are largely publicly funded and often represent the bulk of government spending on active labor market programs. The share of unemployed workers who participate in training is relatively low, and the hours of training are limited compared to the EU-15. The evidence on the effectiveness—value for money—of this training is very limited. The established mechanisms for orienting provision to serve employers' needs often do not operate well in practice (Almeida, Behrman, and Robalino 2012; Mourshed, Farrell, and Barton 2012).

Unlike preuniversity and university education, adult education systems are highly underdeveloped in most of ECA. Adult learning programs have remained a blind spot in education and training policy across much of the ECA region (Sondergaard et al. 2012). In fact, many countries in the region have not yet begun to adequately promote adult learning as a means of addressing the current skills deficit and improving worker productivity in the face of the expected shrinkage of the working-age population. The "second-chance" education programs form a small part of the incipient adult education and training system in ECA countries. Sondergaard et al. (2012) discuss the current situation, challenges, and avenues for expanding this important subsector of education throughout the region.

Ultimately, the response from the supply side of skills—steered by the education and training system—to changes in the demand for skills hinges on market signals to individuals and institutions. Imbalances between the demand and supply for skills would manifest in an increase or decline in the relative wages of workers who possess these skills, although with a lag since the supply (more so than the demand) tends to adjust slowly. This response depends on a number of factors: chiefly, sufficient flexibility in wages to adjust to changing demand and supply, the availability of information on job prospects by type of education and occupation, competitive pressures or accountability for educational institutions to adjust program offerings to the needs of the labor market, and employment services that can effectively match workers to available jobs. The next section examines whether labor market signals reflect the underlying changes in the demand and supply of skills in the ECA countries. Given the unavailability of micro data linking actual measures of skills and earnings of the workforce, the analysis focuses on the returns to tertiary education to assess whether the relative shifts in the skills demand and supply have affected the earnings premia for the skills embodied in workers with tertiary education relative to those of the less educated.

Are Skills Valued? The Returns to Tertiary Schooling

This section focuses on the concern around an alleged overexpansion of tertiary education that is common in the policy debate in many of the region's countries. The supply of tertiary educated workers is said to outpace the demand in the labor market, and there are concerns that tertiary institutions are producing graduates whose skills are not in line with what employers need. It is said that many graduates end up taking jobs that require lower qualifications and skills. A similar concern arose in the late 1970s in the United States when a surge in college graduates from the so-called "baby boom" generation apparently resulted in a substantial reduction in the returns to college. Subsequent analyses of the data proved that concern to be unfounded.[19] In order to assess whether the concern is justified in ECA countries, this report analyzed the evolution and variation in the returns to tertiary education using conventional and novel methodologies (see box 3.3). This analysis fills an important gap as, until recently, there were not comparable earnings data that would allow an assessment of how the college wage premia has evolved since the early 2000s. Figure 3.7 depicts the percentage earnings premia for workers with tertiary education in the low, average, and best paying jobs relative to workers with secondary education (both general and technical) and similar observed characteristics.

There is no systematic evidence that an upsurge in the supply of tertiary graduates drove down the wage premium to college education, although patterns vary by country. In most ECA countries considered, the average college-wage premia remained essentially

---

BOX 3.3

New Measures of the Returns to Tertiary Schooling in ECA

The chapter analyzes the earnings premium to tertiary schooling and their evolution in a sample of ECA countries with available data. It fits Mincer earnings functions for full-time workers in each country for mean earnings and at five percentiles (from the 10th to the 90th) of the earnings distribution, given worker characteristics. This allows assessing how the relative shifts in the demand and supply for skills embodied in workers with tertiary education have affected the earnings premia of workers located at the bottom or the top of the earnings scale, adjusting by differences in their demographics and work experience.

continued

FIGURE 3.8

The Returns to Tertiary Education Can Vary Considerably across Individuals

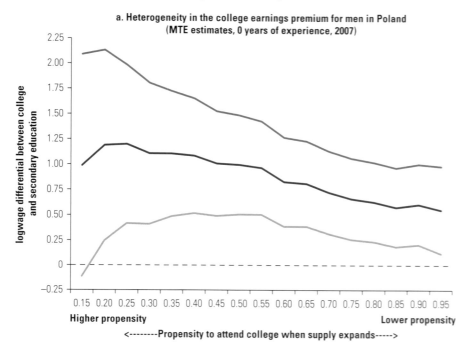

a. Heterogeneity in the college earnings premium for men in Poland
(MTE estimates, 0 years of experience, 2007)

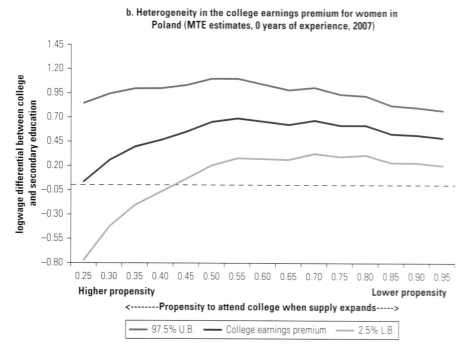

b. Heterogeneity in the college earnings premium for women in
Poland (MTE estimates, 0 years of experience, 2007)

Source: Based on estimates from Carneiro, Arias, and Falcao (2013) using Polish Labor Force Survey (LFS) 2007–10.
Note: MTE = Marginal Treatment Effect; L.B. = lower bounds; U.B. = upper bounds. See box 3.3 for methodological references.

FIGURE 3.9

Returns to College Vary and Carry Different Risks by Field of Study in Bulgaria

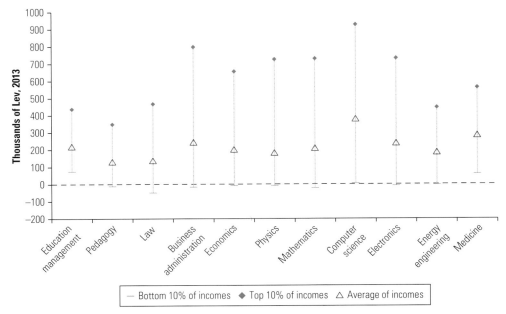

Source: World Bank based on estimates from Open Society Institute 2013.
Note: The results are nonparametric estimates of the net present value of earnings over the projected work life. See box 3.3 for methodological references.

Evidence from Bulgaria reveals a substantial variation in the average returns to different types of college careers and in the risk this entails for graduates. Most college careers yield relatively similar and reasonable average lifetime incomes (and returns that surpass 10 percent per year), with some notable exceptions. Pedagogy and law offer significantly lower returns, while computer science and medicine yield the highest returns (again, netting out tuition and other direct costs). Moreover, neither of the former two careers ends up yielding good value for money for those graduates that end up at the bottom of the earnings scale in each respective field of study. In fact, all careers, except for medicine and education management, result in negative returns when direct costs are factored in. Meanwhile, careers in computer science, business administration, mathematics, physics, economics, and electronics can be quite lucrative if graduates manage to land jobs at the upper tail of the salary scale for each field. Thus, even if average returns to tertiary education are high, at any field, there is considerable risk associated with the investment that can deem the pursuit of a tertiary degree a bad proposition for a nonnegligible group of youth.

Taking together, the results indicate that concerns about the over-supply and/or overqualification of tertiary graduates in the ECA region appear to be misplaced. Tertiary education continues to be a value investment for most youth. However, there is evidence that not all individuals would benefit the same way from a college education. At least in Bulgaria and Poland, the high average returns to tertiary education are not available to everyone alike—in particular, poor families may accrue returns to their investments in higher education significantly below the average market return.

The results for Bulgaria and Poland beg the question of what leads to the wide differences in tertiary returns and whether individuals factor these into their college career decisions. Why are not more youth pursuing more lucrative engineering and technical degrees rather than lower-return diplomas? There are at least two possible explanations. Youth may not have adequate information about the labor market prospects of different careers or degrees from different institutions to wisely select and pursue a course of study. Alternatively, they may know which are the careers and institutions that offer the highest payoffs but their choices are constrained by available funding, limited number of places, and the matching of scholastic requirements to their innate abilities and occupational tastes. Low-income workers may end up in the less technical courses or weaker programs because these are cheaper or even free and also are academically less demanding. As discussed by Sondergaard et al. (2012), the evidence indicates that both explanations hold some truth.

There is therefore a role for policy in providing support, information, and incentives that will direct people into subject areas for which there is relatively high demand in the labor market. There is much need for data collection and diffusion of labor market returns by field of study and even by type of institution attended. Likewise there is a role for policy in understanding and alleviating problems that constrain individuals (especially those from lower socioeconomic groups) from participating in tertiary education, especially in the most profitable fields of study.

The chapter now turns to the policy implications of the findings, and some examples of the types of policies and interventions to strengthen the system of building skills for the workplace in the region.

Conclusions and Policies to Develop Skills for the Workplace

This chapter examines the extent to which workers in the region are prepared to take on new job opportunities by examining two questions: Are skills gaps a constraint to employment in ECA? Who is most affected, youth or older workers? The chapter discussed the extent to which workers have the multiplicity of skills employers want, the role of education and training systems in the ensuing gaps, how these vary for new entrants (youth) and the stock of workers (particularly older workers), and new evidence on how the labor market signals (via returns to tertiary education) reflect the underlying changes in the demand and supply of skills in the ECA countries.

The chapter argues that skills gaps hinder labor performance of both youth and older workers, with varying importance across countries. As in more modern economies, jobs are becoming increasingly intensive in higher-order (new economy) skills—especially in countries more integrated to external markets and with a more skilled workforce—and economic developments post-transition may have rendered obsolete the skills of many older workers. The response from education and training systems has been uneven. Tertiary schooling has expanded fast among youth—delivering diplomas—but with varying quality and relevance. Meanwhile, the legacy of early tracking into technical and vocational education and training (TVET) and labor training with loose market links limits skills upgrading among adults and older workers. As a result, youth and older workers are affected by skills gaps in distinctive ways. Youth do better in acquiring skills, but many often acquire the wrong set (both generic and technical). Many older workers educated for centrally planned economies are at risk of skills obsolescence, which hinders their capacity to tap into new employment opportunities. Emigration of better educated youth compounds skills constraints in some fast-aging countries.

This chapter now turns to a third question: What needs to change to strengthen the system of building skills for the workplace in the region? In a nutshell, reforms and policies should prioritize the development of a strong foundation of generic skills, ensure quality and relevance in expanding tertiary education systems, and make the training system market responsive and age sensitive to enable life-long skills acquisition. These objectives span a wide-ranging policy agenda that goes beyond narrow and fragmented educational, training, and labor policies and integrates them into long-term skills development strategies. The discussion below focuses primarily on key principles and some examples of policies for improving the quality and relevance of education and training systems so that they build market-valued skills, grounded on the life-cycle nature of skills formation. It draws on recent studies by the Bank, including the regional report *Skills Not Just Diplomas* (Sondergaard et al. 2012), as well as work by the European Commission and other regional institutions that delve into more depth.[21] The reader is urged to consult these sources for more detail in the various policy options, conditions for success, and references to lessons on design and implementation issues.

Policy makers could focus on five main strategic policy directions and related priority actions:

1. Preparing new job-market entrants (youth) with strong generic skills foundations
2. Managing the expansion of tertiary education through quality assurance and communication to students about the labor prospects of various careers
3. Addressing market failures that prevent more OJT and incentivizing firms to provide it
4. Addressing technical or job-specific skills gaps of youth and adults through more effective training as part of active labor market policies (ALMPs) and, when needed, through targeted programs focused on disadvantaged groups
5. Creating the conditions for the development of a market for adult education and training services

The first priority is to ensure that new cohorts of youth entering the labor market are equipped with a strong base of generic cognitive and socioemotional skills, by filling gaps in the coverage and quality of early childhood development (ECD) to give all children a level playing field to become school ready and by supporting schools and holding them accountable for achieving results in building these generic skills.

Policy makers throughout the region should direct public resources toward critical investments and interventions during the sensitive periods of a person's life, when cognitive and socioemotional skills are most malleable. Three key policy goals should be achieved: (i) provide adequate early-childhood services in the first three years in the lives of children from low-income families and disadvantaged (in particular Roma) communities; (ii) expand access to quality preschools that provide enriching learning environments, again, especially for disadvantaged children; and (iii) offer quality basic education focused on generic skills for all children through their adolescence. All three are very pressing challenges across late and intermediate modernizer countries, and even most advanced modernizers have to consolidate ongoing progress in these areas. In all countries, this approach is essential to prepare the fewer youth entering a constantly changing labor market for longer and more productive working lives. Moreover, as discussed in chapter 4, high quality ECD programs help boost women's labor market attachment.

Families and communities have, of course, a central role in the early development of generic skills of children. Public policy can support them by providing low-income parents with information on nurturing parenting practices through existing programs and services (counseling in health centers) and schools (through their involvement in community councils). Current key issues for improving access and quality of ECD in the region, including among Roma, are discussed, for instance, in the EC (2011a) "Communication on Early Childhood Education and Care" and World Bank (2011).

Schools also play a fundamental role. The influential McKinsey (2011) report and OECD PISA-based reports on how the best education systems (including general and vocational streams) build valuable skills highlight that, first and foremost, these systems strive for continuous improvement on key fronts: (i) creating institutional arrangements that balance strong oversight and quality assurance functions at a central level—through timely information for performance management—and utilize decentralized management and decision making, empowering schools to achieve results; (ii) empowering effective teachers, through pedagogic support, training, evaluation, and enhanced incentives to attract and retain effective teachers; (iii) providing adequate school curricula, infrastructure, equipment, and pedagogic material; and (iv) establishing financing schemes guided toward outputs and strong accountability systems.

As noted in the World Bank regional report *Skills Not Just Diplomas* (Sondergaard et al. 2012), although countries in the region have undertaken significant reforms, the legacy of central planning inhibits the ability of the basic education systems in the region to develop market-valued skills. Three major factors are at play. First, many systems still operate "in the dark," as they do not systematically collect data on student learning related to generic skills. Even countries with established student assessments often measure only academic content, and several countries still do not participate in international assessments like PISA. Second, despite embracing performance management reforms since the 1980s, the legacy of central planning keeps the governance and management of schools highly centralized and focused on regulatory compliance and input-based financing. Most local education authorities and principals in the region lack the autonomy and authority to decide on key aspects of school management and education delivery, including attracting and retaining effective teachers. And third, financial resources are not used effectively, as few countries have adjusted teacher staffing levels in response to falling student numbers over the past 20 years. Thus, scarce resources go to low salaries of too many staff and maintaining underutilized buildings. While these impediments affect ECA countries differently, none has fully escaped the legacy of central planning. The report discusses policies and reforms, with examples from various countries, in three fronts related to those mentioned above: (i) managing education systems for results, (ii) focusing attention on learning that leads to generic skills, and (iii) deepening autonomy and accountability for results.

One area warranting policy reform is postponing early tracking into TVET to allow youth to acquire stronger generic skills. Some educational systems are still tracking students too early into vocational streams at the expense of generic skills. This is again a vestige of the centralization legacy. Despite country variation, specialized vocational education tended to be provided early and relied heavily on on-site practical experience in state enterprises (Canning, Godfrey, and Holzer-Zelazewska 2007). While the economic structure of countries and existing institutional and budgetary constraints precludes a one-size-fits-all prescription on how to organize an effective TVET system, the evidence points to four broad guidelines: (i) diversify through TVET options only after students have acquired strong generic skills (literacy, numeracy, and socioemotional competence), which for most countries means start at the upper secondary level, at the earliest; (ii) when diversifying in secondary education, provide work competencies that are broad, provide readiness for further in-depth training, and offer flexibility; (iii) postpone occupational training to postsecondary education and promote a diversified supply of courses (from traditional apprenticeship like plumbing and electrical trades to emerging technical white-collar occupations in health care and computing), and providers (e.g., public entities, private firms, nongovernmental organizations) who have strong linkages with employers and the labor market; and (iv) ensure vertical and horizontal pathways between TVET and other tertiary education programs to allow for flexible movement of students between different pathways. Autonomy and timely data that track graduates and labor market needs are particularly needed in vocational education and training so that programs and providers can expeditiously expand or contract course offerings in response to student and employer demand.

Countries can start from a diagnosis of the policy and institutional factors that influence how well the TVET system meets skills demanded by employers. The World Bank's System Assessment and Benchmarking for Education Results (SABER) Workforce Development (WfD) initiative offers a practical and systematic tool for involving stakeholders in assessment and identifying reform

actions in light of international good practices. WfD identifies
9 policy goals and 18 related policy actions in three functional
dimensions: strategic framework, system oversight, and service
delivery. These are benchmarked in four stages of development:
latent, emerging, established, and advanced. Applications are completed for four relevant benchmark countries (Chile, Ireland, the
Republic of Korea, and Singapore), and ongoing applications have
started in the region (Armenia, Bulgaria, Georgia, FYR Macedonia,
and Turkey) as well as in a number of other countries in East Asia.
When applied retrospectively, this tool can provide a useful picture
of how the preemployment TVET system has evolved in various
dimensions, pointing to strengths and gaps, as illustrated in figure
3.10 for Ireland (see also box 3.4).

Countries can build on lessons of TVET systems that feature
strengths in the various dimensions. For instance, Belgium, the

FIGURE 3.10

Benchmarking the System of Workforce Development in Ireland

Scores from application of the System Assessment and Benchmarking for Education Results [SABER]
Workforce Development [WfD] tool, 2012

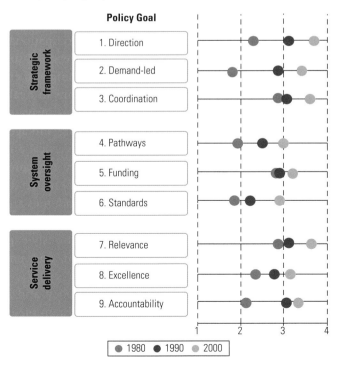

Source: World Bank 2012a.
Notes: 1 = Latent; 2 = Emerging; 3 = Established; 4 = Advanced.

accountability, and performance-based financing more effectively into improving the quality and relevance of higher education.

OECD countries—including Hungary, Italy, and the Netherlands and recently Romania—offer examples on how tracer studies are used to collect and disseminate data on employment and earnings outcomes and how the tertiary sector is performing from a skills perspective. Bulgaria publicly disseminates information about the quality of tertiary institutions, including starting salaries of graduates by field of study and institution attended. Other countries are establishing labor market observatories (including Poland and the Czech Republic and, outside the region, Chile and Colombia), and in cases like the United Kingdom these are integrated with employment services to inform both career choice and training investments and facilitate job search.

Finally, sustaining the financing of further expansions of tertiary education would require options for cost-sharing with student financing (loans, scholarships) to support qualified students (with adequate generic skills) in attending accredited tertiary institutions, based on needs and merits. A cost-sharing system could be accompanied by a comprehensive and income-contingent loans scheme. Since student mobility is growing fast within Europe and from Central Asia to Russia (chapter 5), resulting in high emigration rates of college graduates, this would require cooperation with countries that serve as destinations of young migrants in order to facilitate cost recovery and plausible options for pool financing.

The third priority area is to lay the basis for upgrading lifelong skills, by addressing market failures that prevent firms from OJT training and incentivizing them to do so.

OJT is an important channel through which workers upgrade skills during their working life. It is also a vehicle that can help firms adopt new technologies and new business practices. In aging populations, it is essential to create the right incentives for firms to train their workers, as public funding is unlikely to ensure a stable and adequate level of financing. There is evidence that the incidence of OJT in much of the ECA region is still low (Sondergaard et al. 2012). Identifying the reasons for this in each country context is a prerequisite for designing effective policy responses. Data limitations and the fact that the EU-8 countries are not a homogenous group have led to difficulties in assembling information on vocational education that is fully comparable between countries. The evidence on this area is quite thin in the region, but some basic principles should be considered.[22]

First and foremost, policies should strive to support those firms that, despite positive expected returns, would not train. Some firms may not invest in training simply because it does not pay, that is, the expected rate of return is lower than the (opportunity) cost of funds. This may result from low expected benefits (likely the case for lower productivity firms) from training or high training costs (likely the case for smaller firms). In the former case, the focus should be on policies to promote an enabling environment in which firms can thrive, become more productive, and thus experience positive expected rates of return on training. Other firms may benefit from investments in training but cannot realize these due to market failures. These include concerns of worker turnover, in part due to poaching by other firms, or liquidity constraints.

Payback clauses and apprenticeship contracts can be used to deal with poaching externalities. The former are most common in more advanced economies, where there is capacity to enforce them. Germany offers a paradigmatic example of apprenticeship programs, both school-based and via OJT, which are well-regarded by both workers and employers.

Credits and subsidies are used to deal with liquidity constraints that prevent investments in OJT. Credit programs require considerable information and administrative capacity to target genuinely constrained firms without producing gaming, large deadweight losses, and substitution effects. One possible approach is to allocate subsidies to priority areas based on consultations with enterprises, including small and medium-size firms. Coordination failures occur when private firms refrain from investments in high-potential sectors due to the lack of workers with the right skills, and at the same time workers do not invest in these skills due to the lack of jobs and firms themselves do not take the risk to train them. In this case, training subsidies could be allocated in the form of contributions to match firms' training investments through competitive bidding.

Training funds and tax grants are used to provide training subsidies to firms in some countries in the region. Their use is varied. In Hungary a relatively large sectoral training fund financed from payroll taxes is used to finance preemployment and continuing vocational education and training, while in Poland and Slovenia their use is much more limited. Some countries incentivize firm training by allowing a tax exemption of applicable training expenses up to a maximum of total tax expenditure deductions of the firm in the year. These schemes tend to benefit larger enterprises, as provisions for access of smaller firms are rarely incorporated into the funds' design. Training funds risk excessive centralization and administrative burden, which discourage their use by firms.[23] There is virtually no evidence of whether the resulting training is effective in improving employment outcomes.

These types of schemes have been used effectively to increase firm training in several countries in Western Europe and East Asia, although a few prerequisite elements are common to successful schemes: (i) keeping an effective, simple mechanism for administering tax exemptions through the tax system, because complicated rules lead to employer noncompliance; (ii) ensuring that the training is relevant to market and worker needs by allowing proceeds to be used for in-service training or to purchase training at accredited training institutions and also ensuring a good balance between technical and more generic skills. Employers tend to prefer training that imparts skills that are immediately useful in their business, whereas trainees would benefit from a greater focus on generic skills that are transferable to other jobs and that provide a basis for further learning.

For the fourth priority, address technical or job-specific skills gaps of youth and adults using selective evidence-based training programs with strong ties to labor market needs.

Firm training is less likely to cover general training: for example, on socioemotional skills. Less experienced and less educated workers and small employers tend to benefit substantially less from existing schemes. Moreover, individuals out of jobs are de facto excluded. These gaps in training should be covered by the training offered through ALMPs. An overview of the experiences with training during the transition across countries indicates that the majority of interventions were important and effective (Betcherman, Olivas, and Dar 2004; Card, Kluve, and Weber 2010). However, there is more limited evidence about the cost-effectiveness of current training for the unemployed and inactive. The relatively few rigorous evaluations of these programs in the EU-15 show a mixed record in terms of their impacts on earnings and employment, depending on aspects of their design, and they rarely go through a cost-benefit evaluation.[24]

To address the skills gaps of disadvantaged youth, countries can consider implementing targeted youth labor training to strengthen a core set of technical and socioemotional skills. These programs have a proven track record (from rigorous evaluations in Latin America) in providing valued skills through a combination of classroom and workplace training. Recent developments incorporate explicit training components on behavioral (socioemotional) skills—besides technical and basic cognitive skills—given their malleability through early adulthood. This incorporates features of mentoring and peer-to-peer learning, as there is evidence that they help youth participants develop socioemotional skills.

Labor training of adults can benefit from incorporating insights from emerging findings in various disciplines and recent evaluations of adult training programs in the United States suggesting that these cannot be age-blind. Emerging findings from neurology, psychology, and education challenge many long-held views about adult learning and the effectiveness of adult training (Johnson and Taylor 2006; Maestas and Zissimopoulos 2010). As scientists look deeper into how brains age, they have found that different abilities tend to follow relatively independent paths over the life cycle. Some abilities, like the performance and speed of solving new tasks, are strongly reduced at older ages, while other abilities, like verbal capacities and word fluency, remain at a high functional level until late in life. As people pass middle age, the brain gets better at recognizing the central idea, the big picture, and if kept in good shape, can even find solutions much faster than a younger brain. Prior experience and knowledge play a much more fundamental role in how older workers learn new skills compared to younger individuals.

New insights from this research and promising interventions suggests that with appropriate training strategies, mature brains can learn new skills. In recent evaluations of a range of public and private workforce training strategies in the United States, some focused on the needs of adults have been shown to produce returns as high as 10–26 percent when program impacts are followed over longer periods than in previous evaluations of training programs (see Besharov and Cottingham 2011). Key features of promising strategies to train older workers include establishing clear links to employers beforehand—to ensure relevance but also to overcome any reluctance to hire older workers—and competence-based training organized as series of shorter modules fully built on recognition of prior learning. Older workers can use the tacit know-how and maturity (stronger noncognitive skills) derived from experience and aging to add new skills and contribute effectively to age-diverse teams.

Given the critical importance of identifying effective models of labor training, it would be important for governments, employers, and training providers to engage in serious impact evaluation of new training initiatives. These should include serious cost-benefit analysis and also provide for learning about the duration of program impacts. Most evaluations of ALMPs in Europe provide only a year or two of follow-up. The available evidence on longer-term impacts for the United States suggests that sometimes impacts remain remarkably steady over time for years after an intervention, other times they fade out, and other times they appear only belatedly.[25]

And last but not least, as the fifth priority, countries with aging populations should create the conditions for the development of a market for adult education and training services.

Currently, the participation rates in continuous education in ECA countries are much lower than in the EU-15. Only about 10–20 percent of employees in Estonia, Poland, and Hungary participate in continuous vocational training activities, whereas the lowest share for the EU-15 is 26 percent in Italy. Similar proportions can be observed if the share of the working-age population participating in any educational activity is considered. Hungary has the lowest rates of participation, with only 4.4 percent of the population ages 55–64 continuing to learn, whereas in the EU-15 this share varies from 22 percent (in the United Kingdom) to 35 percent (in Italy).

The development of this adult education sector is important for making training effective in upgrading skills throughout a person's working life. Lifelong training is central to the region's economic growth strategy, particularly in more advanced ECA countries that are facing a shrinking and aging workforce. Only few countries have started to plan for the development of this sector. Building such systems will require a shift away from government-driven programs and toward a well-regulated market of private and public providers that deliver training services with close involvement of employers. Governments will continue to play a role in education and training for those out of work, increasingly relying on contracting private providers to deliver training services. Successful systems require a high degree of coordination and partnership between government agencies and the private sector, as well as giving the demand side of training—that is, businesses and individuals—a strong voice in determining training policy. Once a solid adult learning sector is established, governments can then provide the oversight by monitoring data on program quality, encouraging autonomy and accountability, and improving the efficiency of government financing in the sector.

In less advanced economies in the region that are experiencing a demographic decline (many of those in Southeastern Europe and the middle-income CIS countries) the goal is to introduce a strategic policy framework for adult learning and create the tools needed to implement this strategy (e.g., coordination mechanisms plus initial steps toward regulation). Less advanced economies in the region that are not facing a demographic decline (low-income CIS countries) may limit efforts to establishing a strategic policy framework and coordination mechanism for this sector.

For all countries, participating in the OECD's PIAAC or the World Bank's STEPs skills measurement study would be an important first step in understanding the current skills and competencies of their adult work force. The PIAAC surveys are currently underway in several of the New Member States, and STEPs is being implemented in Azerbaijan, FYR Macedonia, Armenia, Georgia, and Ukraine.

In sum, priorities three, four, and five call for a fundamental rethinking of vocational education, training, and lifelong learning systems. This comprises three key directions: (i) a stronger policy coordination among government, training providers, and the enterprise sector, with a sound regulatory regime for the development of private provision; (ii) appropriate incentives for firms to engage more in training of adults and older workers; and (iii) a concerted effort by employers, governments, and workers to invest more effectively in training at older ages. Building the demand side—employer buy-in— is a key challenge. Relevant experiences are those of the United Kingdom and some EU-15 countries of setting up sector employer councils and of East Asian countries in setting up independent apex training authorities (such as Singapore's Institute for Technical Education) that have strong partnerships with employers and other stakeholders.

These and other specific actions can help address the market and institutional failures affecting skills formation and insertion of youth and older workers into the region's labor market. Prepared with the skills needed to tap into new job opportunities, workers must see that work actually pays and be able to access jobs that fit their skills, including by being willing to move to places with the greatest job creation potential. These issues are the subject of chapters 4 and 5. The next chapter, in particular, lays out the basis on which to design tax and social benefits that are compatible with strong work incentives and adequate protection against employment and income shocks.

Annex 3A: Evolution in the Skills Intensity of Jobs

TABLE 3A.1

Evolution in the Skills Intensity of Jobs in Selected ECA Countries

	a. Cohort born after 1974					b. Cohort born before 1955				
	Nonroutine cognitive: Analytical	Nonroutine cognitive: Interpersonal	Routine cognitive	Routine manual	Nonroutine manual physical	Nonroutine cognitive: Analytical	Nonroutine cognitive: Interpersonal	Routine cognitive	Routine manual	Nonroutine manual physical
BGR-Bulgaria										
2002	50	50	50	50	50	50	50	50	50	50
2003	50	54	50	50	54	50	50	49	48	50
2004	50	48	50	50	54	50	50	49	48	50
2005	50	48	52	50	54	50	48	50	48	50
2006	50	48	50	50	50	50	49	48	48	50
2007	50	54	52	50	50	50	49	48	48	50
2008	50	54	52	50	50	50	50	48	48	50
2009	58	57	52	47	50	50	50	48	48	46
2010	50	54	50	50	50	50	50	48	48	46
Average	51.0	52.1	51.0	49.6	51.5	50.0	49.5	48.5	48.0	49.0

continued

TABLE 3A.1
Continued

CZE-Czech Republic

| | a. Cohort born after 1974 | | | | | b. Cohort born before 1955 | | | | |
	Nonroutine cognitive: Analytical	Nonroutine cognitive: Interpersonal	Routine cognitive	Routine manual	Nonroutine manual physical	Nonroutine cognitive: Analytical	Nonroutine cognitive: Interpersonal	Routine cognitive	Routine manual	Nonroutine manual physical
2002	50	50	50	50	50	50	50	50	50	50
2003	50	50	50	51	50	50	50	50	50	57
2004	53	50	50	48	50	50	50	50	50	57
2005	53	50	50	51	50	50	50	50	50	57
2006	53	50	50	48	50	50	50	50	57	57
2007	61	50	50	50	50	62	53	50	50	50
2008	61	50	50	48	50	62	53	50	50	50
2009	61	56	50	45	50	62	50	50	50	50
2010	61	56	50	48	50	50	53	50	50	50
Average	56.6	51.5	50.0	48.6	50.0	54.5	51.1	50.0	50.9	53.5

	a. Cohort born after 1974					b. Cohort born before 1955				
	Nonroutine cognitive: Analytical	Nonroutine cognitive: Interpersonal	Routine cognitive	Routine manual	Nonroutine manual physical	Nonroutine cognitive: Analytical	Nonroutine cognitive: Interpersonal	Routine cognitive	Routine manual	Nonroutine manual physical
EST-Estonia										
2002	50	50	50	50	50	50	50	50	50	50
2003	50	61	48	50	50	49	48	53	50	50
2004	55	52	48	45	50	52	50	53	50	50
2005	56	61	48	44	50	49	50	50	50	50
2006	55	61	48	48	50	49	55	53	50	46
2007	56	61	48	49	50	45	50	52	50	46
2008	56	61	48	49	50	49	55	52	50	46
2009	61	61	49	45	38	53	55	50	45	46
2010	61	61	48	42	38	49	50	50	50	50
Average	56.3	59.9	48.1	46.5	47.0	49.4	51.6	51.6	49.4	48.0

continued

TABLE 3A.1
Continued

	c. Cohort born after 1974					d. Cohort born before 1955				
	Nonroutine cognitive: Analytical	Nonroutine cognitive: Interpersonal	Routine cognitive	Routine manual	Nonroutine manual physical	Nonroutine cognitive: Analytical	Nonroutine cognitive: Interpersonal	Routine cognitive	Routine manual	Nonroutine manual physical
HUN-Hungary										
2002	50	50	50	50	50	50	50	50	50	50
2003	50	55	50	49	50	50	50	51	50	50
2004	50	55	48	49	50	50	50	51	50	50
2005	54	55	48	49	50	50	50	51	50	50
2006	50	55	48	49	50	50	50	53	50	50
2007	55	55	48	49	50	50	55	53	50	48
2008	57	55	48	49	50	50	55	50	50	50
2009	57	59	48	40	42	50	55	50	50	48
2010	56	56	48	49	50	50	55	50	50	50
Average	53.6	55.6	48.3	47.9	49.0	50.0	52.5	51.1	50.0	49.5
LTU-Lithuania										
2002	50	50	50	50	50	50	50	50	50	50
2003	47	50	48	50	50	50	50	50	49	50
2004	50	50	50	50	50	50	50	50	49	50

	c. Cohort born after 1974					d. Cohort born before 1955				
	Nonroutine cognitive: Analytical	Nonroutine cognitive: Interpersonal	Routine cognitive	Routine manual	Nonroutine manual physical	Nonroutine cognitive: Analytical	Nonroutine cognitive: Interpersonal	Routine cognitive	Routine manual	Nonroutine manual physical
2005	50	50	50	50	50	50	50	50	49	50
2006	47	50	50	50	48	50	50	59	49	50
2007	50	64	50	46	48	50	50	59	49	50
2008	65	64	59	40	39	60	50	59	49	40
2009	65	72	59	40	34	60	50	59	39	40
2010	72	72	59	30	31	61	66	59	39	40
Average	*55.8*	*59.0*	*53.1*	*44.5*	*43.8*	*53.9*	*52.0*	*55.6*	*46.5*	*46.3*
LVA-Latvia										
2002	50	50	50	50	50	50	50	50	50	50
2003	49	50	50	56	54	50	50	50	50	50
2004	50	50	50	56	50	50	50	55	50	50
2005	49	52	54	50	50	50	50	50	50	50
2006	50	55	54	50	50	50	50	50	50	50
2007	58	59	54	47	50	55	50	55	50	50
2008	58	59	54	50	50	55	50	55	50	50
2009	64	59	50	45	42	55	50	50	43	44
2010	64	59	50	46	41	55	50	50	43	44
Average	*55.3*	*55.4*	*52.0*	*50.0*	*48.4*	*51.9*	*50.0*	*51.3*	*48.3*	*48.5*

continued

TABLE 3A.1
Continued

	e. Cohort born after 1974					f. Cohort born before 1955				
	Nonroutine cognitive: Analytical	Nonroutine cognitive: Interpersonal	Routine cognitive	Routine manual	Nonroutine manual physical	Nonroutine cognitive: Analytical	Nonroutine cognitive: Interpersonal	Routine cognitive	Routine manual	Nonroutine manual physical
POL-Poland										
2002	50	50	50	50	50	50	50	50	50	50
2003	50	53	50	49	48	50	50	50	47	47
2004	50	50	50	49	48	50	50	56	47	47
2005	50	50	50	45	48	50	50	56	50	50
2006	50	50	50	45	48	50	50	60	46	47
2007	50	53	50	45	48	50	50	58	50	50
2008	50	53	50	45	44	50	50	56	50	50
2009	62	68	50	45	42	50	50	56	47	47
2010	62	68	50	45	42	50	50	59	46	47
Average	53.0	55.6	50.0	46.0	46.0	50.0	50.0	56.4	47.9	48.1
ROM-Romania										
2002	50	50	50	50	50	50	50	50	50	50
2003	50	50	49	50	49	50	50	50	50	50

	e. Cohort born after 1974					f. Cohort born before 1955				
	Nonroutine cognitive: Analytical	Nonroutine cognitive: Interpersonal	Routine cognitive	Routine manual	Nonroutine manual physical	Nonroutine cognitive: Analytical	Nonroutine cognitive: Interpersonal	Routine cognitive	Routine manual	Nonroutine manual physical
2004	50	50	50	50	49	50	50	50	50	50
2005	50	50	50	50	47	50	50	50	50	50
2006	50	50	50	50	47	50	50	50	50	50
2007	50	50	50	50	39	50	50	50	50	50
2008	50	50	50	50	39	50	50	50	50	50
2009	50	50	50	50	39	50	50	50	50	50
2010	50	50	50	50	39	50	50	50	50	50
Average	50.0	50.0	49.9	50.0	43.5	50.0	50.0	50.0	50.0	50.0
SVK-Slovak Republic										
2002	50	50	50	50	50	50	50	50	50	50
2003	50	55	50	50	50	49	50	50	50	50
2004	50	55	50	50	50	50	53	50	50	46
2005	51	55	50	47	50	49	53	50	50	50
2006	50	55	50	50	50	49	50	50	50	50
2007	52	55	50	52	50	49	50	50	50	50
2008	52	55	50	50	50	48	50	50	50	50
2009	55	57	50	47	50	48	53	48	50	50
2010	57	65	50	47	50	50	53	50	50	46
Average	52.1	56.5	50.0	49.1	50.0	49.0	51.5	49.8	50.0	49.0

continued

TABLE 3A.1
Continued

	g. Cohort born after 1974					h. Cohort born before 1955				
	Nonroutine cognitive: Analytical	Nonroutine cognitive: Interpersonal	Routine cognitive	Routine manual	Nonroutine manual physical	Nonroutine cognitive: Analytical	Nonroutine cognitive: Interpersonal	Routine cognitive	Routine manual	Nonroutine manual physical
SVN-Slovenia										
2002	50	50	50	50	50	50	50	50	50	50
2003	50	55	50	48	50	54	50	54	48	44
2004	50	55	50	48	50	54	50	54	48	49
2005	50	55	50	50	50	50	50	54	48	49
2006	50	55	50	49	50	50	50	50	48	49
2007	56	55	50	48	50	50	50	41	50	86
2008	59	58	45	48	50	50	50	47	50	58
2009	60	58	45	48	40	50	50	41	50	57
2010	70	58	45	38	40	50	50	41	50	57
Average	55.6	55.8	48.1	47.1	47.5	51.0	50.0	47.8	49.0	56.1

	g. Cohort born after 1974					h. Cohort born before 1955				
	Nonroutine cognitive: Analytical	Nonroutine cognitive: Interpersonal	Routine cognitive	Routine manual	Nonroutine manual physical	Nonroutine cognitive: Analytical	Nonroutine cognitive: Interpersonal	Routine cognitive	Routine manual	Nonroutine manual physical
GEO-Georgia										
2002	50	50	50	50	50	50	50	50	50	50
2007	62	59	58	50	50	45	48	50	58	59
2010	62	61	65	50	50	45	48	46	58	59
Average	62.0	60.0	61.5	50.0	50.0	45.0	48.0	48.0	58.0	59.0
HRV-Croatia										
2001	50	50	50	50	50	50	50	50	50	50
2002	50	50	55	50	50	50	50	50	50	50
2003	57	50	55	50	50	50	50	47	77	53
2004	57	50	55	55	50	50	50	47	77	55
2008	64	58	56	50	50	50	50	47	77	53
Average	57.0	52.0	55.3	51.3	50.0	50.0	50.0	47.8	70.3	52.8

continued

TABLE 3A.1
Continued

	g. Cohort born after 1974					h. Cohort born before 1955				
	Nonroutine cognitive: Analytical	Nonroutine cognitive: Interpersonal	Routine cognitive	Routine manual	Nonroutine manual physical	Nonroutine cognitive: Analytical	Nonroutine cognitive: Interpersonal	Routine cognitive	Routine manual	Nonroutine manual physical
MKD-Macedonia, FYR										
2007	50	50	50	50	50	50	50	50	50	50
2008	50	50	50	51	51	48	50	47	54	55
2009	51	66	50	46	47	47	50	50	54	53
2010	54	66	46	46	46	45	50	47	54	56
2011	60	66	43	48	48	47	50	46	54	54
Average	53.8	62.0	47.3	47.8	48.0	46.8	50.0	47.5	54.0	54.5
UKR-Ukraine										
2001	50	50	50	50	50	50	50	50	50	50
2004	50	50	50	50	50	50	49	50	58	59

Notes

1. Examples of comprehensive studies covering countries in Europe and Central Asia are European Commission (2012b); Cedefop (2012c); OECD 2012a; Mourshed, Farrell, and Barton (2012); Sondergaard et al. (2012).
2. As noted in the recent EC (2012b); OECD (2012a); Sondergaard et al. (2012).
3. This is the proportion of firms answering affirmatively to the question "Did your establishment encounter any of the following problems related to personnel: (a) Difficulties in finding staff for skilled jobs; (b) Difficulties in finding staff for low-skilled or unskilled jobs." The figures are simple averages for each country group computed from data reported in EC (2012b).
4. Eurobarometer (2010). The survey covered all 27 EU member states, as well as Norway, Iceland, Croatia, and Turkey. Companies included in this study had recruited higher education graduates in the past five years and/or were planning to recruit such graduates in the next five years.
5. These figures are rescaled percentages among the recruiters who answered what the two most important challenges are when filling their vacancies. Nineteen percent of graduate recruiters did not answer the question, while 33 percent and 25 percent of those surveyed chose a shortage of applicants with the right skills and the difficulty in offering a competitive starting salary as answers.
6. See for example the recent Eurobarometer report, *Employers' Perception of Graduate Employability* (2010). See Bowles and Gintis (1998) for evidence of employer surveys from the United States and the United Kingdom; Blom and Saeki (2011) for a study for India; and Aedo and Walker (2012) for evidence from Latin America.
7. See Borghans et al. (2008) for a literature review; Brunello and Schlotter (2011) for Europe; Heckman, Stixrud, and Urzua (2006) for the United States; and Aedo and Walker (2012) for Latin America.
8. The obsolescence of skills arises when these are no longer adequate to maintain effective performance in the job, because they depreciate or become outdated over time due to aging, there is a diffusion of new technologies, there are new forms of work organization, and career interruptions occur (De Grip and van Loo 2002; Kaufman 1974).
9. The estimations are done for two other cohorts: those born between 1955 and 1964 and those born between 1965 and 1974. The results for the former cohort tend to mimic those found for the oldest cohort, while the second cohort shows mixed results—in some cases mimicking the young cohort and in others behaving more like the older cohort.
10. The results are broadly aligned with other existing studies on the demand for skills in some ECA countries (summarized in Sondergaard et al. 2012), although these rely on data from changes in occupations and education levels not on the various skills-intensities of jobs.
11. EC (several years); Cedefop (several years); OECD (several years); among others.
12. Idem.
13. The questions on skills constraints in firm surveys generally do not specify to employers which segment of the labor force to focus on when answering.

14. Heritability and environmental influence both determine how these skills are developed. See Heckman and Cunha (2007).
15. For example, the forthcoming Russia skills and education study (World Bank 2013a) and the Europe 2020 study (World Bank 2011).
16. World Bank (2013b).
17. World Bank (2012b); EC (2012a);
18. Idem.
19. At the center of this debate was Richard Freeman's book "The Overeducated American," published in 1976. See Berg (1970); Freeman (1975), (1976); Smith and Welch (1978).
20. The results from the Mincer analysis show that returns to secondary education (general and technical) over primary are smaller, and fell, rose only slightly, or stagnated in these countries during this period.
21. Skills development is prominent in the "smart and inclusive growth" pillars of the Europe 2020 Strategy and related policy documents (Lisbon agenda, Europe 2020); in the strategies devised in the Bologna Process, of which virtually all ECA countries are part; and in national development strategies (e.g., the human capital strategy of Poland). See Arnhold et al. (2011).
22. The foregoing discussion is based on Almeida, Behrman, and Robalino (2012).
23. For example, Gill, Fluitman, and Dar (2000) report that in Hungary employers felt that government exerted excessive control over funds and that this limited their effectiveness.
24. See the recent review by Smith (2011). Munch, Skipper, and Jespersen (2008) provide a notable Danish example, while Raaum, Torp, and Zhang (2002) do the same for Norway. Osikominu (2009) shows a more common situation, with only a very rudimentary comparison of costs and impacts.
25. This was actually the case in the evaluation of German training programs by Lechner, Miquel, and Wunsch (2011).

Bibliography

Acemoglu, Daron, and David Autor. 2011. "Skills, Tasks and Technologies: Implications for Employment and Earnings." In *Handbook of Labor Economics*, edited by David Card and Orley Ashenfelter, 1043–171. Vol. 4 (part B). Philadelphia, PA: Elsevier.

Aedo, Cristian, Jesko Hentschel, Javier Luque, and Martin Moreno. 2012. "Skills around the World: Structure and Recent Dynamics." Background paper for the *World Development Report 2013*, World Bank, Washington, DC.

Aedo, Cristian, and Ian Walker. 2012. "Skills for the 21st Century in Latin America and the Caribbean." World Bank, Washington, DC.

Almeida, K. Rita, and Reyes Aterido. 2010. "Investment in Job Training: Why Are SMEs Lagging So Much Behind?" World Bank Policy Research Working Paper 5358, Washington, DC.

Almeida, K. Rita, Jere Behrman, and David Robalino. 2012. "The Right Skills for the Job? Rethinking Training Policies for Workers." World Bank Publications 13075, Summer.

Arnhold, Nina, Itzhak Goldberg, Natasha Kapil, Marcin Piatkowski, and Jan Rutkowski. 2011. "Europe 2020 Poland: Fueling Growth and Competitiveness in Poland Through Employment, Skills, and Innovation." World Bank, Washington, DC.

Autor, H. David. 2001. "Why Do Temporary Help Firms Provide Free General Skills Training?" *Quarterly Journal of Economics* 116 (4): 1409–48.

Autor, H. David, Frank Levy, and Richard J. Murnane. 2003. "The Skill Content of Recent Technological Change: An Empirical Exploration." *Quarterly Journal of Economics* 118 (4): 1279–333.

Barrick, R. Murray, and Michael K. Mount. 1991. "The Big Five Personality Dimensions and Job Performance: A Meta-Analysis." *Personnel Psychology* 44 (1): 1–26. doi:10.1111/j.1744-6570.1991.tb00688.x.

———. 1993. "Autonomy as a Moderator of the Relationships between the Big Five Personality Dimensions and Job Performance." *Journal of Applied Psychology* 78 (1): 111–18.

Barrick, R. Murray, Michael K. Mount, and Timothy A. Judge. 2001. "Personality and Performance at the Beginning of the New Millennium: What Do We Know and Where Do We Go Next?" *International Journal of Selection and Assessment* 9 (1–2): 9–30.

Bennett, Jessica, and Seamus McGuinness. 2009. "Assessing the Impact of Skill Shortages on the Productivity Performance of High-Tech firms in Northern Ireland." *Applied Economics* 41 (6): 727–37.

Berg, Ivar. 1970. *Education and Jobs: The Great Training Robbery*. New York: Praeger.

Besharov, J. Douglas, and Phoebe H. Cottingham, eds. 2011. *The Workforce Investment Act: Implementation Experiences and Evaluation Findings*. Kalzamazoo, MI: Upjohn Institute for Employment Research.

Betcherman, Gordon, Karina Olivas, and Amit Dar. 2004. "Impacts of Active Labor Market Programs: New Evidence from Evaluations with Particular Attention to Developing and Transition Countries." Social Protection Discussion Paper 0402, World Bank, Washington, DC.

Blom, Andreas, and Hiroshi Saeki. 2011. "Employability and Skill Set of Newly Graduated Engineers in India." World Bank Policy Research Working Paper Series 5640.

Borghans, Lex, Angela Lee Duckworth, James J. Heckman, and Bas ter Weel. 2008. "The Economics and Psychology of Personality Traits." *Journal of Human Resources*, University of Wisconsin Press, 43(4).

Bowles, Samuel, and Herbert Gintis. 1998. "Schooling, Skills and Earnings: A Principal-Agent Approach." In *Meritocracy and Economic Inequality*, edited by Kenneth Arrow, Samuel Bowles, and Steven Durlauf. Princeton, NJ: Princeton University Press.

Bowles, Samuel, Herbert Gintis, and Melissa Osborne. 2001. "The Determinants of Earnings: A Behavioral Approach." *Journal of Economic Literature* 39 (4): 1137–76.

Brunello, Giorgio, and Martin Schlotter. 2011. "Non Cognitive Skills and Personality Traits: Labour Market Relevance and their Development in Education & Training Systems." IZA Discussion Paper 5743, Institute for the Study of Labor, Bonn, Germany.

Business Europe. 2012. "Plugging the Skills Gap: The Clock Is Ticking (Science, Technology and Maths)." http://www.businesseurope.eu /Content/default.asp?pageid=568&docid=28659.

Campos, Nauro, and Dean Jolliffe. 2007. "Earnings, Schooling, and Economic Reform: Econometric Evidence from Hungary (1986–2004)." *World Bank Economic Review* 21(3): 509–26.

Canning, Mary, Martin Godfrey, and Dorota Holzer-Zelazewska. 2007. *Vocational Education in the New EU Member States: Enhancing Labor Market Outcomes and Fiscal Efficiency*. Washington, DC: World Bank.

Card, David, Jochen Kluve, and Andrea Weber. 2010. "Active Labour Market Policy Evaluations: A Meta-Analysis." *Economic Journal* 120 (548): F452–77.

Carneiro, Pedro, Omar Arias, and Natasha Falcao. 2013. "Average and Marginal Returns to Education in Poland." Background paper for this book. World Bank, mimeo.

Carneiro, Pedro, Karsten T. Hansen, and James J. Heckman. 2003. "Estimating Distributions of Treatment Effects with an Application to the Returns to Schooling and Measurement of the Effects of Uncertainty on College Choice," IZA Discussion Paper 767, Institute for the Study of Labor, Bonn, Germany.

Caroli, Eve, and John Van Reenen. 2001. "Skill-Biased Organizational Change? Evidence from a Panel of British and French Establishments." *The Quarterly Journal of Economics* 116 (4): 1449–92.

CASEL (Collaborative for Academic, Social, and Emotional Learning). 2011. *Student Self-Report Scale of Social and Emotional Competence*. Chicago, IL: CASEL.

Cedefop (European Center for the Development of Vocational Training). 2008. "Sectoral Training Funds in Europe." Cedefop Panorama Series 156, Luxemburg.

———. 2010. "Employer-Provided Vocational Training in Europe." Cedefop Research Paper 2, Publications Office of the European Union, Luxembourg.

———. 2011. *Learning while Working: Success Stories on Workplace Learning in Europe*. Luxembourg: Publications Office of the European Union.

———. 2012a. *From Education to Working Life: The Labour Market-Outcomes of VET*. Luxembourg: Publications Office of the European Union.

———. 2012b. Skills Forecasts Online Tool. http://www.cedefop.europa.eu /EN/about-cedefop/projects/forecasting-skill-demand-and-supply/skills -forecasts.aspx.

———. 2012c. "Skill Mismatch: The Role of the Enterprise." Cedefop Research Paper 21, Publications Office of the European Union, Luxembourg.

———. Forthcoming. *The Labour Market Outcomes of VET in Europe: Evidence from the LFS Survey*. Luxembourg: Publications Office of the European Union.

Cunha, Flavio, James J. Heckman, and Susanne Schennach. 2010. "Estimating the Technology of Cognitive and Noncognitive Skill Formation." IZA Discussion Papers 4702, Institute for the Study of Labor, Bonn, Germany.

De Grip, Andries, and Jasper van Loo. 2002. "The Economics of Skills Obsolescence: A Review." In *The Economics of Skills Obsolescence: Theoretical Innovations and Empirical Applications,* edited by Andries de Grip, Jasper van Loo, and Ken Mayhew. Research in Labor Economics 21: 1–26.

Dearden, Lorraine, Howard Reed, and John Van Reenen. 2000. "Who Gains when Workers Train? Training and Corporate Productivity in a Panel of British Industries." CEPR Discussion Papers 2486.

Duckworth, L. Angela, Christopher Peterson, Michael D. Matthews, and Dennis R. Kelly. 2007. "Grit: Perseverance and Passion for Long-Term Goals." *Journal of Personality and Social Psychology* 92 (6): 1087–101.

Durlak, A. Joseph., Roger P. Weissberg, Allison B. Dymnicki, Rebecca D. Taylor, and Kriston B. Schellinger. 2011. "The Impact of Enhancing Students' Social and Emotional Learning: A Meta-Analysis of School-Based Universal Interventions." *Child Development* 82 (1): 405–32.

EC (European Commission). 2011a. *Communication on Early Childhood Education and Care: Providing All Our Children with the Best Start for the World of Tomorrow.* COM (2011) 66. Brussels: EC.

———. 2011b. *Satisfying Labour Demand through Migration.* Brussels: European Migration Network, EC. http://ec.europa.eu/home-affairs/policies /immigration/docs/Satisfying_Labour_Demand_Through_Migration _FINAL_20110708.PDF.

———. 2012a. "Apprenticeship Supply in the Member States of the European Union." Directorate-General for Employment, Social Affairs, and Inclusion.

———. 2012b. *Employment and Social Developments in Europe 2012.* Brussels: Directorate-General for Employment, Social Affairs, and Inclusion, European Commission.

Eurobarometer. 2010. *Employers' Perception of Graduate Employability.* Flash Eurobarometer Series #304.

European Training Foundation. 2006. *Financing Vocational Education and Training in the EU New Member States and Candidate Countries: Recent Trends and Challenges.* Turin, Italy: European Community.

Flabbi, Luca, Stefano Paternostro, and Erwin R. Tiongson. 2007. "Returns to Education in the Economic Transition: A Systematic Assessment Using Comparable Data." Policy Research Working Paper Series 4225, World Bank, Washington, DC.

Freeman, B. Richard. 1975. "Overinvestment in College Training?" *Journal of Human Resources* 10 (3): 287–311.

———. 1976. *The Overeducated American.* New York: Academic Press.

Gill, Indermit, Fred Fluitman, and Amit Dar, eds. 2000. *Vocational Education and Training Reform: Matching Skills to Markets and Budgets.* New York: Oxford University Press for the International Labour Organization and World Bank.

Goos, Maarten, and Alan Manning. 2007. "Lousy and Lovely Jobs: The Rising Polarization of Work in Britain." *The Review of Economics and Statistics* 89 (1): 118–33.

Goos, Maarten, Alan Manning, and Anna Salomons. 2009. "Job Polarization in Europe." *American Economic Review* 99 (2): 58–63.

Grossman, M. Gene, and Esteban Rossi-Hansberg. 2008. "Trading Tasks: A Simple Theory of Offshoring." *American Economic Review* 98 (5): 1978–97.

Handel, J. Michael. 2012. "Trends in Job Skill Demands in OECD Countries." OECD Social, Employment and Migration Working Papers 143, OECD Publishing. http://dx.doi.org/10.1787/5k8zk8pcq6td-en.

Hanushek, A. Eric, and Ludger Woessmann. 2009. "Schooling, Cognitive Skills, and the Latin American Growth Puzzle." NBER Working Paper w15066, Cambridge, MA.

Hanushek, A. Eric, Ludger Woessmann, and Lei Zhang. 2011. "General Education, Vocational Education and Labor Market Outcomes over the Life Cycle." NBER Working Paper w17504, Cambridge, MA.

Heckman, J. James. 2008. "Schools, Skills and Synapses." *Economic Inquiry* 46 (3): 289–324.

Heckman, J. James, and Flavio Cunha. 2007. "The Technology of Skill Formation." *American Economic Review* 97 (2): 31–47.

———. 2010. "Investing in Our Young People." NBER Working Paper w16201, Cambridge, MA.

Heckman, J. James, Lance Lochner, and Christopher Taber. 1998. "Explaining Rising Wage Inequality: Explorations with a Dynamic General Equilibrium Model of Labor Earnings with Heterogeneous Agents." NBER Working Papers 6384, Cambridge, MA.

Heckman, J. James, Lance Lochner, and Petra E. Todd. 2003. "Fifty Years of Mincer Earnings Regressions." IZA Discussion Paper 775, Institute for the Study of Labor, Bonn, Germany.

———. 2006. "Earnings Functions, Rates of Return and Treatment Effects: The Mincer Equation and Beyond." In *Handbook of the Economics of Education,* edited by Eric Hanushek and Finis Welch, Chapter 7. Vol. 1. Philadelphia, PA: Elsevier.

Heckman, J. James, Jora Stixrud, and Sergio Urzua. 2006. "The Effects of Cognitive and Noncognitive Abilities on Labor Market Outcomes and Social Behavior." *Journal of Labor Economics* 24 (3): 411–82.

Jakubowski, Maciej, Harry Anthony Patrinos, Emilio Ernesto Porta, and Jerzy Wisniewski. 2010. "The Impact of the 1999 Education Reform in Poland." Policy Research Working Paper Series 5263, World Bank, Washington, DC.

Johnson, Sandra, and Kathleen Taylor. 2006. *The Neuroscience of Adult Learning. New Directions for Adult and Continuing Education.* Jossey-Bass.

Katz, Lawrence F, and Kevin M. Murphy. 1992. "Changes in Relative Wages, 1963–1987: Supply and Demand Factors." *The Quarterly Journal of Economics* 107 (1): 35–78.

Kaufman, G. Harold. 1974. *Obsolescence and Professional Career Development.* New York: AMACOM.

Lechner, Michael, Ruth Miquel, and Conny Wunsch. 2011. "Long-Run Effects of Public Sector Sponsored Training In West Germany." *Journal of the European Economic Association* 9 (4): 742–84, 08.

Leuven, Edwin, and Hessel Oosterbeek. 2011. "Overeducation and Mismatch in the Labor Market." IZA Discussion Paper 5523, Institute for the Study of Labor, Bonn, Germany.

Levy, Frank, and Richard J. Murnane. 1996. "With What Skills Are Computers a Complement?" *American Economic Review* 86 (2): 258–62.

Maestas, Nicole, and Julie Zissimopoulos. 2010. "How Longer Work Lives Ease the Crunch of Population Aging." *Journal of Economic Perspectives* 24 (1): 139–60, Winter.

McKinsey. 2011. "How the World's Most Improved Systems Keep Getting Better." McKinsey, Washington, DC.

Mitra, Pradeep, Marcelo Selowsky, and Juan Zalduendo. 2010. *Turmoil at Twenty: Recession, Recovery, and Reform in Central and Eastern Europe and the Former Soviet Union.* Washington, DC: World Bank. https://openknowledge.worldbank.org/handle/10986/2682.

Mourshed, M., D. Farrell, and D. Barton. 2012. "Education to Employment: Designing a System That Works." McKinsey Center for Government, Washington, DC.

Munch, R. Jakob, Lars Skipper, and Svend Jespersen. 2008. "Costs and Benefits of Danish Active Labour Market Programmes." Labour Economics 15: 859–84.

OECD (Organisation for Economic Co-operation and Development). 2009. "Learning for Jobs: OECD Policy review of Vocational Education and Training" (Initial Report). OECD, Paris.

———. 2010. "PISA 2009 Results: Learning Trends. Changes in Student Performance since 2000" (Volume V). OECD, Paris.

———. 2011a. "Right for the Job: Over-Qualified or Under-Skilled?" In *OECD Employment Outlook,* 191–233. Paris: OECD.

———. 2011b. *OECD Science, Technology and Industry Scoreboard 2011.* Paris: OECD. http://www.oecd-ilibrary.org/science-and-technology/oecd-science-technology-and-industry-scoreboard-2011_sti_scoreboard-2011-en.

———. 2012a. *Better Skills, Better Jobs, Better Lives: A Strategic Approach to Skills Policies.* Paris: OECD. http://dx.doi.org/10.1787/9789264177338-en.

———. 2012b. *Connecting with Emigrants: A Global Profile of Diasporas.* Paris: OECD. http://www.oecd-ilibrary.org/content/book/9789264177949-en.

Open Society Institute. 2013. "Net Returns to Higher Education in Bulgaria." Open Society Institute, Sofia.

Osikominu, Aderonke. 2009. "Quick Job Entry or Long-Term Human Capital Development? The Dynamic Effects of Alternative Training Schemes." IZA Discussion Paper 4638, Institute for the Study of Labor, Bonn, Germany.

Raaum, Oddbjorn, Hege Torp, and Tao Zhang. 2002. "Do Individual Programme Effects Exceed the Costs? Norwegian Evidence on Long Run Effects of Labour Market Training." Memoranda, 15/2002, Department of Economics, University of Oslo.

Roberts, W. Brent, Nathan R. Kuncel, Rebecca Shiner, Avshalom Caspi, and Lewis R. Goldberg. 2007. "The Power of Personality: The Comparative Validity of Personality Traits, Socioeconomic Status, and Cognitive Ability for Predicting Important Life Outcomes." *Perspectives on Psychological Science* 2 (4): 313–45.

Rutkowski, Jan. 1996. "High Skills Pay Off: The Changing Wage Structure during Economic Transition in Poland." *Economics of Transition* 4: 89–112. doi:10.1111/j.1468-0351.1996.tb00163.x.

———. 2001. "Earnings Inequality in Transition Economies of Central Europe. Trends and Patterns during the 1990s." Social Protection Discussion Paper 0117, World Bank, Washington, DC.

Smith, P. James, and Finis Welch. 1978. "The Overeducated American? A Review Article." UCLA Economics Working Papers 147, UCLA Department of Economics.

Smith, Jeffrey. 2011. "Improving Impact Evaluation in Europe." In *The Workforce Investment Act: Implementation Experiences and Evaluation Findings*. Besharov, Douglas J., and Phoebe H. Cottingham, eds. Kalamazoo, MI: W.E. Upjohn Institute for Employment Research.

Sondergaard, Lars, Mamta Murthi, with Dina Abu-Ghaida, Christian Bodewig, and Jan Rutkowski. 2012. *Skills, Not Just Diplomas: Managing Education for Results in Eastern Europe and Central Asia*. Directions in Development. Washington, DC: World Bank.

Staneva, V. Anita, Reza Arabsheibani, and Philip D. Murphy. 2010. "Returns to Education in Four Transition Countries: Quantile Regression Approach." IZA Discussion Paper 5210, Institute for the Study of Labor, Bonn, Germany.

UK Department for Business, Innovation and Skills. 2011. *STEM Graduates in Non-STEM Jobs*. London: UK Department for Business, Innovation and Skills.

UK Department for Innovation, Universities and Skills. 2009. *The Demand for Science, Technology, Engineering and Mathematics (STEM) Skills*. London: UK Department for Innovation, Universities and Skills.

UNESCO (United Nations Educational, Scientific and Cultural Organization). 2003. *Global Education Digest*. Institute for Statistics.

———. 2012. *Global Education Digest*. Institute for Statistics.

World Bank. 2009. *Ukraine: Labor Demand Study*. Washington, DC: World Bank.

———. 2011. "Europe 2020: The Employment, Skills and Innovation Agenda." World Bank Technical Note No. 60847.

———. 2012a. "Ireland—Workforce Development." Systems Approach for Better Education Results (SABER) multiyear country report 2012. World Bank, Washington, DC. http://documents.worldbank.org/curated /en/2012/01/18104048/ireland-workforce-development.

———. 2012b. *World Development Report 2013: Jobs*. Washington, DC: World Bank.

———. 2013a. "Developing Skills for Innovative Growth in the Russian Federation." Report No: ACS1549.

———. 2013b. "Reforming Technical and Vocational Education and Training (TVET)? A Practical Primer." Education Sector in the ECA Region. World Bank, Washington, DC.

CHAPTER 4

Getting More People into Productive Jobs: Addressing Disincentives and Barriers to Employment

Introduction

Imagine a poor young woman, mother of two, in an urban area of a country in the Europe and Central Asia (ECA) region. It is often hard for such a woman to search for and find a job outside her home. Social norms in her community, for one, dictate that women are responsible for household and family care. These norms inevitably influence her labor market choices and opportunities and limit the time that she can dedicate to working outside the home, particularly when affordable child care options are not available. Even if she could and decided to work, she would very likely earn less than men with the same qualifications and, in some settings, face a tax system that penalizes part-time, low-wage, and second earners such as her. Besides these obstacles and disincentives, this woman could possibly face many others—e.g., lack of flexible work arrangements, inadequate skills, and discrimination—further excluding her from labor markets. If she belonged to an ethnic minority, her opportunities to search for and find a job would be even slimmer in many cases. Many of these disincentives and barriers to work are faced not only by women in ECA but also by younger and older workers and ethnic minorities.

There are too few people in productive jobs and self-employment in ECA, particularly among younger and older workers, women, and ethnic minorities. Precrisis, less than two-thirds of household income came from work in ECA; this is around 10 percentage points lower than for Latin American countries.[1] Earlier chapters in this report have shown that a large part of the jobs problem in ECA stems from weak net job creation in the private sector. However, there is also an important set of disincentives and barriers to work that contribute to poor employment performance among particular groups. Labor market institutions, tax and social protection systems, and the rules and norms that govern employment today have been designed mainly for prime-age male workers, thus inadvertently excluding many from work and limiting the employment and growth potential of the region.

The average labor force participation (LFP) rate in ECA countries masks large inequalities across gender, education, and age groups (figure 4.1). As described in chapter 1, younger workers are more likely to be out of work than prime-age workers, due to both inactivity (particularly among young females) and unemployment (particularly among young males). Youth also have been particularly hard hit by unemployment in recent years amid the economic crisis. In most ECA countries where data are available, youth unemployment rates have increased more than twice as much as adult unemployment rates since the onset of the crisis. Similarly, older workers drop out of the labor force earlier in ECA than in other regions, resulting in many years of productive life lost. Moreover, as in many other parts of the world, women continue to have poorer labor market outcomes than men, not only with lower participation rates, but also with significantly lower earnings.[2] Finally, ethnic minorities, such as Roma, which represent a growing share of the young population in several countries in ECA, also often experience unemployment and joblessness rates that are considerably higher than those among the rest of the population.[3]

Longer and more productive (formal) working lives are critical to the health and sustainability of the ECA growth and social models. Low employment rates coexist with extensive social welfare systems, primarily driven by high pension spending.[4] While playing a key role in protecting the poor and the vulnerable, and helping individuals make efficient labor market transitions, these programs can be better aligned with work. Moreover, high informality in some countries means that relatively few people financially support these welfare systems. For each person contributing to social security, on average, almost three are not (figure 4.2). This dependency ratio is more than twice that of OECD countries and will worsen over time due to the region's demographic trends.

FIGURE 4.1

Average Labor Force Participation (LFP) Rates Mask Large Inequalities

LFP by group in selected ECA countries

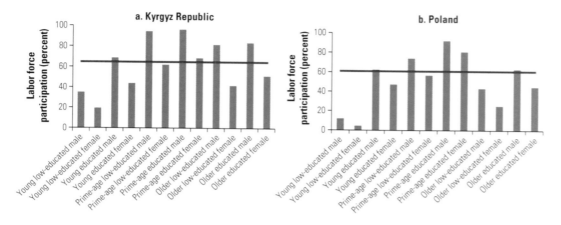

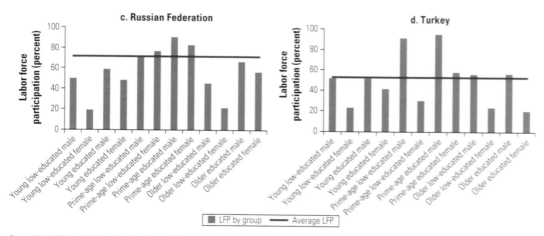

Source: World Bank calculations based on household and labor force surveys.
Note: Young refers to ages 15–24; *prime-age* to 25–49; and *older* to 50–64 years. *Low-educated workers* refers to those who have completed secondary education or less.

This will mean that ever larger pools of retirees will need to be financed by smaller and smaller pools of workers (World Bank forthcoming b). Hence, the challenge for policy makers is to encourage longer working lives and to bring in new labor market entrants—younger and older workers, women, and ethnic minorities. This will not only contribute to the sustainability of the system but, more broadly, as argued in the *World Development Report 2013,* it will improve living standards, productivity, and social cohesion (World Bank 2012l).

FIGURE 4.2

Few People Financially Support Social Security Systems in ECA

Noncontributing versus contributing populations (all ages) to ECA social security, 2007–10

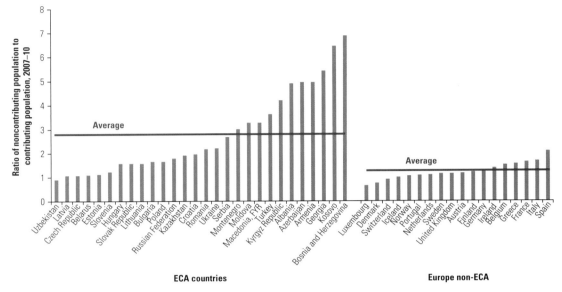

ECA countries   **Europe non-ECA**

Source: Calculations with data from World Development Indicators and the World Bank pensions database.
Note: Contributors correspond to individuals contributing to social security or accruing pension rights even if they are not contributors; the estimates presented here are, therefore, a lower bound. Data are for latest year available between 2007 and 2010, with the exception of Estonia (2004), Georgia (2004), Slovak Republic (2003), and Uzbekistan (2005).

This chapter focuses on two main questions:

1. Do tax and social protection systems in ECA undermine work incentives? Policies aimed at removing constraints to firms' growth (chapter 2) are important, but firms must also feel that it is financially worthwhile to hire and workers must feel it is worthwhile to seek (formal) work. Labor taxes and social protection systems (social assistance programs, unemployment benefits, and pensions),[5] along with labor regulations (discussed in chapter 1), could create disincentives to work and make labor markets less competitive. To support job creation, attract people into (formal) work, and promote more inclusive labor markets, the chapter argues, first, that it is the design of labor taxes and social protection systems that has the highest potential to create disincentives to work. Critically, this can be done without reducing coverage or generosity of social protection systems. It would also be desirable to reduce the burden of labor taxation where there is fiscal space to do so, make it more progressive and responsive to differences in hours worked and household structure that currently penalize low-wage, part-time, and second earners. Overall pension reform and improvements to

the design of social assistance and unemployment benefits, particularly by removing explicit bans or penalties to (formal) work, are also central to the jobs agenda.

2. Are there additional barriers to productive employability affecting younger and older workers, women, and ethnic minorities? While disincentives arising from tax and benefit systems can be important, they leave unsolved a large part of the jobs problem: Beneficiaries of most social programs in ECA represent only a small share of the overall population out of work and, even if these systems do discourage employment, they are likely to be only one of the multiple factors affecting labor market outcomes. This chapter argues that barriers among younger and older workers, women, and ethnic minorities include lack of adequate skills (chapter 3); low mobility (chapter 5); lack of child and elder care options; limited flexible work arrangements; imperfect access to productive inputs, networks, and information; and/or adverse attitudes and social norms. Besides their own impact on limiting access to jobs, these barriers often reinforce each other (figure 4.3)

FIGURE 4.3

Mutually Reinforcing Barriers to Employment for Younger and Older Workers, Women, and Ethnic Minorities

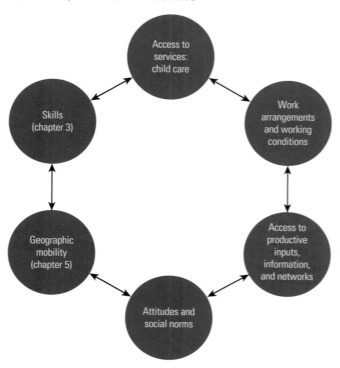

and interact with disincentives from labor tax and social protection systems to further exacerbate exclusion from labor markets. Younger and older workers, women, and ethnic minorities thus face twin problems: disincentives to work from labor taxes, regulations, and social protection systems, and market, social, and institutional barriers to employment. Targeted, evidence-based activation policies that go beyond welfare dependency and overcome employability barriers are fundamental to promoting employment in the region.

The remainder of the chapter is organized as follows. The second section discusses the role of taxes and social protection systems in creating disincentives to (formal) employment and puts forward some policy options for countries in the region. The third section argues for the importance of promoting inclusive labor markets; identifies key obstacles to employability for younger and older workers, women, and ethnic minorities; and presents policy alternatives to overcoming these barriers to employment. The fourth and final section presents a summary of the proposed policy agenda.

Do Taxes and Social Protection Systems in ECA Create Disincentives to Work?

To get people into jobs, it has to pay to work and to hire workers. People will be more willing to get a (formal) job and work longer if they are able to appropriate the fruits of their efforts;[6] firms, in turn, will be more willing to hire if labor costs are linked to labor productivity. High and distortive labor taxation could lead to less hiring, lower LFP, fewer hours worked, and more informality.[7] Work disincentives can also arise from social protection benefits. These transfers are additional resources for the household and reduce its reliance on labor income as a source of livelihood. The design of social programs and pensions—including eligibility criteria and the abrupt withdrawal of social benefits as the person starts working or works longer—can further discourage work. Moreover, in the case of pensions, early retirement schemes and overall low retirement ages can push people into inactivity, even if they are in fact still healthy and productive. Hence, in order to attract more people into (formal) work and make labor markets more inclusive, it is necessary to reform tax and social protection systems in such a way that they promote employment rather than deter it.

High Labor Taxation in Some Countries Can Discourage Work, Especially Among Low-Wage Earners

There is large variation in labor taxation rates across ECA countries, with high rates concentrated mostly in EU-10 countries. On average, ECA countries tax away 36.8 percent of labor costs in the form of income taxes, payroll taxes, and social contributions (figure 4.4). This is the so-called tax wedge. Labor tax rates are lower than in OECD European countries but significantly higher than in other developed countries: in ECA, the tax wedge is 13 percentage points higher than in non-European OECD countries. Taxes on labor are particularly high in the Czech Republic, Hungary, Latvia, Romania, and Slovenia, with rates above 40 percent. In recent years, a number of countries with high taxation rates have actually increased them in the context of the crisis. Since 2007, Latvia, Romania, and Estonia have increased

FIGURE 4.4

Labor Taxation Is High in Many ECA Countries, Driven Mostly by Social Contributions
The "tax wedge" as a percentage of wages, 2011

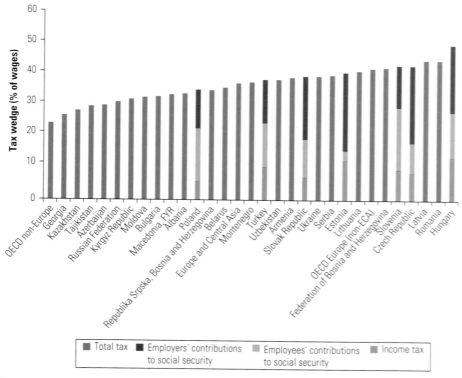

Sources: OECD 2012a; Institute for the Study of Labor (IZA) Database.
Note: Tax wedge calculated for a single person without children at the average wage. For ECA countries outside the EU or the Western Balkans, the tax wedge is calculated at 67 percent of the average wage for 2007. For Bosnia and Herzegovina, FYR Macedonia, and Serbia data are for 2009; for Bulgaria, Latvia, Lithuania, and Romania, data are for 2010. Bosnia and Herzegovina comprises two political entities: (a) Federation of Bosnia and Herzegovina; and (b) Republika Srpska, Bosnia and Herzegovina.

their tax wedge by 2.4, 1.3, and 1.2 percentage points, respectively. Other countries, however, have reduced the tax wedge; in particular, in Poland it fell by 3.7 percentage points while in Lithuania and Slovenia it fell by 2.4 percentage points during this period (Eurostat 2011). In FYR Macedonia, a significant tax reform effort has gradually reduced the tax wedge by more than 10 percentage points since 2008.

High labor taxes are driven mostly by high social contribution rates. In Poland, for example, social contributions (both employers' and employees') add up to 28.4 percent of wages, accounting for more than four-fifths of total labor taxation. These high contributions are used mostly to finance pension systems. In Ukraine, for example, contributions to old age, disability, and survivors pensions are approximately 36 percent of wages, taking up almost all labor taxes.[8] On average, in ECA countries, pension contributions account for more than two-thirds of all social security contributions (World Bank 2007a).

Labor taxes are not only often high in ECA but also less progressive than in Western European and other OECD countries. A number of countries, such as Bulgaria and Montenegro, have flat labor income tax rates that tax any additional euros earned from work the same, regardless of the level of earnings. In most other ECA countries, the tax wedge increases with wages but less sharply than in Western Europe (see figure 4.5). In some countries, such as FYR Macedonia and Serbia, this is driven by artificially high social contribution rates for low-wage earners through the so-called reference wages.[9] One exception to low progressivity in the region is Hungary: the tax wedge at the average wage is almost 15 percentage points higher than it is at one-third of the average wage (EC 2012c). Low progressivity in labor taxation is particularly harmful for young and older workers, women and ethnic minorities, who are most likely to be low-wage earners or part-time workers. In addition, particularly in a system with high taxes, low progressivity not only creates disincentives for low-wage earners to work or work formally but also means that hiring a low-wage earner is relatively more costly for employers.

Hence, labor taxes in the region are disproportionately high for the "wrong" groups—those whose employment is most sensitive to taxation.[10] On the one hand, low-wage earners—especially younger and older workers and women—are most responsive to tax and benefit changes. Young and older workers have alternative livelihood options outside the (formal) labor market: living with other working family members, working informally, or living off pension income in the case of older workers. Women face particularly steep work disincentives as they often live in households with other working adults and have a relatively high opportunity cost of working outside

FIGURE 4.5

Labor Taxation in ECA Countries Is Less Progressive Than in Western Europe

(Gap in tax wedge between average and low wage earners, 2008)

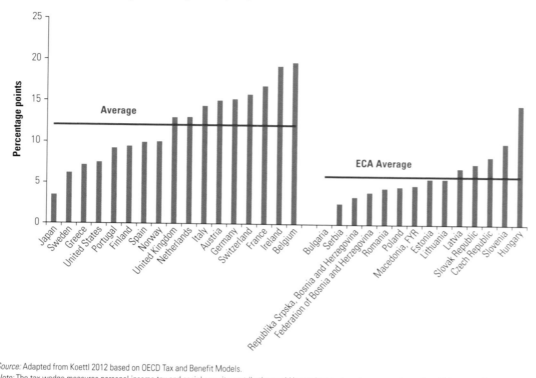

Source: Adapted from Koettl 2012 based on OECD Tax and Benefit Models.

Note: The tax wedge measures personal income tax and social security contributions paid by workers and employers as a share of total labor costs. The figure shows progressivity of labor taxation, as the tax wedge difference between average and low wage earners (for a single person with no children at 100 percent or 33 percent of average wage, respectively). Progressivity refers to the increase of the tax wedge in percentage points. Bosnia and Herzegovina comprises two political entities: (a) Federation of Bosnia and Herzegovina; and (b) Republika Srpska, Bosnia and Herzegovina.

the home given household and family responsibilities. On the other hand, these are groups for whom labor demand is more elastic: the market for this set of workers is often tighter than at higher wage and skills levels. This means that, often, higher labor taxation translates into higher labor costs for firms, thus potentially reducing employment among these groups.

The evidence shows that the average impact of labor taxation is generally modest and varies considerably depending on a country's level of development, links between social insurance and labor markets, labor market conditions, labor market institutions, and the quality of public services received (see spotlight 4.1).[11] Labor taxation appears to matter most when deciding whether to work or not and whether to do so formally or informally, rather than for decisions on hours worked. Importantly, the effects of taxation are very heterogeneous and impacts are found to be larger among younger and older workers, low-skilled and/or low-wage workers, and women—precisely the groups that show worst performance on general labor market outcomes and where reforms payoffs are likely to be the largest.[12]

For Social Protection, It Is Structure and Design That Matter Most

Rigorous empirical evidence on the labor market impacts of social protection benefits remains scarce. While the literature often finds that pensions can weaken work incentives among all members of the household, the evidence is more mixed for social assistance and unemployment benefits (spotlight 4.2). For example, social assistance programs have been found to create disincentives to participation and formal work, but mostly in high-income countries and particularly if benefits are close to wages of low-paid jobs (Adema 2006).[13] The very limited and scattered evidence available for developing countries, which includes some low- and low-middle-income ECA countries, suggests, however, that these effects are less important in these contexts given the usual low generosity of these benefits. While further research is needed, there appears to be significant room to make social protection systems more work compatible as they expand, especially in terms of their structure and design.

Social protection systems in ECA have—with the exception of pensions—low coverage and generosity, limiting the work disincentives that they can generate (spotlight 4.2). Social protection—including unemployment benefits, social assistance, and pensions—plays an important role in shielding households from poverty and overall vulnerability across the region. However, in terms of coverage and generosity, there is wide variation across countries and programs. Unemployment benefits have, on average, low coverage and low generosity in ECA, amounting to 24.2 percent of average earnings for low-wage workers. Similarly, social assistance benefits, although they sometimes cover a significant share of the population, are usually not very generous.[14] In cases where benefits are more generous relative to local wages, however, they do have the potential to discourage work: In Montenegro, for example, social assistance transfers accounted until recently for 75 percent of the minimum wage.[15] Contrary to unemployment benefits and social assistance, pensions in the region have high coverage (39.7 percent on average in ECA), driven not only by demographics (figure 4.6), but also by flexible eligibility criteria that allow for early retirement and for pensions beyond those associated with old-age.[16] Further, pensions can be generous. On average, for countries with available

FIGURE 4.6

ECA Pensions in the Region Have High Coverage, Driven Not Only by Demographics

Households reporting social benefits, including pensions, as source of income, 2010

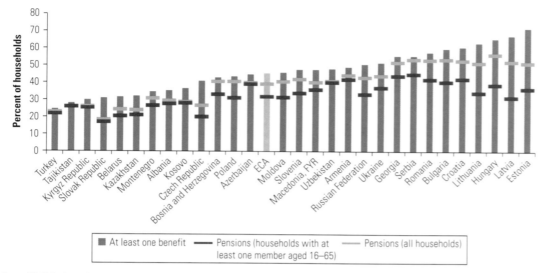

Source: World Bank calculations from Life in Transition Survey (LiTS) (EBRD and World Bank 2010).

Note: "Pensions (households with at least one member aged 16–65)" refers to households in which there is at least one member 16–65 years old; therefore, it excludes households composed only of elderly members. For countries where data from Household Budget Surveys is available, LiTS seems to underestimate the share of households receiving social benefits. The numbers in the figure could, therefore, be considered lower-bound estimates.

data, the net pension replacement rate for average earners is 80 percent, 11 percentage points higher than the OECD average.[17]

Beyond coverage and generosity, work disincentives can arise from eligibility criteria that effectively prohibit or discourage work. Exclusionary filters—designed to better target benefits to those most in need—can in practice have adverse results by, for example, excluding families in which any one member is economically active or has a (formal) job. One common filter is proof of unemployment status or registration with the public employment services (PES). Kosovo, for example, applies an unemployment status filter in its last resort social assistance program. In Albania, where the main social assistance program (Ndihma Ekonomike) excluded households with any working adult (except for rural households), conditions are being reformed to focus on a means test without exclusionary filters like this one (World Bank 2011e). Beyond requirements related to labor force status, these filters also often penalize households that own assets that could be critical for their productive lives (e.g., land and cars).

In many countries, eligibility criteria for social benefits or health insurance lead many to register as unemployed without really being active job seekers. This is the case when unemployment registration is a precondition for accessing these benefits. In the Western Balkans,

FIGURE 4.7

In Many Countries, Especially in the Western Balkans, There Are Strong Incentives to Register as Unemployed

Ratio of registered unemployed to total unemployed in ECA, 2009

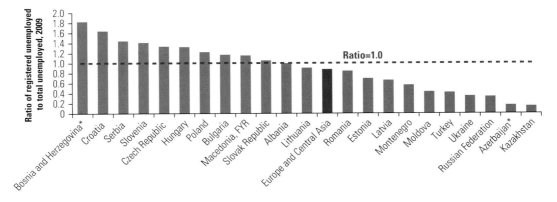

Source: Kuddo 2010.
Note: *2008 data.

the Czech Republic, Hungary, and Poland the ratio of registered unemployed to total unemployed according to labor force surveys is above 1.0 (figure 4.7). Some of these countries have moved to delinking some of the social benefits from unemployment registration, but the practice is still common.

Even when eligibility criteria do not explicitly prohibit work, social programs in the region often remove benefits too abruptly from people when starting to work. "I could earn 3000 denars a month working [informally] in a manufacturing factory; from all social assistance programs, I receive 2300 denars. For 700 denars a month, I will not leave my family and children."[18] This was the calculation done by a female social assistance beneficiary in her mid-40s in a focus group in FYR Macedonia when asked why she was not working. Indeed, in some countries, if a person starts to work, even one hour per week, social assistance or unemployment benefits are fully withdrawn. In other countries, social assistance benefits are withdrawn very abruptly as formal labor income increases. If workers have little to gain from starting to work formally or work more, they will have few incentives to come out of inactivity, open unemployment, or informality.

Work disincentives can be exacerbated by the fact that, in many cases, benefits are open-ended or of very long duration. In the Russian Federation, Serbia, and Slovenia, a person could be receiving unemployment benefits for up to two consecutive years; in Poland, for 18 months (U.S. Social Security Administration 2012). In most countries in the region, there are no explicit limits for benefit duration in social assistance as long as the eligibility conditions continue to be met. In Serbia it is estimated that approximately 90 percent of the able-bodied beneficiaries of its last-resort program reapply on a regular basis and have been beneficiaries for more than five years (World Bank 2011e). In some countries outside the region, reforms have moved toward instituting time limits for social transfers. In the United States, for example, reforms have mandated a five-year lifetime time limit on cash assistance and require recipients to (re)commence work after two years (U.S. Personal Responsibility and Work Opportunity Reconciliation Act and Associated Legislation 1996). Similarly, in Germany, reforms in the mid-2000s included reductions in unemployment benefits' duration, particularly for older workers, along with means-tested basic income support; these reforms were successful in reducing unemployment rates (Lo, Stephan, and Wilke 2012). Some countries in ECA have introduced reforms to, if not limit benefits, reduce their generosity over time. In FYR Macedonia, for instance, the social assistance benefit to able-bodied beneficiaries falls by half after three years in the program (World Bank 2011e). In Russia, during the second 12-month period, the monthly benefit falls to 30 percent of the local minimum subsistence level.

In the case of pensions, early retirement and increasing life expectancy can lead to many years of inactivity, especially among women. The average statutory retirement age in ECA is 59 years for women and 62.5 for men, with significant variation across countries. These official ages for retirement are lower than the OECD average of 64 for women and 65 for men.[19] The effective retirement age is even lower in some countries due partly to several early retirement schemes,[20] and in a number of countries retirement at the statutory age is mandatory for the private sector (e.g., Bosnia and Herzegovina, Croatia, FYR Macedonia, Romania, and Uzbekistan).[21] In Poland and Russia, for example, qualitative work found that tax and pension benefit rules are a reason for older workers to fully retire upon reaching retirement age.[22] If the gap in life expectancy between ECA and advanced OECD countries (about 10 years) is closed, workers in the region are bound to spend an ever greater time in inactivity and as pension beneficiaries in the decades ahead.

Beyond the individual effects of labor taxation and social protection systems on employment decisions, their interaction is likely to matter most. As argued above, labor taxation remains not only high but also only weakly progressive in many ECA countries. This means that for (potential) low-wage earners, labor taxation can be disproportionately high; since, in addition, these are also often the recipients of social benefits, they are faced with two sources of disincentives. This chapter analyzes these interactions next. Due to data limitations, most of the evidence comes from EU new member states and the Western Balkans. However, these issues are relevant even in cases where welfare states remain relatively small, such as in Central Asia, as these countries move to expand their social protection systems to better protect the poor and the vulnerable.

The Interaction between Labor Taxes and Social Benefits Can Exacerbate Disincentives[23]

When analyzed together with labor taxes, there are significant costs to accepting a formal job and foregoing social assistance benefits, especially for low-wage and part-time earners. This is particularly the case in Lithuania, Slovenia, and Latvia, where 85, 75, and 71 percent of labor income for average wage earners, respectively, is taxed away through a combination of income tax and lost benefits. This is the

FIGURE 4.8

The Costs of Moving Out of Social Assistance Could Be High, Especially for Low-Wage Earners and Part-Time Workers (the "Inactivity Trap")

Average effective tax rate, 2010: income tax plus lost benefits as a percentage of gross labor income

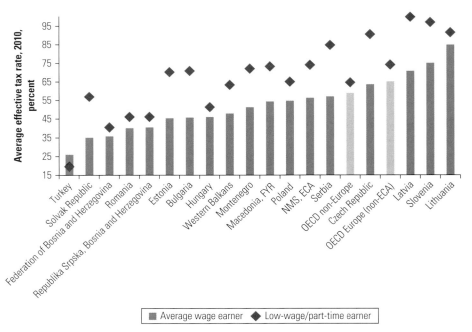

Source: Calculations, based on OECD Tax and Benefit Model.

Note: Calculations are based on one-earner couples with two children. They measure the share of gross income of the accepted formal job—including in-work benefits—that is taxed away through personal income tax, social security contributions, and lost benefits (social assistance, family, and housing benefits). Children are assumed to be ages 4 and 6. The data for Bosnia and Herzegovina, FYR Macedonia, and Serbia are from 2009 and for Montenegro from 2011. *Low-wage earner* refers to those earning 50 percent of the average wage. Bosnia and Herzegovina comprises two political entities: (a) Federation of Bosnia and Herzegovina; and (b) Republika Srpska, Bosnia and Herzegovina; NMS stands for New EU Member States.

so-called inactivity trap. In ECA overall, the inactivity trap appears less severe for average earners than in OECD countries (figure 4.8). However, formal work disincentives are disproportionately high for low-wage earners and part-time workers on social assistance (70 percent, on average). In Latvia, for example, low-wage earners on social assistance gain literally nothing from taking on a formal job, a result of having an implicit tax of 100 percent. In the Western Balkans, FYR Macedonia, Montenegro, and Serbia have tax rates above 70 percent for low-wage earners; that is, a household's total income increases by only 30 percent of the workers' potential new earnings when starting a (formal) job.

Whereas in non-ECA OECD countries disincentives arise primarily from either social assistance or taxes, in ECA it is the combination of taxation, traditional social assistance programs, and housing benefits that appear to induce an inactivity trap (figure 4.9). In some countries, reforms have moved in the right direction: in the Slovak Republic, the implicit work tax rate for those on social assistance fell by 52 percentage points (to 43 percent) between 2001 and 2010; in the Czech Republic and Hungary, this tax rate fell by 10 percentage

FIGURE 4.9

Work Disincentives in ECA Countries Arise from a Mix of Labor Taxation and the Design of Traditional Social Assistance Programs and Housing Benefits

Average effective tax rate (% of gross labor income), by source, 2010

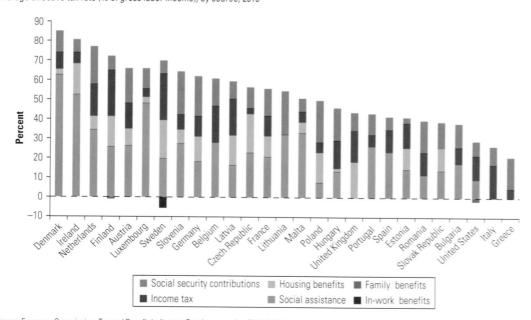

Source: European Commission, Tax and Benefit Indicators Database, version 2012-04-24.
Note: Calculations refer to one-earner couples at average earner wage with two children. Values below zero refer to benefits that increase with formal work.

points in the same period and, critically, fell significantly more (33 percentage points) for low-wage earners. The impact of these reforms on labor markets needs to be the subject of further research.

The move out of unemployment seems to be even more difficult than the move out of inactivity in ECA. Even if unemployment benefits overall are not very generous, they are often abruptly withdrawn when people start to work formally. In ECA countries, on average, almost two-thirds of labor income for average wage earners is effectively taken away when shifting from unemployment benefits to formal employment (figure 4.10). This "unemployment trap" is significantly higher than in non-European OECD countries. Work disincentives when moving out of unemployment benefits could be especially damaging in Bulgaria, Latvia, FYR Macedonia, Serbia, and Slovenia, with more than 73 percent of income "taxed away." As with the inactivity trap, work disincentives derived from this "unemployment trap" are especially high for low-wage and part-time earners; however, this

FIGURE 4.10

There Are Significant Work Disincentives for the Unemployed, Especially for Low-Wage and Part-Time Earners (the "Unemployment Trap")

Average effective tax rate, 2010: income tax plus lost unemployment benefits as a percentage of gross labor income

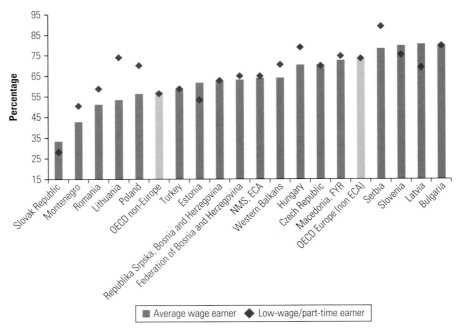

Source: Calculations based on OECD Tax and Benefit Model.

Note: Calculations are based on one-earner couples with two children. They measure what share of gross income of the accepted formal job—including in-work benefits—is taxed away through personal income tax, social security contributions, and lost benefits (unemployment, family, and housing benefits). No social assistance is assumed to be available in either the in-work or out-of-work situations. Children are assumed to be ages four and six. The data for Bosnia and Herzegovina, FYR Macedonia, and Serbia are from 2009; for Montenegro, from 2011. Bosnia and Herzegovina comprises two political entities: (a) Federation of Bosnia and Herzegovina; and (b) Republika Srpska, Bosnia and Herzegovina; NMS stands for New EU Member States.

Making social protection systems more work-compatible calls for improving their design rather than cutting benefits: consolidating programs, improving the targeting of benefits, and tying transfers more closely to active job searching. Social protection systems in the region are often fragmented and most benefits are categorical, leading to many benefits going to nonpoor, nonvulnerable households. For instance, 10 percent of total social assistance benefits are, on average, received by the richest quintile in ECA; these leakages can be as high as 28 percent in Belarus, 21 percent in Tajikistan, 17 percent in Bosnia and Herzegovina, and 15 percent in the Russian Federation.[25] More consolidation and better targeting can strengthen the poverty and vulnerability reduction functions of social protection while reducing potential work disincentives. In Germany, a significant reform effort was made between 2003 and 2005 aimed at reducing high unemployment rates. The reform package (referred to as Hartz IV reforms) included reductions in unemployment benefits' generosity and duration to make these benefits more work compatible. A large part of the reduction in unemployment in Germany has been attributed to the changes in unemployment benefits introduced as part of Hartz IV (Gill and Reiser 2012; Krebbs and Scheffel 2013).

A well-designed social protection system can facilitate labor market transitions and can be used as a mechanism for getting people into work.

- Eliminating or reducing instances where social benefits are abruptly withdrawn when a person starts to work formally. To address this issue, some governments have introduced only gradual reductions in benefits as a person starts to work or "earnings disregards" that exclude some labor income from being counted as taxable or toward determining eligibility and benefit levels of social programs and pensions (annex 4A). Moving in this direction could help in getting people into (formal) work while in due time, reducing fiscal pressures. Romania is a case in point, where the last resort social assistance program is being reformed through income disregards and in-work benefits. Other possible, more far-reaching reforms would move in the direction of social assistance programs in Latin America, for which eligibility is based on an income or asset means test but where, once eligible, the benefit remains flat (i.e., independent of additional income below the threshold).

- Eliminating one-off filters that make a household ineligible for a benefit if one of its members is employed and delinking social benefits eligibility from unemployment registration. For example, in 2011 the Slovak Republic introduced changes to its maternal benefits, allowing benefits to be combined with work and offering slightly higher payments to partly reimburse child care costs. In the presence of enough supply of child care centers, this reform is expected to increase women's labor force participation, as opposed to subsidizing them to stay at home.[26]

- Continuing pension reform efforts that rethink, for example, eligibility criteria, retirement ages, benefits, and financing of the system. For older workers, the pension system is arguably the most relevant source of (formal) work disincentives. Since most disincentives from pensions arise from low mandatory retirement ages and an income effect on the household, increases in the retirement age and reductions in the benefit package resulting from fiscal and demographic pressures will help in better aligning pensions with work.[27] In general, policies should aim at discouraging early retirement and supporting workers who want to stay active.[28] Most countries in the region have introduced important reforms in pension systems in the past two decades: increasing retirement age, indexation reforms, and changes in benefit rates and contribution rates, among other measures. However, as argued in a parallel World Bank report on pensions in the region, *The Inverted Pyramid: Pension Systems in Europe and Central Asia Facing Demographic Challenges,* although useful, these reforms need to go further to keep up with fiscal, competitiveness, and demographic pressures.

Active labor market measures and the overall work of social welfare centers and PES are also central to making social protection more work compatible. Tailored activation plans for social assistance beneficiaries, but more generally for the unemployed and the inactive, can help address the multiplicity of barriers that they face (EC 2012b). The case of Jobcentre Plus in the United Kingdom, which integrates coaching, mediation, referral services, and monitoring, exemplifies the direction in which these initiatives are moving (box 4.2). The ECA region spends relatively little on active labor market policies (box 4.3), and existing evidence suggests that there is still room for improving their effectiveness.[29]

Given the current limited coverage of social assistance and unemployment benefits, in particular, the impact of policy changes solely focused on addressing welfare dependency is likely to be limited at the aggregate level in the short term. However, as these programs expand, making them more work compatible becomes increasingly important.

BOX 4.2

UK's Jobcentre Plus: A Comprehensive and Tailored Approach to Activation

Citizens of the United Kingdom have the right to employment benefits and support in finding work. Job search assistance is provided through Jobcentre Plus, which was created in 2002 as part of the Department of Work and Pensions. Jobcentre Plus provides career advice, access to job vacancy databases, occupational training, sector-based work academies, and access to internships, apprenticeships, and volunteer programs. Additional training is provided for those interested in starting their own business.

The assistance provided intensifies with the duration of unemployment. After three months of unemployment, clients enter into a directed job search, and approximately 60 percent of clients find a job within six months. After six months, a supported job search is provided, in which personal advisors assist with both the job search and with other employment barriers such as homelessness in order to craft a holistic approach. Advisors tailor the job search and skills training support to individual needs, while also explaining the benefits available to clients. Additionally, clients receive further support once employed in order to help them stay in their job. However, if a client remains unemployed after a year, he or she is referred to private providers with more comprehensive services to tackle barriers to employment. An incentive structure determines payment of these providers so that they receive payment both when a person joins the program and when that person has been employed for six months. Additionally, as the client retains the job, monthly payments are made to the provider over the first 24 months of continued employment. These positive incentives for the private sector are considered one of the program's strengths. Finally, the program requires periodic performance reports and provides a grievance mechanism, which allow for increased transparency and effectiveness.

Beyond these innovations, the program continues to test and try new approaches to activation at the local level. In parts of Essex recently, an experimental variant of the program incorporating lessons from behavioral economics was implemented. Two thousand beneficiaries were divided into two groups with one receiving the traditional program, while for the rest Jobcentre staff got claimants not only to identify and write down what they were going to do to find work in the following two weeks but also to craft a detailed action plan on how and when they were going to do it. At the end of the pilot, those taking part in the new service were approximately 15 percent more likely to be in work within 13 weeks.

Upcoming revisions to the UK welfare system are expected to take into account the success of local, individualized solutions. Changes are expected to include giving greater freedom to Jobcentre Plus advisers to determine what clients need. There is also an effort to provide local solutions to local labor market challenges, giving greater autonomy to district managers to design their programs according to local needs and available partnerships. The government expects increased partnerships with local colleges, adult learning providers, recruitment agencies, authorities, and community organizations as this localized and customized approach is credited for the program's successes thus far.

Sources: Evans and Simmonds 2012; Great Britain Department for Work and Pensions 2010; Wright 2013.

BOX 4.3

Active Labor Market Programs Can Work, but More Evidence Is Needed

Active labor market programs (ALMPs) are a combination of policy tools that support and incentivize job-searching and job-finding, productive participation in society, and becoming and remaining self-sufficient and less dependent on public income support. ALMPs can strengthen the motivation, the capabilities, and the opportunities of a targeted population. ALMPs cover a wide range of interventions that can target labor supply with, for example, training programs, and labor demand through, for example, public works projects or employment subsidies. They can also foster the matching of workers and jobs through intermediation services.

The level of spending on ALMPs differs significantly between countries, independently from the level of unemployment. Average spending in ECA is about 0.5 percent of gross domestic product (GDP). But expenditures greatly vary within this region. While Poland spends about 0.6 percent of its GDP, Georgia, for instance, lacks ALMPs. The new EU member states spent about 0.3 of their GDP in 2009, while in EU 27 and OECD countries average spending is 0.7 percent of GDP.

The type of programs under ALMPs in ECA differs from those in OECD countries. Prior to the economic downturn, OECD countries' spending on ALMPs was driven mainly by public employment services (PES) job-search assistance and placement and training, with about 25 percent of the total spending going to each. In the EU-10, employment incentives (subsidies to private employment) were the second most important type of expenditure after PES. Training accounted for just over 10 percent of ALMPs' budget in these countries. Together, direct-job creation and programs targeting disabled people absorbed about 22 percent of the total spending on ALMPs in EU-10 countries.

ALMPs are often tailored to certain population segments, for example, youth or the long-term unemployed. Evidence suggests that well-designed ALMPs can have a positive impact on employment outcomes for participants. Success stories in ALMPs come from a variety of countries: while a work requirement in tandem with subsidization of private sector employment had positive outcomes on youth income in UK's New Deal program, effective public employment and relocation services characterized the Romanian experience. Positive outcomes are also found in married women who are required to search for a job (for example in Hungary) or receive child care support (as in the CCT Chile Solidario). Similarly, long-term unemployed social assistance beneficiaries can become active with mandatory intensive counseling (Denmark and Norway) or temporary sanctions (the Netherlands). However, many programs also fail for a variety of reasons, like low take-up rates, claimants' failure to comply with program requirements, weak design of programs, bad matching of programs and beneficiaries, and others. The existing evidence, while limited, also suggests differential impacts of programs by type of beneficiary. For example, returns from training programs appear to be consistently higher among women than men, maybe partly due to lower starting levels of education among female participants or higher motivation in the training courses.

continued

FIGURE 4.14

The Gender Gap in Labor Force Participation Starts Early and Remains throughout the Life Cycle

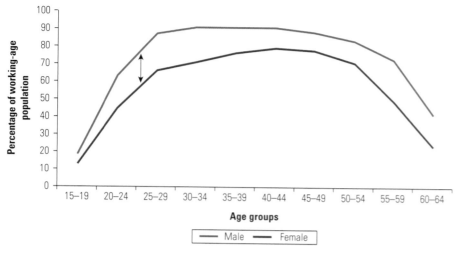

Source: Based on Labor Force and Households Surveys, latest years (2009–11; for Albania, data is for 2008).
Note: Simple average for available ECA countries: Albania, Armenia, Bulgaria, the Czech Republic, Estonia, Georgia, Hungary, the Kyrgyz Republic, Latvia, Lithuania, FYR Macedonia, Moldova, Poland, Romania, Russian Federation, Slovak Republic, Slovenia, Turkey, and Ukraine.

Expanding good-quality and affordable child care can help bring women into work. Providing households, and particularly women, with cost-effective alternatives for child (and elder) care services can help reduce the opportunity cost of working outside the home. Several studies have established the positive effect that affordable child care options can have on boosting female labor supply (see, for example, Attanasio, Low, and Sanchez-Marcos 2008; Nollenberger and Rodríguez-Planas 2011; Sánchez-Mangas and Sánchez-Marcos 2008). A few countries in the region are moving toward actively expanding child care options, including by expanding operating hours of child care centers to meet the needs of full-time working parents. EU-10 countries have recommitted, along with other European countries, to the 2002 Barcelona targets of child care provision as part of the European Pact for gender equality (2011–20).[34] Given the region's demographics, a similar expansion in elder care services is also critical and is most urgent in fast-aging countries.

Flexible Work Arrangements and Adequate Working Conditions

Limited flexibility in work arrangements and inadequate working conditions can further limit access to economic opportunities.

Today's workplace and job market have been designed mainly for prime-age male workers who can work full time, have limited family and household responsibilities, have completed their formal education, and have significant work experience. As a result, the preferences and needs of other types of workers who want or require additional flexibility and who are more likely to have an intervallic work life are often not accounted for (OECD 2010a). For youth enrolled in educational programs, these rigidities in the current setup of the labor market are particularly restrictive, as the lack of flexibility in work schedules makes it difficult to combine work and studies and, hence, to gain the necessary experience to facilitate a full entry into the labor market. For older workers, the scarcity of options in part-time and home-based employment prevents individuals from remaining active for longer and often result in an abrupt exit from the labor market once the retirement age is reached, or even before that. Indeed, qualitative work in Croatia and Poland found that half of those between ages 55 and 70 would have liked to delay retirement but that appropriate arrangements, such as part-time contracts, were not always available (World Bank 2012d, 2012e). Finally, for women, especially those in childbearing age and those with young children, the lack of alternatives in work arrangements—including part-time and home-based work—makes it difficult to hold a job.

Making it easier and less costly to work part-time can be advantageous for both employers and workers and can help to bring more people into the workforce.[35] Part-time work gives employers more flexibility to adjust hours worked to the economic cycle and workers more options for work-life balance.[36] Notwithstanding the potential benefits of part-time work, however, it remains limited in many countries in the region, not even reaching, on average, 10 percent of the employed.[37] Part-time employment ranges from less than 3 percent in Bulgaria and the Kyrgyz Republic to 17 percent in Georgia. In the EU in 2011, 18.8 percent of workers were engaged in part-time, with rates as high as 49 percent in the Netherlands, 34 percent in Switzerland, 27 percent in Norway, and 26 percent in the U.K.[38] Women work part-time more often than men in many ECA countries such as Russia (25 percent of employed women versus 13 percent of employed men); Turkey (23 percent versus 6 percent); and Poland (11 percent versus 5 percent). Youth and older workers also have relatively higher part-time rates on average in ECA, at 14 and 12 percent, respectively, compared to around 7 percent for other workers (figure 4.15). Some of the constraints to

FIGURE 4.15

Younger Workers, Older Workers, and Women Are Most Likely to Take Up Part-Time Work

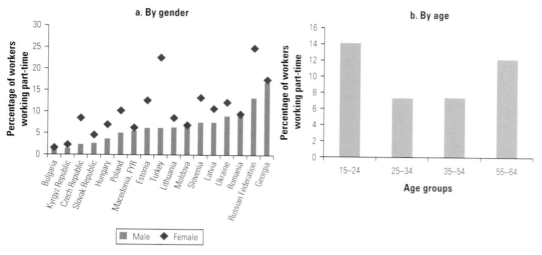

Source: Calculations based on household and labor force surveys for 17 ECA countries for years between 2009 and 2011.

part-time work arise from labor legislations. For example, in Montenegro part-time work cannot be less than one-fourth (10 hours per week) of a full-time engagement. In some countries it is a statutory right of employees to increase (or decrease) part-time working hours, while in other countries this is more difficult (Eurofound 2011). Constraints to part-time work also arise from the tax and benefit systems, as previously discussed. In Serbia, the "reference" wage (determining a minimum social contribution) is not adjusted for hours worked, meaning that social contributions are disproportionately high for part-time workers. Policy makers can aim at improving conditions for part-time work (and the transition to full-time work, if desirable) while also minimizing some of the potential negative effects.[39]

Some countries are already making labor markets more flexible to allow for part-time work. In Hungary, for example, since the beginning of 2010 it has been compulsory in the public sector to provide the option of part-time employment on a 20-hour weekly basis to employees returning from maternity leave, at least until the child is three years old.[40] In other countries like Armenia, Latvia, Montenegro, and Russia, employees with minor children have additional legal rights to a flexible or part-time work arrangement.[41] Reforms will need to go beyond labor regulations to make part-time work pay. For example, it is important for firms to offer training and development opportunities for part-time workers, who are usually at a disadvantage (Lyonette, Baldauf, and Behle 2010). This could mini-mize potential scarring effects associated with less than full-time employment and increase take up of part-time work in countries in which inactivity is the alternative.

Modern technology and new management practices have opened up a wide array of alternative and more flexible work arrangements. For white-collar workers, computers, mobile devices, Internet access, and video conferencing have made it possible to work productively outside of the traditional office space. E-work, increasingly common through services like ODesk, have brought workers and firms closer through online matching services. Similarly, for blue-collar workers, technological advances have automated many processes that allow for more flexible shifts. Technological advances have also made it possible to have new forms of contractual arrangements: on-call contracts, freelance contracts, and telework (Kuddo 2009). For exam-ple, an experimental pilot on home-based work in a 16,000-employee travel agency in China found a 13 percent increase in performance for employees working from home, both from working longer and from higher productivity. Based on this success the program was rolled out to the whole firm (Bloom et al. 2013).

Beyond making work schedules more flexible, the work environ-ment can be better tailored to the changes in needs and preferences that occur during the life cycle, without sacrificing productivity. In ECA, this is particularly important for older workers. The type of job, arrangements, and work environment for older workers might need to be adapted to maintain and increase productivity. Changing health and physical conditions could impact older workers' produc-tivity, especially in jobs that are physically demanding or that require activities and tools designed for younger and prime-age workers. Some firms have risen above the aging challenge and have adapted working conditions and environment accordingly. For example, the German car company BMW has piloted a production line with older workers, incorporating specific interventions to address the health, skills, workplace environment, and other chal-lenges associated with their aging workforce. Such changes included, for example, special chairs to alternate physical strain, magnifying lenses, and stackable transport containers, resulting in a 7 percent increase in line productivity in one year and matching productivity levels of younger workers (box 4.5). Finally, adapting the work environment to the needs of other groups, such as breast-feeding mothers or religious workers, could foster more inclusive and productive labor markets.

BOX 4.5

"The 2017 Line": How BMW Is Defusing the Demographic Time Bomb

In 2007, the German car company BMW started to worry about the seemingly inevitable decline in labor productivity at its power train plant in Dingolfing (Lower Bavaria), due to the aging of its workforce. The average age of the plant's workers, in fact, was expected to rise from 39 in 2007 to 47 in 2017. As older workers are more likely to call in sick and their productivity is usually lower, such an increase in the average age would have threatened the plant's production targets and BMW's overall strategy of enhancing competitiveness.

Since early retirement was not politically feasible and moving older workers into less physically demanding jobs could not be easily implemented within the plant, the BMW production management had to come up with an innovative solution to this issue.

A production line was selected for a pilot project to develop productivity-improving changes. These were grouped along five dimensions: health management, skills, workplace environment, retirement policies, and change in processes. The line, relatively small but highly labor intensive, was operated by 42 employees and produced rear-axle gearboxes for medium-size cars. Despite the initial resistance, the project team persuaded 20 workers already on the line to stay and enlisted 22 more to switch from their old positions for a year. The average age of the line was 47 years, thus reflecting the projection for 2017.

Following consultations with the Workers Council, the project team held a workshop for its workers, who could describe their main health concerns and express opinions on what they would change on the line. The outcome of the workshops was a prioritized action list, created by the workforce itself. Seventy changes in design and equipment were implemented on the line, in cooperation with an ergonomist and process engineers. Such changes included, among other things, a new wooden floor, special chairs to alternate physical strain, orthopedic footwear, magnifying lenses, stackable transport containers, and larger typeface on computer screens. All such changes were meant to reduce wear and tear on workers' bodies, thus diminishing the likelihood that workers would call in sick. Additionally, job rotation between more and less physically demanding workstations was introduced.

With a total cost of €20,000, the BMW line improved its productivity by 7 percent in one year, reaching the productivity level of lines staffed by younger workers. Absenteeism related to health and rehabilitation dropped from 7 percent in 2008 to 2 percent in 2009. Given this success, BMW is now introducing similar projects in other plants.

The "2017 line" is a remarkable case of a firm's adaptation to the new demographic challenges. The model adopted at BMW, with line workers creating the solutions to the issues raised by the management, shows that the barriers to employability for older workers are not insurmountable.

Source: Based on Bauer and Mauermann 2010.

Access to Productive Inputs, Information, and Networks

Access to economic opportunities, particularly in the form of entrepreneurship, can also be hindered by a limited access to productive inputs. As discussed in chapter 2, enabling conditions for productive entrepreneurship is critical to address ECA's job challenge. For young workers, women, and ethnic minorities, lack of access to credit and land, for example, can represent an important barrier to tapping their entrepreneurial potential and achieving gainful employment. Women in ECA, and in many countries worldwide, are less likely than men to obtain credit (IFC 2013; Sattar 2012; and World Bank 2011f); when they do, it is often under more stringent conditions than men. In Tajikistan, for example, women are charged interest rates that are 12 percentage points higher than men for long-term loans, linked to women's lack of assets and overall poorer labor market outcomes (Sattar 2012). Similarly, youth are disproportionately likely to be credit constrained (World Bank 2012j). Moreover, limited access to land can make it more difficult to obtain credit or to directly use it for production. Evidence from ECA shows, for example, that in Albania, Bulgaria, and Tajikistan, female heads of household are less likely to own land compared to male heads. Even when the legal provisions and procedures are gender neutral, women are often at a disadvantage in securing property rights.[42] Ensuring access to productive inputs, especially for those facing more severe constraints to do so, is therefore critical to promoting employment and productivity.[43]

In addition to traditional inputs, access to labor market information and networks is also key in linking people to jobs. Lack of information about where jobs can be found or about potential wages, as well as having weak professional network ties can make job searching more difficult. This is particularly important in the case of internal migrants (see chapter 5). Incomplete information in the labor market has been shown to have detrimental effects on the quality of matches between firms and workers by, for example, influencing workers' educational choices, firms' final selection of workers, or the time that it takes to fill vacancies (Jensen 2010; Kaas and Manger 2010; World Bank 2012j). Similarly, personal and professional connections are considered an important entry point to jobs: In ECA, two-thirds of the working-age population report that having connections is critical to getting either a public or private job (EBRD and World Bank 2010).

Facilitating information flows and strengthening networks are likely to be particularly important for youth and ethnic minorities. Young workers, almost by definition, are often first-time job-seekers and arrive to the labor market without extensive work experience or strong professional networks. Since educational systems in the region provide little practical experience, as internships and apprenticeships might do, professional connections are not formed prior to a full entry into the labor market. Moreover, employers' uncertainty about young workers' potential productivity can further limit their employment opportunities or lead to many youth being hired at lower wages than appropriate (Pallais 2013; World Bank 2012j). Ethnic minorities, in turn, could be cut off from a number of jobs due to the lack of extensive social and professional networks, and access to information beyond their kin—both sometimes further limited by language barriers. On the side of employers, a similar mechanism is at play: The observed differences in labor market access across ethnic groups may in part reflect incomplete information about the potential productivity of minority groups. In Germany, for example, a randomized study of discrimination in the labor market using variations from Turkish-sounding versus German-sounding names found that the initial 14 percent gap in callback probabilities between the groups disappeared once the study was restricted to applications which included reference letters with favorable information about the candidate (Kaas and Manger 2010).

Countries in ECA and in other regions have taken different approaches to improving information flows in the labor market. Countries have aimed at strengthening the capacity of PES and social welfare centers to better serve their clients. Some countries have increased the number of staff in PES (e.g., Estonia and Russia) and some others have increased the proportion of staff working directly with job seekers (Latvia, Bulgaria, Moldova, and Azerbaijan) (Kaas and Manger 2010). Further, countries are looking to improve the effectiveness and better monitor the results of active labor market policies with, for example, a stronger involvement of the private sector and a more tailored and personalized service, in which case workers develop individual employment plans, following the UK model (box 4.1). However, PES still face many challenges across the region related to, for example, staffing constraints (in Kosovo, there are around 1,900 job seekers per staff member)[44]; reaching out to unemployed job seekers that do not register; and providing adequate services to those particularly difficult to employ (e.g., younger workers, ethnic minorities, the long-term unemployed, and low-skilled workers).[45]

In addition, countries have looked to improve the quantity and quality of labor market information available to all actors—students, workers, firms, and government agencies. In particular, some countries in the region such as Poland have introduced "employment observatories" that provide information on job availability, wages, career prospects, and hiring expectations. Observatories can start with a small office in charge of collecting labor market information and conducting specialized labor-related analysis, as in Poland, and then further develop into more sophisticated outfits able to provide information about wages, labor conditions by sectors, and types of firms and jobs as in countries like Chile and Colombia. Other interventions aimed at improving information flows have been discussed in chapter 3.

Similarly, there are steps that countries can take to improve youth's and ethnic minorities' access to professional networks and jobs. Creating tax and other incentives to increase the availability of paid apprenticeships for youth that build experience and networks can ease the transition for youth from school to work (see also OECD 2011). Further, connecting these groups to mentors and networks can help raise aspirations, motivation, and even school performance. For example, two programs in the United States target Hispanic high-school students to provide information on career paths and university life, facilitate the creation of networks among students and professors, and link Hispanic youth to role models among local successful Hispanic business leaders.[46] Other unconventional approaches, such as organizing sports events to link unemployed youth and employers,[47] have been carried out in some countries. Some countries regularly hold job fairs that help bring together firms and job searchers, especially youth. Such interventions can also contribute to addressing adverse attitudes toward youth and ethnic minorities (or others) and lack of information about these groups.

Attitudes and Social Norms

In ECA, as in other regions around the world, attitudes and social norms can be a barrier to productive employment, both on the side of employers and on the side of (potential) workers. Attitudes and social norms strongly influence the functioning of markets and institutions, and shape individuals' and families' decisions, including those related to the labor market. In particular, attitudes and social norms can influence a firm's decision to hire or not to hire a worker or determine the level of pay, but they can also determine individuals' decisions on whether to look for a job outside the home or in which sector or occupation to work. Outright discrimination is one manifestation of negative attitudes,[48] and it persists, particularly in terms of ethnicity, age, and gender. Negative attitudes toward certain population groups can

reducing labor taxation levels across the board in countries where it remains high. Also, social programs, while providing adequate protection to the poor and vulnerable, need to be made more work compatible and benefits linked more closely to job search and activation measures by (a) eliminating or reducing instances where social benefits are abruptly withdrawn when a person starts to work formally and improving benefit targeting; (b) eliminating one-off filters that make a household ineligible for a benefit if one of its members is (formally) employed and delinking social benefits eligibility from unemployment registration; (c) continuing pension reform efforts that rethink, for example, retirement ages, benefits, and financing of the system; and (d) strengthening active labor market measures and the overall work of social welfare centers and PES.

Beyond the tax and social protection systems, especially in countries where barriers are systematically high, a cross-sectoral policy agenda aimed at removing group-specific barriers to employment for younger and older workers, women, and ethnic minorities is required. It should build relevant skills along the life cycle (chapter 3); facilitate geographic mobility (chapter 5); provide access to affordable child care; encourage more flexible and adequate work environments; improve access to productive inputs, information, and networks; promote positive attitudes; and reshape social norms. Beyond their individual impacts, resolving barriers in these areas will most likely have a mutually reinforcing effect. Policies should ensure that markets, institutions, and culture reward talent and effort rather than having economic opportunities be determined by an individual's circumstances. See figure 4.20 for a potential policy agenda.

Strengthening the evidence base for policy design regarding incentives and barriers to work should also be high in the agenda. Critical knowledge gaps remain in three particular areas: (a) better measuring the actual impact—beyond simulations—of tax and benefits systems on employment decisions in ECA countries where evidence is currently limited; (b) identifying the types of active labor market programs that are most effective at increasing employability for different socioeconomic and educational groups; and (c) understanding the marginal gain in implementing measures, especially short-term ones, that remove barriers to work, such as those linked to extending the provision of child care and creating flexible work arrangements.

Going forward, rebalancing longer and more productive work lives with social welfare systems that still protect the vulnerable and that help workers in transition is arguably the critical challenge to prosperity in the ECA region.

FIGURE 4.20

A Policy Agenda for Removing Disincentives and Barriers to Employment in ECA

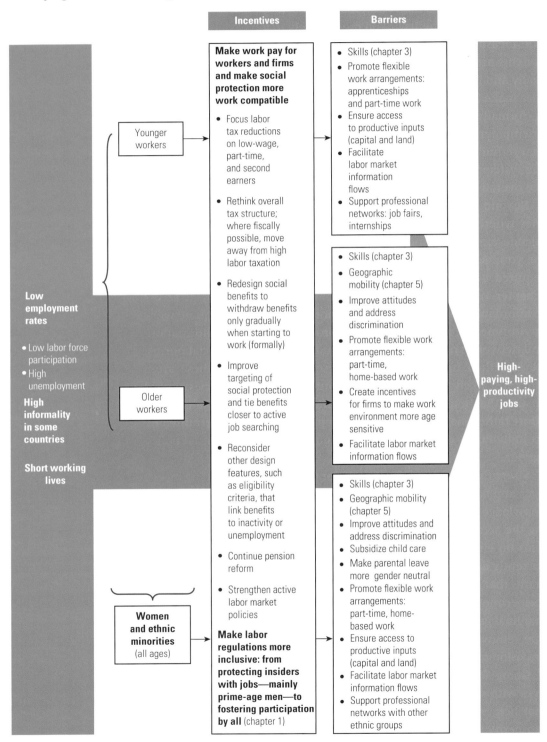

Annex 4A: Examples of Countries with Income Disregards in Social Assistance

Cyprus	Income earned from the following sources are exempted: Income from work up to €85.43, up to €512.58 if the applicant or spouse has disabilities, up to €170 if the person is over 63 years of age or has mental health problems, and up to €256.29 if the claimant is a single parent; income from dependent children.
Czech Republic	To provide an incentive to work, only 70 percent of income from gainful activity and 80 percent of sickness benefit or unemployment benefit are taken into account.
Denmark	Income is deducted krone to krone (euro to euro), e.g., a pro rata pension is deducted as any other income. Income from work is deducted except an amount of DKK 14.57 (€1.95) per working hour. For those receiving a starting allowance (starthjælp): DKK 35.51 (€4.76) per working hour. This rule concerns only 160 hours per month.
Finland	The following income is not taken into account: salaries and benefits deemed insignificant, regular income of a child under the age of 18, income corresponding to travel to work and other expenses related to working, certain benefits (maternity benefits and disability allowances).
Germany	For assistance toward living expenses and a needs-based pension supplement in old age and in the event of reduced earning capacity, the equivalent of 30 percent of the income from self-employed or not employed activities of the beneficiary are to be deducted, within the limit of 50 percent of the rate for the head of the household. When working in a sheltered workplace for disabled persons the amount deductable from the wage is one-eighth of the rate for the head of the household plus 25 percent of the wage exceeding this amount. Basic security benefits for job seekers (Grundsicherung für Arbeitsuchende): Persons who are working can deduct €100 of the monthly earned income. For earned income between €101 and €1,000, 20 percent is deducted, and for earned income between €1,001 and €1,200 (for families with children), 10 percent is deducted.
Hungary	Monthly income deriving from occasional work is exempted.
Lithuania	In order to be granted cash social assistance, the following resources are exempted (among others): * wages of pupils studying at general education schools and vocational institutions according to general education or vocational training curricula and * income from agricultural land the total area of which does not exceed 1 hectare. Amounts paid for the maintenance of a child (alimony) is included in the income of a person who receives such alimony.
Netherlands	Work and Social Assistance Act (Wet Werk en Bijstand, WWB) and Investment in the Young Act (Wet investeren in jongeren, WIJ): All income is taken into account. However, under the WWB, 25 percent of income from work (up to a maximum of €190) is left untouched.
Portugal	Social integration income (rendimento social de inserção): Only 80 percent of income from work is taken into account.
Slovak Republic	The following family resources are disregarded: * 25 percent of earnings, * incidental income and community help up to two times the amount of the subsistence minimum (Životné minimum), * activation allowance for voluntary service, and * earnings of students not exceeding 1.2 times the subsistence minimum in the last 12 months, etc.
Sweden	As a general rule, all income and benefits, whatever the nature and the origin, are taken into account. However, with a view to stimulating the labor market attachment, income below a half-price base amount (prisbasbelopp) per year earned during vacation by young persons of school age shall not be taken into account when assessing their need of social assistance.
Switzerland	Determining income for the calculation of the supplementary benefits, the following is exempted: * two-thirds of income from gainful employment insofar as it exceeds per year CHF 1,000 (€815) for persons living alone, CHF 1,500 (€1,223) for couples/registered partners and for persons with children; * pensions, family allowances; and * maintenance payments under family law.

Source: EC 2011b.

Annex 4B: Indices for Work Disincentives, Barriers to Employment, and Protection—Methodology

The indices for work disincentives, barriers, and protection were obtained as the average of indicators that capture these three different aspects. The countries considered are the ECA countries and the European OECD countries. For each index, a higher value means a higher level of disincentives, barriers, or protection, respectively. Each indicator was standardized by subtracting the mean and dividing by the standard deviation, so that all indicators have a mean of zero and standard deviation of one. Then, each index was estimated as the arithmetic average of the indicators via the following formula:

$$Index_{l,i} = \frac{1}{K} \sum_{j=1}^{K} (-1)^{m_j} * Standardized\_Indicator_{j,i}$$

where $l = \{Disincentives, Barriers, Protection\}$, i indicates each country in the sample, $m_j = \{0,1\}$ depending on whether the indicator j enters directly (0) or inversely (1) into the index, K is the number of indicators used for each index, and $Standardized\_Indicator_j$ is each indicator j standardized according to this formula:

$$Standardized\_Indicator_{j,i} = \frac{Indicator_{j,i} - Average\,(Indicator_j)}{Standard\,Deviation\,(Indicator_j)}$$

The list of indicators used and the direction in which each affects the indices are indicated below.

TABLE 4B.1

Indicators Used for Indices

Indicator	Description	Source	Direction of the effect		
			Disincentives	Barriers	Protection
Tax wedge	Income tax (net of any tax credits) for a single earner with no children at 67 percent of average wage.	For OECD countries, 2011 data from OECD. For the rest, 2007 data from IZA.	(+)		
Hiring and firing flexibility	How would you characterize the hiring and firing of workers on your country? [1=impeded by regulations, 7=flexibility determined by employers] 2011–12 weighted average.	World Economic Forum, The Global Competitiveness Report 2012–2013.	(−)		
Minimum wage	Ratio of minimum wage to average value added per worker.	Employing Workers (Doing Business indicators on labor) 2012.	(+)		

continued

TABLE 4B.1
Continued

Indicator	Description	Source	Direction of the effect		
			Disincentives	Barriers	Protection
Retirement age	Statutory retirement age (arithmetic average by gender).	OECD.	(−)		
Social assistance coverage*	Coverage (direct and indirect beneficiaries).	For non-OECD countries: ECA Social Protection Database, World Bank. The figures are for 2004 for EST, HUN; 2006 for MKD; 2007 for BIH, BGR, GEO, KAZ, KOS, KYR, SRB; 2008 for ALB, ARM, BLR, HRV, LTU, RUS, UKR; 2009 for LVA, MDA, MNE, ROM, TUR; and 2010 for POL. For OECD countries, 2008 Statistics on Income and Living Conditions (SILC).	(+)		(+)
Social assistance targeting*	Percentage of benefits distributed in the lowest quintile (targeting accuracy).		(−)		(+)
Social assistance generosity*	Benefits as percentage of post-transfer consumption (all quintiles).		(+)		(+)
Pensions spending	Expenditure by active beneficiary divided by GDP per capita.	World Bank Pensions Database, different years (2005–10).	(+)		(+)
Child care availability	Are there laws establishing the public provision of child care, or does the state subsidize child care for children under the age of primary education?	Women, Business and the Law Dataset, the World Bank.		(−)	
Ethnic prejudice	To what extent do you agree with the following statements? The presence of people from other ethnic groups (a)is a cause of insecurity (b) increases unemployment. [1=Strongly disagree, 5=Strongly agree. Indicator reports the arithmetic average of these two questions.]	EBRD 2010 Life in Transition Survey. For OECD non-ECA countries, the average for FRA, GBR, DEU, ITA, and SWE was imputed.		(+)	
Temporary contracts	Fixed-term contracts prohibited for permanent tasks?	Employing Workers (World Bank Doing Business indicators on labor) 2012.		(+)	
Ease of access to loans	How easy is it to obtain a bank loan in your country with only a good business plan and no collateral? [1=very difficult, 7=very easy] 2011–12 weighted average.	World Economic Forum, The Global Competitiveness Report 2012–2013.		(−)	
Importance of networks in the labor market	Some people, because of their job, position in the community, or contacts, are asked by others to help influence decisions in their favor. In general, how important is it in your country to have the support of such people to influence decisions in: (a) Getting a good job in the government sector (b) Getting a good job in the private sector. [1=Not important at all, 5=Essential. Indicator reports the arithmetic average of these two questions.]	EBRD 2010 Life in Transition Survey. For OECD non-ECA countries, the average for FRA, GBR, DEU, ITA, and SWE was imputed.		(+)	

* Two different sources were used to construct these indicators. Compatibility checks showed them to be comparable.

Note: EBRD = European Bank for Reconstruction and Development; ECA = Europe and Central Asia; GDP = gross domestic product; IZA = Institute for the Study of Labor; OECD = Organisation for Economic Co-operation and Development.

Correlations

To check how well the indices are correlated with labor market outcomes, we estimated linear regressions of those outcomes and the disincentives and barriers indices. Results are presented in table 4B.2.

TABLE 4B.2

Linear Regressions: Labor Market Outcomes and Disincentives and Barriers Indices

	Disincentives index			Barriers index		
	(1)	(2)[+]	(3)[+]	(4)	(5)[+]	(6)[+]
Dependent Variable: Labor Force Participation Rate						
Disincentives/Barriers Index	−10.826***	−8.795*	−8.551*	3.781	−0.12	0.565
	(2.785)	(4.231)	(3.713)	(3.363)	(4.426)	(3.586)
MALE Labor Force Participation Rate						
Disincentives/Barriers Index	−10.331***	−6.923	−7.730*	5.809	−1.619	−0.539
	(3.100)	(4.427)	(3.965)	(3.744)	(4.631)	(3.829)
FEMALE Labor Force Participation Rate						
Disincentives/Barriers Index	−11.234***	−10.919	−9.591	1.775	1.912	2.198
	(3.788)	(6.263)	(5.701)	(4.575)	(6.552)	(5.506)
Gender Gap LFPR (As Percentage of Male LFPR)						
Disincentives/Barriers Index	5.327	7.455	4.634	3.573	−4.641	−3.894
	(5.430)	(8.388)	(7.932)	(6.558)	(8.775)	(7.661)
15–24 Labor Force Participation Rate						
Disincentives/Barriers Index	−7.952**	−7.271	−9.585	2.682	−4.362	0.886
	(3.516)	(6.009)	(6.271)	(4.246)	(6.287)	(6.056)
55–64 Labor Force Participation Rate						
Disincentives/Barriers Index	−19.746***	−22.536*	−16.591	4.072	12.124	5.266
	(4.798)	(10.411)	(9.655)	(5.794)	(10.892)	(9.325)
Unemployment						
Disincentives/Barriers Index	6.109	0.75	1.557	−7.782*	−4.246	−5.863
	(3.727)	(4.882)	(4.390)	(4.093)	(4.501)	(4.145)
15–24 Unemployment						
Disincentives/Barriers Index	14.006**	6.3	8.46	−16.525**	−7.648	−11.694
	(6.611)	(8.117)	(7.563)	(7.260)	(7.484)	(7.141)
Barriers Index	X	X	X			
Disincentives Index				X	X	X
Log (GDP per capita PPP)		X	X		X	X

continued

TABLE 4B.2
Continued

	Disincentives index			Barriers index		
	(1)	(2)[+]	(3)[+]	(4)	(5)[+]	(6)[+]
EBRD Transition Index		X			X	
Doing Business Std. Index			X			X
Mobility Rate (last 10 years)		X	X		X	X
PISA 2009: Math Score		X	X		X	X
PISA 2009: Reading Score		X	X		X	X
PISA 2009: Science Score		X	X		X	X

* p<0.10, ** p<0.05, *** p<0.01. + Sample size falls from 24 to 17 for LFPR regressions, and from 21 to 16 for unemployment regressions.
Note: EBRD = European Bank for Reconstruction and Development; GDP = gross domestic product; LFPR = labor force participation rate; PISA = Program for International Student Assessment; PPP = purchasing power parity.

Data

ECA countries	Tax wedge	Hiring and firing flexibility	Min. wage (% VA per worker)	Retirement age	Social assistance coverage
Albania	33.4	4.7	0.406	63.0	9.7
Armenia	38.5	5.0	0.232	59.5	18.5
Azerbaijan	29.8	5.4	0.168	57.5	
Belarus	35.5		0.159	65.0	54.9
Bosnia and Herzegovina	34.9	4.4	0.954	61.5	12.4
Bulgaria	33.0	4.2	0.239	62.5	38.2
Croatia	40.3	3.1	0.313	61.8	25.2
Czech Republic	39.6	3.4	0.211	61.7	42.0
Estonia	39.0	4.5	0.228	62.0	51.8
Georgia	26.7	5.0	0.081	62.0	13.2
Hungary	45.2	4.2	0.249	63.0	64.4
Kazakhstan	28.2	4.7	0.137	65.0	29.1
Kosovo			0.000	60.5	10.9
Kyrgyz Republic	31.6	4.8	0.109	62.0	13.5
Latvia	41.8	4.2	0.237	61.3	51.5
Lithuania	40.6	3.3	0.238	63.0	56.7
Macedonia, FYR	41.4	4.3	0.322	59.5	12.1
Moldova	32.4	3.7	0.523	67.0	30.6
Montenegro	40.2	4.1	0.095	62.5	5.6
Poland	33.3	3.5	0.265	62.5	39.6
Romania	42.2	3.6	0.216	57.5	57.4
Russian Federation	31.0	3.7	0.139	62.5	56.0
Serbia	42.2	3.6	0.253	60.8	16.2
Slovak Republic	36.0	3.5	0.238	62.0	59.8
Slovenia	38.6	2.3	0.371	62.0	59.1
Tajikistan	29.6	4.2	0.144		
Turkey	36.2	4.3	0.465	59.0	26.1
Turkmenistan				57.5	
Ukraine	39.2	4.9	0.376	57.5	44.4
Uzbekistan	38.0		0.170		

Social assistance targeting	Social assistance targeting (SILC)	Social assistance generosity	Social assistance generosity (SILC)	Spending in pensions	Child care	Ethnic prejudice	Forbidden temporary contracts	Ease of access to loan	Import. of network
78.1		25.7		35.9	1	2.75	1	1.8	3.2
53.6		16.2		19.1	1	2.70	1	2.8	3.6
48.8				22.6	0	2.84	0	3.0	3.3
20.0		8.7		21.4	1	2.89	0		3.2
36.8		13.2		73.9	1	2.67	0	2.0	3.5
45.2	33.8	12.7	6.8	22.4	1	3.21	0	3.3	4.0
53.6		10.4		30.4	1	2.68	1	2.5	3.8
48.8	51.6		12.0	17.7		3.60	0	2.9	3.1
40.4	28.1	12.1	8.3	23.2		3.01	1	2.8	3.1
53.0		23.3			1	3.22	0	2.5	3.3
43.7	44.0	16.7	15.2	26.8		3.50	0	2.3	4.1
40.0		10.9		9.6	0	2.95	0	2.3	3.4
72.9		31.7			1	3.14	0		3.0
47.3		4.7		14.1	1	2.77	1	1.7	2.8
44.9	20.1	8.0	6.1	17.5	1	3.02	1	2.8	3.9
40.6	30.3	6.7	7.9	21.8	1	2.97	1	2.3	3.4
45.0		12.7		40.3	1	3.00	0	2.8	3.6
39.6		10.3		39.4	1	2.71	1	2.4	2.9
72.9		26.6		38.2	1	2.75	0	3.3	3.3
62.4	53.0	11.0	10.6	26.6		3.04	0	2.5	3.0
49.1	36.9	12.3	7.2	26.4	1	2.88	1	2.7	3.4
28.8		6.2		23.2	1	3.45	1	2.6	3.4
63.6		16.2		51.7	1	2.71	1	2.4	4.0
48.8	44.6		5.7	23.9		3.19	0	3.0	3.3
48.8	42.9		9.5	28.7		2.91	1	2.2	3.5
48.8					0	2.79	1	3.1	2.9
44.0		8.4		30.3	0	3.19	1	3.0	3.4
48.8						3.00			
47.4		8.3		67.6	1	3.07	1	2.3	3.3
48.8				12.1	1	2.88	1		2.9

continued

Data

Continued

Benchmark countries	Tax wedge	Hiring and firing flexibility	Min. wage (% VA per worker)	Retirement age	Social assistance coverage
France	47.1	2.5	0.140	60.0	
Germany	45.6	3.1	0.213	65.0	52.9
Italy	44.4	2.8	0.356	62.5	37.9
United Kingdom	28.7	4.5	0.345	62.8	55.7
Sweden	40.7	2.9	0.213	65.0	58.4
Australia	20.6	3.2	0.239	64.5	
Austria	43.8	3.5	0.124	62.5	55.8
Belgium	50.5	2.9	0.305	65.0	52.7
Denmark	36.8	5.3	0.000	65.0	62.4
Finland	36.6	3.9	0.361	65.0	58.0
Greece	38.6	3.3	0.288	63.5	17.8
Iceland	29.4	5.2	0.320	67.0	62.8
Ireland	19.9	3.9	0.332	66.0	78.6
Luxembourg	29.4	3.2	0.264	65.0	61.8
Netherlands	33.3	3.1	0.174	65.0	61.8
Norway	34.3	2.8	0.335	67.0	57.6
Portugal	32.2	2.9	0.261	65.0	45.4
Spain	36.7	3.0	0.273	65.0	11.3
Switzerland	19.0	5.6	0.000	64.5	
Median values	Median values (proportion for binary variables)				
ECA Countries	37.1	4.2	0.237	62.0	34.4
Benchmark Countries	36.6	3.2	0.264	65.0	56.7
All Countries	36.6	3.7	0.238	62.5	48.4
Standard deviation					
ECA Countries	4.9	0.7	0.2	2.3	19.5
Benchmark Countries	9.2	0.9	0.1	1.7	17.0
All Countries	6.9	0.8	0.2	2.5	20.2

Social assistance targeting	Social assistance targeting (SILC)	Social assistance generosity	Social assistance generosity (SILC)	Spending in pensions	Child care	Ethnic prejudice	Forbidden temporary contracts	Ease of access to loan	Import. of network
				31.5	1	2.90	1	3.0	3.2
	41.2		10.8	24.4	0	3.10	0	3.2	3.1
	26.7		4.7	37.5	1	3.45	1	2.0	3.3
	59.2		13.0	11.5	0	2.30	0	3.1	2.5
	48.6		14.2	15.3	0	3.40	0	4.6	2.6
				7.2	1	3.03		3.7	2.9
	37.4		11.9	26.6	1	3.03	0	3.2	2.9
	35.8		10.0	22.2	1	3.03	0	3.8	2.9
	51.7		10.1	9.8	1	3.03	0	3.1	2.9
	50.4		11.9	18.6	1	3.03	1	4.4	2.9
	32.3		9.1	34.3	1	3.03	1	1.7	2.9
	40.5		7.0	3.6	1	3.03	0	2.7	2.9
	45.5		12.5	8.4	1	3.03	0	1.8	2.9
	38.8		10.9	10.5	0	3.03	1	4.1	2.9
	65.7		11.0	9.9	1	3.03	0	3.7	2.9
	47.6		10.1	9.6	1	3.03	1	4.4	2.9
	34.3		5.3	22.5	1	3.03	1	2.3	2.9
	22.9		7.4	24.3	1	3.03	1	2.1	2.9
				12.0	1	3.03	0	3.7	2.9
48.8	39.9	12.1	8.1	25.1	0.83	2.96	0.55	2.6	3.3
–	40.8	–	10.5	15.3	0.79	3.03	0.44	3.2	2.9
48.8	40.8	12.1	10.1	22.6	0.81	3.03	0.51	2.8	3.1
12.1	10.6	7.0	3.0	15.4	–	0.2	–	0.4	0.4
–	11.3	–	2.7	10.0	–	0.2	–	0.9	0.2
12.1	11.0	7.0	2.8	14.4	–	0.2	–	0.7	0.4

SPOTLIGHT 4.1

How Powerful Are the Disincentives from Labor Taxes and Social Protection?

At the aggregate level, income taxation has often been linked to lower employment levels, higher unemployment, and higher informality (see for example Keane and Rogerson 2011; Davis and Henrekson 2004; Flaig and Rottman 2011; World Bank 2007a). Davis and Henrekson (2004), for example, find that among OECD countries a one-standard-deviation increase in tax rates (12.8 percentage points) leads to 122 fewer market work hours per adult per year, a drop of 4.9 percentage points in the employment-population ratio, and a rise in the shadow economy equal to 3.8 percent of GDP. It also leads to 10–30 percent lower employment and value added shares in the retail, hotel-restaurant, and industry sectors. More broadly, it has been shown that labor taxation partly explains the persistence of relatively high unemployment rates in Western Europe in the past decades.[57] The effects of labor taxation at the aggregate level do vary in magnitude. Results from a meta-analysis of multiple studies suggest that a 10 percent decrease in labor taxation in middle-income and developed countries is, on average, associated with an increase half as large in total employment.[58] In Turkey, for example, estimated impacts from labor taxation reform are of similar magnitude and take place mostly in less than 18 months. An evaluation of social contribution subsidies in low-income provinces in the country found that reductions in total labor costs significantly increased registered employment in eligible provinces (Taymaz 2006). Overall, estimates of the impact of labor taxation on employment appear to be lower in developing and transition economies (Vroman and Brusentsev 2005). Higher labor taxation is also linked to higher informality. A meta-analysis of 22 studies in OECD countries found that tax and social security contributions explain around half of the cross-country variation in the size of the informal economy. Critically, the effect of labor taxation on informality is reduced by around one-fifth after taking into account the quality of public services received in exchange for the taxes and contributions paid (Schneider 2012, see also Schneider 2003, 2005, and 2009; Dell'Anno 2003; Giles and Tedds 2002; Mummert and Schneider 2001).

At the individual and firm levels, labor taxation has also been found to impact labor market decisions. As discussed in chapter 2, tax rates are seen as a major obstacle for ECA firms' growth and performance. In particular, World Bank Enterprise surveys for 2007 and 2009 reveal that, on average, 16 percent of firms in ECA cite tax rates as the biggest obstacle to doing business and thus creating (formal) jobs, going as high as 35 and 27 percent in Lithuania and Kazakhstan, respectively. On the side of workers, higher income taxation reduces disposable income and—if arising from higher labor taxation—take-home pay. In a survey of EU countries, taxes and social security contributions were reported as key factors considered when deciding whether or not to work formally. For example, in Hungary and Lithuania, around one-third of respondents cited labor taxation as the most important factor behind informality. In other countries, labor taxation seemed less relevant than competing factors such as low wages and stringent government control in the formal sector (World Bank 2012k, based on

continued

Eurobarometer EC 2007). Further, as noted, labor taxation is particularly relevant in determining the choice of participating or not, more often than the decision on how many hours to work (Eissa and Hoynes 1998; and Eissa and Liebman 1996). The effects of tax reforms on labor market outcomes, for both firms and workers, is likely to increase with time as economic agents adapt to the changes.

The extent to which reducing labor costs through lower labor taxation can boost formal employment will depend on whether the tax reform leads to lower costs for firms or to higher take-home pay for workers (Gruber and Krueger 1990). The effects of lowering labor taxation on employment would be less than expected if a significant portion of the reduction is captured by workers through higher wages.[59] This was, in fact, the case in Chile when a major labor tax reform in the early 1980s had virtually no employment impact (Heckman and Pagés 2004). Conversely, in the case of Colombia, the incidence of labor taxation changes over the 1980s and 1990s primarily fell on employers with subsequent effects on employment (Kugler and Kugler 2008).

The effects of labor taxation on labor markets will also depend on labor market institutions. Evidence for ECA countries suggests that labor market flexibility can mitigate the negative employment effects of labor taxation. Labor market institutions influence the balance of power between employers and workers, affecting whether a reduction in labor taxation gets translated into higher wages or higher employment. Stronger trade unions, binding minimum wages, and rigid labor laws, for example, could increase workers' bargaining power, protecting wages at the expense of employment (World Bank 2007b).

In practice, the effects of labor taxation on employment appear to be larger among low-wage/low-skilled, part-time, and female workers. The market for this set of workers is often tighter than the market at higher wages and skill levels. Therefore, lower labor taxation does not translate into higher wages but rather into lower labor costs for firms, potentially boosting employment for this group. In Bulgaria, the Czech Republic, Estonia, Latvia, Poland, and the Slovak Republic, a higher labor tax and a more aggressive withdrawal of social benefits were linked to lower formal employment. This effect was especially high for workers earning less than a third of the average wage in the country.[60] The literature also finds larger employment effects among women.[61] This means that there is likely to be a larger pay-off in terms of employment from targeting reductions in labor taxation at the low end of the wage distribution than from doing so across the board. This is most relevant for countries with relatively high labor taxation for low-wage earners (e.g. Bulgaria, Estonia, Latvia, FYR Macedonia, Montenegro, and Serbia) and countries where this set of workers represents a large share of the working-age population.

Social assistance has been found to create disincentives to work or work formally, but the evidence is scarce and mostly for developed countries. In a set of high-income countries (the United Kingdom, Canada, Norway, Sweden, and Denmark), benefit generosity has been found

continued

to have a negative effect on labor force participation (LFP), particularly if benefits are close to wages of low-paid jobs (Adema 2006). Further, evidence for the United States shows a negative impact of social assistance programs on the decision to work formally for low-wage earners (Eissa and Hoynes 2005; Eissa and Liebman 1996; Meyer and Rosenbaum 2001). The scarce evidence available for developing countries has found the effects to be less important. Program evaluations for Brazil (Bourguignon, Ferreira, and Leite 2003), Mexico,[62] and some African (Adato and Hoddinott 2008) countries have found no significant effects on labor market decisions. Some evidence in Latin America does point to increased informality (Gasparini, Haimovich, and Olivieri 2007; Mason 2007). In ECA, the available evidence is for low and low-middle income countries where smaller or no disincentive effects would be expected given overall low income. In Tajikistan, social assistance transfers have actually been found to increase adult employment rates in female-headed households, possibly by providing a much needed safety net to transition into employment from either inactivity or informality (World Bank forthcoming a). In Armenia, the social assistance program does not affect LFP or decisions on formality; some potential negative impact on hours worked is found for rural workers only (World Bank 2011a). In Georgia, the targeted social assistance program—relatively generous compared to similar programs in the region—is associated with a decrease of 7 percentage points in the probability of working or looking for a job, with the effect higher among men than women (9 versus 5 percentage points). However, accounting for the fact that all social assistance beneficiaries also receive free health insurance, the effect disappears. This suggests that it is the provision of health insurance that is really affecting labor market decisions (World Bank, forthcoming c).

In terms of unemployment benefits, findings on the existence of work disincentives remains mixed, with most of the evidence available from developed countries. Across OECD countries, the evidence shows that benefit generosity and duration have a positive impact on unemployment (Addison and Portugal 2008; Dlugosz, Stephan, and Wilke 2013; Flaig and Rottman 2011; Katz and Meyer 1990; Lo, Stephan, and Wilke 2012; Nickell 1998). Other studies, including for Estonia and Slovenia, also link unemployment benefits to disincentives for job search (Lauringson 2011; Van Ours and Tuit 2010; Van Ours and Vodopivec 2006). However, in Germany a recent study finds an impact on the length of unemployment but also reports that those with longer benefit duration are also able to find jobs at higher wages and longer tenure—possibly suggesting the role of unemployment benefits in allowing workers to find better matching jobs.[63] Conversely, other studies find no support for an effect of unemployment benefits on unemployment (Howell and Rehm 2009).

Pension benefits appear to weaken work incentives, even among members of the household aside from the pensioner. The available literature is limited, but suggests important labor market effects of pensions. For instance, Gruber and Wise (2004) find that, in nine Western European countries, increasing the pension age by three years is likely to reduce

continued

SPOTLIGHT 4.1 *continued*

the proportion of inactive men aged 56–65 by up to 36 percent. In the United States, the labor supply of older workers has been found to respond to changes in retirement incentives, especially taxation (French and Jones 2010). In Brazil, changes in pension eligibility and generosity for rural male workers reduced male LFP by 38 percentage points (Carvalho Filho 2012). Similarly, in the Czech Republic, a decrease of 2–3 percent in early retirement benefits in 2001 led to a similar decrease the probability of inactivity for male workers eligible for early retirement (Kocourek and Pertold 2009). The universal increase in old-age pension benefits in Ukraine in 2004, analyzed with a quasi-experimental design, also increased the probability of retiring at the statutory pension age by 30–47 percent, particularly among the low-skilled and men. The magnitude of the effects on hours worked was smaller—partly driven by limited choices in working arrangements—but larger among women and the least educated. Other studies find effects of pensions on other household members. A cross-country analysis of ECA countries finds an increased probability of inactivity among households' members ages 18–65 in households receiving pensions (figure S4.2.5).[64] For South Africa findings point to modest, negative impacts on participation and employment on average, but a pronounced, positive migration impact (Bertrand, Mullainathan, and Miller 2003; Sienaert 2008). In Georgia, where about 53 percent of all households include at least one pensioner, results from a quasi-experimental study suggest a four percent decline in household-level activity rate as a female household member becomes eligible for pensions (World Bank 2011b).

SPOTLIGHT 4.2

Social Protection Systems

Social protection—including unemployment benefits, social assistance, and pensions—plays an important role in shielding households from poverty and overall vulnerability. Social protection schemes in the region cover a relatively large share of the population, barring a few countries. Forty-six percent of households in ECA receive either social assistance or pension income. Most of this coverage is driven by pensions. Social protection systems help households combat poverty and reduce vulnerability. In Hungary, Romania, and Estonia, for example, social assistance is associated with a 5 percentage point reduction in poverty rates (figure S4.2.1). Social benefits, more generally, can help workers manage unemployment risks and uncertainty in earnings. They also play a fundamental role in fostering more efficient labor transitions by providing workers with a financial cushion that can help them make better employment decisions and move to better jobs.[65] Pensions also play an important role in preventing old-age poverty (World Bank forthcoming b).

continued

SPOTLIGHT 4.2 *continued*

FIGURE S4.2.1
Social Benefits Help Combat Poverty

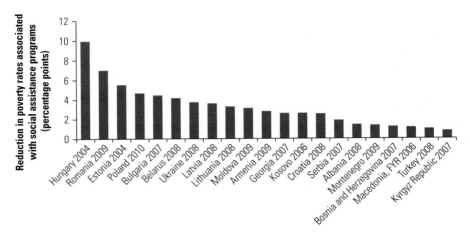

Source: Sundaram and Strokova forthcoming.

Notes: To facilitate comparison across countries, performance indicators for ECA are calculated using a standardized methodology that ranks individuals into quintiles based on harmonized consumption aggregates and pretransfer consumption per capita. The baseline poverty line is determined by consumption at the 20th poorest percentile. The poverty rate that would exist if there were no social assistance is based on the number of households that moves below that poverty line once the amount of transfers received is subtracted from consumption.

First, coverage and generosity of unemployment benefits, in and of themselves, are unlikely to create work disincentives.[66] Unemployment benefits cover a relatively small share of the unemployed (figure S4.2.2). In Poland, Ukraine, the Slovak Republic, and Turkey, for example, less than a fifth of the unemployed receive benefits. In other countries, like Georgia, unemployment benefits do not exist. Unemployment benefits are also relatively low across the board, with the possible exception of Serbia. On average, they amount to 24.2 percent of average earnings for low-wage workers in ECA (figure S4.2.2). However, beyond generosity and coverage, unemployment benefits—given their duration, eligibility, and withdrawal schedule—can in fact give rise to work disincentives.

Second, social assistance programs could discourage (formal) work, although mostly in countries with high coverage and relatively generous benefits. Most social assistance programs in the region are categorical, where benefits are not means-tested (figure S4.2.3). Within these categorical benefits, child and family, maternity, disability, and housing are often the largest.[67] Generally, social assistance programs in the region do cover a significant share of the population but are not very generous. National household surveys indicate that, on average, one-third of all households and more than half of those in the poorest quintile receive social assistance. Coverage is particularly high in the Slovak Republic, Slovenia, Hungary, and Romania (above 57 percent), while it is the lowest in the Western Balkans, the South Caucasus, and the Kyrgyz Republic

continued

SPOTLIGHT 4.2 *continued*

(figure S4.2.4). Although not very generous on average,[68] social assistance benefits can create work disincentives in cases where they are high relative to local wages. This is likely to be the case in Montenegro, for example, where transfers are generous vis-à-vis the minimum wage (74.8 percent).[69]

FIGURE S4.2.2

Unemployment Coverage Is Relatively Low in ECA, and in Most Cases Benefits Are Not Very Generous

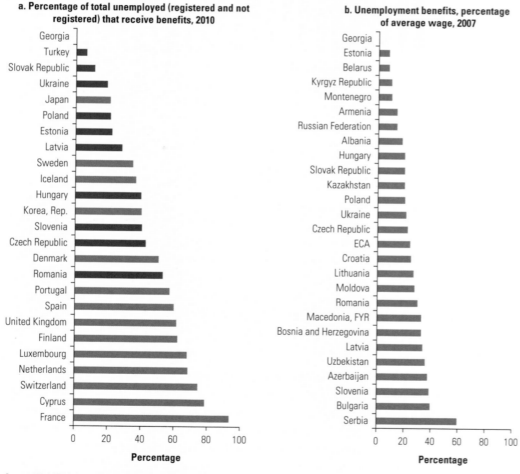

a. Percentage of total unemployed (registered and not registered) that receive benefits, 2010

b. Unemployment benefits, percentage of average wage, 2007

Sources: World Bank, based on ILO data; OECD (2012a) and IZA database.
Notes: ECA is the simple average of countries in the region included in the figure. Calculations made for a single earner with no children at 67 percent of average wage. Data for Georgia is not missing but zero. In panel a, ECA countries have red bars.

continued

SPOTLIGHT 4.2 *continued*

FIGURE S4.2.3

Most Social Assistance Programs Are Not Means Tested

Coverage of the poorest quintile by program types

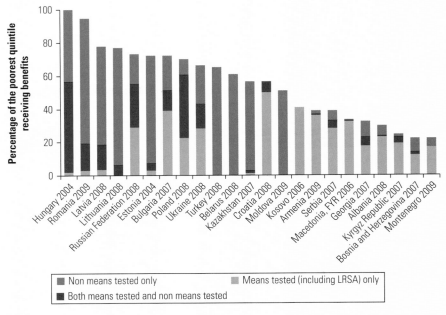

Source: EC 2011b.
Note: LRSA refers to last-resort social assistance.

Third, contrary to unemployment benefits and social assistance, pensions in the region can be generous and an important source of income for many households, potentially creating work disincentives both for recipients and other household members. Coverage is high for pensions, driven not only by demographics, but also by generous eligibility criteria that allow for early retirement and for pensions beyond those associated with old-age. This means that a large number of people live in households with pensioners; if pensions do create work disincentives, they have the potential to affect many.

As figure S4.2.5 suggests, households that receive pensions have a larger share of members out of the labor force compared to nonrecipient households. Across ECA countries, on average 39.7 percent of households receive pension income; more than half of all households do in Bulgaria, Croatia, Georgia, Hungary, Latvia, Lithuania, Romania, and Serbia. Even when excluding households with only members 65 or older, pensions remain prevalent. Further, pensions are very generous in most countries (figure S4.2.6). Other indicators show that, on average, for countries with available data, net pension replacement rates for average earners is 80 percent, 11 percentage points higher than the OECD average. In Hungary, Romania, and Turkey net

continued

SPOTLIGHT 4.2 *continued*

FIGURE S4.2.4

Coverage of Social Assistance Is High in EU Member States but Low in Western Balkans, South Caucasus, and the Kyrgyz Republic

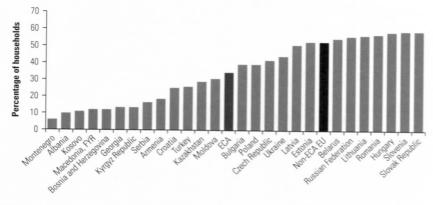

Source: EC 2011b.

Note: Social assistance includes the following benefits: last-resort social assistance, housing allowances, family and disability benefits, and any other noncontributory programs. For non-ECA EU, Slovenia, and the Slovak Republic, social assistance includes education, housing, family and child benefits, and social exclusion benefits not elsewhere classified.

FIGURE S4.2.5

Pensions Could Create Work Disincentives in the Region, Both for Recipients but Also for Other Household Members

Share of household members 18–65 in inactivity in households with at least one member of working age

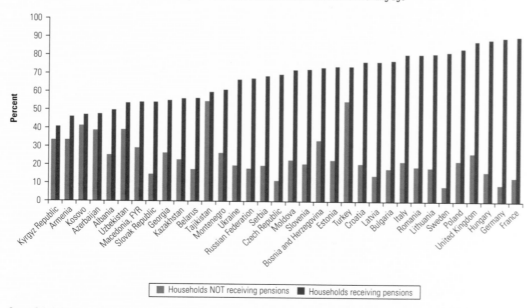

Source: Calculations using LiTS (EBRD 2010).

continued

SPOTLIGHT 4.2 *continued*

FIGURE S4.2.6

Pension Generosity Is High in Many ECA Countries, Even When Compared to OECD Countries

Pension spending per person 65 or older, GDP per capita, 2009

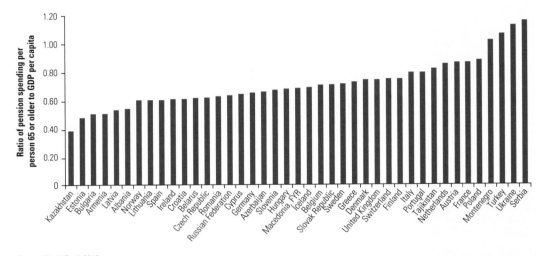

Source: World Bank 2012g.
Note: ECA = Europe and Central Asia; GDP = gross domestic product; OECD = Organisation for Economic Co-operation and Development.

replacement rates are well above 100 percent. As a result, pensions are a critical income source in many households, accounting, for example, for an average 36 percent of household income in Serbia, 25 percent in Ukraine, and 22 percent in Belarus and Poland. The high cost of pensions drive up social contribution and labor taxation rates. As a result, work disincentives associated with pensions are exacerbated as hiring costs rise and take-home pay shrinks.

Notes

1. World Bank staff calculations based on household surveys. Data for Latin America and the Caribbean is for 2010. In ECA, household nonlabor income primarily consists of income from social benefits and pensions, although remittances are also important in some countries. In Moldova, the Kyrgyz Republic, and Tajikistan, for example, remittances are an important source of income for many households and account for 24, 27, and 40 percent of GDP (World Bank 2010c).
2. In a sample of ECA countries, on average men earn 31 percent more than women (authors' calculations using labor force surveys, accounting for self-selection and controlling for age, education and location).

3. World Bank (2010b, forthcoming [a]).
4. Pensions represent more than a third of total household income in some countries, driven partly by demographics. Pensions are reported as the main source of income by many households in Lithuania (38 percent of households), Estonia (41 percent), and Romania and Hungary (45 percent) (calculations based on EBRD and World Bank 2010).
5. Social assistance includes, for example, disability benefits; family, child, and birth allowances; minimum income programs; social pensions; and heating, utilities, and housing benefits. Social insurance benefits refer to pensions, unemployment and disability insurance, maternity leave and sickness, and invalid and survivor insurance. This report focuses here on overall social assistance and unemployment and pension insurance benefits.
6. In countries where public services and government expenditures are effective, individuals are more likely to be willing to accept higher taxation. Across ECA countries, there are important variations in the quality of government spending and governance. These factors, and their interaction with government taxation, are discussed in Gill and Raiser (2012) and Koettl and Weber (2012).
7. A change in labor taxation can have both an income and a substitution effect on labor supply. On the one hand, higher labor taxation leads to lower net wages and could therefore make it more necessary to work longer to maintain a given level of net income. On the other hand, higher labor taxation also reduces the opportunity cost from not working since the payoff from working is now lower. Which effect dominates is an empirical question and is likely to depend on various individual and labor market factors. This evidence is discussed in spotlight 4.1. In addition to this direct impact, labor taxation also partly determines the relative cost of capital with respect to labor, another channel that matters for employment.
8. Calculations using data from U.S. Social Security Administration (2012).
9. This reference wage is used as a notional wage to calculate minimum social security contributions for workers earning below a certain level. In FYR Macedonia, it is set at 50 percent of the average wage and in Serbia at 35 percent. In Serbia, however, the reference wage is not adjusted by hours worked, further penalizing part-time workers. In these countries, the reference wage is used as a second-best solution to addressing the issue of under-reporting of wages by creating a wage floor for reporting social contributions.
10. See, for example, McClelland and Mok (2012); Bargain, Orsini, and Peichl (2011); and Heckman (1993) for reviews of this literature.
11. A limiting factor of the literature is that, overall, the available evidence stems primarily from developed countries. Where evidence from developing countries does exist, it covers mostly low- and low-middle income economies.
12. Koettl and Weber (2012). Similar results were obtained by Behar (2009) where the impact of tax and benefits on employment was found only for low-wage earners, particularly youth. Kugler and Kugler (2008) also

document larger effects of labor taxation changes among low-skilled, low-wage earners. For the effect on women workers, see Morawski and Myck (2010) for the case of the "kiln" Polish reforms. For a survey of the literature see Keane (2011).

13. Within social assistance, it is important to recognize that the relationship between benefit and work is likely to vary significantly depending on the program. Maternity, disability, and housing benefits, for example, can affect labor market decisions differently.

14. ECA Social Protection Database (World Bank 2012b).

15. World Bank (2011e). The system in Montenegro is currently under reform.

16. Most countries have additional types of pensions, especially for disability and survivors; in others, there are some special categories of the population receiving pensions, such as war veterans.

17. OECD 2010b; data covers EU new member states, Croatia, and Turkey.

18. Quote from focus group discussions carried out by the World Bank in FYR Macedonia in 2012.

19. The Women, Business and the Law Database (World Bank 2012i).

20. In the Slovak Republic and Hungary, for example, women retire more than four years earlier than the age designated by law; in Poland, men retire three and a half years earlier (OECD).

21. World Bank (2012i); qualitative work conducted by the World Bank in Croatia and Poland showed that a high proportion of older workers (between 55 and 70 years old) retire "by default" when they reach the retirement age, even when not mandatory (World Bank 2012d, 2012e).

22. World Bank (2012e, 2012f).

23. To analyze the interaction of taxation and benefits with labor income, the report relies on the OECD Tax and Benefit Model. This model provides a description of what workers and their employers have to pay in taxes and contributions and the benefits workers can get when inactive, unemployed, or employed, depending on their gross income and family type. The model calculates the individual's entitlements to benefits such as social assistance, unemployment, housing, family, and in-work benefits according to the various income levels. In recent years, the World Bank has cooperated with the OECD to develop the same model for non-OECD members.

24. For a more detailed discussion on policies addressed at fighting informality, see World Bank (2012k).

25. World Bank (2012b). Data for Belarus is from 2008, for Tajikistan 2012, for Bosnia and Herzegovina 2007, and for the Russian Federation 2008.

26. In some instances, countries may also need to rethink the overall composition of social assistance programs. For example, in the case of family benefits, rethinking the balance between subsidies to social services and provision of cash benefits. In Denmark and Iceland, for example, of the total public spending on family benefits (3.7 and 3.5 percent of GDP, respectively), approximately 60 percent is spent on services—50 percent more than on cash benefits (OECD 2012c).

27. It is important to note, however, that potential disincentives to (formal) work could arise among younger workers as benefits are reduced and retirement ages increased.

28. For a more detailed discussion see World Bank (forthcoming [b]).

29. For a more detailed discussion of active labor market policies in ECA and OECD countries, see Brown and Koettl (2012) and Immervoll (2012).

30. Further evidence points to differences in the wage gap during these years. See for example, Pastore, Sattar, and Tiongson (2012) for the case of Kosovo.

31. When women do work, parental leave regulations in some ECA countries—which usually include different provisions for mothers and fathers—can put women at a disadvantage regarding their labor market trajectory. Most countries in ECA provide maternity leave, but there is wide variation in length, percentage of leave that is paid, and who pays for it. Conversely, only six countries in ECA provide paid paternity leave, and in those that do, the duration is limited to an average of 13 days. Countries may consider reducing the gender gap in parental leave— depending on the case by decreasing maternal leave, increasing paternal leave, or both—as a means of leveling the playing field for women in the job market. In addition, countries may also consider reforming the financing of parental leave by shifting from a system based on payroll taxation and employers to one where paid leave is financed through general taxation. This shift would also address the additional costs that employers incur when hiring women in childbearing age.

32. World Bank (2012i).

33. World Bank (2012i) reports that only the Kyrgyz Republic has child care tax credits among the 23 countries covered.

34. The Barcelona targets of 2002 set the provision of child care by 2010 to at least 90 percent of children between three years and the mandatory school age, and at 33 percent, at least, for children under three (EC 2012b).

35. According to the ILO, part-time work is "regular, voluntary work carried out during working hours distinctly shorter than normal," usually less than 35 or 30 hours per week.

36. Using quasi-experimental evidence from a cash for care transfer program, N. Drange and M. Rege (2012) show that women in Norway who left the labor market to raise children were able to re-engage in fulltime work in large part because they stayed in part-time work in between transitions.

37. Authors' calculations with household and labor force data for 17 ECA countries between 2009 and 2011.

38. Eurostat.

39. Part-time work is, however, not a full solution, given that it could have scarring effects on wages (Fouarge and Muffels 2009) or present obstacles into transitioning into full-time work. In a survey of employers in 21 EU countries, it was found that, on average, 27 percent of managers reported that part-time employees could easily get a full-time job while the same proportion said that there was "no chance" of this happening.

The remaining 43 percent said that this could happen only exceptionally. Countries where the highest proportion of managers said that this could be done quickly included the Czech Republic, Cyprus, Italy, and Belgium (Eurofound 2011).

40. These policies, however, need to account for the fact that they effectively increase the cost of hiring women, especially in cases where social contributions are not adjusted by hours worked.

41. World Bank (2012i).

42. World Bank (2012c).

43. A more detailed analysis of how to improve access to credit, land, and other inputs is beyond the scope of this chapter. However, for discussion on these issues see World Bank (2011f); World Bank (2012l); and Sattar (2012).

44. Compared to 1:150 in the European Union and 1:100 as the recommended ILO standard (Kuddo 2012).

45. Ibid.

46. This refers to the Steps to College Program and Junior Achievement Hispanic Outreach Program in Dalton, Georgia (OECD 2011).

47. This refers to the Jobmarathon in Brussels (OECD 2011).

48. Most ECA countries have the legal frameworks in place that mandate nondiscrimination on the basis of gender, age, race, and other criteria. However, gender wage gaps, for example, persist for workers with the same qualifications. Authors' calculations based on household and labor force surveys.

49. Other factors, not included in the empirical analysis, may also help explain unequal outcomes, e.g. women's willingness to commute given travel options, work experience, and work hour compatibility with school times.

50. Calculations based on EBRD (2010).

51. Qualitative work in Poland conducted in 2010 for the *World Development Report* 2012 (World Bank 2011f).

52. Authors' calculations with data from LiTS (EBRD 2010). Data for Western Europe includes France, Germany, the United Kingdom, Italy, and Sweden.

53. This initiative is being supported by the World Bank through the Turkey Technical Assistance on "Promoting Gender Equity in the Private Sector."

54. The Youth Employment Inventory (YEI) is a joint effort of the World Bank's Human Development Network/Labor Team (WB/HDN), the German Ministry of Economic Cooperation and Development (BMZ), the Inter-American Development Bank (IADB), the International Labour Organization (ILO), and the Youth Employment Network (YEN).

55. More details available at http://ec.europa.eu/justice/newsroom/discrimination/news/120523_en.htm. Last accessed February 12, 2013.

56. Protection in this context refers narrowly to coverage and generosity without considerations of fiscal cost or efficiency (beyond labor market incentives). As such, the index should not be taken as an indicator of overall desirability of a social protection system. See annex 4B for full methodological details of this index.

Fiszbein, A., and N. Schady. 2009. *Conditional Cash Transfers Reducing Present and Future Poverty*. Policy Research Report. Washington, DC: World Bank.

Flaig, G., and H. Rottman. 2011. "Labour Market Institutions and Unemployment. An International Comparison." CESifo Working Papers 3558, Munich.

Fouarge, D., and R. Muffels. 2009. "Working Part-Time in the British, German and Dutch Labor Market: Scarring for the Wage Career?" *Schmollers Jahrbuch* 129 (2): 217–26.

Freije, S., R. Bando, and F. Arce. 2006. "Conditional Transfers, Labor Supply, and Poverty: Microsimulating Oportunidades." *Economia* 7 (1): 73–124.

French, E., and J. Jones. 2010. "Public Pensions and Labor Supply over the Life Cycle." Federal Reserve Bank of Chicago, Working Paper 2010–09.

Gasparini, L. F. Haimovich, and S. Olivieri. 2007. "Labor Informality Effects of the Programa Jefes de Hogar." CEDLAS Working Paper 53, Centre for Distribution, Labor and Social Studies (CEDLAS), National University of La Plata, Buenos Aires.

Giles, D. E. A., and L. M. Tedds. 2002. "Taxes and the Canadian Underground Economy." Canadian Tax Paper 106, Canadian Tax Foundation, Toronto, Canada.

Gill, I. S., and M. Raiser. 2012. "Golden Growth: Restoring the Luster of the European Economic Model." World Bank, Washington, DC.

Great Britain Department for Work and Pensions. 2010. "Delivering Universal Credit: A Better Deal for Everyone." Chap. 4, *Universal Credit: Welfare that Works*, Cm 7957, London. http://www.dwp.gov.uk/docs/universal-credit-full-document.pdf.

———. 2011. "Jobcentre Plus Delivery Plan 2011 to 2012," London. http://www.dwp.gov.uk/docs/jcp-delivery-plan-2011-2012.pdf.

Gruber, J., and A. Krueger. 1990. "The Incidence of Mandated Employer-Provided Insurance: Lessons from Workers' Compensation Insurance." Working Paper 279, Industrial Relations Section, Princeton University, NJ.

Gruber, J. and D. Wise, eds. 2004. *Social Security Programs and Retirement around the World: Micro-Estimation*. University Of Chicago Press, Chicago.

Gutiérrez-Domenech, M. 2005. "Employment after Motherhood: A European Comparison." *Labour Economics* 12 (1): 99–123.

Heckman, J. J. 1993. "What Has Been Learned about Labor Supply in the Past Twenty Years?" *American Economic Review* 83 (2): 116–21.

Heckman, J. J., and C. Pagés. 2004. *Law and Employment: Lessons from Latin America and the Caribbean*: Cambridge, MA: NBER Books.

Hotz, J. V., and J. K. Scholz. 2001. "The Earned Income Tax Credit." NBER Working Paper 8078, Cambridge, MA, January. http://www.nber.org.libproxy-wb.imf.org/papers/w8078.pdf?new_window=1.

Howell, D. R., and B. M. Azizoglu. 2011. "Unemployment Benefits and Work Incentives: The US Labour Market in the Great Recession," *Oxford Review of Economic Policy* 27 (2): 221–40.

Howell, D. R., and M. Rehm. 2009. "Unemployment Compensation and High European Unemployment: A Reassessment with New Benefit Indicators." *Oxford Review of Economic Policy* 25 (1): 60–93.

IFC (International Finance Corporation). 2013. "Assessing Private Sector Contributions to Job Creation and Poverty Reduction." IFC Jobs Study, Washington, DC.

Immervoll, H. 2012. "Activation Policies in OECD Countries: An Overview of Current Approaches." Social Protection & Labor Policy Note 14, World Bank, Washington, DC, June.

Islam, R., and K. Smits. 2013. *Fiscal Recovery? Managing in a Risky World.* Washington, DC: World Bank.

IZA (Institute for the Study of Labor). IZA Database Employment Protection Legislation, Bonn.

Jensen, R. 2010. "The (Perceived) Returns to Education and the Demand for Schooling." *Quarterly Journal of Economics* 125 (2): 515–48.

Kaas, L., and C. Manger. 2010. "Ethnic Discrimination in Germany's Labor Market: A Field Experiment." IZA Discussion Paper 4741, Institute for the Study of Labor, Bonn, Germany.

Katz, L. 1998. "Wage Subsidies for the Disadvantaged." In *Generating Jobs: How to Increase Demand for Less Skilled Workers,* edited by P. Gottschalk and R. B. Freeman. New York: Russell Sage Foundation.

Katz, L., and B. Meyer. 1990. "The Impact of Potential Duration of Unemployment Benefits on the Duration of Unemployment." NBER Working Paper 2741, National Bureau of Economic Research, Cambridge, MA.

Kaygusuz, R. 2010. "Taxes and Female Labour Supply." *Review of Economic Dynamics* 13 (4): 725–41.

Keane, M. P. 2011. "Labor Supply and Taxes: A Survey." *Journal of Economic Literature* 49 (4): 961–1075.

Keane, M. P., and R. Rogerson. 2011. "Reconciling Micro and Macro Labor Supply Elasticities: A Structural Perspective." NBER Working Papers 17430, National Bureau of Economic Research, Cambridge, MA.

Kocourek, D., and F. Pertold. 2009. "The Impact of Early Retirement Incentives on Labor Market Participation: Evidence from a Parametric Change in the Czech Republic." Czech National Bank, Prague.

Koettl, J. 2012. "Work Disincentives in Montenegro: Results from the 2011 OECD Tax and Benefit Model for Montenegro." Technical Note for the Government of Montenegro, World Bank, Washington, DC.

Koettl, J., and M. Weber. 2012. "Does Formal Work Pay? The Role of Labor Taxation and Social Benefit Design in the New EU Member States." *Research in Labor Economics* 34: 167–204.

Krebs, T., and M. Scheffel. 2013. "Macroeconomic Evaluation of Labor Market Reform in Germany." IMF Working Paper 13/42, International Monetary Fund, Washington, DC.

Kuddo, A. 2009. "Labor Laws in Eastern European and Central Asian Economies: Minimum Norms and Practices." Social Protection Discussion Paper 0920, World Bank, Washington, DC.

Kuddo, A. 2010. *Labor Market Monitoring in Eastern Europe and Central Asia Countries: Recent Trends (Round Three)*. Washington, DC: World Bank.

———. 2012. "Public Employment Services, and Activation Policies." Social Protection Discussion Paper 1215, World Bank, Washington, DC.

Kugler, A., and M. Kugler. 2008. "Labor Market Effects of Payroll Taxes in Developing Countries: Evidence from Colombia." NBER Working Paper 13855, National Bureau of Economic Research, Cambridge, MA.

Kvist, J., and L. Pedersen. 2007. "Danish Labour Market Activation Policies." *National Institute Economic Review* 202: 99.

La Cava, G., and S. Michael. 2006. *Youth in the Northern Caucasus: From Risk to Opportunity.* World Bank: Washington, DC.

Laderchi, C. R., A. Olivier, and C. Trimble. 2013. *Balancing Act: Cutting Energy Subsidies while Protecting Affordability.* Washington, DC: World Bank.

Lauringson, A. 2011. "Disincentive Effects of Unemployment Insurance Benefits: Maximum Benefit Duration versus Benefit Level." *Baltic Journal of Economics* 11 (1): 25–49.

Lee, J., M. Lundberg, D. Margolis, D. Newhouse, D. Robalino, F. Rother, and A. Tasneem. 2012. *Youth Employment: A Human Development Agenda for the Next Decade.* World Bank, Washington, DC.

Liebman, J. 1996. "The Impact of the Earned Income Tax Credit on Labor Supply and Taxpayer Compliance." PhD dissertation, Harvard University, Cambridge, MA.

Lo, S., G. Stephan, and R. Wilke. 2012. "Estimating the Latent Effect of Unemployment Benefits on Unemployment Duration." IZA Discussion Paper 6650, Institute for the Study of Labor, Bonn, Germany.

Lyonette, C., B. Baldauf, and H. Behle. 2010. *Quality Part-Time Work: A Review of the Evidence.* Institute for Employment Research, University of Warwick, U.K.

Maani, S. A. 1993. "Post-unemployment Wages, the Probability of Re-Employment, and the Unemployment Benefit." *New Zealand Economic Papers* 27 (1): 35–55.

Mason, A. D. 2007. "Informality, Social Protection, and Antipoverty Policies." In *Informality: Exit and Exclusion,* edited by G. E. Perry, W. F. Maloney, O. S. Arias, P. Fajnzylber, A. D. Mason, and J. Saavedra-Chanduvi, 179–211. Washington, DC: World Bank.

McClelland, R., and S. Mok. 2012. "A Review of Recent Research on Labor Supply Elasticities," *Working Paper* 2012–12, Congressional Budget Office, Washington, DC.

Meyer, B. D., and D. T. Rosenbaum. 2001. "Welfare, the Earned Income Tax Credit, and the Labor Supply of Single Mothers." *Quarterly Journal of Economics* 116 (3): 1063–114.

Morawski, L., and M. Myck. 2010. "'Klin'-ing Up: Effects of Polish Tax Reforms on Those in and on Those Out." *Labour Economics* 17 (3): 556–66.

Mummert, A., and F. Schneider. 2001. "The German Shadow Economy: Parted in a United Germany?" *Finanzarchiv* 58: 260–85.

Nickell, S. 1998. "Unemployment: Questions and Some Answers." *Economic Journal* 108 (448): 802–16.

Nickell, S., L. Nunziata, and W. Ochel. 2005. "Unemployment in the OECD since the 1960s: What Do We Know?" *Economic Journal* 115 (1): 1–27.

Nollenberger, N., and N. Rodríguez-Planas. 2011. "Child Care, Maternal Employment and Persistence: A Natural Experiment from Spain." IZA Discussion Paper 5888, Institute for the Study of Labor, Bonn, Germany.

OECD (Organisation for Economic Co-operation and Development). 2010a. *OECD Employment Outlook 2010*. OECD, Paris.

————. 2010b. *Tax and Benefit Model. Data for EU New Member States*. Paris: OECD.

————. 2011. "Ensuring Labor Market Success for Ethnic Minority and Immigrant Youth." OECD Local Economic and Employment Development (LEED) Working Papers 2011/09, OECD, Paris.

————. 2012a. Labor Force Statistics Database, OECD, Paris. http://www .oecd.org/std/labour-stats/labourforcestatistics1989-20092010editionoecd .htm.

————. 2012b. OECD Stat (database), OECD, Paris. http://stats.oecd.org/.

————. 2012c. Social Expenditure Database, OECD, Paris. http://www.oecd .org/els/soc/socialexpendituredatabasesocx.htm.

O'Higgins, N. 2010. "Youth Labor Markets in Europe and Central Asia." IZA Discussion Paper 5094, Institute for the Study of Labor, Bonn, Germany. http://ftp.iza.org/dp5094.pdf.

Pallais, A. 2013. "Inefficient Hiring in Entry-Level Labor Markets." NBER Working Paper 18917, National Bureau of Economic Research, Cambridge, MA.

Pastore, F., S. Sattar, and E. R. Tiongson. 2012. "Gender Differences in Earnings and Labor Supply in Early Career: Evidence from Kosovo's School-to-Work Transition Survey." Photocopy, World Bank, Washington, DC.

Rodríguez-Planas, N., and J. Benus. 2009. "Evaluating Active Labor Market Programs in Romania." *Empirical Economics* 38 (1): 65–84.

Saint-Paull, G. 2004. "Why Are European Countries Diverging in Their Unemployment Experience?" *Journal of Economic Perspectives* 18 (4): 49–68.

Sánchez-Mangas, R., and V. Sánchez-Marcos. 2008. "Balancing Family and Work: The Effect of Cash Benefits for Working Mothers." *Labour Economics* 15 (6): 1127–42.

Sattar, S. 2012. *Opportunities for Men and Women in Emerging Europe and Central Asia*. Washington, DC: World Bank.

Schneider, F. 2003. "Shadow Economy." In *Encyclopedia of Public Choice*, vol. 2, edited by C. K. Rowley and F. Schneider, 286–96. Dordrecht, Netherlands: Kluwer Academic Publishers.

———. 2005. "Shadow Economies around the World: What Do We Really Know?" *European Journal of Political Economy* 21 (4): 598–642.

———. 2009. "Size and Development of the Shadow Economy in Germany, Austria and Other OECD Countries: Some Preliminary Findings." *Revue Economique* 60: 1079–116.

———. 2012. "Work in the Shadow: What Do We (Not) Know?" Johannes Kepler University of Linz and IZA Discussion Paper 6423, Institute for the Study of Labor, Bonn, Germany.

Sienaert, A. 2008. "The Labor Supply Effects of the South African State Old Age Pension: Theory, Evidence and Implications." Southern Africa Labour and the Development Research Unit, WP20, SALDRU, University of Cape Town, Cape Town.

Skoufias, E., and V. Di Maro. 2008. "Conditional Cash Transfers, Adult Work Incentives, and Poverty." *Journal of Development Studies* 44 (7): 935–60.

Stovicek, K., and A. Turrini. 2012. "Benchmarking Unemployment Benefits in the EU." IZA Policy Paper 43, Institute for the Study of Labor, Bonn, Germany.

Sundaram, R. 2013. *Improving Access to Jobs and Earning Opportunities: The Role of Activation Policies*. Internal presentation, Washington, DC: World Bank.

Sundaram, R., and V. Strokova. Forthcoming. *Patchy Protection: Performance of Social Assistance Programs in Europe and Central Asia*. A World Bank Study. Washington, DC: World Bank.

Tatsiramos, K. 2006. "The Effect of Unemployment Insurance on Unemployment Duration and Subsequent Employment Stability." IZA Discussion Paper 2280, Institute for the Study of Labor, Bonn, Germany.

Taymaz, E. 2006. "Labor Demand in Turkey." Photocopy, World Bank, Washington, DC.

Terrell, K., and R. K. Almeida. 2008. "Minimum Wages in Developing Countries: Helping or Hurting Workers?" World Bank Employment Policy Primer 10, World Bank, Washington, DC, December.

Trampe, P. 2007. "The EITC Disincentive: The Effects on Hours Worked from the Phase-Out of the Earned Income Tax Credit." *Econ Journal Watch* 4 (3): 308–20.

Tsounta, E. 2006. "Why Are Women Working So Much More in Canada? An International Perspective." IMF Working Paper 06/92, International Monetary Fund, Washington, DC, April.

UNECE. 2012. UNECE Statistical Database, UNECE, Geneva, Switzerland. http://w3.unece.org/pxweb/?lang=1.

U.S. Personal Responsibility and Work Opportunity Reconciliation Act and Associated Legislation. 1996. Available at http://www.gpo.gov/fdsys/pkg /PLAW-104publ193/html/PLAW-104publ193.htm, accessed 15 April 2013.

U.S. Social Security Administration. 2012. *Social Security Programs throughout the World: Europe, 2012.* Woodlawn, MD. http://www.ssa.gov/policy/docs /progdesc/ssptw/, accessed 15 April 2013.

Van Ours, Jan C., and S. Tuit. 2010. "How Changes in Unemployment Benefit Duration Affect the Inflow into Unemployment." *Economics Letters* 109 (2): 105–7.

Van Ours, Jan C., and M. Vodopivec. 2006. "How Shortening the Potential Duration of Unemployment Benefits Affects the Duration of Unemployment: Evidence from a Natural Experiment." *Journal of Labor Economics* 24 (2): 351–78.

Van Reenen, J. 2004. "Active Labor Market Policies and the British New Deal for the Young Unemployed in Context." In *Seeking a Premier Economy: The Economic Effects of British Economic Reforms, 1980–2000,* edited by D. Card, R. Blundell, and R. B. Freeman, 461–96. Cambridge, MA: National Bureau of Economic Research.

Vroman, W., and V. Brusentsev. 2005. *Payroll Taxes, Labor Taxes and Employment in Turkey: Revised Report.* A World Bank Study, Washington, DC.

Williams, P., J. Larrison, V. Strokova, and K. Lindert. 2012. "Social Safety Nets in Europe and Central Asia: Preparing for Crisis, Adapting to Demographic Change, and Promoting Employability." Europe and Central Asia Knowledge Brief vol. 48, World Bank, Washington, DC, April.

World Bank. 2007a. *Fiscal Policy and Economic Growth: Lessons for Eastern Europe and Central Asia.* A World Bank Study. Washington, DC: World Bank.

———. 2007b. "Miles to Go: A Quest for an Operational Labor Market Paradigm for Developing Countries." World Bank/HDNSP, draft, World Bank, Washington, DC.

———. 2009a. *Economic and Sector Work Report.* A World Bank Study. Washington, DC: World Bank.

———. 2009b. *Estimating the Impact of Labor Taxes on Employment and the Balances of the Social Insurance Funds in Turkey.* World Bank Report 44056-TR. Washington, DC: World Bank.

———. 2009c. *A Gender Perspective on Access to Land and Finance in Tajikistan.* A World Bank Study. Washington, DC: World Bank.

———. 2010a. *Economic Costs of Roma Exclusion.* A World Bank Study, Europe and Central Asia Region. Washington, DC: World Bank.

———. 2010b. "Roma Inclusion: An Economic Opportunity for Bulgaria, Czech Republic, Romania and Serbia." ECA Policy Note, World Bank, Washington. DC: World Bank.

———. 2010c. World Development Indicators (database), World Bank, Washington, DC. http://data.worldbank.org/data-catalog/world -development-indicators.

———. 2011a. *Armenia: Social Assistance Programs and Work Disincentives.* World Bank Report 63112-AM. Washington, DC: World Bank.

———. 2011b. *Georgia Demographic Change: Implications for Social Programs and Poverty.* World Bank Report 63156-GE. Washington, DC: World Bank.

————. 2011c. "Kosovo: Minimum Wage Discussion." Photocopy, World Bank, Washington, DC.

————. 2011d. *Gender and Economic Choice Making Economic Choices Republic of Moldova Country Synthesis Report, Adult and Youth, Women and Men.* World Bank Country Report. Washington, DC: World Bank.

————. 2011e. *Social Safety Nets in the Western Balkans: Design, Implementation and Performance.* World Bank Report 54396-ECA, Europe and Central Asia Region. Washington, DC: World Bank.

————. 2011f. *World Development Report 2012: Gender Equality and Development.* Washington, DC: World Bank.

————. 2012a. *Closing the Early Learning Gap for Roma Children in Eastern Europe.* A World Bank Report. Washington, DC: World Bank.

————. 2012b. Europe and Central Asia Social Protection Database, World Bank. Washington, DC: World Bank.

————. 2012c. "Gender and Land Administration: Issues and Responses." Europe and Central Asia Knowledge Brief vol. 53, World Bank, Washington, DC, June.

————. 2012d. *Older Worker Labor Force Participation and Employment: Croatia.* A World Bank Study. Washington, DC: World Bank.

————. 2012e. *Older Worker Labor Force Participation and Employment: Poland.* A World Bank Study. Washington, DC: World Bank.

————. 2012f. *Older Worker Labor Force Participation and Employment: Russia.* A World Bank Study. Washington, DC: World Bank.

————. 2012g. Pension Database, World Bank, Washington, DC, http://web .worldbank.org/WBSITE/EXTERNAL/TOPICS/EXTSOCIALPROTECTION /EXTPENSIONS/0,,contentMDK:23231994~menuPK:8874064~pagePK :148956~piPK:216618~theSitePK:396253,00.html.

————. 2012h. *Protecting the Poor and Promoting Employability: An Assessment of the Social Assistance System in the Slovak Republic.* A World Bank Study, Europe and Central Asia Region. Washington, DC: World Bank.

————. 2012i. Women, Business and the Law Database, World Bank, Washington, DC. http://wbl.worldbank.org/.

————. 2012j. *Youth Employment: A Human Development Agenda for the Next Decade.* A World Bank Study. Washington, DC: World Bank.

————. 2012k. *In from the Shadow: Integrating Europe's Informal Labor.* A World Bank Study. Washington, DC: World Bank.

————. 2012l. *World Development Report 2013: Jobs.* Washington, DC: World Bank.

————. Forthcoming(a). *Ethnicity, Conflict and Development Outcomes in the ECA Region.* A World Bank Study. Washington, DC: World Bank.

————. Forthcoming(b). *The Inverted Pyramid: Pension Systems in Europe and Central Asia: Facing Demographic Challenges.* A World Bank Study. Washington, DC: World Bank.

————. Forthcoming(c). *Labor Market Inequalities in Eastern Europe and Central Asia.* A World Bank Study. Washington, DC: World Bank.

World Economic Forum. 2012. *The Global Competitiveness Report 2012–2013.* Geneva, Switzerland: World Economic Forum.

Wright, O. 2013. "Job Seekers Get a Nudge in Planning to Find Work." *Independent*, London, UK, March 8. http://www.independent.co.uk/news /uk/politics/job-seekers-get-a-nudge-in-planning-to-find-work-8527271 .html, last accessed 2 April 2013.

CHAPTER 5

Labor Mobility:
Leading Workers to Jobs

Introduction

This chapter discusses labor mobility in Europe and Central Asia, highlighting its centrality to the jobs agenda. As emphasized in chapter 2, fostering entrepreneurship and ensuring a high-quality business environment are keys to creating new and better employment in the region. Also, policies that facilitate and promote economic agglomeration will allow firms to become more productive and provide more and better jobs. Chapter 3 then argued that workers need to be equipped with the right set of skills to take advantage of the newly created, modern jobs. Moreover, social protection and taxation systems need to provide the right incentives to actively participate in the labor market and workers must have access to productive jobs (chapter 4). However, this is not enough. To contribute to higher employment and productivity, people have to be in the "right place"; workers should be able and prepared to move to the centers of economic activity where jobs and opportunities are. In doing so, they bring together knowledge and human capital that can generate productivity gains through agglomeration and create better labor market matching; this, in turn, opens opportunities for better wages and higher living standards for the workers and their families

(Moretti 2012; World Bank 2009). Mobility also entails great personal costs related to losing one's social ties or imposing big changes on partners and children (EC 2009). Skills mismatch and overqualification may be additional problems for international migrants. Mobility also poses a number of societal risks such as brain drain or increased demographic pressures in aging societies that need to be carefully managed.

Labor mobility can take place both within and across countries. International migration is very common in the region, particularly among Commonwealth of Independent States (CIS) countries and, in the context of EU integration, from EU-10 to EU-15 countries. It has been well researched and is increasingly receiving due policy attention (IOM 2009; World Bank 2010). In contrast, internal labor mobility—across localities and regions within a country—is less well understood and is often neglected in policy discussions, despite the fact that many times more people move internally than externally.

This chapter focuses largely on internal mobility. In contrast to international mobility, it plays a key role in fostering local agglomeration economies and can be important in alleviating demographic pressures if it offers an alternative to people who would otherwise have moved abroad. A focus on internal mobility may be a means to bring to the forefront issues that are too often neglected in the policy debate. The chapter draws lessons from the literature on international migration, when relevant. Internal and international mobility are often analyzed separately, but there are important linkages between the two. For example, within-country mobility from rural to urban areas often precedes cross-border mobility. More generally, internal and international mobility need not be perfect substitutes but can rather complement each other. Despite the high levels of international mobility in the region, internal mobility still has a key role to play. First, not everybody can move abroad. Second, persistent and growing regional labor market and socioeconomic disparities suggest substantial gains to be made from moving internally.

Low internal labor mobility can inhibit efficient labor matching and overall productivity growth. First, the chapter discusses internal mobility patterns, mainly drawing on recent surveys (EBRD 2010; EC 2009), harmonized administrative data (Eurostat), and country-specific studies. This is followed by a discussion of policy options available to governments to increase labor mobility within countries. In particular, the discussion will focus on existing barriers to migration and how these barriers can be removed so that people who want to move can do so. Given the linkages with international migration, the chapter concludes with a brief discussion on how smart immigration policies can help countries in Europe and Central Asia to succeed in the international race for talent.

Is Labor Mobility Low in Europe and Central Asia?[1]

Internal labor mobility in the region is low by international norms. Cross-country comparisons of labor mobility rates, particularly internal mobility, are plagued with difficulties (box 5.1). The internal migration rate varies with the size of the region or locality—many more people move across municipalities than between regions. Yet, by available metrics, spatial labor mobility is low in most European

---

BOX 5.1

The Pitfalls in Measures of Labor Mobility

There are a number of caveats on migration statistics, their definition, and their measurement, since data availability is limited for both international migration and internal mobility. To the extent that migration data is available, concepts, definitions, and underlying data sources often differ across countries (and sometimes time), making it difficult to arrive at regionwide consistent estimates.

Internal Migration

Data on internal migration are often unavailable. When the data do exist, there are a number of caveats that need to be considered when comparing across countries:

1. Differences in migration intervals: Measures of migration often differ between the national census and household surveys. This is particularly relevant given the different types of migration: short-term versus long-term and seasonal and circular migration (Janiak and Wasmer 2008).

2. Differences in spatial units: As discussed in Bell and Muhidin (2009), territorial units are not always comparable. While the EU tries to unify its statistics by using the concept of Nomenclature of Territorial Statistical Units (NUTS), this classification is based primarily on population density and administrative aspects rather than size or geographical distance. In countries outside the EU, this issue is even more complex, since there is no international agreement on defining territorial units.

3. Administrative versus survey data: As discussed in Brauw and Carletto (2012), many countries use administrative data to report on internal mobility. Yet, these only include information on households and individuals that officially register their movements with the authorities.

continued

BOX 5.1 *continued*

Since the likelihood of reporting moves varies significantly across countries, this data source is difficult to compare internationally or within countries with other sources such as household surveys.

International Migration

There are four main ways of classifying someone as an international migrant: (a) place/country of birth, citizenship, or ethnicity; (b) whether or not a person resides at the place of birth; (c) household membership by an expansive definition of household; and (d) duration of stay away from the residence. These definitions have implications, particularly for countries in the region, given discontinuities in the classification of countries because of the change in political borders following the political and economic transition. For instance, most immigration statistics for the United States are based on country of birth, and it is still possible to state the USSR as one's country of birth. This causes changes in the time series of the number of immigrants by origin due to the classification and not actual changes. Disentangling the two reasons for changes in the numbers is often impossible.

and Central Asian countries. Figure 5.1 shows that, even after adjusting for differences in the size of geographic units across countries (or population size), countries in the region have internal migration rates below the expected cross-country trend; the population in other parts of the world, such as Australia, Canada, Chile, China, the United States, and some countries in Northern and Western Europe, is much more likely to move internally.

Between 10 to nearly 20 percent of the population in the region moved out of their birthplaces over the past 20 years. Based on data from the 2010 Life in Transition Surveys (LiTS), figure 5.2 presents nationally representative indicators of mobility that are comparable across Europe and Central Asia.[2] Respondents were asked if they had ever moved out of their place of birth and, if so, when they had moved last. The figure shows that, by these indicators, except for Estonia, the Kyrgyz Republic, and Turkey, European and Central Asian countries have mobility rates lower than those of Western Europe.

Mobility is low despite positive attitudes toward migration. A Eurobarometer survey in 2009 (EC 2009) revealed that people in the region view geographical mobility positively and consider it important to European integration, the economy, and labor markets. However, when asked about their willingness to move for employment reasons, a large majority (74 percent) had no intention of going elsewhere in the country for a job (figure 5.3), significantly below

FIGURE 5.1

The Population in Europe and Central Asia Is Less Internally Mobile Than Populations in the Rest of the World

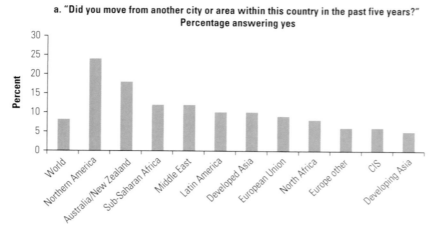

a. "Did you move from another city or area within this country in the past five years?"
Percentage answering yes

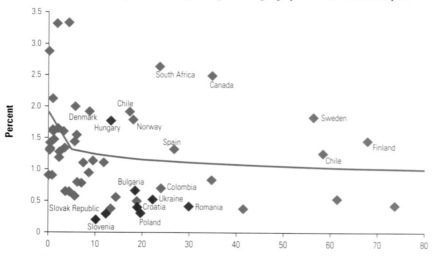

b. Internal migration rates by average size of geographic units, most recent year

Average size of unit of measurement like settlement, district, or region (in km², thousands)

Sources: Esipova, Pugliese, and Ray 2013; World Bank 2012b; based on UN, Eurostat, and national data.
Note to *panel b:* Countries display differing internal migration rates, depending on the size of the unit of measurement. For example, internal migration measured at the village level (that is, movements from one village to another) is much higher than migration measured across larger geographic areas, like districts or regions. Some countries in the figure have more than one observation, corresponding to migration rates measured at different levels, like settlements and oblasts in the case of Ukraine. European and Central Asian countries are highlighted in red. The solid line represents a log trend approximation of the average relationship between internal migration rates and the size of the geographic unit of measurements. The United States has migration rates much higher than the regression line (not shown in the graph). Results are robust to adjustments to regions' population size.

the corresponding figures for Western Europe. Tellingly, the share of people with no intention to move internationally for employment is even higher (78 percent). These high rates of immobility partly reflect—as discussed below—demographic factors and the socialist legacy in the region.

FIGURE 5.2

Low Rates of Internal Mobility in Many Countries after the Transition

Percentage of population 18 and older that moved to a different city in the past 20 years

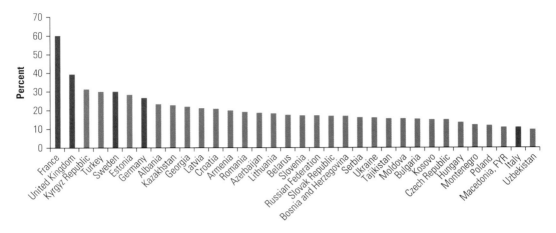

Source: World Bank calculations using LiTS (EBRD 2010).

FIGURE 5.3

Less Than 30 Percent of People Are Willing to Migrate Internally for Employment

Percentage of population ages 18–64 willing to move internally for employment reasons

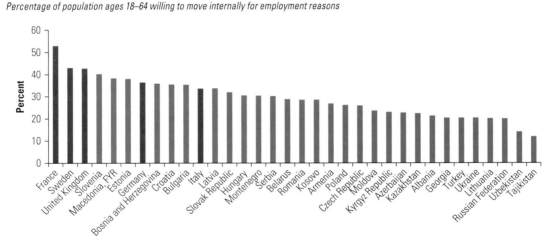

Source: Bank calculations using LiTS (EBRD 2010).

Internal migration in the region does not always lead to the types of agglomeration economies that are crucial to economic development. This is especially the case in intermediate and late modernizers where, respectively, 47 and 37 percent of all migration takes place from urban to rural areas and within rural areas (compared to 28 and 31 percent in early modernizers and Western European countries, respectively) (figure 5.4). Since productivity growth is often concentrated in cities, this type of migration is likely

FIGURE 5.4

Urban Areas Account for Most Mobility, but There Is Also Significant Migration from and within Rural Areas

Breakdown of migration patterns among population 18 and older in the past 20 years

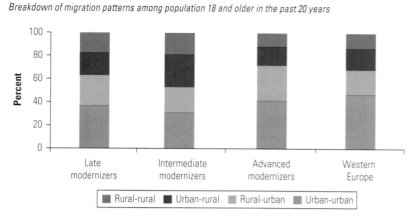

Source: Bank calculations using LiTS (EBRD 2010).

to have only limited effects on growth and living standards. In fact, in some countries, most of the migration is not to urban areas: in Estonia and Poland, over half of all migration (55 percent) is to or within rural areas; in Tajikistan, the rate is almost three-quarters (72 percent). In the case of Ukraine, where more detailed analysis exists, labor market conditions only partially explain internal mobility. People appear only slightly more likely to go to areas with low unemployment, and wages at destination have no effect on internal migration decisions. That is, people are not moving to leading regions with high wages and employment opportunities.

International migration and commuting are alternatives to internal labor mobility. Low internal labor mobility partly reflects the particular economic geography of Europe and Central Asia: in many cases, physical, economic, and cultural distance between localities in neighboring countries may be de facto shorter than between localities within the same country. The presence of two economic powerhouses in the region—the EU and the Russian Federation—makes international migration more attractive. On average, about 10 percent of the population in Europe and Central Asia is living in countries other than their country of birth (figure 5.5). By this metric, several countries appear quite mobile. People from Azerbaijan, Kazakhstan, the Kyrgyz Republic, Tajikistan, and Ukraine often move to Russia, and among EU-10 countries, many Romanians move to Italy and Polish natives to Germany (table 5.1). The economic crisis appears to have increased people's willingness to move abroad for work.

FIGURE 5.5

International Migration Is High in Many European and Central Asian Countries

Percentage of the native-born population living outside the country, 2010

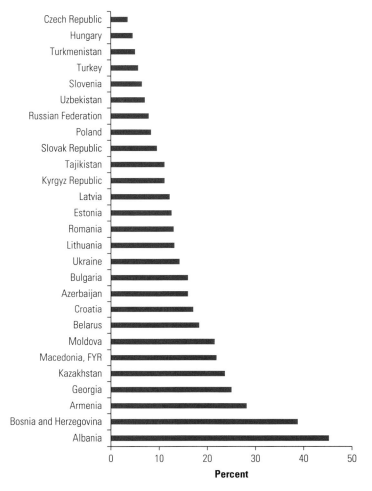

Source: Heleniak 2012 using World Bank 2010.

In Estonia and Latvia, where the crisis hit particularly hard, people's willingness to migrate elsewhere increased by at least 8 percentage points between 2009 and 2011.[3] Given the worsening economic conditions in home countries, people—especially youth—may be more willing to consider searching for jobs abroad. Since the crisis hit many traditional destination countries within Europe, the patterns of the most recent migration flows are likely to be different, with fewer people going to places like Spain, Italy, or the United Kingdom in favor of new destinations even outside Europe.

TABLE 5.1

Russia and Western Europe Are Main Destinations for International Migrants

Main destinations of migrants from Europe and Central Asia, 2010

Origin	Main destination
Armenia, Azerbaijan, Belarus, Georgia, Kazakhstan, Kyrgyz Republic, Latvia, Lithuania, Moldova, Tajikistan, Turkmenistan, and Ukraine	Russian Federation
Croatia, Hungary, Poland, Serbia, Slovenia, and Turkey	Germany
Macedonia, FYR; and Romania	Italy
Albania	Greece
Bulgaria	Turkey
Russian Federation	Ukraine
Slovak Republic	Czech Republic
Czech Republic	Slovak Republic

Source: Heleniak 2012 using data from World Bank 2010.

In some cases, commuting is also a common form of labor mobility. Available data from household surveys show that commuting is important in the Czech Republic, Hungary, the Kyrgyz Republic, and the Slovak Republic, though mainly among men (figure 5.6). Commuting is marginal in Romania, Bulgaria, and Poland. It is noteworthy that there is not a systematic relationship between the different forms of labor mobility. For instance, in the Czech Republic internal and external mobility are low while commuting is more important. In Romania, external mobility is more important while internal mobility and commuting are more modest. Poland has low internal mobility, but relatively higher commuting and international migration rates.

However, international migration and commuting are not perfect substitutes for internal mobility. While commuting and emigration can help relieve labor market pressures and improve resource utilization, they cannot substitute for healthy rates of internal mobility. Emigration can deprive the local economy of increasingly scarce local talent and exacerbate demographic shifts in rapidly aging countries with shrinking working-age populations (figure 5.7). In countries like Bulgaria, Romania, and Ukraine both forces are already reducing the size of the potential work force. Commuting, on the other hand, generally occurs across localities that are not so distant and rarely across distant provinces or regions. It cannot, therefore, be expected to reduce all gaps in economic opportunities between leading and lagging regions within a country; importantly, commuting is often a second-best response to barriers and constraints to full internal mobility. Crucially, neither commuting nor international migration are conducive to the agglomeration economies and resource reallocations that internal labor mobility can help foster.

FIGURE 5.6

Commuting Rates Can Be Important in Some Countries, Especially among Men

Percentage of employed of working age (18–64) who work in a different region than they reside in, 2010

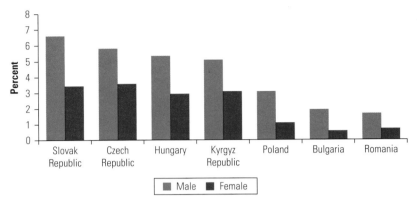

Source: World Bank calculations using EU-LFS 2012 and the Kyrgyz Republic 2010 data.

FIGURE 5.7

Population Shrinkage and Negative Net Migration Are Already Having Significant Impacts on the Size of the Labor Force in Some Countries

Percentage change in the total population from population's natural increase and net migration in the early 2000s

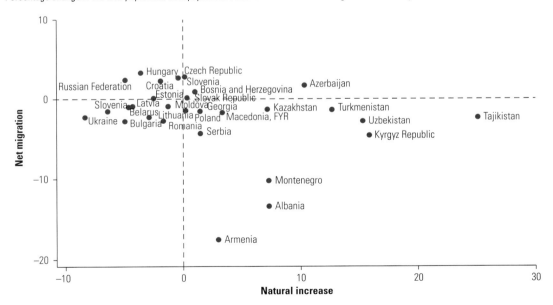

Source: Adapted from Heleniak 2012 using data from UNICEF, Transmonee database, and countries' national statistical offices.

Even factoring in emigration and commuting, labor mobility remains far below potential, given the extent of economic integration and the aspirations for a single market among EU member states and accession countries. A 2008 report on labor mobility in Europe adopted a broad definition of geographic mobility that included changes of residency within countries and across borders as well as cross-border and regional commuting (Bonin et al. 2008). Even with this more expansive metric, workers' mobility within the EU-27 was barely 1 percent each year between 2000 and 2005, again far below that observed in Australian and U.S. states (which exceed 2 and 3 percent, respectively). When rates of movement between territories (at NUTS2 level) within EU countries are considered, approximately 21 percent of the EU population has lived in a territory or country other than where they were born. Even by this figure, labor mobility is lower than in the United States, where 32 percent of the population lives outside their state of birth. As highlighted in World Bank (2012a), with data from the EC's Eurobarometer of 2005, even after the EU accession, migrants between EU countries constitute a small share of the population. In 2008, about 2 percent of the EU labor force was born in a different member state than their current state of residence; approximately 4 percent of the EU population has lived in another EU country at some point; only 3 percent has lived in a country outside the EU. Thus, despite the importance ascribed to labor mobility in the EU fabric, the numbers indicate that there is ample room for further integration and a more fluid labor market in Europe.

Looking ahead, countries in the region will have to counteract the aging and shrinking of their working-age population through smart migration policies that complement efforts to boost internal migration. Countries in or candidates to the EU and countries in the European Free Trade Association and in the Eastern European Partnership will lose 50 million workers between now and 2060. Over the next 20 years their labor force will fall by 15 million (5 percent), largely workers below the age of 40, followed by an additional loss of 14 million in the 2030s, mainly among the labor force ages 40 and older (World Bank 2012a). As noted in chapter 1 of this report, this has significant implications for long-term growth and the ability to create jobs in an aging economy. As noted in World Bank (2012a), even with radical policy and behavioral changes that improve participation of those currently outside the labor market, smart immigration policy will be needed to better manage these trends. This chapter returns to this issue and the associated policy considerations in the policy section.

Internal Labor Mobility Is Low—Why Does It Matter?

There are numerous reasons why a mobile labor force matters for labor market performance and the economy. Labor mobility matters for productivity, economic growth and labor market performance (box 5.2). A more mobile labor force improves resource allocation as it facilitates a better match between workers and firms. More mobile workers make it easier for firms to find the right skills for the job. As labor moves toward more dynamic or higher-potential locations and activities in a country, it helps ignite the forces of agglomeration that are critical for productivity growth. As discussed in chapter 2, generating new jobs also triggers a multiplier effect, raising the local employment and income levels mainly through an increasing demand for services. The size of the employment multiplier depends on several factors, including the required skill level and in which

BOX 5.2

Labor Mobility Is Key for Productivity and Long-Term Growth

"When an industry has thus chosen a locality for itself, it is likely to stay there long: so great are the advantages which people following the same skilled trade get from neighborhood to one another" (Marshall 1920, 271).

The economic concentration of capital, knowledge, and labor leads to greater specialization and shared learning which, in turn, fosters productivity and long-term growth. Think Silicon Valley in California, Route 128 near Boston, or Silicon Docks in Dublin. Agglomeration of workers and economic production has been shown to lead to productivity gains through scale production, higher specialization, and better human capital matching (Baldwin and Martin 2004; Gill and Kharas 2007; Martin and Ottaviano 1999; Rosenthal 2004; World Bank 2009). Bringing together capital and (better) educated workers makes everyone more productive. These human capital spillovers have been shown to drive productivity increases, especially among industries that are economically more linked to each other. In particular, Moretti (2004) finds that plants' productivity growth was significantly higher when located in cities in the United States where the share of college graduates had increased markedly; critically, productivity gains spillovers across industries were larger when these industries were economically linked through value chains, inputs, or technology. In France, Germany, Italy, Spain, and the United Kingdom, a 1 percent increase in employment density has been linked to an increase of 4.5 percent in labor productivity—an elasticity that is only slightly lower than that identified for the United States (Ciccone 2002).

Potential growth and productivity gains from agglomeration are likely to depend on level of development, specialization patterns, and type of settlement. New products and industries are likely to benefit more from a diversified environment while mature industries gain more from concentrating (they can delocalize, but only when their production is standardized). Paci, Marrocu, and Usai (2011) have examined the case of agglomeration spillovers in the case of EU-15 and EU-12 countries, among which there are critical differences in economic development levels and structure. The authors find that, in EU-15 countries, specialization externalities on low-tech

continued

BOX 5.2 *continued*

---

industries are negatively related to growth (congestion effect) while diversity externalities on high-tech industry in urban centers are positively related to productivity growth. In contrast, in the EU-12, there is still a strong positive growth effect of specialization spillovers, especially in low-tech manufacturing, with a negative growth effect from diversity across industries. This suggests that EU-12 countries can still benefit significantly from further agglomeration.

Increased internal labor mobility, coupled with the agglomeration of capital and other productive inputs, is a fundamental ingredient for productivity and long-term economic growth. Human capital earns higher returns where it is plentiful; the sharing of inputs across firms creates incentives for specialized producers of intermediate goods to compete and become more productive; the concentration of economic activities makes it easier for firms to find the right workers; and knowledge spillovers across firms facilitate the spread of new technologies, ideas, and products. These gains from agglomeration of capital and labor can, thus, raise productivity and economic growth. Across countries, there is a positive association between internal labor mobility and economic growth (see World Bank 2009, fig. 5.7). For example, it is estimated that output in the United States would be twice as high if there were no actual costs of geographic and intersectoral labor mobility (Lee and Wolpin 2006). Similarly, Gang and Stuart (1999), examining "closed" cities in the former Soviet Union to which migration was explicitly limited, find that "uncontrolled" cities grow significantly faster than "closed" ones. Sharpe, Arsenault and Ershov (2007) have similar findings for Canada where, interprovincial migration is estimated to have increased trend labor productivity growth by 1.6 percentage points over the 1987–2006 period and actual labor productivity growth by 6.2 percent in 2006. In the developing world, Lall and Chakravorty (2005), for example, estimate that the mobility of over 20 million people in India from rural to urban areas in the 1990s accounts for 30 percent of national urban growth. Internal migration has also been found to have contributed to economic growth in Asia (Anh 2003) and raised productivity in Brazil (Timmins, 2005).

Bertola (2000) documented the role of internal mobility in balancing labor market outcomes and living standards across regions, concluding that low labor mobility in the EU is a key factor behind unemployment differentials across European regions. The evidence of the contribution of internal labor mobility to spatial income convergence exists for countries as diverse as Canada, France, Japan, India, the Russian Federation, the United Kingdom, and the United States (Barro and Sala-I-Martin 1992; Brown 1997; McInnis 1966; Tabuchi 1988; World Bank 2009). Historical evidence on labor mobility and convergence in living standards exists for the United States, France, and England (World Bank 2009). In Canada, for instance, labor mobility narrowed per capita income differences among Canadian provinces in early 20th century; convergence in income slowed down when internal migration slowed down (McInnis 1966). Although at early stages of development increased agglomeration of economic resources—including labor—is associated with higher spatial inequality in socioeconomic indicators within a country, in time it is expected that it becomes an equalizer (World Bank 2009).

sector the job was generated. Similarly, the elasticity of the local labor supply, which in turn is determined by labor mobility and labor market institution, for example the generosity of unemployment benefits, determines the magnitude of the multiplier. In the case of the United States and Sweden, it was estimated that one additional high-skilled job in the high-technology sector generates between 3 and 5 jobs in the long run (Moretti 2012; Moretti and Thulin 2013). The shift from agriculture to manufacturing and services is one such channel in the development process. Migrants often create critical links between leading and lagging areas through remittances or local investments. This in turn can result in new job opportunities both in leading and lagging regions. The lack of internal mobility is often blamed for keeping unemployment high in lagging areas while labor shortages may drive up wages in leading regions. In addition, mobility can help countries in absorbing economic shocks: As discussed in World Bank (2012a), in much of Europe, the adjustment to negative regional shocks has often taken place through reductions in labor force participation or persistent unemployment; in contrast, in a very mobile country like the United States, labor mobility has traditionally enabled a more balanced distribution of the adjustment burden between unemployment and wages.

Labor mobility and labor market performance reinforce each other. People move to places with better job opportunities in the form of higher wages and lower unemployment. At the same time, internal mobility can improve labor market outcomes through a better matching of workers and firms and through increases in productivity. As a result, there is a two-way causal relationship between mobility and labor market outcomes that is difficult to disentangle empirically.[4]

There are significant employment and productivity gains to be realized from higher internal labor mobility in Europe and Central Asia. There are important—and persistent—regional gaps within countries in terms of unemployment rates and labor productivity, and these gaps, especially on labor productivity, are larger in European and Central Asian countries than in EU-15 countries (figure 5.8). In Ukraine, for example, the most productive regions are more than twice as productive as the rest of the country (World Bank 2012b).

With more labor mobility, workers could move to more productive jobs and sectors. Productivity growth associated with labor reallocation has been a key ingredient for East Asia's success story in the past decade, for example. On average, 42 percent of the overall growth in productivity in East Asia has been due to jobs reallocations across

FIGURE 5.8

There Are Significant Regional Disparities in Unemployment and Labor Productivity in Europe and Central Asia

Regional disparities in labor productivity and unemployment, 2002 and 2009

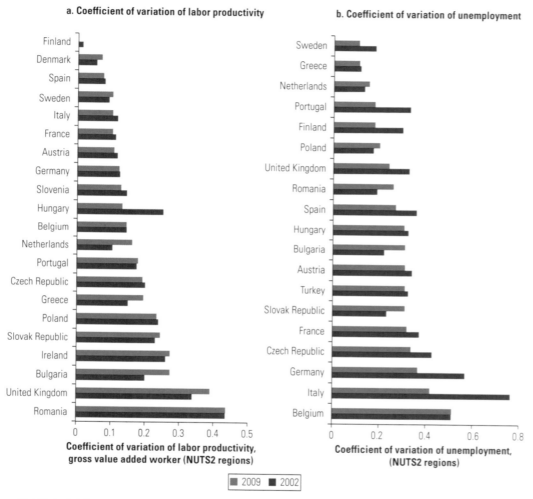

Source: World Bank calculations using Eurostat data.

Note: The coefficient of variation is the ratio of the standard deviation to the mean and is a measure of inequality. The larger the coefficient, the larger the regional disparities. Data on unemployment for Turkey refers to 2006 and 2009; data on productivity for Sweden refers to 2002 and 2007.

sectors. Again, much of this reallocation takes the form of shifts in the labor share in agriculture and low productivity services in rural and lagging areas to more productive uses in manufacturing and services in urban and leading zones. In Central and Southeastern European countries, while annual labor productivity growth has been close to levels estimated for South Asia and East Asia, only 6 percent of productivity gains are associated with cross-sector labor mobility (figure 5.9). The untapped potential exists: enterprise surveys show that firms located in large cities in Europe and Central Asia, where capital and labor is agglomerated, grow faster. Realizing the gains from increased mobility is particularly relevant for late modernizers who still need to complete economic restructuring. Higher internal labor mobility correlates with lower unemployment, overall higher employment rates, and earning opportunities. This is illustrated for the EU countries in figures 5.10 and 5.11. A recent EU study finds that countries where workers move often across jobs, occupations, and sectors have higher employment and lower long-term unemployment rates. For many of these moves, geographical mobility is often a first-step. In 24 out of 35 countries covered by the *World Development Report 2009*, migrants were more likely to be in the labor force and employed. In Ukraine, unemployed men and inactive women—after controlling for a set of socioeconomic characteristics—are more likely to move internally than those that have a job (World Bank 2012b). Beyond employment outcomes, internal mobility is also associated with higher wages. In the United Kingdom, for example, it is estimated that the long-run wage premium for men who

FIGURE 5.9

Labor Reallocations as a Driver of Productivity Growth across the World, 1999–2008

Annual labor productivity growth, percentage, various regions

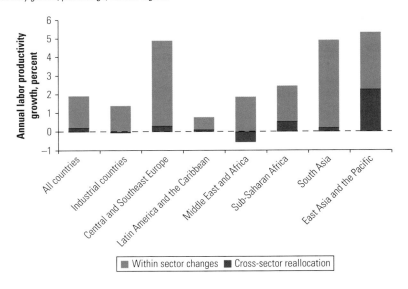

Source: World Bank 2012c.

Note: The figure presents the decomposition of labor productivity growth in 81 countries over 1999–2008. Seven sectors are considered: agriculture, hunting, forestry, and fishing; mining and utilities; manufacturing; construction; trade, restaurants, and hotels; transport, storage, and communication; and other services. The regional growth rates are weighted averages, with weights based on a country's share in regional GDP.

BOX 5.3 *continued*

construction sector or health care sector in Italy. Since 2005, migrants were younger and more likely to have tertiary education than the average Romanian and relied less on networks in their destination. They went to different host countries in Northern Europe and the non-European Anglophone world, often found employment in the formal service sector, including banking and finance, and were able to advance their careers upon migration. Migrants like these are less likely to remit or return to their home country. The dynamics are different in Tajikistan, a country that experienced several waves of international migration since independence. Until the mid-1990s, highly educated people moved mainly to Russia to escape deteriorating living conditions. By the end of the 1990s, the rural population also started to migrate to the Russian Federation, as the countryside was devastated by the civil war; but these migrants were older and less educated than the first generation (Jones, Black, and Skeldon 2007). During the early 2000s, emigration has been steadily increasing and it is estimated that in 2008, around 12 percent of Tajikistan's population was working abroad. Around 70 percent of all migrants are below the age of 35, many with only general secondary education. More than 90 percent are men who work in the construction sector in Russia or other low-skilled, agricultural jobs. To a large extent, migration is seasonal, and almost half of the respondents had migrated more than once between 2001 and 2007.

Sources: Davis 2012; IBS 2013; Kartseva and Kuznetsova 2013.

FIGURE 5.14

Wage Premium Required to Accept a Job in a Different Country or Region

Increase in wages required to accept a job elsewhere, by percentage of wage

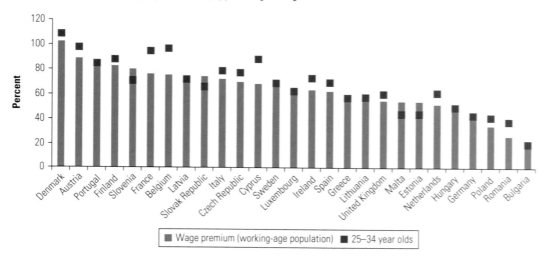

Source: Based on Eurobarometer 2009 data (EC 2009).

Note: Original question was: "Compared to what you earn or could earn here, what income would one need to offer to you in order to take up a job in another country or region?" Answers are adjusted by purchasing power parity (PPP) to account for differences in cost of living across countries. Sample is restricted to working-age population individuals who report willingness to accept a job elsewhere.

internal migration rates are among the lowest in the region, the gap between intentions and actions suggest that people may be constrained in their ability to move internally (figure 5.15). In other countries, for example, Tajikistan and Uzbekistan, the lack of willingness to move internally may itself reflect a perception of low potential gains from moving or barriers to doing so.

Low internal mobility is closely related to contextual factors in the region, particularly its demographics and socialist legacy. There are significant differences in mobility behavior between young and older workers, and within these groups, across gender and educational levels (figure 5.16). Analyzing these differences can help shed light on mobility barriers. Beyond demographics, market and institutional features stemming from the region's socialist past—in housing and credit markets, social benefits, regional policies, skills, information and networks, labor market institutions and urban policies—also contribute to low mobility within countries.

Demographic factors partly explain low labor mobility in Europe and Central Asia. As in other parts of the world, internal mobility is

FIGURE 5.15

For Some Countries, Intentions to Migrate for Work Are Higher Than Predicted by Previous Migration Patterns

Actual internal labor migration versus labor migration intentions

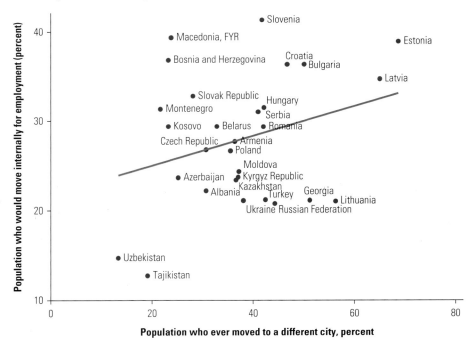

Source: World Bank calculations using LiTS micro data (EBRD 2010).

FIGURE 5.16

Demographics, Education, Risk Attitudes, and Home Ownership Matter For Internal Mobility

Odds ratios of internal migration in the 1990–2010 period

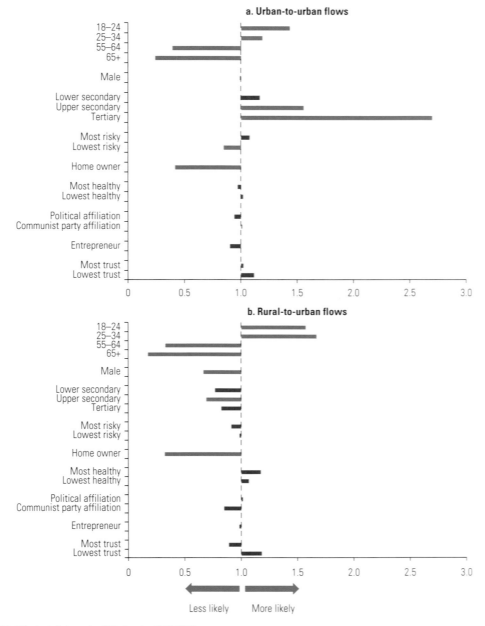

Source: World Bank calculations using LiTS micro data (EBRD 2010).

Note: Statistically significant coefficients at the 10% level or lower are shown in blue. The coefficients show the odds of urban-urban or rural-urban migration given an individual's characteristics and are obtained from multinomial logit regressions. Country dummies were included. Complete regression results including flows to or within rural regions are available from the authors upon request. The reference group is a prime-age (35–54) woman, with average health, risk propensity and trust; less than lower secondary education, no political affiliation or affiliation to the Communist Party in the family, and without any previous entrepreneurial experience. Most (lowest) risky, healthy, and trusting are self-defined based on a within-country distribution, where the most (lowest) 25% in each index are given a value of 1 and the others a value of 0.

more common among youth than among prime-age workers and, especially, older workers. Thus, low labor mobility partly stems from the region's older and more rapidly aging population. Figure 5.16 shows that young people entering the labor market (18–24 years old) are 42 percent more likely to have migrated between urban areas during the past 20 years than prime-age workers (35–54 year olds) and more than six times more likely than workers above 65. In rural-to-urban migration flows, critical for agglomeration economies, a similar demographic pattern is observed. This is consistent with results in the literature, as younger workers are more likely than prime-age or older workers to be risk takers and healthy and less likely to have their own dwelling.[5] All of these factors are correlated with higher mobility intentions (figure 5.16).

Not only are younger workers more likely to move, but when they do so, they are more likely to follow economic opportunities rather than move away from them (table 5.2). Analysis of precrisis administrative data from Bulgaria, the Czech Republic, Hungary, Poland, and Romania shows that young and prime-age migrants are pulled to places with better economic conditions (higher per capita GDP in the case of youth and low unemployment in the case of prime-age workers). This is consistent with the fact that migration

TABLE 5.2

Migration Flows and Responsiveness to Regional Incentives, 2000–07

Outcome variables	Correlates	Age groups					
		15–24	25–34	35–44	45–54	55–64	15–64
In-migration rate $\frac{\text{Inflows}_{i,t}}{\text{Population}_{i,t}} * 100\%$	Unemp. Rate			−			
	GDP	+	+				+
	No. Doctors						
	Population Density			+	+	+	
Out-migration rate $\frac{\text{Outflows}_{i,t}}{\text{Population}_{i,t}} * 100\%$	Unemp. Rate						
	GDP		−	−		+	−
	No. Doctors	−	−		−		−
	Population Density	+	+	+	+	+	+
Net migration rate $\frac{\text{Inflows}_{i,t} - \text{Outflows}_{i,t}}{\text{Population}_{i,t}} * 100\%$	Unemp. Rate				−		
	GDP	+	+	+		−	+
	No. Doctors	+					
	Population Density			−	−		−

Note: Each column reports results from separate panel regressions for each age group. A + or − indicates a positive or negative significant effect of the respective independent variables (lagged one year to reduce endogeneity concerns). Subscript i indicates the region (NUTS 2 level), subscript t refers to the year. Variables are measured as the deviation from the national average. Number of doctors is a proxy measure for access to services in the region. Population density was included to control for migration flows between regional centers. Regional random effects and year dummies were included. Full regression results are available upon request.

BOX 5.4

Youth on the Move: The Growing Phenomenon of Global Student Mobility

Many young people become migrants for the first time when they move elsewhere to study. This early migration is often a step into further migration waves. When people move to study, they gain experiences, skills, and networks that make it more likely that they will be mobile in the future. According to the 2009 Eurobarometer, 38 percent of those who had ever studied abroad for more than two months report that they were willing to migrate for employment reasons; this is twice as high as among those who had only national education and training.

The phenomenon of student mobility is not trivial in Europe and Central Asia. In 2009, over 465,000 students from the region were enrolled in higher education outside their home country, up from about 260,000 only 10 years earlier. Almost half of these students were enrolled in a foreign country within the region (including 94,000 in the Russian Federation and 73,000 in the EU-10 countries); the others were mostly based in Western Europe and the United States. Destinations in East Asia are attracting an increasing number of students. Meanwhile, approximately 130,000 students from other parts of the world pursued university courses in the region's higher education institutions in 2009.

Russia, the leading recipient of foreign students in Europe and Central Asia and one of the top three countries in the region for sending students overseas, offers an interesting example. In 2009 alone, almost 25,000 students from Kazakhstan, 20,000 from Belarus, 13,000 from Ukraine, 10,000 from Uzbekistan, and approximately 25,000 from elsewhere in the region came to Russia to study in higher education institutions. Most often, these students already speak Russian and are very familiar with the Russian labor market and norms. At the same time, Russian students overseas amounted to 28,000 in 2000 and increased to 47,000 in 2009, a year in which a quarter of them were studying in Germany, about 11 percent in the United States, 8 percent in France, 7 percent in the United Kingdom, 15 percent in other Western European countries, and 30 percent in other European and Central Asian countries. Numbers on student "return rates" are limited. The Organisation for Economic Co-operation and Development (OECD) has explored this issue in somewhat greater detail, finding that an average of about 25 percent of foreign students in selected OECD countries remained there upon completion of their studies in 2008/2009.

Source: UNESCO 2009, ISCED 5 and 6, table 18A.

for younger cohorts is typically associated with student mobility and that attractive higher education institutions are most likely to be located in economic centers (box 5.4). In contrast, older migrants (closer to retirement age) tend to leave wealthier regions to go to less well-off regions (GDP per capita below national average), which is consistent with the high shares of rural-to-rural and urban-to-rural migration reported earlier. Again, this is consistent with anecdotal evidence that some older individuals, particularly those entering

FIGURE 5.17

Demographics and Other Socioeconomic Factors Matter for Migration Intentions

Odds ratios for intentions to migrate internally for employment reasons

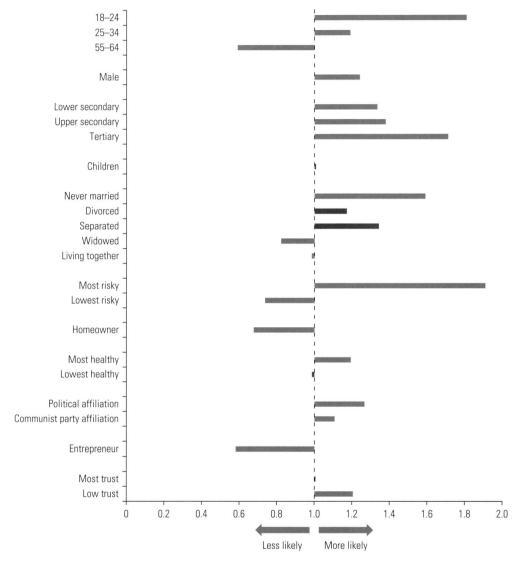

Source: Based on multivariate regressions using LiTS (EBRD 2010)

Note: Statistically significant coefficients at the 10% level or lower are shown in blue. The coefficients show the odds of being willing to migrate internally for employment reasons and were obtained from multinomial logit regressions. Country dummies were included. The reference group is a prime-age (35–54) woman, with average health, risk propensity, and trust; less than lower secondary education; no political affiliation or affiliation to the Communist Party in the family; and without any previous entrepreneurial experience. Most (lowest) risky, healthy, and trust are self-defined based on a within country distribution, where the most (lowest) 25% in each index are given a value of 1 and the others a value of 0.

retirement, move to places with lower costs of living. Looking into the future, internal labor migrants are likely to be disproportionately young, male, single, and well educated. Intentions to migrate for employment reasons decrease with age and increase with higher educational attainment or among nonmarried (figure 5.17).

Across age groups, higher education facilitates mobility. Holders of a tertiary level degree are 1.7 times more likely to have migrated between urban areas than people with lower levels of educational attainment, reflecting the importance of skills as a portable human capital investment. As discussed in chapter 3, better skills make the workforce more adaptable to economic changes and make it easier for workers to seize work opportunities, especially in cities that are becoming increasingly specialized in new sectors.

Internal mobility patterns also differ by gender. Across the region, women have had a slightly higher propensity to move internally between 1990 and 2010; the largest gender gap of nearly 10 percentage points can be found among low-income CIS countries. In particular, women were more likely to move from rural to urban areas (figure 5.16). Women and men often also move for different reasons. In the case of Ukraine, for example, most female internal migrants enroll in higher educational institutions in the urban centers; men, on the other hand, are more likely to directly move for labor market reasons (World Bank 2012b).

In addition to demographics, the region's socialist legacy poses a number of specific challenges for labor mobility. As discussed earlier, workers need to have the right skills to succeed in highly competitive labor markets in leading regions and economic centers. Even if workers have the right skills, however, existing market, institutional, and policy failures constitute significant barriers to mobility in the region. In contrast, in the United States—one of the countries with highest internal mobility and immigration rates—the costs of internal migration are relatively low, with a fluid housing, rental, and mortgage market; as in other countries, such as Ireland, flexible labor laws also allow for high job turnover rates and flexible wages that prompt people to relocate to where economic opportunities are.

The relevant literature discusses five areas as loci for barriers that affect internal mobility:

- Housing and credit markets, which—when underdeveloped— increase the cost of migration, especially for those with liquidity constraints

- Social benefits and regional policies, which can subsidize the lack of mobility but which, if designed correctly, can actually foster it

- Skills, information, and networks, which are critical for successful labor market transitions, are a barrier to moving when workers do not have the skills demanded by firms in leading regions or when there are no functioning formal institutions that provide reliable and timely information about job vacancies and requirements or living conditions at potential destinations[6]

- Labor market institutions, which—if too rigid—can make labor markets less dynamic by making it difficult for those with no employment to find a job or which dampen wage signals by compressing wages and thereby reducing potential payoffs from moving (OECD 2010; Paci et al. 2007; World Bank 2005, 2009, 2011a, 2012a, 2012b)

- Urban policies, which sustain functional cities that provide the benefits of agglomeration economies but limit the downsides of urbanization

---

BOX 5.5

Labor Mobility and Institutional Barriers: The Case of Ukraine

Ukraine's economy lacks dynamism, with job creation and job destruction rates significantly below those of its peers. This is both the cause and the effect of people not moving. The rate at which Ukrainians move from one region to another within the country is only half of what one would expect when comparing it to other countries. Given significant regional disparities in unemployment rates and wages, internal labor mobility is low. Migrants are not leaving lagging areas with poor labor market outcomes, and they are not necessarily going to regions with better job conditions. Instead, they seem to be pushed out by low levels of social spending in their home regions. This suggests that certain barriers prevent people from seeking economic opportunity, but also that significant gains could be realized from greater internal labor mobility.

The main barriers to internal mobility in Ukraine are institutional: (a) administrative procedures that require people to be officially registered at their place of residence, although many people prefer not to register a new residence for various reasons; (b) underdeveloped housing and credit markets, which make it difficult for people to rent or buy housing in leading regions; (c) inadequate human capital, as people in lagging regions often lack the necessary skills to access better economic opportunities in high-productivity, modern sectors in the leading regions; (d) weak formal labor market institutions that reduce dynamism in the labor market, stimulate informal work arrangements, and do not provide workers with enough reliable information about job openings and labor market conditions; and (e) social benefits, housing, and services that are often tied to the place of residence and that could, in some cases, discourage labor force participation (figure B5.5.1).

continued

BOX 5.5 *continued*

FIGURE B5.5.1
The Most Important Barriers to Internal Mobility in Ukraine
Percentage of respondents who listed the barrier as one of the three most important

Percentage of respondents

Addressing these institutional bottlenecks that affect internal mobility will allow people—especially the poor—to access more and better jobs in leading regions. As they do so, aggregate productivity and economic growth will accelerate and living standards in both leading and lagging regions will continue to rise.

Source: World Bank 2012b.

Several of these have been extensively documented in a recent World Bank study for Ukraine. See box 5.5 for a summary of the main findings.

Barriers affect some groups more than others. For example, in many societies the mobility of women is largely determined by very traditional social norms concerning women's role in the household and in the economy. Chapter 4 has discussed how different groups—youth, older workers, women, and ethnic minorities—often face specific barriers to employability and access economic opportunities at home, in other localities in their home countries, or abroad.

Below, the chapter discusses in detail the first two areas listed above. Readers are referred to chapters 1, 2, 3, and 4 in this report for a discussion on the remaining areas. The scope for governments to remove these barriers and facilitate labor mobility is discussed in the next section. It should be pointed out that the discussion on mobility barriers related to the socialist legacy of the region and available policy options to overcome these obstacles warrant further study.

Underdeveloped Housing and Credit Markets

Housing constraints can span issues related to housing costs, under-developed real estate, rental and mortgage markets, and high home ownership rates. In particular, high costs for home ownership, cou-pled with lack of affordable rental housing, can slow down the pace of internal mobility. In many countries of the region, housing is a largely informal market; in many cases, supply is limited by zoning restrictions that contribute to making renting and owning more expensive (figure 5.18) and markets shallower. In qualitative sur-veys done in Ukraine, for example, housing and lack of credit were identified as the second most critical barriers to internal mobility—especially in the case of Kiev.[7] In Warsaw, the cost of renting a stu-dio apartment accounts for around 70 percent of the average monthly net wage of a low-skilled worker (World Bank 2005). A survey of internal labor mobility conducted in Russia, Ukraine,

FIGURE 5.18

Buying a House in Europe and Central Asia Is Relatively Expensive

House price to annual income ratio, 2010

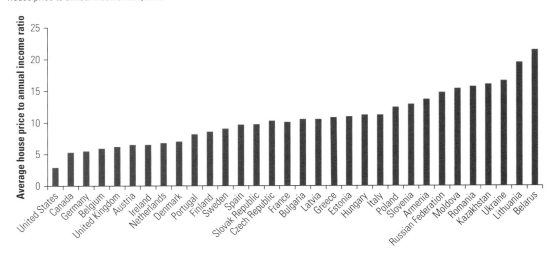

Source: Komarov 2012 based on data from Numbeo.
Note: The price to income ratio is the ratio of median apartment price to median disposable family income, expressed as years of income. For example, in the United States the median house price equals 2.5 times the median annual income while the ratio between house price and annual income is 10 in Latvia and greater than 20 in Belarus.

Bulgaria, and Serbia showed that even with a 1.5 times increase in salary, 80 percent of respondents in Russia and Ukraine would still not move; the share was close to 50 percent in Bulgaria and Serbia. Interestingly, most respondents report that they would move under those conditions if offered free housing (Synovate 2010). Housing availability and housing prices in other countries have also been found to matter for mobility (Dragunova and Maidanik 2009; Fidrmuc and Huber 2003; Ghatak, Mulhern, and Watson 2007). The overall high rates of commuting in the region documented earlier also partly reflect the high cost of buying a house in economic centers; in that sense, commuting is a suboptimal solution for a family that wants to access better economic opportunities but cannot afford to live and work in the same community.

Overall, underdeveloped credit and housing markets have been shown to deter migration, especially in a context of high home ownership. Home ownership rates, at above 80 percent in most EU-10 countries or above 95 percent in countries like Ukraine, are high by international standards (figure 5.19). This partly reflects a legacy from the transition when homes were transferred to their occupants at little or no cost. High homeownership can discourage (internal) migration by increasing the costs of moving, including transaction costs related to buying or selling but also emotional costs related to leaving behind a place considered "home." Critically, these costs are higher in countries where housing was heavily or fully subsidized and where there were no functional housing markets before transition. Home ownership has been found to be associated with lower labor mobility in a variety of countries (Bloze 2009; Fidrmuc and Huber 2003; Green and Hendershott 2001). Based on the 2010 LiTS data, it can be shown that homeowners in general are 32 percent less likely than people who do not own their homes to report migration intentions. More specifically, homeowners are about half as likely as non-homeowners to have any urban-to-urban migration experience. Similarly, recent work in Ukraine finds that home ownership is the most important correlate of internal migration among men and the second most important one among women.[8] In addition to home ownership effects, this reflects thin housing markets both for rental and ownership. For the Czech Republic and the Slovak Republic, OECD has found that the high share of the population living in owner-occupied dwellings, mixed with stringent regulations in the rental market, hinders labor mobility through the creation of large regional price differentials in housing—especially by generating housing shortages in economic centers (OECD 2004a, 2004b).

FIGURE 5.19

Home Ownership Is Relatively High in the Region

Owner occupancy rates, 2009

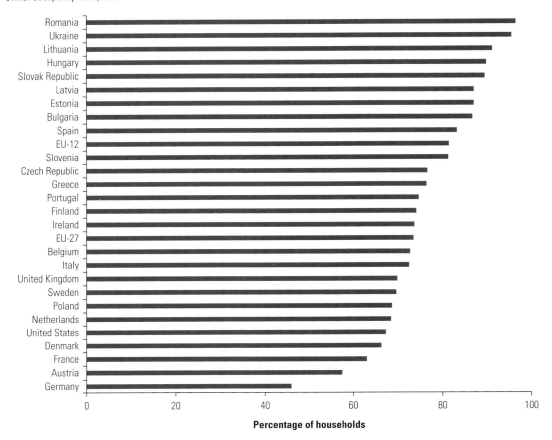

Source: Komarov 2012.

The Role of Social Benefits and Regional Development Policies

Social benefits and regional policies could have both positive and negative effects on migration. If designed well, social benefits and insurance—like pensions, unemployment and health insurance, and social assistance—and regional development policies can help people overcome financial constraints and can connect them with better jobs in leading regions. If poorly designed, however, social benefits can end up limiting internal mobility by decreasing incentives to work or move. The key is to find the right balance in the design of these policies such that they keep protecting people while not tying them to lagging regions.

mobility is also likely to increase. International migrants, however, face additional obstacles, such as language and cultural barriers, lack of international recognition of professional qualifications and previous work experience, and strict rules for licensing in professions and occupations (figure 5.20).

The lack of social and professional networks and imperfect information about socioeconomic conditions at the destination country can also hamper international mobility: The 2009 Eurobarometer (EC 2009) survey finds, for example, that, among the 36 percent of respondents who knew other migrants, almost one-third was willing to migrate (compared to only 16 percent among those who did not know any migrants). On the other hand, fostering greater immigration is most critical for new EU member states that send many prime-age workers to Western Europe while its population at home shrinks and gets older. A similar urgency exists in countries like Belarus, Moldova, and Ukraine that are also aging rapidly and sending a great number of younger workers outside, mostly to Russia. The remainder of this section will therefore briefly reflect on barriers that affect the decision to move to another country and how policy can be shaped to remove them or lessen their detrimental effects on international mobility.

FIGURE 5.20
Difficulties with Language, Housing, and Finding Employment limit Mobility
Top three cited practical difficulties expected when going to work abroad, % of respondents

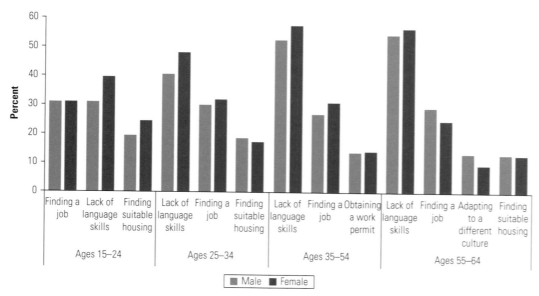

Source: World Bank based on Eurobarometer 2009 (EC 2009).

Europe is perhaps the most integrated region of the world, but other subregions are also becoming more integrated. The freedom of movement for workers is one of the policy chapters of the *acquis communautaire* of the EU and one of its four economic freedoms: free movement of goods, services, capital, and labor. In 2008, 37 percent of non-nationals in EU-27 countries were citizens of another member state. But labor markets are also well integrated beyond the EU: Russia, Belarus, and Kazakhstan also share free movement of workers among the three countries.

The competition for talent is not only internal or within the region, but global. While international migration rates are relatively high within the region, as argued earlier in this chapter, there is less integration between European and Central Asian countries and the world outside the EU (World Bank 2012a). Removing barriers to this type of mobility is crucial, especially for countries where demographic conditions mean that the population is decreasing and/or rapidly aging and where sustained immigration can partly—although not fully—help rebalance the demographic pyramid.

Language and cultural barriers clearly play a role (figure 5.20). Technological advancements that make it easier to connect with family and friends back home, investments in infrastructure that connect countries and reduce the cost of traveling, and the strengthening of foreign language courses in schools are keys to improving migration attitudes and enhancing the migration experience. The experience of the EU points to useful policy approaches to tackle these barriers.

Many EU policies and institutions contribute to fostering mobility across the union, and could be strengthened, be extended, and serve as an example for other economic areas in the region. Programs like ERASMUS can foster educational exchanges among youth and cohesion funds focused on interregional and cross-border infrastructure can contribute to connecting people to others and bringing leading and lagging regions closer together. Expanding these initiatives but also expanding school exchange and internship programs between EU and non-EU countries—or at the subregional level—can be useful tools for exposing future workers early to the experience of living abroad. Similarly, international cooperation in cross-border infrastructure projects would be beneficial for mobility.

Migration policy in the region needs to get smarter to complement efforts to increase internal mobility. As discussed above, despite integration, Europe and Central Asia still attract fewer immigrants from outside the region than many other OECD countries. Since the competition for talent is really global, there are lessons to be drawn from these successful immigration countries: Australia,

Canada, New Zealand, and the United States, for example, where not only is immigration higher but also the typical migrant is better educated. Almost half of the adult EU immigrant population originating from outside the EU has only primary education, while only 25 percent have secondary education and 21 percent have tertiary education. In contrast, about 40 percent of immigrants to Australia, New Zealand, and the United States have a tertiary education.[14] To compete successfully, immigration policies need to become smarter: proactive in searching out talent and flexible in adapting to changing labor market conditions (box 5.6).

Critical for an integrated, smart migration policy is the strengthening of links between the diasporas and the local economy and creating incentives for migrants to return and invest productively at

---

BOX 5.6

Smart Immigration Policies: Good Practices

Across Europe and the rest of the world, several countries are getting immigration policy right. Australia, Canada, Ireland, New Zealand, and the United Kingdom, for example, are competing with the United States in the global race for talent. Canada and Ireland attract by far the highest relative share of tertiary educated migrants (40 percent); the United States, with its demand-driven temporary worker programs for specialized migrants, attracts the bulk of secondary educated migrants. What do these countries' immigration policies have in common? Immigration policies and institutions are shaped by history, culture, geography, and economic conditions. However, today's success stories share common principles:

They focus on attracting talent, the best of the best. Borders remain open for international migrants who bring the skills that are missing in the domestic labor market. Ireland, Sweden, and the United Kingdom were the only three countries that did not impose quotas on workers from the new EU member states at the time of enlargement. The United Kingdom has introduced a points-based system, focusing on the quality of immigrants rather than quantity. Canada, similarly, has a points system for visa applications that prioritizes certain features of labor force and characteristics of workers: having a job offer or tertiary education grants additional points. Also, in order to attract highly skilled labor, talented immigrants can be admitted to the country without having a job offer yet. Once in, migrants in these new migration countries are attracted by cities that are livable and open to foreigners.

The leading countries focus on attracting future workers early on in the migration process, often at the time of higher education studies. The United Kingdom is one of the hotspots for international students: it hosted an annual average of 132,700 international students between 2003 and 2008. New migration countries invest heavily in centers of excellence in higher education

continued

BOX 5.6 *continued*

and facilitating the transition from university to work. Between 15 and 20 percent of foreign students remain in Canada and start working.

Successful recruiting countries focus not only on being open to foreigners but equally on equipping its workforce for the international race for talent. In Ireland, the ability of its population to react to economic developments by moving internally and internationally has served the country well in the past, including during the recent crisis. The Irish are the most mobile of all Europeans, with nearly 15 percent of Ireland's population having moved within the EU.

These countries support migrants in integrating into society. The Canadian system is designed to treat all immigrants equally, regardless of ethnicity, race, religion, or nationality. Permanent immigrants have the same access to work opportunities as Canadian citizens. Immigration policy provides stable solutions for fostering family reunion. Another important aspect of integration policy is the universal access to education for all children living in the country, regardless of immigration status.

The countries have systems that remain flexible, able to adapt to changing economic conditions. Successful immigration systems are based on a strong demand-driven mechanism that responds quickly to shifting labor market needs in the host country, including also temporary work permits and immigration arrangements. Typically, employers play a central role in designing the demand-driven mechanism and can initiate the request for an entry visa and work permission. Points systems can include demand-driven components by granting additional credit to migrants with an existing job offer, as the Australian system does. A visa type granted even to visitors interested in job hunting makes the Australian immigration system even more responsive to shifting labor market needs.

Source: Based on World Bank 2012a.

home. Remittances already have a large impact in some countries, for example in Moldova, the Kyrgyz Republic, and Tajikistan; the challenge for policy makers now is to create incentives for gearing remittances toward more productive investments and to strengthen the links with the diasporas.[15] Many workers may also want to return to their home countries, and public policies can try to make those transitions easier, focusing, for example, on making it easier to maintain social benefits, buy property, and start a business.

A comprehensive policy approach to mobility that (a) removes barriers when people want to move in search of better opportunities, (b) makes portable investments in people, and (c) supports links across citizens regardless of borders will help European and Central Asian countries seize the many opportunities available for more productive employment and will, in due time, contribute to better living standards everywhere.

In pursuing a more effective policy approach to mobility, important knowledge gaps remain, however. First and foremost, data on internal mobility need to be collected more often, more systematically, and more widely. This would allow countries to identify who is moving (or not), where to, and why, which—as argued in this chapter—is the first step in identifying and removing obstacles to accessing more and better jobs. Beyond strengthening data collection, there is an important research agenda in identifying evidence-based policy interventions that can help remove existing barriers to mobility, especially in lagging regions, and better target interventions to the specific obstacles faced by specific subgroups of the population.

Notes

1. The discussion in this session builds on World Bank (2012b, chapter 6).
2. The microdata identify only whether the last movement of the respondent was from a rural or an urban area, regardless of the country of origin.
3. Eurobarometer (EC 2009, 2011). These numbers are lower-bound estimates, since in 2009 the question refers to migration intentions anywhere in the world, while in 2011 the destinations are restricted to only the EU.
4. Most of the empirical evidence on the relationship between labor mobility and labor market outcomes is based on spatial, cross-country, or time-series correlations. Disentangling the causal effects is an active area of empirical research.
5. See Zaiceva and Zimmermann (2008) for similar previous studies covering the EU-10 members.
6. Established in 1993, EURES—the European network of public employment services—is a job mobility portal now offering comprehensive services in 27 EU countries. The network provides information, advice, and job-matching services for both workers and employers, but also operates a database with details on living costs, comparability of qualifications, finding accommodation, etc. Almost 64 percent of potential migrants from EU-10 countries are unaware of its services (EC 2009).
7. World Bank (2012b). The number one barrier was the registration system.
8. Voznyak (2008). Among women, the most influential factor to migrate internally is to be young (15–29 years old).
9. In Ukraine, for example, leading regions, like Kiev and Sevastopol, have relative housing prices that are twice as high as those in other parts of the country. Renting a benchmark one bedroom apartment costs approximately 43 percent of the average household monthly disposable income in Kiev and 44 percent in Sevastopol, compared to only half that in Zaporizhzhya or Uzhgorod (Komarov 2012).

10. See also Janiak and Wasmer (2008).

11. Portability of benefits can be defined as "Ability to preserve, maintain and transfer vested social security and private rights or rights in the process of being vested, independent of profession, nationality and country of residency, with 2 elements: 1) The full receipt of vested and eligible social security rights as well as rights under private sector arrangements based on acquired rights through prior contributions/premiums or residency criteria in any chosen residency and 2) The full transfer of social security rights as well as rights under private sector arrangements that are in the process of being vested before eligibility has been established based on acquired rights through prior contributions/premiums or residency criteria in any chosen residency" (Holzman and Koettl 2012).

12. Despite the possibility of transferring social benefits across borders, doing so may not be straightforward. In fact, more than 40 percent of respondents with transfer experience rated the transfer as "fairly difficult" (EC 2011). As past experiences affect the probability of moving abroad again (d'Addio and Cavalleri 2013), governments should work toward uniform and efficient standards in relation to benefit portability.

13. Holzman, Koettl, and Chernetsky (2005). For a more detailed discussion on reform options and trade-offs, see Holzman and Koettl (2012).

14. Database on Immigrants in OECD Countries (OECD 2008).

15. For a more detailed discussion on the links between diasporas and development, see World Bank (2011b).

Bibliography

Andrews, M., K. Clark, and W. Whittaker. 2007. "The Employment and Earnings of Migrants in Great Britain." IZA Discussion Paper 3068, Institute for the Study of Labor (IZA), Bonn, Germany.

Anh, D. N. 2003. "Migration and Poverty in Asia, with Reference to Bangladesh, China, the Philippines, and Viet Nam." Paper presented at the Ad Hoc Expert Group Meeting on Migration and Development, Bangkok, August 27.

Avato, J., J. Koettl, and R. Sabates-Wheeler. 2009. "Social Security Regimes, Global Estimates, and Good Practices: The Status of Social Protection for International Migrants." *World Development* 38 (4): 455–66.

Baldwin, R. E., and P. Martin. 2004. "Agglomeration and Regional Growth." In *Handbook of Regional and Urban Economics: Cities and Geography*, edited by V. Henderson and J. F. Thisse. Amsterdam: Elsevier.

Barro, R. J., and X. Sala-I-Martin. 1992. "Convergence." *Journal of Political Economy* 100 (2): 223–51.

Bell, M., and S. Muhidin. 2009. "Cross-National Comparisons of Internal Migration." UNDP Human Development Research Paper 2009/30, United Nations Development Programme, New York.

Bertola, G. 2000. "Labour Markets in the European Union." *IFO Studien* 46: 99–122.

Bloze, G. 2009. "Interregional Migration and Housing Structure in an East European Transition Country: A View of Lithuania 2001–2008." *Baltic Journal of Economics* 9 (2): 47–66.

Bonin, H., W. Eichhorst, C. Florman, M. Hansen, L. Skioeld, J. Stuhler, K. Tatsiramos, H. Thomasen, and K. Zimmermann. 2008. *Geographic Mobility in the European Union: Optimising Its Economic and Social Benefits*. IZA Research Report 19, Institute for the Study of Labor, Bonn, Germany.

Brauw, A., and C. Carletto. 2012. "Improving the Measurement and Policy Relevance of Migration Information in Multi-Topic Household Surveys." Photocopy, World Bank, Washington, DC.

Brown, A. N. 1997. "The Economic Determinants of the Internal Migration Flows in Russia during Transition." Working Paper 89, William Davidson Institute, Ann Arbor, MI.

Ciccone, A. 2002. "Agglomeration Effects in Europe." *European Economic Review* 46 (2): 213–27.

Colleo, A. L., and M. C. P. Branca. 2008. "Portability of Pension Benefits as a Means to Foster Trans-National Labour Mobility." Work Package 4, Activity 4.4, NOMISMA—Societa di Studi Economici S.P.A., Bologna, Italy.

Coulson, N., and L. Fisher. 2009. "Housing Tenure and Labor Market Impacts: The Search Goes On." *Journal of Urban Economics* 65 (3): 252–64.

D'Addio, A. C., and M. C. Cavalleri. 2013. "Labour Mobility and the Portability of Social Rights in the EU." CESifo Working Paper: Social Protection 4153, CESifo Group, Munich, Germany.

Danish Technical Institute. 2008. *Job Mobility in the European Union: Optimising Its Social and Economic Benefits*. Copenhagen, Denmark: Danish Technical Institute.

Davis, S. 2012. "Romanian Migration during the 2000s." Photocopy, World Bank, Washington, DC.

Dragunova, T., and I. Maidanik. 2009. "Present Trends and Determinants of Migration of Population in Kyiv Oblast." *Demography and Social Economy* 1 (11): 125–35.

EBRD (European Bank for Reconstruction and Development). 2010. Life in Transition Survey II (LiTS database), EBRD, London.

EC (European Commission). 2009. Eurobarometer (database) 72 (5). EC, Brussels.

———. 2011. Eurobarometer (database) 75 (1). EC, Brussels.

Esipova, N., A. Pugliese, and J. Ray. 2013. "The Demographics of Global Internal Migration." *Migration Policy Practice* 3 (2): 3–5.

EU-LFS (European Union Labour Force Survey). 2012. European Union Labour Force Survey (database). EC, Brussels.

Fidrmuc, J., and P. Huber. 2003. "The Puzzle of Rising Regional Disparities and Falling Migration Rates during Transition." Photocopy, Austrian Institute for Economic Research, Vienna.

Gang, I. N., and R. C. Stuart. 1999. "The Political Economy of Russian City Growth." *Economic Development and Cultural Change*, University of Chicago Press, 50 (3): 491–508.

Ghatak, S., A. Mulhern, and J. Watson. 2007. "Interregional Migration in Transition Countries: The Case of Poland." Economics Discussion Paper 2007/7, School of Economics, University of Kingston, London.

Gill, I., and H. Kharas. 2007. *An East Asian Renaissance: Ideas for Economic Growth*. Washington, DC: World Bank.

Green, R., and P. Hendershott. 2001. "Home Ownership and the Duration of Unemployment: A Test of the Oswald Hypothesis." Working Paper, University of Aberdeen, United Kingdom, London.

Haurin, D., and L. Gill. 2002. "The Impact of Transaction Costs and the Expected Length of Stay on Homeownership." *Journal of Urban Economics* 51: 563–84.

Heleniak, T. 2012. "Migration Trends in the Europe and Central Asia Region since 2000." Background paper for this report, World Bank, Washington, DC.

Hoj, J. 2011. "Improving the Flexibility of the Dutch Housing Market to Enhance Labour Mobility." OECD Working Paper 833, Organisation for Economic Co-operation and Development (OECD), Paris.

Holzman, R., and J. Koettl. 2012. "Portability of Pension, Health, and Other Social Benefits: Facts, Concepts, and Issues." CESifo Working Paper Series 4002, CESifo Group, Munich, Germany.

Holzman, R., J. Koettl, and T. Chernetsky. 2005. "Portability Regimes of Pension and Health Care Benefits for International Migrants: An Analysis of Issues and Good Practices." Social Protection Discussion Paper 0519, World Bank, Washington, DC.

IBS (Institute for Structural Research). 2013. *Country Case Study for Poland for the Regional ECA Jobs Report*. Warsaw.

IFC (International Finance Corporation). 2013. *Assessing Private Sector Contributions to Job Creation*. An IFC Open Source Study, World Bank, Washington, DC.

IOM (International Organization for Migration). 2009. *The Impact of the Economic Crisis on Migration Trends and Migration Policy in the Russian Federation and the Eastern Europe and Central Asia Area*. Moscow.

Janiak, A., and E. Wasmer. 2008. "Mobility in Europe: Why It Is Low, the Bottlenecks and the Policy Solutions." European Commission Economic Papers 340, EC, Brussels.

Jones, L., R. Black, and R. Skeldon. 2007. "Migration and Poverty Reduction in Tajikistan." Globalisation and Poverty Working Paper C11, Development Research Centre (DRC) on Migration, Brighton, U.K.

Kartseva, K. 2013. *Country Case Study for Tajikistan for the Regional ECA Jobs Report*. Background paper for this report, World Bank, Washington, DC.

Komarov, V. 2012. "Housing Market and Labor Mobility." Photocopy, Background paper for this report, World Bank, Washington, DC.

Kuddo, A. 2011. "Unemployment Registration and Benefits in ECA Countries." ECA Knowledge Brief Vol. 37, World Bank, Washington, DC.

Kyrgyz Republic. 2010. Household Budget Survey (database), National Statistical Committee of the Kyrgyz Republic, Bishkek.

Lall, S. V., and S. Chakravorty. 2005. "Industrial Location and Spatial Inequality: Theory and Evidence from India." *Review of Development Economics*. 9 (1): 47–68.

Lee, D., and K. Wolpin. 2006. "Intersectoral Labor Mobility and the Growth of the Service Sector." *Econometrica, Econometric Society* 74 (1): 1–46, 01.

Marshall, A. 1920. *Principles of Economics*. London: Macmillan.

Martin, P., and G. Ottaviano. 1999. "Growing Locations: Industry Location in a Model of Endogenous Growth." *European Economic Review* 43: 281–302.

McInnis, R. M. 1966. "Regional Income Differentials in Canada, 1911–1961." *Journal of Economic History* 26 (4): 586–8.

Moretti, E. 2004. "Workers' Education, Spillovers, and Productivity: Evidence from Plant-Level Production Functions." *American Economic Review* 94 (3): 656–90.

Moretti, E. 2012. *The New Geography of Jobs*. New York: Houghton Mifflin Hartcourt.

Moretti, E., and P. Thulin. 2013. "Local Multipliers and Human Capital in the United States and Sweden." *Industrial and Corporate Change* 22 (1): 339–62.

National Statistical Committee of the Kyrgyz Republic. 2009. "Population and Housing Census of the Kyrgyz Republic of 2009" (accessed August 2012). http://cod.humanitarianresponse.info/country-region/Kyrgyzstan.

OECD (Organisation for Economic Co-operation and Development). 2004a. *OECD Economic Surveys: Slovak Republic*. Paris: OECD.

———. 2004b. *OECD Territorial Reviews: Czech Republic*. Paris: OECD.

———. 2008. Database on Immigrants in OECD Countries (DIOC). http://www.oecd.org/els/mig/databaseonimmigrantsinoecdcountriesdioc.htm.

———. 2010. "Labor Mobility and Development Dynamics in OECD Regions." Discussion paper for the 19th session of the OECD Working Party on Territorial Indicators, OECD, Paris.

Oswald, A. 1999. "The Housing Market and Europe's Unemployment: A Nontechnical Paper." Photocopy, University of Warwick, Warwick, U.K.

Paci, R., M. Marrocu, and S. Usai, 2011. "Productivity Growth in the Old and New Europe: The Role of Agglomeration Externalities." ERSA Conference Papers, European Regional Science Association, Louvain-la-Neuve, Belgium.

Paci, P., E. Tiongson, M. Walewski, J. Liwirnski, and M. Stoilkova. 2007. "Internal Labor Mobility in Central Europe and the Baltic Region." World Bank Working Paper 105, World Bank, Washington, DC.

Rosenthal, S. 2004. "Evidence on the Nature and Sources of Agglomeration Economies." In *Handbook of Regional and Urban Economics*, Vol. 4, edited by J. Vernon Henderson and J. Thisse. Amsterdam: North-Holland.

Sharpe, A., A. Arsenault, and D. Ershov. 2007. *The Impact of Interprovincial Migration on Aggregate Output and Labour Productivity in Canada, 1987–2006.* CSLS Research Report 2007–02, Ottawa: Centre for the Study of Living Standards.

Synovate. 2010. *Survey of Labour Mobility in Russia, Ukraine, Bulgaria and Serbia.* Synovate, London.

Tabuchi, T. 1988. "Interregional Income Differentials and Migration: Their Interrelationships." *Regional Studies* 22 (1): 1–10.

Timmins, C. 2005. "Estimable Equilibrium Models of Locational Sorting and Their Role in Development Economics." *Journal of Economic Geography* 5 (1): 59–83.

UNESCO. 2009. Education Statistics (database). www.uis.unesco.org.

United Nations. 2011. "International Migration in a Globalizing World: The Role of Youth. Department of Economic and Social Affairs." Technical Paper 2011/1, UNESCO, New York.

Van Leuvensteijn, M., and P. Koning. 2004. "The Effect of Home Ownership on Labor Mobility in the Netherlands." *Journal of Urban Economics* 55 (3): 580–96.

Voznyak, R. 2008. "Who Moves: A Micro-Level Study of Migration in Ukraine." EERC (KSE) MA thesis, Kyiv School Of Economics, Ukraine, (accessed July 1, 2013). http:// kse.org.ua/uploads/file/library/2008/voznyak.pdf.

Wasmer, E., and J. von Weiszäcker. 2007. "A Better Globalization Fund." Bruegel Policy Brief 2007–01, Bruegel, Brussels.

World Bank. 2005. *Enhancing Job Opportunities: Eastern Europe.* Washington, DC: World Bank.

———. 2009. *World Development Report: Reshaping Economic Geography.* Washington, DC: World Bank.

———. 2010. *Taking Stock of Recent Migration Flows in the European Union.* Washington, DC: World Bank.

———. 2011a. "Russia: Reshaping Economic Geography." Photocopy, World Bank, Washington, DC.

———. 2011b. *Harnessing the Diaspora for Development in Europe and Central Asia.* Mirpal Discussion Series, World Bank, Washington, DC.

———. 2012a. *Golden Growth: Restoring the Lustre of the European Economic Model.* Washington, DC: World Bank.

———. 2012b. *In Search of Opportunities. How a More Mobile Workforce Can Propel Ukraine's Prosperity.* Washington, DC: World Bank.

———. 2012c. *World Development Report 2013: Jobs.* Washington, DC: World Bank.

Zaiceva, A., and K. Zimmermann. 2008. "Scale, Diversity, and Determinants of Labour Migration in Europe." IZA Discussion Paper 3595, Institute for the Study of Labor, Bonn, Germany.